Affect: Psychoanalytic Perspectives

Affect:
Psychoanalytic Perspectives

EDITED BY

Theodore Shapiro, M.D. and Robert N. Emde, M.D.

INTERNATIONAL UNIVERSITIES PRESS, INC.
Madison Connecticut

Library of Congress Cataloging-in-Publication Data

Affect: psychoanalytic perspectives/edited by Theodore Shapiro and
Robert N. Emde.
p. cm.
Includes bibliographical references and indexes.
ISBN 0-8236-0116-1
1. Affect (Psychology) 2. Emotions. 3. Psychoanalysis.
I. Shapiro, Theodore. II. Emde, Robert N.
[DNLM: 1. Affect. 2. Emotions. 3. Psychoanalytic Interpretation.
WM 460.7 A256]
RC455.4.E46.A33 1992
152.4—dc20
DNLM/DLC
for Library of Congress 92-49359
CIP

Manufactured in the United States of America

CONTENTS

GENERAL INTRODUCTION

THEODORE SHAPIRO AND ROBERT N. EMDE

IT IS NOT POSSIBLE TO THINK of a human being without addressing the emotional and affective components of being alive. Vibrant, sentient, sensuous, sensual, are each descriptors of dimensions of existence that encompass affect, feelings, and emotion. Psychoanalysts have long been aware of the centrality of emotion in psychoanalytic theory, but we have never satisfactorily integrated the crucial memorial, cognitive notions we cherish with what has been learned in the past 25 years about affects, and emotions, their social significance, regulatory function, and expression.

Nonetheless, from the beginning, analysts did speak of abreaction, catharsis, impounded affect, affective dissociation, isolation of affect, and cathexis, implying investment of ideas with drive energy experienced as emotional valence. Thus, while acknowledging the centrality of affect, Freud and his followers did not develop a coherent model accounting for affectivity in clinical theory and even less so in metapsychology. Initially, drives became affects, and libidinal drives were converted to affects such as anxiety under conditions that were thought about metaphorically in terms of damming. Later the affect, anxiety, took on a central role in symptom formation as a mediational way station with the introduction of signal anxiety, while manifest anxiety appeared clinically as a pathological breakthrough of the defensive attempts to protect the ego from the onslaught of the drives.

When the structural theory was proffered and the concept of signal anxiety stated in 1926, it took another decade or more for ego psychology and for adaptation to become central themes of psychoanalysis. With those achievements Hartmann and his followers sought to make psychoanalysis a general psychology that could encompass not only the human in conflict, but his autonomous ego as well. Then with later developments in object relations theory and self psychology, psychoanalysis had to attend further to the special vantage of the analyst who is enmeshed in a relationship viewed from the special perspective of a dyad in an empathic field. The analyst's emotions and thought processes now came under special scrutiny both in countertransference phenomena and in interactions with patients. Words such as empathy and projective identification appeared more frequently in our literature as a prompt to consider the emotional climate of the analytic situation. Metaphors of sterile surgical fields and the analyst as an external observer gave way to context-bound Heisenberg-like phenomena and interactive emotional fields as well as shared unconscious fantasy and even intersubjectivity.

Just as clinical analysis has been reanalyzed, the developmental propositions of psychoanalysis have also adopted new "emotion words" and "affective tone." Mahler and her followers wrote about the emotional exuberance of the practicing subphase of the separation-individuation process and the *low keyedness* of rapprochement. Others introduced the emotional responses to early castration reactions and complexes, and analysts studying early attachment joined developmental psychologists to pursue Bowlby's unique variation of psychoanalytic theory by beginning studies of mother-infant interaction and their consequences on secure and insecure attachment. Psychoanalysts also reexplored the arts and other artifacts that emerged from the human spirit and hand. They also for the first time used psychoanalytic propositions to illuminate emotional experiences such as love and romance and the emotional pull and compulsion of hate and the emotional tone and relatedness in perversion.

A current overall perspective has it that affects are organized and organizing aspects of mental functioning. From an adaptive standpoint, affects need to be viewed in context, taking into account patterns that are biological, social, and developmental. From a clinical standpoint, we also need to view affects in context, taking into account current defenses, signal affects, emotional communication with the analyst, and various regulatory influences. The latter include influences of particular emotional patterns (e.g., anger, fear, sadness, or surprise) as well as the influence of more general emotional states (e.g., anxiety or pleasure).

This volume celebrates these many ideas, inventions, and discoveries. It provides the most recent reformulations of our theories in terms of emotional and affective life. Each author, whether developmental psychologist, scientific empiricist, cognitive scientist, linguist, anthropologist, or clinical psychoanalyst, approaches the topic of affect and emotion in accord with the primary interest and study area that stamps his or her work. They have each sought to provide a contemporary integrative statement about how affect and emotion are organized, experienced, and expressed, and, in turn, how the psychoanalytic experience depends on mobilization, taming, and reintegration of affects into cognitive schemas, personality style, and even temperament.

For convenience, the volume is structured in three segments, but each individual author has had the license to explore his or her unique viewpoint. Initially, we offer developmental perspectives on affectivity. The interplay of cognition and affect is highlighted as the organism grows and the person develops.

We reintroduce the segmentation of primary Darwinian affects and the emergence of self-consciousness as determinants of later more complex emotions. We will be "surprised" by the idea that positive, pleasurable, affective systems are organized separately from negative emotions and may even have different biological substrates. We will reexamine aggression as a drive and hostile aggression as a separate line of development. We will reexamine the organization of feelings in relation to object relations and then reciprocally do a double take when we see how temperament organizes caretaker behavior.

We then move into the clinical arena in the second section and reciprocally examine the effect of theory on clinical practice and try to decipher what can be learned from practice about affects and emotions. We will reacquaint ourselves with scholarly arguments about unconscious affects and whether defenses may be elicited by depression as well as anxiety. We will be forced to reconsider how we organize emotion around unconscious fantasies, schemas, and themes. New data on internalized person schemas will be explored to guide practice, and we will then augment our ideas about hatred as expressed in the analytic situation. We will also see how basic affects continue to drive behavior in relation to behavioral constellations. If we miss some of the older language of psychoanalysis in these essays, it is because we are beginning to recast our models, discard nonheuristic notions, and describe the phenomena of our clinical experience differently—in a way that will guide practice better.

The final section encompasses an array of integrative essays ranging across explorations of romance and love, the driving emotions of love and perversion, the role of language, and the influence of cognitive bioscience. These later essays try to convince us that psychoanalysts could do well to integrate the newest information from other disciplines. Anthropology, neuroscience, linguistics, cognitive science, and literary criticism are but a few of the areas begging for attention.

A word is necessary about usage of terms. We have not constrained our authors with prescribed specific definitions. Still, a convention of approximate usage is apparent throughout the volume, and making it explicit at the outset may be helpful to the reader. The term "affect" is used to refer, abstractly, to a general domain of mental functioning. It is therefore often used in its adjectival form. The term "emotion" is used to refer to phenomena that are more "experience-near" or are observable patterns of behavior. Emotions encompass such states and patterns as joy, surprise, interest, anger, fear, sadness, disgust, shame, guilt, anxiety, depression, envy, jealousy, and the like. The term "feeling" is used to connote a subjective state that may or may not be communicated to others.

Finally, we are moved to frame our volume with one other point. If Hartmann failed in his wish to make of psychoanalysis a general science, he certainly was prescient, as was Freud, that psychoanalysis has a compelling scope that can encompass many other human endeavors. Psychoanalysis keeps moving, however, not only because of its scientific method, but also because of its humanistic epistemology. Psychoanalysis as a clinical science embraces the notion that human beings cannot be understood or helped without consideration of their emotive, sentient, and intentional selves. It is to such a consideration that this volume is devoted.

I. DEVELOPMENTAL PERSPECTIVES

INTRODUCTION

THEODORE SHAPIRO, M.D. AND ROBERT N. EMDE, M.D.

THIS SECTION PRESENTS SELECTED new perspectives on development, some of which may be less familiar to the general psychoanalytic reader. An overview of common developmental principles may therefore be useful. We will then comment on more specific linkages to psychoanalysis.

Human developmental processes involve increasing organization over time. Thus, developmentalists see individuals moving toward increasingly organized complexity in their emotional development. Processes include both *differentiation* (an increasing number of organized patterns for emotional experience and expression) and *integration* (an increasing overall control and regulation of these patterns). Developmental processes also include both *continuity* (an "affective core" of patterning that persists as it undergoes incremental increases in organizations) and *transformation* (new emotional patterns that appear and change the organization of one's experience). Other dialectical polarities concern the contexts for such processes. Contexts for development include the *biological* (our Darwinian evolutionary givens for the emotional patterning of experience) as well as the *social* (the internalization of emotions through relationship experiences, changes in emotional organization stemming from particular experiences with others, and trauma). They also include the *intrapsychic* (the development of signal affects, defensive organizations, and more complex, goal-oriented, emotional systems) as well as the *interpersonal* (the development of emotional communication systems, resonance, and empathy as well as more complex states such as shame and social responsibility).

The authors of this section discuss more particular issues that will be familiar to analysts such as those dealing with the emergence of self-awareness, issues of temperament, and the development of particular emotional patterns and states. Empirical perspectives arising from social cognition (Lewis) and from drive development (Parens) supplement those arising from observations of positive emotions (Emde) and changing patterns of affectivity (Kagan). The reader will undoubtably see many points of convergence in theory and in views about the state of our knowledge. But there is also divergence and a lack of connectedness among views.

The contributors of the section emphasize early development. This results from several factors. First, there has been more recent research and thinking in this area than others. Second, early emotional development not only has temporal priority, it takes place in the context of early relationship experiences that are formative (i.e., they are experienced and internalized for the first time). Third, the changes in early emotional development are rapid, lively, and substantive. But we are aware that we have overemphasized early development. We are pleased to have a contribution on emotional development in the adolescent (Hauser), an area that can use increasing attention. Current perspectives are also much needed on emotional development during the oedipal period, and during the primary school years. There also needs to be more attention given to emotional development during adulthood and throughout the life-span—an area that we think will require increasing psychoanalytic focus in the future. The contributions on romantic love in Section III concern an important aspect of adult emotional development, but more needs to be done.

POSITIVE EMOTIONS FOR PSYCHOANALYTIC THEORY: SURPRISES FROM INFANCY RESEARCH AND NEW DIRECTIONS

ROBERT N. EMDE, M.D.

Contemporary psychoanalytic thinking about motivation is likely to give positive emotions an increasingly prominent place. This essay reviews the basis for this statement in the author's infancy research, as well as in other recent research that is developmental, neurophysiological, and experimental. New directions include reformulating the drive theory with our knowledge about positive emotions in incentives, scripts, and fantasy formation. Developmental motives involving exploration and "getting it right" about an expanding world must be considered as well as experiences involving negentropy pleasure. New perspectives may guide clinical practice as they generate surprise and new questions.

IT HAS BEEN SAID that there is not much *Freude* (German for joy) in Freud's psychoanalytic psychology. Correspondingly, Freud's ideas about pleasure have been among the most criticized aspects of his theories. Freud himself was unsatisfied. As several excellent reviews have documented, from 1900 to 1938 Freud maintained the idea that unpleasure resulted from an increase in energy (or drive tension) and that pleasure derived from its decrease (Fenichel, 1945; Rapaport, 1953, 1959; Saussure, 1959; Needles, 1964; Ducey and Galinsky, 1973). But forepleasure in sexual activity did not fit into such a discharge model, nor did Freud's periodic awareness that pleasure might have its own qualities separate from those

---

Professor of Psychiatry, University of Colorado Health Sciences Center, School of Medicine, Denver, Colorado.

Supported by the National Institute of Mental Health project grant MH22803, Research Scientist Award 5 K02 MH36808, and the John D. and Catherine T. MacArthur Foundation Network on Early Childhood Transitions.

of avoiding unpleasure. At different times Freud attempted to account for seeming exceptions to his tension-discharge formulation of pleasure by invoking ideas of changing rhythms of discharge or ideas of discharge to an optimal level. These explanations were incomplete, however, and today's reader senses Freud's continuing unhappiness with what has been referred to as his "unpleasure-pleasure principle" (e.g., Freud, 1920, 1924, 1940).

Two lines of psychoanalytic thinking since Freud's time have addressed the problem of pleasure in psychoanalytic theory. One has been predominant, and has used metapsychology to continue the idea that pleasure is explained through tension discharge. Pleasure from seeking stimulation (and thereby from increasing tension, for example, in foreplay) is acknowledged but is still seen as secondary to an overall form of tension discharge. Mechanisms that are invoked to explain pleasure seeking include changing rhythms and thresholds (following Freud's earlier tentative ideas); moreover, other abstract aspects of metapsychology are also brought to bear (see Fenichel, 1945; Rapaport, 1959; Saussure, 1959; Ducey and Galinsky, 1973). This line of thinking remains unsatisfactory in several respects. First, it is extraordinarily complex and, at best, is difficult to follow logically. Second, it does not account in any straightforward way for the separate quality of pleasure that is such a part of everyday life. Third, it lacks face validity: we know we seek pleasure; we use positive emotions continually for communicating with others; and we find pleasure in exploring and solving problems.

The other line of thinking since Freud's time has not achieved prominence within the psychoanalytic mainstream, perhaps because of a reluctance on the part of many to abandon a core aspect of classic metapsychology. This line of thinking in its various forms agrees on one point: *pleasure must be acknowledged as a qualitatively separate domain of mental functioning.* Significant aspects of pleasure do not have to do with avoiding unpleasure or with drive discharge, and these aspects need to be understood in their own terms. Thus, some theorists linked pleasure to different sources of motivation, such as pleasure from work (Hendrick, 1934) and from an independent "effectance motivation" (White, 1963)—ideas that led to infancy studies of what later came to be known as "mastery pleasure" (see review in Morgan and Harmon, 1984). Earlier ideas of a "pleasure in functioning" set forth by Karl Bühler were also influential (for example, see Hartmann, 1939; Spitz, 1965). But other theorists were even more direct. A basic pleasure system was postulated for guiding behavior, and it supplemented a basic unpleasure system (see Jacobson, 1953; Heath, 1964; Rado, 1964—also by implication Erikson, 1950; Maslow, 1971).

I believe that the second line of thinking since Freud's time is one that can now be extended and that it should be accepted as a basis for new theory-building. It is more in accord with the facts, with common sense, and it is simpler. It is internally consistent and, although questions remain, it promises to be more useful for psychoanalysis. These points will be illustrated with personal observations from infancy research and also with findings from neurophysiology and animal research. I will conclude with a view of new directions for psychoanalytic theory.

An Observer of Infancy Learns about Positive Emotions

I have come to realize that positive emotions are what drives a researcher. Curiosity, interest, and pleasure in discovery are major contributors but, perhaps most of all, is the emotion of surprise. I therefore begin the substantive part of my essay by telling about several early surprises I experienced in my infancy research.

Activation and Excitement

The first surprise was how much joy normatively surrounds the arrival of a new baby. This occurs in spite of the baby's crying and the physical discomfort of the mother, and is particularly prominent in today's natural childbirth settings that permit unmedicated babies who are alert and who typically soon engage mother and others in eye-to-eye contact with mother and others. Families show pleasure and excitement and joy is expressed, experienced, and communicated with or without distress. When I began to study smiling babies, I then discovered something more about joy. I ask the reader to imagine a 3-month-old smiling baby. Even if you are reminded of a favorite snapshot, you do not have a static picture in mind. You imagine a baby who is soon going to have bicycling movements of the arms and legs, with eyes that are sparkling as you continue looking at them, and you may imagine the baby cooing in response to your delight. The dynamic feature of smiling is impossible to restrain. There is an activation to excitement that is expressed by the baby and conveyed to both caregiver and researcher. Smiling babies convinced me very early that the idea of positive emotions having to do with tension discharge did not seem right. Smiling had to do with activation. After being engaged in this way by babies for several years, my colleagues and I finally got around to conducting a study that looked at activation and smiling. We carefully looked at smiling in 5-month-olds and 9-month-olds, comparing the time during smiling with the time immediately before and after smiling. We indeed found a higher level of motoric activity during smiling. We also found evidence of an activation of heart rate during smiling, with accelerations in the 5-month-old being recorded independent of movement (Emde et al., 1978).

Realizing that infant smiling involves increasing activation rather than decreasing activation was only one surprise. Another came from our studies of early infant smiling. We found two different types of smiling before the onset of the well-known regular social smile that blossoms at 2 months of age, is so celebrated by parents, and was documented so well by the research of Spitz and Wolf (1946). The newborn observations of Wolff (1959) had pointed to the existence of earlier smiling that called for research and understanding. In studying such early smiling, we were surprised to find two types that were organized expressions unrelated to frowning, fussing, or crying. One type we labeled *early endogenous smiling.* Such smiling is linked to rapid eye movement (REM) states and appears within minutes after birth. It occurred on the average of 11 per 100 minutes of REM states and, according to our measurement, this type of smiling occurred whether or not the infant had his eyes open, providing there was an accompanying REM state physiology. REM smiles "clocked along" in a spontaneous (i.e., not elicited) manner and had a clear tendency to occur in bursts (Emde and Koenig, 1969a, 1969b). At first we thought such inborn smiles might be mediated by the limbic cortex, but our hypothesis was proven wrong by subsequent observations. We found more REM smiling in prematures, who had less limbic cortex, than in full-terms who had more limbic cortex (Emde et al., 1971). We then observed a microcephalic infant who, during life, had comparable amounts of endogenous smiling as did healthy newborns of the same postconceptional age (Harmon and Emde, 1972). The infant in question came to postmortem examination, and brain anatomical study revealed virtually no cortex, limbic or otherwise. The conclusion that forced itself upon us was that REM smiling is mediated by midbrain and lower diencephalic structures (this conclusion will undoubtedly be clarified now that the brain-imaging techniques make *in vivo* studies possible).

What is the adaptive function of early endogenous smiling? It was regular in its occurrence, yet hardly seemed noticed by mothers and others. The teleological view we were left with was that endogenous REM smiling may be a sort of a "practicing" or "tooling up" form of smiling that exists in the first 2 postnatal months prior to social smiling. Our longitudinal observations documented that this form of smiling becomes inhibited over the early months of postnatal life, on a similar time course to the inhibition of other REM-related behaviors in early infant "active" sleep (Stern et al., 1969).

We also studied *early exogenous smiling.* This form of smiling begins in the earliest postnatal days and occurs in response to external stimulation but is irregular. It seems to have a "maturational push" over the first 2 months, increasing in frequency as a response to a variety of sensory modalities. Our studies documented an upsurge in this smiling immediately preceding the time of onset of the specific social smiles elicited by the human face that Spitz and Wolf (1946) described as a response to the specific "essential Gestalt" (Emde and Harmon, 1972). The strict automatic response tendency that Spitz described probably lasts a few days only; learning then supervenes, bringing important modifications as other studies have illustrated (Polak et al., 1964a, 1964b).

What can we infer about the significance of these two types of early infant smiling? The infant's earliest endogenous smiling is inborn and biologically organized in such a way that it must be regarded as a "spontaneous activity" that accompanies REM states. As this form of smiling becomes inhibited, the other form of irregular nonspecific smiling arises as a biological response to stimulation; exogenous smiling then comes to have increasing features of activation and gives a potential excitement in social interaction.

Other developmental researchers have shown that the infant has an apparent inborn tendency to experience pleasure in the midst of exploration and "getting it right" about the environment. Piaget (1936) linked infant smiling to cognitive assimilation, and so-called "smiles of assimilation" have since been noted to occur in the infant's first year (Kagan et al., 1978; McCall, 1972) as well as in the second year during more complex mastery tasks (Morgan and Harmon, 1984; Kagan, 1981). Similarly, laughter and smiling have been shown to occur in response to incongruous distortions or exaggerations of familiar events, providing they are not too discrepant (Sroufe and Wunsch, 1972).

Does the propensity for expressing pleasure in actively engaging others have adaptive significance? Clearly so. Other studies have confirmed the meaning of infant smiling to caregivers. In addition to families with normal infants, we studied families with Down syndrome infants in whom smiling is delayed in onset and dampened. It seemed clear that the adaptive significance of the smiling, in addition to other things, was to facilitate bonding in the loving relationship, to add feelings of warmth and pleasure so that the caregiver could get feedback that things are going well. The smile of the infant seems to say, "Keep it up, I like it." From the point of view of survival, it seems fortunate that elicited regular social smiling develops only after the initial 2 postnatal months. Elicited crying is present earlier, at birth, and is a more biologically crucial biological expression. It gives a peremptory universal emotional communication to the caregiver. Unlike the smile, the cry says, "Change something now!" It calls immediate attention to the need for change and is a communication device important for survival with respect to the regulation of fundamental physiological systems. We speculated, in fact, that if the infant had exogenous, socially elicited smiling at birth, there could be a false sense of caregiving security with a message of "things are all right"; correspondingly, more children would be at risk of having vital needs neglected.

The picture that began to emerge was that positive emotions had a separately organized set of adaptive functions as compared with negative emotions. But aside from *expression*, would they have a separate influence on *performance* of the infant? To jump ahead a bit in time, a few years ago we collaborated with Professor Meng Zhao-Lan of Beijing University in studies of 15- and 16-month-old infants. Our studies both in Denver and in Beijing demonstrated the influence of mild mood manipulations on performance during a cognitive task. The task was one in which the child had to push a lever one way in order to get an interesting object to come around the other way. This task seems counterintuitive—pushing one way to get something from the opposite direction—and children solve this problem at varying rates during the second year of life. Our mood manipulation consisted of, on the one hand, a peek-a-boo game with mother, followed by the lever task after several minutes and, on the other hand, a separation from the mother followed by the lever task after several minutes. We found clear differences in performance based on prior mood manipulations, even though the affect expressions of the child were not measurably different during the performance itself. The positive emotion precondition was associated with enhanced performance, whereas the negative emotion was not. But more interestingly, there were two different patterns of affective arousal relationships with the performance itself. With respect to negative emotion, we found a straightforward negative correlation between performance and the intensity of prior mood arousal. That is, the more negative the emotion the child expressed during the earlier manipulation, the less successful was the subsequent performance. On the other hand, there was quite a different curve with respect to the positive emotion manipulation. The intensity of positive emotion prior to the task showed a curvilinear trend with subsequent performance instead of a linear one. In these results, low levels of positive emotion had some enhancing affect, moderate levels of positive emotion had still more of an enhancing effect on performance, but high levels of positive emotion in the earlier mood manipulation was associated with a decrement in performance.[1]

Taken together, these findings from infancy give a clear picture of a separately organized, biologically based system for positive emotion. This system is associated with the expression of activation and excitement, and it may also facilitate performance in ways that are quite different from a negative emotion system.

[1]Interestingly, these results indicate that the so-called Yerkes-Dodson Law that describes the inverted U-shape function of performance level in relation to the level of arousal may be modified by the separate hedonic states.

Behavioral Regulation

The next surprise concerned behavioral regulation. Here the results of our studies in several areas may be the most dramatic of all in supporting the idea of an independently organized system of positive emotion.

The first area of behavior regulation has to do with what we refer to as social referencing. Social referencing is a phenomenon we have defined as follows: An individual of any age encountering a situation of uncertainty looks to a significant other person for an emotional signal in order to resolve the uncertainty and to regulate behavior accordingly. All of these elements in our definition are teased apart experimentally in studies where we construct situations of uncertainty, experimentally manipulate emotion signals of others around the infant, and measure behavioral regulation. Because of our advances in measuring emotional expression, we can manipulate emotions as independent variables, teaching mothers or testers to give clear facial or vocal expressions of emotion. Thus, for example, in a situation of uncertainty involving a toy robot coming into a room, a child will typically look to the robot and then look to mother or to the tester for an emotional signal. If the individual smiles, expressing joy, the child will approach the uncertain stimulus. If the mother expresses interest, most of the children will also approach or explore. On the other hand, if the mother expresses fear or anger, children typically will not approach the toy robot. Experimentally, we have used uncertainty stimuli which have involved strangers approaching, a visual cliff, a collapsing toy house, and toy dolls that come apart. All have produced results in which social referencing has shown behavioral regulatory effects that are different for positive and for negative emotions (Sorce et al., 1985; Klinnert, 1984; Klinnert et al., 1986; Boccia and Campos, 1983).

Social referencing has been studied by others (Feinman

and Lewis, 1983; Feinman, 1985; Gunnar and Stone, 1983; Walden and Baxter, 1989) and has been related to the development of shared periods of attention and meaning between caregiver and infant. Such shared meaning has components of shared emotions, shared intentions, and a shared sense of what is appropriate in any given context. Referred to as "intersubjectivity," this aspect of development has been the subject of increasing research (Trevarthen, 1979; Bretherton and Beeghly, 1982; Bruner, 1982; Kaye, 1982). Stern (1985), in a like manner, has included the matching of positive emotions between caregiver and infant in his concept of "affect attunement," proposing that such a process reflects an important, biologically adaptive tendency in social species.

Another aspect of behavior regulation also illustrates the adaptive independence of positive emotions from negative emotions and is closely related to Stern's affective attunement. It concerns what we have referred to as "positive affect sharing." We have found that toward the end of the first year of life, children in our normative samples tend to look to a significant other and share a positive affect. During our playroom observations, for example, children may share a smile in the midst of an exploration or an accomplishment. There are considerable individual differences in this form of behavior, and it seems to us as though it gives way in the course of development to a sort of "puffing up of pride" expression that children begin to display in the middle of the second year of life. In one longitudinal study conducted in our laboratory playroom, we found moderate levels of positive affect sharing at 12 months of age, quite high levels at 18 months of age, and then moderate levels again at 24 months of age. In a study of a risk population involving offspring of teenage mothers, Joy Osofsky employed some of our laboratory paradigms and found almost no evidence of positive affect sharing. Instead, most affect sharing was negative, which, in turn, was unusual in our studies with normal children.

The psychoanalytic reader will be reminded of the importance of caregiver affirmations according to the different concepts of "mirroring" as proposed by Winnicott (1971), Lacan (1966), and Kohut (1971), and now considered such an important aspect of self psychology. The point to be emphasized is that positive emotion communications may provide separate sources of encouragement from the absence of negative emotion communications.

This leads us to another area of behavioral regulation that emphasizes the separate importance of positive emotions in development, namely, the emotional availability of caregiver for infant. Over a decade ago we did a study that we called our "library study" because we set up our playroom as a reading room that mother entered with her toddler. The room was one in which another woman was already sitting reading a newspaper, and mother soon sat down and also began reading a newspaper. The library-playroom was an uncertain situation of a sort in which we demonstrated that the infant's exploration and level of play depended on whether mother was reading the newspaper or not. When she was not reading the newspaper—in other words, when mother was emotionally available and could express interest and perhaps an occasional smile—her 15-month-old infant engaged in more exploration and the developmental level of play was higher (Sorce and Emde, 1981). In clinical consultation, we have developed a more general impression. Emotional availability is one of the best overall barometers as to whether development is going well in early childhood. We find it a good screening indicator. If development is going well, we expect to see evidence of a range of emotions and a balance of interest and pleasure going back and forth between caregiver and child. If one does not see that, the clinician becomes concerned and thinks of looking further for specific pathology. We do know that when there are behavioral problems, it is characteristic for there to be little positive affect with a dampening of range in emotions. One may see "turning off" behaviors involving gaze aversion and withdrawal, as Brazelton et al. (1975), Tronick et al. (1978), and Tronick and Gianino (1986) have decribed, and there may be a global lesser amount of interest in the environment. In assessing problems in caregiver emotional availability, a lack of positive emotions may be a more sensitive indicator of problems than an excess of negative emotions.

Play is another area of behavioral regulation in the infant and young child that illustrates the independent adaptive organization of positive emotions. Some play does occur, according to Freud's model (1920), as a repetition in the service of mastery—as an active reexperiencing of separation from caregivers and other distressing experiences. But one is struck that a great deal of play seems distant from distress and instead seems motivated by the kind of excitement in games where the child reaches a shared goal with another. I believe this is the aspect of play that has been emphasized by Winnicott (1971) and more recently by Shor (1990). Child development researchers are now coming to realize that play is an unappreciated dimension of the child's earliest relationships (Stern, 1977; Dunn, 1988; Emde, 1989). The home observations of Dunn vividly document the amounts of time the 2-year-old spends in delight and humor with others and how such positive emotions vary systematically with particular family relationships.

Interestingly, we found that more positive emotion words were expressed by 24-month-old toddlers than negative emotion words. Twenty-six children were carefully observed by their mothers using a systematic child language inventory (Bretherton and Bates, 1984) and were found to express a mean of 12 positive emotion words and 7 negative emotion words per child. The greater number of positive emotion words may reflect the mother's "scaffolding" with prideful encouragement of the child's positive emotional states and developmental accomplishments. Indications are that this is different with populations of families under stress where negative words and expressions outweigh positive ones.

In sum, the observations of behavioral regulation also indicate a strong, separately organized, adaptive role for positive emotions in infancy. Social referencing, positive affect sharing, emotional availability, and play all illustrate the infant's use of positive emotions found in significant others as incentives for action.

Individual Differences

The next area continues our theme of separately organized positive emotions and makes links with emerging research on individual differences, temperament, and personality.

A major surprise for me (but not now for the reader) resulted from our longitudinal studies of individual differences in emotionality. In three different samples we measured the intensity and style of emotional signaling in mothers, fathers, and young children. We collected data in our playroom and in the home, and we analyzed data from videotapes as well as from reports from parents. In all instances, we found that correlations between positive and negative emotions across cases were essentially zero. Our findings replicated for several ages and were true for infants, toddlers, and adults, whether in home or in laboratory. In other words, under normal conditions of low stress, positive emotions are measurably independent of negative emotions. Another finding concerns a different pattern of longitudinal consistency. There is more individual consistency for negative emotions over time than there is for positive emotions over time. We have interpreted the latter finding according to our growing sense that positive emotions are more variable than negative emotions in terms of reflecting changes in environmental context.

Findings from behavioral genetic studies of infant temperament are consistent with the above picture. Evidence from twin studies indicates substantial heritability with respect to negative emotionality (most notably for fearfulness and anger/aggression) but weak heritability with respect to positive emotionality (see Plomin, 1986; Goldsmith and Campos, 1986). Again, there seems to be a relative independence of emotion systems, and there seems to be greater environmental variation for positive emotions.

Temperament research, armed with a new set of methods, is currently a productive area of investigation. Future discoveries will undoubtedly link early temperament to a new wave of research on personality dimensions in adults. Although we take our argument beyond infancy at this point, it seems worth noting that two dimensions of personality have survived recent critical scrutiny. From the work of Eysenck (1981), these dimensions have been labeled as neuroticism and extroversion. More recently, Jeffrey Gray (1982) has reviewed this work and put it in a neuropsychological context of separate functional brain systems. The case is made that these two dimensions of personality might best be thought of as separate dynamic predispositions toward negative and positive affects. (In Gray's model, the tendency for extroversion is in line with the positive affect tendency.) Tellegan (1984) and colleagues, with a variety of scaling studies of their own, have reached similar conclusions, as have Costa and McCrae (1980). The main dimensions of personality can be thought of in terms of positive affectivity and negative affectivity; a bias toward negative affectivity results in a risk of psychopathology and, in contrast, a bias toward positive affectivity results in an inclination for sociability and outgoing adaptation.

Another related trend in research concerns stress and coping (Garmezy and Rutter, 1983). It has been suggested that the outcome of stress for a given individual may be determined by whether there is a previous personality organization clustered around negative emotional traits (see Patterson and Dishion, 1988; Caspi and Elder, 1988). Although speculative, it may also be that those who have positive emotional traits "buffer themselves" during times of stress and have more resiliency.

Early Moral Development

Another telling area of our infancy research has to do with early moral development. Surprisingly, a lot of moral development occurs prior to 3 years and much of it involves learning what to do as compared with learning what not to do. Positive emotions (interest, curiosity, pleasure, delight, and pride) have a significant role in mediating this developmental pathway.

Reciprocity is a major feature of this aspect of moral development, and it has a strong biological preparedness. The human infant has inborn organized capacities for initiating, maintaining, and terminating social interactions. These become exercised and expanded through everyday caregiving interactions. The basic procedures of turn-taking behavior are learned in the midst of early, back-and-forth, interested looking, smiling, vocalizing, and laughing with mother prior to 6 months, and they then become expanded with anticipatory games (Brazelton et al., 1975; Stern, 1977). Through the positive emotional "scaffolding" of caregivers who extend the infant's capacities in repeated turn-taking encounters, the infant comes to internalize the basis for the fundamental procedures of communication (Bruner, 1982; Kaye, 1982). This becomes a basis not just for the later development of language, but the later development of moral systems. Think about it. A fundamental basis of all moral systems has to do with reciprocity. It has to do with a sense of fairness—variations of "the golden rule"—do unto others as you would have them do unto you.

Infants, in addition, come to internalize a considerable amount about everyday "rules"—where things belong, how they look, and how things are supposed to happen—in other words, rules about context and what is appropriate. There is a strong interest and positive propensity for "getting it right" about the environment and about one's interactions with it. The emotions of mastery pleasure, positive emotion sharing, and pride are particular incentives for "getting it right."

This leads to another feature of early moral development that I believe should be considered from the standpoint of positive emotionality—i.e., early tendencies for reparative behavior and prosocial actions. We might say that these are positive emotion sequences since, although they begin with negative emotions, they proceed to behaviors most would consider positive.

The first such sequence involves *empathy*. Beginning in the latter part of the second year, infants, when faced with the distress of another, may show helping, comforting, and sharing behaviors. The original observations of Zahn-Waxler and Radke-Yarrow (1982) have now been replicated in a number of laboratories, including our own; they indicate that there is considerable individual variability to this response. Research needs to be done, but one believes the variability is dependent on the quality of infant/caregiver relationship. The fact that empathy appears normatively in development suggests a biologically prepared, positive system for prosocial inclination which to the extent it is universal may provide a nonrelativistic platform for moral development, as Kagan (1981) and Hoffman (1977) have put it.

Another new emotional response sequence is also observed regularly toward the end of the second year. This seems to be a continuation of the infant's developmental line of "getting it right" about the environment. Infants can be observed at this time to show distress when encountering a familiar toy or object that is out of place, flawed in some way, or dirty (Kagan, 1981; Dunn, 1988). From the point of view of early moral development, Kagan has emphasized how this milestone indicates that the toddler has internalized a standard and shows distress upon the violation of that standard. From the perspective of this essay, the point is that positive inclinations for reparation are set in motion (all moral systems involve internalized standards and internalized uneasiness when these standards are violated and propensities for reparation). The psychoanalytic reader may also recognize convergence with another point of view—namely, that of the toddler's regulations of behavior during anality (Freud, 1905; Erikson, 1950).

Developmentalists are now giving attention to the paradoxical idea of guilt as a positive interpersonal emotion. Even in the preschooler, guilt can be seen as a moral regulating emotion that is based on an empathic desire to make things better when another is hurt. This is especially so when the child believes he or she is the cause of the hurt in the other or could make it better (Damon, 1988; Zahn-Waxler and Radke-Yarrow, 1982).

Note that the above features of early moral development do not necessarily involve conflict. Other aspects of early moral development involve positive emotionality in the midst of conflict. Much of early moral development during the second and third years occurs in the context of parental prohibitions. The child begins to touch a wall socket, a fragile lamp, or the knobs of the hi-fi and experiences conflict in the form of hearing "no's" and "don't's." We have studied such prohibitions in home and laboratory and have observed the many forms of negotiations that occur with toddlers "testing" and asserting their wills in varying contexts with varying outcomes. But here we would emphasize the role of positive emotions. Positive affect-sharing and pride are expressed with children sharing smiles and sparkling-eyed pleasures with caregivers after specific actions that have involved effort in mastering a restraint subsequent to a prohibition. Smiling and a proud erect posture with social referencing of the significant other become increasingly prominent during the second year. Pride, along with shame, is a more complex emotion that is based on experience and on some sense of struggle, dilemma, or conflict; pride and shame are anticipatory, portending the consequences of an intended outcome. Here the positive and negative emotions complement each other. They provide evidence for a "pull" as well as a "push" we might say from a motivational standpoint. Pride exerts a positive pull, indicating that a standard or rule has been successfully applied in a given situation; shame exerts a negative push, indicating an experience of unpleasure (with a limpness) after carrying out a prohibited act. Both emotions operate in the presence of a significant other and presumably after the developmental onset of reflective self-awareness (see Lewis, this volume).

Experiences of interpersonal conflict around prohibitions and related contexts with parents (and often with siblings) are a prominent part of the child's life in the second and third years during the time when language develops. By 36 months, the child has the capacity for narrative discourse, and we can probe for moral understanding of affective themes. When given "story stems" in which stories are begun with dolls and the children complete them in play, a normal middle-class sample of children we studied produced a rich set of story completions. As we expected, the stories showed us internalized coherent themes involving rules, standards, reciprocity, and empathy. But another result was most surprising: most children also showed us that they understood a moral dilemma. Our prototypic story stem for the dilemma was one in which a prosocial inclination was pit against a binding rule. The story begins with the tester and two dolls of the same sex as the child. One doll falls and hurts herself and says, "Oh, I hurt my leg. Get me a Band-Aid." The other child says, "Okay, oh, but Mom says I can't go on the bathroom shelf where the Band-Aids are." The tester then asks the child, "Show me and tell me what happens now." More than three-quarters of our children struggled with the dilemma, and some reached prosocial responses. Many did not. Still, the engagement with the moral dilemma itself was surprising. Researchers had only recently demonstrated that preschoolers can hold two possible alternative solutions in mind (Flavell et al., 1986; Wellman et al., 1986).

We also observed 36-month-old children in a standardized prohibition situation when mother is absent. The situation is as follows. Mother brings in a set of new toys in a playroom that has many other toys and says to the child and the tester, "These toys are not to be played with now." Mother then leaves the room. The tester plays with a puppet doll that begins to express a desire to play with the new toys. Most children, at least for a while, resist the temptation of involving the new toys in doll play. Not surprising. But something dramatic occurred to us one day when we realized that a number of children said to the tester in effect, "I can't play with those toys, you can't either. Didn't you hear my Mommy? We can't play with those toys." What occurred to us was that a fascinating development had taken place. It seemed as if the child had developed an executive sense of "we." Referring to a similar positive sense, George Klein (1967) once pointed out that psychoanalysis needs a theory of "we-go" to supplement its theory of "ego." We refer to an executive sense of "we" to emphasize the positive sense of togetherness, power, and control that exists for guiding behavior and for resisting temptation. Does not an executive sense of "we" call for further research? Has not this sense been underemphasized in our Western self-other culture as compared with Eastern culture and experience (see Doi, 1973)? Perhaps future research can discover the extent to which this development, with its positive emotionality, is related to a caregiver-child relationship that is prideful and generates experience of a shared positive meaning.

Thus far, my essay has reflected a personal odyssey about research surprises concerning positive emotions in early development. Because of my area of research, I have focused on infant with caregiver, but peers and sibs will soon occupy more and more of the child's world of emotions and morality. Piaget

(1932), in fact, believed the child's peer experiences to be the crucial arena for moral development—especially with respect to equity and fairness. Let me therefore mention a positive aspect of early peer interactions research that continues a line we have been discussing—namely, sharing.

Damon (1988) summarizes that by 4 years of age most children have internalized a standard about sharing. Children of this age evidence a sense of obligation to share with others; and there is now an internal belief that sharing is an obligatory part of any social relationship. Interestingly, when 4-year-olds are interviewed about the reasons for their belief about sharing, the most common reason given is based on a consideration of feelings in the other: there is sharing because it makes the other "happy" or the other will be "sad" if I don't share.

Whatever else, it would seem that positive emotions continue to play an enlivening role in relationships beyond infancy and caregiving. It is expectable that positive emotions will vary according to context, show increasing complexity, and occasionally be "swamped" by negative emotions. And the extent to which later individual differences in positive emotions represent continuities with earlier individual differences and positive emotions—either from temperament or from early caregiving experiences—remains an open question. I hope the reader agrees that we have made a strong case for theoretical coherence, but more development research needs to be done.

Biological Research

Infant behavior has shown us that positive emotions are separately organized from negative emotions. Moreover, positive emotions are crucial for adaptation; they provide significant incentives for learning, communication, and development. For the infant and for the caregiver positive emotions are rewarding and have motivational effects that are independent of "relief" or the discharge of negative emotions. In this section we will see to what extent there is a basis for these formulations in neurobiology and in studies of animal behavior. In the first instance we will consider biology in its more specific sense of physiological mechanisms and processes. In the second instance we will consider biology in its larger sense of evolutionary preparedness and those aspects of adaptive functioning for which the study of controlled animal behavior is relevant.

Human Studies of Neurophysiology

Are there separate systems in the human brain for organizing positive and negative emotions? The evidence seems to mount that such is the case. The studies of patients with temporal lobe epilepsy in whom electrical stimulation of the cortex was done while the patients were awake and under local anesthesia have been suggestive. Penfield and Perot (1963), reviewing the classic studies done at the Montreal Neurological Institute, cite some examples of positive emotion in the midst of hallucinatory experiences of watching familiar people laughing or singing. More recent brain stimulation studies have probed below the temporal lobe cortex with deeper electrical stimulation in the limbic system and have provided mixed results. Two such studies reported elicited emotional experiences that were unpleasant and not pleasurable (Halgren et al., 1978; Gloor et al., 1982). In a recent review McGeer et al. (1987) cite two other studies in which stimulation of deeper structures did produce specific positive emotion experiences. In one such study Hassler and Reichert (1961) observed that stimulation of the thalamus could produce smiling or laughing, a response that could not be suppressed on command from the surgeon. In another study, Mark and Ervin (1970) observed that stimulation of the amygdala generated discrete responses with the patient experiencing feelings of elation and floating at one point, warm and pleasant feelings at another point, and then unpleasant feelings at still another stimulation point. Thus, under these special circumstances, there appears to be evidence for a separate anatomical organization of the hedonic systems.

Other studies in humans provide a more convincing picture of a separate organization. These concern the lateralization of brain function., To summarize findings: the left anterior hemisphere has been implicated in organizing approach behavior and positive affect and the right anterior hemisphere in organizing withdrawal behavior and negative affect. (See reviews in Trevarthen, 1984; Nass and Gazzaniga, 1987; Davidson, 1988; and Silberman and Weingartner, 1986.) From earlier studies of unilateral carotid Amytal anesthesia, it was known that patients with left hemispheric anesthesia tend to become depressed and disphoric, whereas patients with right-sided anesthesia tend to become euphoric. Lesion studies from clinical populations showed a similar differential hedonic pattern. Patients with left frontal lesions tend to have depressive symptomatology, while comparable lesions in the right frontal area are often associated with indifference or euphoria.

Recent EEG studies have noted asymmetries in response to affect-eliciting stimuli in normal subjects. Perhaps most compelling has been a set of EEG studies done by Fox and Davidson (1984, 1987, 1988; Davidson and Fox, 1982, 1989). These studies have documented an affective valence-dependent anterior asymmetry that is present during the first year of life. Not only has the EEG activation of the left anterior frontal area been associated with positive affect and the corresponding right area with negative affect during the presentation of pleasant and unpleasant stimuli respectively, but also base line differential right frontal activation has been effective in predicting the extent of distress during a subsequent maternal separation!

Other physiological data bearing on our question come from two other research domains. Although a separate organization for hedonic systems is compatible with data from each of these domains, the research stories are preliminary and incomplete. One domain concerns the autonomic nervous system (ANS) where Ekman et al. (1983) found that patterns of ANS responsiveness distinguished between positive and negative affects as well as among particular negative affects. This research, however, awaits independent replication. Another domain concerns that of brain neurochemistry. The earlier discovery of endogenous opioids and their receptors excited the imagination of investigators concerning a possible separate biochemical basis for positive emotions and self reward. This field, however, is fast-moving and complex with many pathways and neurotransmitters under study; thus specific functions and activities are unclear at this time.

Animal Studies of Motivation

Whereas human neurophysiological studies have provided evidence for a separately organized positive emotion system at the *correlational* level, animal studies have gone further. Experimental manipulations have allowed researchers to probe for mechanisms of behavior and this has led squarely to considerations of motivation.

Studies of animal behavior have provided strong evidence for two major classes of hedonically distinct motivated behavior. Research over the past three decades and more has led to a veritable "sea change" in psychological thinking about motivation and, as we shall see, this thinking has direct implications for the biology of emotions.

The work of three pioneers, namely, Berlyne (1960), Harlow (1953), and Hebb (1949), demonstrated that a good deal of motivated animal behavior cannot be accounted for by biological deficits or imbalances of homeostasis (i.e., by drive reduction). Much behavior was found to be exploratory, manipulative, and stimulus seeking. Over the years this has led to a shift from a psychology largely concerned with internal deficit signals as behavior instigators to one increasingly concerned with the role of environmental incentive stimuli and expectations about them.

Another boost for this line of thinking came from the discovery of central reinforcing systems in the brain (Olds and Milner, 1954; Delgado et al., 1954). These studies demonstrated that brain self-stimulation was positively reinforcing; moreover, such self-stimulation occurred independently of drive state or drive reduction. Paradoxically, animals were even found to self-stimulate in regions of the brain that at the same time increased their hunger, thirst, or sexual tension. Olds and Milner in their original report found that reward centers and punishment centers were widely dispersed in the brain, with 35 percent of rat brain cells having reward activity (areas the rat would work to get stimulation in) and 5 percent punishment activity (areas in which the rat would work to avoid stimulation in). In a recent review (McGeer et al., 1987) it has been noted that since the original experiments thousands of self-stimulation studies have been done in rats and that self-stimulation occurs in virtually all areas of the limbic system, with the median forebrain bundle being the most preferred region of all. Comparable studies have been done in cats, monkeys, and dolphins, and there are some studies from subcortical electrical stimulation in conscious human patients with tumors, epilepsy, and intractable pain. A quoted statement from the review seems apt:

> Reward centers have been found in the human associated with intense, but non-specific, feelings of well-being, with pleasant sensations ascribed to distinct parts of the body, and with sexual arousal. Punishment areas have also been found, the stimulation of which can elicit terror, anger, or pain (Delgado, 1976; Sem-Jacobsen, 1976). The implication of all these studies is that much learning and decision-making, which presumably takes place chiefly in the cortex, are directed toward stimulating pleasure centers and away from stimulating punishment centers. In other words, the cells that are "neutral" for reward or punishment are marshaled to direct the animals' behavior in such

a way as to provide a sensory input that is "just right" for pleasure and punishment cells [p. 530].

As a result of this and other work a change in theorizing has come about in which two classes of motivation are seen. One concerns those motivated behaviors initiated by deficit stimulation, and the other concerns those motivated behaviors initiated by incentive stimulation (Mogenson and Phillips, 1978). The later class relates to the expectation of intrinsic reward. It is based on the "pulling power" of stimulus association and adds to the predictive power of behavior as compared to a concept based exclusively on the push provided by internal drive states brought about by homeostatic imbalances (Firbirger and Phillips, 1986). In some ways the concept is similar to that of conditioned positive reinforcement. For our purposes the importance of this is that a biologically significant aspect of the control of behavior can be accounted for by the anticipation of positive reward. Thus, according to a theory of incentive motivation, some stimuli may be projected directly to limbic or other structures concerned with positive reinforcement; the activation of such pathways would thereby cause the stimulation to be experienced as rewarding.

New Directions for Theory

We have seen that contemporary research-oriented thinking about motivation has undergone vast changes as a result of considering positive emotions. Similarly, contemporary psychoanalytic thinking about motivation is likely to give positive emotions an increasingly prominent place. Not only are positive emotions involved in special activities and mastery pleasure as Hendricks, White, and others saw, but they are involved in everyday activities of interest, curiosity, and surprise. The latter emotions guide the seeking of the new and the assimilation of the new to the familiar. Positive emotions activate and guide behavior, are separately organized from negative emotions, and are often associated with incentive motivations (i.e., expectations about sought-after environmental stimuli). As we have seen, these matters are quite fundamental—consistent both with everyday experience and with research that is developmental, neurophysiological, and experimental.

A New Look at Drives and a Separate Role for Positive Emotions in Incentives, Scripts, and Fantasy

A significant direction of psychoanalytic thinking involves a new look at the drives in which affects are considered organizing features of early representations involving self in relation to other in the context of need satisfaction. Not surprisingly, such thinking incorporates a stream of psychoanalytic clinical insights from both the "object relations" and "ego psychology" traditions. Rather than recapitulating this stream of thinking, however, I will discuss two contemporary theories that provide particularly cogent and integrative views. Both views offer separate organizing roles for positive and for negative emotions and both offer potential linkages to developmental research outside of psychoanalysis.

The theory of Otto Kernberg (1976) views early experiences of peak affect states with the caregiver as marking the beginnings of drive organization as well as structuralized object relations (see also this volume). In other words, affects are seen to organize representations of self in relation to others and these become components or building blocks for the later formation (after infancy) of more complexly organized, libidinal and aggressive drives. Moreover, in Kernberg's view, such early peak affect states represent *either* extremely desirable (i.e., pleasurable) *or* extremely undesirable (i.e., painful) experiences; these in turn motivate corresponding wishes either to repeat or avoid similar affective experiences.

Kernberg's contribution in this volume details the organization and developmental fate of early, negative, peak emotional states having to do with infantile rage elicited in the context of repeated experiences of frustration and pain with the caregiver. Such experiences lead to internalized object relationships revolving around attachments to a bad or traumatizing object (in what is referred to as a process of "fixation to the trauma"). This contrasts with the organization and developmental fate of early, positive emotional states experienced in the context of love and elation with the caregiver—although Kernberg does not spell out the latter. From the point of view of this essay, Kernberg's theory, while masterful in integrating an array of previous psychoanalytic theorizing and providing new directions for thinking about positive emotions, has certain shortcomings. It focuses on peak affective experiences and leaves out those everyday or less-than-peak affective experiences considered important by many infancy researchers (e.g., Stern, 1985; Sameroff and Emde, 1989). It also uses the abstract language of metapsychology that suggests bridging to research in other fields but makes it difficult because of its metaphorical and unspecified nature.

Related theorizing by Joseph Sandler (1978) addresses a simpler language that allows for such bridging. Using an object relations theory perspective, Sandler translates the psychoanalytic notion of "drive" or "need" into the terms of a represented wish, one that includes the desired or expected response of the significant other (i.e., the response of the "object"). In other words, the very notion of "wish" implies a set of expectations—with goals and actions of others in relation to self in an imagined scenario. And positive pleasurable outcomes with others are often imagined. Not only does this model have a place for positive as well as negative emotion scenarios, but it also has the virtue of representing experience as organized nonmechanically in a way that integrates the dynamic past and the future (i.e., according to expectations). Current theorizing in the cognitive sciences, as well as in some areas of psychoanalysis, is making use of similar models that deal with sequences of expectation and dynamic themes of self in relation to other (for example, see the "role relationship models" conceptualized by Horowitz, 1987, and the "core conflictual relationship themes" conceptualized by Luborsky, 1977).

The Sandler model is convergent with another major line of thinking now occupying the cognitive sciences, psycholinguistics, and the study of emotions. This concerns script theory. Based on research showing that knowledge is stored according to event sequences (Tulving, 1972; Shank and Abelson, 1977), script theory has attempted to articulate the real-life scenarios of stored sets of expectations of self in relation to others. Tomkins (1979) proposed scripts as affectively based sequences and, more recently, Nelson and colleagues (1986) advanced our knowledge of the child's acquisition and use of scripts in relation to representations of events and developing memory. Most recently, integrated developmental approaches have discussed scripts according to affective themes and the child's emerging cognitive and linguistic capacities (Fischer et al., 1990; Nelson, 1989). In other words, research has shown that, soon after language is acquired, the child organizes representations of experience according to expectations of goal-sequences of what will happen with actors in relation to self. The 3-year-old, when asked by a skilled play-interviewer, tells of represented experiences in terms of intentions of actors and affective themes. For example, the child tells what Mommy does when a child doll plays and does not take a nap in his room as he is supposed to do, or what happens when a child doll spills juice at the family table. Tomkins has pointed out that, to a large extent, these tellings can be thought of as motivation scripts based on "affect programs." From the point of view of this essay, many of these are experienced as expectations of positive emotion scenes or desired outcomes concerning people, events, or accomplishments. To be sure, some fantasies are concerned with overcoming fears, obstacles, and distress. But others are concerned with pleasant outcomes.

Does this not sound familiar to the psychoanalyst? Fantasy is central in psychoanalytic work. And wish fulfillment in fantasy is quite often a matter of represented positive affective outcomes with respect to imagined action scripts. We are continually having fantasies that involve positive emotions. One is reminded of another essay of Sandler and Sandler (1987) in which the metaphor is invoked of an everyday preconscious fantasy "gyroscope"; the gyroscope is adaptive in periodically bringing to conscious view a small portion of the nonconscious fantasies that exist in everyday life.[2]

Negentropy Pleasure

We now come to the basic issue raised in our introduction. Freud's concept of motivation was centered around his unpleasure-pleasure principle: unpleasure resulted from an increase in drive tension and pleasure from its decrease. This principle has often been referred to as the principle of entropy (Rapaport, 1959) since motivation was seen in terms of a discharge of energy or a running down to a lower level of organization. Freud's psychobiological model was based on a physics that specified entropy as the second law of thermodynamics. But modern biology has brought us to a changed viewpoint. Organized complexity is now a central concept and, correspondingly, modern developmental biology is considered a biology of increasingly organized complexity. In other words, *negentropy* characterizes developmental systems. Although it is rare for negentropy to be discussed directly, a number of contemporary models for psychoanalytic theoriz-

[2]Script representations are affective themes that are as much interpersonal (guiding real interactions) as they are intrapsychic (guiding expectations and goals). As such they are useful metaphors for family therapists as well as for individual psychotherapists (Byng-Hall, 1986). Scripts evoke a metaphor from the theater with actors involved in dramatic encounters. I believe this metaphor is apt; represented experiences are dynamic, sequential, and goal-directed as well as expectant of final outcome scenes. There are dreaded outcomes represented in tragedies, but there are also representations of happy endings. In real life as well as in plays, there is comedy as well as tragedy, there is a wished-for happy ending as well as an expectant sad or sober one.

ing have changed in accordance with this viewpoint (for example, see Peterfreund, 1971; Bowlby, 1969; Emde, 1980; Lichtenberg, 1989), particularly when a developmental orientation is adopted. But I would like to make two additional points. First, although the principle of negentropy has not been integrated into psychoanalytic theory, it has, beginning with Freud, been included in it. Second, when we consider negentropy more directly, we can see that a good deal of pleasure is connected with it.

An early unacknowledged version of negentropy can be seen in Freud's (1905) theorizing about increasingly organizing psychosexual stages and especially about the transformations of puberty; it may also be that Freud's occasional viewing of the libido as life instinct as contrasted with the death instinct can be seen in this light. Hartmann's theory (1939) about increasing differentiation and structuralization of the ego is clearly a theory of increasing organization and complexity in development. Similarly, Spitz (1959), following Hartmann, made use of concepts of successive differentiation in development and spoke of the sequential appearance of organizers of the ego in new fields of integration. Erikson (1950) along quite similar lines formulated his ideas of epigenesis throughout the life-span—with changing and more complex levels of organization between self and society at each level.

Loewald (1960, 1971), in theorizing about therapeutic action, has brought concepts of higher levels of integration from development into the process of psychoanalytic therapy itself. Finally, I might mention that Fenichel (1945) and Rapaport (1953)—who might be thought of as the arch expositors of their time for the standard corpus of metapsychology—discussed increasing countercathexis in development and, hence, implicitly acknowledged a model that required increasing complexity rather than its decrease.

This brings us to a clarification of the psychoanalytic theorist's understanding of homeostasis. When Freud made use of Fechner's "constancy principle" in 1924, he introduced the concept of threshold to understand pleasure. Thus, one got pleasure not from the fullest discharge of excitation, but from discharge to an optimum level. Most psychoanalytic writers since have assumed that this idea is the same as a homeostatic regulatory principle (Fenichel, 1945; Saussure, 1959; Ducey and Galinsky, 1973), but this is not the case, as has been pointed out by Needles (1964). Homeostasis as set forth by the physiologist Walter Cannon (1932) requires energy and often operates so as to increase energy. Regulatory control occurs in two directions, not just one. Freud assumed one direction only, toward decreasing energy and organization. The reader only has to consider homeostatic states wherein feedback mechanisms are set in motion so as to increase energy, such as results in shivering during the cold or in seeking new food when hungry. Thus, negentropy or increasing organization occurs everyday during processes of regulation as well as across development.

Now we come to a straightforward point. A good deal of pleasure, perhaps most of it, is linked to negentropy, not entropy. It is exploratory, expectant of novelty, stimulus seeking, often linked to a variety of specific sensations, and it is organizing in its functions. Even in the psychoanalytic setting, there is pleasure not only in finding relief from tension but pleasure in finding and making new insights.

Negentropy pleasure also has a role in therapeutic action. The analyst, through emotional scaffolding, can be thought of as helping to reinstate a capacity for negentropy pleasure in the patient—i.e., a capacity for pleasure in experiencing and in integrating what is new. Such a process takes energy, if you will, and that energy comes from the outside—from another who helps one gain from new experiences (or "metabolize" them to use the biological metaphor that was a favorite of Piaget).

Developmental Considerations

Elsewhere, I described a set of basic motives that operate in the midst of increasing complexity throughout development

(Emde, 1988). From the perspective of an individual's experience, they are continual processes that orient and reorient one's position in an expanding world. The descriptive labels I gave to such motives are: (1) activity; (2) self-regulation; (3) social fittedness; and (4) affective monitoring. Although they are inborn, they are practiced, nourished, and given shape within the context of the infant-caregiver relationship, and they require an emotionally available caregiver.

From the point of view of this essay, these basic motives involve positive emotions as well as negative emotions. And I now want to add a fifth basic motive—one that gives further emphasis to positive emotions and links with my prior discussion on incentive motivation. The additional motive is that of cognitive assimilation. Piaget, in his masterful edifice of cognitive-developmental theory, considered assimilation to be the "basic fact of life." The motive of cognitive assimilation refers to the biological propensity to process information, to structuralize such information according to what is familiar, and, more broadly, to seek out novelty. Other researchers have viewed cognitive assimilation in terms of the infant's tendency to reduce cognitive discrepancy (Kagan et al., 1978; McCall, 1972). In this view, the infant is motivated to act according to a perceived discrepancy from what is expected; thus there is a future orientation in this motivation much like we have seen in incentive motivation. I believe the basic motive of cognitive assimilation can be thought of in relatively simple terms: as a tendency for the child to "get it right" in the midst of increasing exploration. The child expands knowledge with an increasingly organized view of the world. And, most importantly, "getting it right" involves positive emotions—interest, engagement, pleasure, and surprise, to name only a few.

As with all other psychological domains, cognitive assimilation operates according to principles of regulation. Affects are central mediators in this regulatory activity, and we can see the separate functioning of positive emotions. If the environmental event is mildly or moderately discrepant from what is known, it is experienced as interesting; if it is extremely discrepant, it is experienced as frightening. Something familiar, appearing in an unexpected context (providing it is not too abrupt), is experienced as surprising and may even become joyful. Where there is restriction or restraint imposed on one's plans to resolve a discrepancy, there can be frustration and anger. Finally, pleasure and mastery, in their various forms, can occur when a plan is carried out and a discrepancy resolved (Morgan and Harmon, 1984).

Concluding Questions

With today's emphasis on affirmation, empathy, and enhancing development in therapeutic work, it is appropriate that we now integrate positive emotions into our clinical theory. But unsettling questions remain for research and clinical discovery. To what extent do individual differences in early positive emotion experiences go forward in development to enhance adaptation and buffer against stress? To what extent do they generalize to other relationships and in what contexts? How much of what goes forward in development depends upon the match between the child's temperament and particular experiences with emotionally available caregivers?

Another set of questions needing research concerns questions related to developmental psychopathology. If positive emotion experiences with primary caregivers are fundamental for enhancing early developmental modes including early moral development, to what extent can early deficits in such experiences be compensated for by later salutary relationships and experiences? What is the role of early deficits in emotional availability and positive emotion experience in predisposing toward later disorder of conduct and emotion? What about the role of distortions of such early experiences and trauma? Considering today's widespread existence of broken homes, emotional deprivation of children, and traumatic child abuse, these questions are in urgent need of clinical research so that we may have better theories and targeted areas for preventive intervention. It is important for us to note that deficits and distortions in early experiences such as those we are discussing must be considered risk factors for the later development of psychopathology as opposed to markers of such pathology itself. Only a proportion of such children who later encounter the addition of other stress and risk factors (Sameroff and Emde, 1989) will develop the psychopathology. It is up to research to determine what leads to what under what circumstances so that we may target our intervention efforts for prevention.

Finally, there are many questions about the role of the child's developing negative emotions in the context of intimacy, being excluded, aggression, and sexuality. In other words, there is a major need for studying the developing oedipus complex from this framework. The child's integration of negative emotional experiences and positive emotional experiences is in need of more research and theoretical work as we bare the dynamics of an internalized morality.

We have many questions that will guide our interest and explorations for a while. Undoubtedly, there will be more surprises, not only from infancy research but also from oedipal, adolescent, and life-span research. There will certainly be more surprises from the clinical situation. Practitioners of psychoanalysis use positive emotions in spite of what sometimes seems to be a sober theory (Reik, 1937; Shor, 1990). Surprise, interest, pleasure, and a sense of irony spur creativity and allow for new views. Psychoanalytic work is often difficult, painful, and taxing, but it is not in the main a matter of entropy: we are activated by our work and enjoy it. Otherwise, it would be difficult to engage ourselves in what would be a grim and sleepy enterprise.

REFERENCES

BERLYNE, D. E. (1960). *Conflict, Arousal, and Curiosity.* New York: McGraw-Hill.

BOCCIA, M. & CAMPOS, J. J. (1983). Social referencing: Impact of emotional communication between mother and infant on reactions to strangers. Presented at the meetings of SRCD, Detroit, Michigan.

BOWLBY, J. (1969). *Attachment and Loss,* vol. 1. New York: Basic Books.
BRAZELTON, T. B., TRONICK, E., ADAMSON, L., ALS, H., & WEISE, S. (1975). *Early Mother-Infant Reciprocity.* Parent-Infant Interaction, CIBA Foundation Symposium 33. Amsterdam: Elsevier.
BRETHERTON, I. & BATES, E. (1984). The development of representation from 10 to 28 months: differential stability of language and symbolic play. In *Continuities and Discontinuities in Development,* ed. R. N. Emde & R. J. Harmon. New York: Plenum.
——— & BEEGHLY, M. (1982). Talking about internal states: The acquisition of an explicit theory of mind. *Develpm. Psychol.,* 18:906–921.
BRUNER, J. (1982). *Child's Talk: Learning to Use Language.* New York: Norton.
BYNG-HALL, J. (1986). Family scripts: A concept which can bridge child psychotherapy and family therapy thinking. *J. Child Psychother.,* 12:3–13.
CANNON, W. (1932). *The Wisdom of the Body.* New York: Norton.
CASPI, A. & ELDER, G. H., JR. (1988). Emergent family patterns: The intergenerational construction of problem behavior and relationships. In *Relationships within Families: Mutual Influences,* ed. R. Hinde & J. Stevenson-Hinde. Oxford, England: Oxford Science Publications.
COSTA, P. & MCCRAE, R. (1980). Still stable after all these years: Personality as a key to some issues in adulthood and old age. In *Life-Span Development and Behavior,* vol. 3, ed. P. Baltes & O. Brimm. New York: Academic Press, pp. 65–102.
DAMON, W. (1988). *The Moral Child.* New York: Free Press.
DAVIDSON, R. J. (1988). EEG measures of cerebral asymmetry: Conceptual and methodological issues. *Int. J. Neurosci.,* 39:71–89.
——— & FOX, N. A. (1982). Asymmetrical brain activity discriminates between positive versus negative affective stimuli in human infants. *Science,* 218:1235–1237.
——— ——— (1989). The relation between tonic EEG asymmetry and ten month old infant emotional responses to separation. *J. Abnorm. Psychol.,* 98:127–131.
DELGADO, J. M. R. (1976). Brain stimulation in man. In *Brain-Stimulation Reward,* ed. A. Wauquier & E. T. Rolls. Amsterdam: North-Holland Publishing; New York: American Elsevier Publishing.
——— ROBERTS, W. W., & MILLER, N. E. (1954). Learning motivated by electrical stimulation of the brain. *Amer. J. Physiol.,* 179:587–593.
DOI, T. (1973). *The Anatomy of Dependence.* New York: Harper & Row.
DUCEY, C. & GALINSKY, M. D. (1973). The metapsychology of pleasure. *J. Amer. Psychoanal. Assn.,* 21:495–525.
DUNN, J. (1988). *The Beginnings of Social Understanding.* Cambridge: Harvard Univ. Press.
EKMAN, P., LEVENSON, R. W., & FRIESEN, W. V. (1983). Autonomic nervous system activity distinguishes among emotions. *Science,* 221:1208–1210.
EMDE, R. N. (1980). A developmental orientation in psychoanalysis: Ways of thinking about new knowledge and further research. *Psychoanal. & Contemp. Thought,* 3:213–235.
——— (1988). Development terminable and interminable: I. Innate and motivational factors from infancy. *Int. J. Psychoanal.,* 69:23–42.
——— (1989). The infant's relationship experience: Developmental and affective aspects. In *Relationship Disturbances in Early Childhood: A Developmental Approach,* ed. A. J. Sameroff & R. N. Emde. New York: Basic Books.
——— CAMPOS, J. J., REICH, J., & GAENSBAUER, T. J. (1978). Infant smiling at

five and nine months: Analysis of heart rate and movement. *Infant Behav. & Develpm.,* 1:26–35.
——— & HARMON, R. J. (1972). Endogenous and exogenous smiling systems in early infancy. *J. Amer. Acad. Child Psychiat.,* 11:177–200.
——— & KOENIG, K. L. (1969a). Neonatal smiling and rapid eye movement states. *J. Amer. Acad. Child Psychiat.,* 8:57–67.
——— ——— (1969b). Neonatal smiling, frowning, and rapid eye movement states: II. Sleep-cycle study. *J. Amer. Acad. Child Psychiat.,* 8:637–656.
——— MCCARTNEY, R. D., & HARMON, R. J. (1971). Neonatal smiling in REM states: IV. Premature study. *Child Develpm.,* 42:1657–1661.
ERIKSON, E. H. (1950). *Childhood and Society.* New York: Norton.
EYSENCK, H. J. (1981). *A Model for Personality.* Berlin: Springer.
FEINMAN, S. (1985). Emotional expression, social referencing, and preparedness for learning in infancy: Mother knows best, but sometimes I know better. In *The Development of Expressive Behavior: Biology-Environment Interactions,* ed. G. Zivin. New York: Academic Press, pp. 291–318.
——— & LEWIS, M. (1983). Social referencing at ten months: A second-order effect on infants' responses to strangers. *Child Develpm.,* 54:878–887.
FENICHEL, O. (1945). *The Psychoanalytic Theory of Neurosis.* New York: Norton.
FIRBIRGER, H. C. & PHILLIPS, A. G. (1986). Reward, motivation, cognition: Psychobiology of mesotelencephalic dopamine systems. *The Handbook of Physiology: Section 1. The Nervous System,* 4:647–675.
FISCHER, K. W., SHAVER, P., & CARNOCHAN, P. (1990). How emotions develop and how they organize development. *Cognition and Emotion,* 4:81–127.
FLAVELL, J. H., GREEN, F. L., & FLAVELL, E. R. (1986). Development of knowledge about the appearance-reality distinction. *Monogr. Soc. Research Child Develpm.,* 51(1), Serial No. 212.
FOX, N. A. & DAVIDSON, R. J., eds. (1984). *The Psychobiology of Affective Development.* Hillsdale, N.J.: Erlbaum.
——— ——— (1987). EEG asymmetry in ten month old infants in response to approach of a stranger and maternal separation. *Develpm. Psychol.,* 24:230–236.
——— ——— (1988). Patterns of brain electrical activity during the expression of discrete emotions in ten month old infants. *Develpm. Psychol.,* 24:230–236.
FREUD, S. (1905). Three essays on the theory of sexuality. *S. E.,* 7:125–243.
——— (1920). Beyond the pleasure principle. *S. E.,* 18:3–64.
——— (1924). The economic problem of masochism. *S. E.,* 19:159–170.
——— (1940). An outline of psycho-analysis. *S. E.,* 23:141–207.
GARMEZY, N. & RUTTER, M., eds. (1983). *Stress, Coping, and Development in Children.* New York: McGraw-Hill.
GLOOR, P., OLIVER, A., QUESNEY, L. F., ANDERMANN, F., & HOROWITZ, S. (1982). The role of the limbic system in experiential phenomena of temporal lobe epilepsy. *Ann. Neurol.,* 12:129–144.
GOLDSMITH, H. H. & CAMPOS, J. J. (1986). Fundamental issues in the study of early temperament: The Denver twin temperament study. In *Advances in Developmental Technology,* ed. M. Lamb & A. Brown. Hillsdale, N.J.: Erlbaum, pp. 232–283.

GRAY, J. A. (1982). *The Neuropsychology of Anxiety.* New York: Oxford Univ. Press.

GUNNAR, M. R. & STONE, C. (1983). The effects of maternal positive affect on one-year-olds' reactions to toys: Is it social referencing? Paper presented at the meetings of SRCD, Detroit, Michigan.

HALGREN, E., WALTER, R. D., CHERLOW, D. G., & CRANDALL, P. D. (1978). Mental phenomena evoked by electrical stimulation of the human hippocampal formation and amygdala. *Brain,* 101:83–117.

HARLOW, H. F. (1953). Mice, monkeys, men and motives. *Psychol. Rev.,* 60:23–32.

HARMON, R. J. & EMDE, R. N. (1972). Spontaneous REM behaviors in a microcephalic infant: A clinical anatomical study. *Perceptual and Motor Skills,* 34:827–833.

HARTMANN, H. (1939). *Ego Psychology and the Problem of Adaptation.* New York: Int. Univ. Press, 1958.

HASSLER, R. & REICHERT, T. (1961). *Nervenarzt,* 32:97–109. As cited in McGeer, Eccles, & McGeer (1987). *Molecular Neurobiology of the Mammalian Brain,* 2nd ed. New York: Plenum.

HEATH, R. G. (1964). Pleasure response of human subjects to direct stimulation of the brain: Physiologic and psychodynamic considerations. In *The Role of Pleasure in Behavior,* ed. R. G. Heath. New York: Harper & Row.

HEBB, D. O. (1949). *The Organization of Behavior.* New York: Wiley.

HENDRICK, I. (1934). *Facts and Theories of Psychoanalysis.* New York: Knopf, 2nd ed., 1939.

HOFFMAN, M. L. (1977). Moral internalization: Current theory and research. In *Advances in Experimental Social Psychology,* vol. 10, ed. L. Berkowitz. New York: Academic Press.

HOROWITZ, M. H. (1987). *States of Mind: Configurational Analysis of Individual Psychology.* New York: Plenum.

JACOBSON, E. (1953). The affects and their pleasure-unpleasure qualities, in relation to the psychic discharge processes. In *Drives, Affects, Behavior,* ed. R. M. Loewenstein. New York: Int. Univ. Press, pp. 38–66.

KAGAN, J. (1981). *The Second Year: The Emergence of Self-Awareness.* Cambridge: Harvard Univ. Press.

——— KEARSLEY, R., & ZELASO, P. (1978). *Infancy: Its Place in Human Development.* Cambridge: Harvard Univ. Press.

KAYE, K. (1982). *The Mental and Social Life of Babies: How Parents Create Persons.* Chicago: Univ. Chicago Press.

KERNBERG, O. F. (1976). *Object Relations Theory and Clinical Psychoanalysis.* New York: Aronson.

KLEIN, G. S. (1967). Peremptory ideation: Structure and force in motivated ideas. In *Psychol. Issues,* monogr. 18/19. New York: Int. Univ. Press.

KLINNERT, M. D. (1984). The regulation of infant behavior by maternal facial expression. *Infant Behavior and Develpm.,* 7:447–465.

——— EMDE, R. N., BUTTERFIELD, P., & CAMPOS, J. J. (1986). Social referencing: The infant's use of emotional signals from a friendly adult with mother present. *Develpm. Psychol.,* 22:427–432.

KOHUT, H. (1971). *The Analysis of the Self.* New York: Int. Univ. Press.

LACAN, J. (1966). *Ecrits.* Paris: Editions du Seuil.
LICHTENBERG, J. D. (1989). *Psychoanalysis and Motivation.* New York: Analytic Press.
LOEWALD, H. W. (1960). On the therapeutic action of psychoanalysis. *Int. J. Psychoanal.,* 41:16–33.
——— (1971). On motivation and instinct theory. *Psychoanal. Study Child,* 26:91–128.
LUBORSKY, L. (1977). Measuring a pervasive psychic structure in psychotherapy: The core conflictual relationship theme. In *Communicative Structures and Psychic Structures,* ed. N. Freedman & S. Grand. New York: Plenum.
MCCALL, R. B. (1972). Smiling and vocalization in infants as indices of perceptual-cognitive processes. *Merrill-Palmer Q.,* 18:341–348.
MCGEER, P. L., ECCLES, J. C., & MCGEER, E. G. (1987). *Molecular Neurobiology of the Mammalian Brain.* New York: Plenum, 2nd ed.
MARK, V. H. & ERVIN, F. R. (1970). *Violence and the Brain.* New York: Harper & Row.
MASLOW, A. H. (1971). *The Farther Reaches of Human Nature.* New York: Viking Press.
MOGENSON, G. & PHILLIPS, A. (1978). Brain-stimulation reward after twenty-five years. *Canad. J. Psychiat.,* 31:54–57.
MORGAN, G. A. & HARMON, R. J. (1984). Developmental transformations and mastery motivation: Measurement and validation. In *Continuities and Discontinuities in Development,* ed. R. N. Emde & R. J. Harmon. New York: Plenum, pp. 263–291.
NASS, R. D. & GAZZANIGA, M. S. (1987). Cerebral lateralization and specialization in human central nervous system. In *Handbook of Physiology: Section I. The Nervous System.* Bethesda: American Psychological Society.
NEEDLES, W. (1964). Comments on the pleasure-unpleasure experience. *J. Amer. Psychoanal. Assn.,* 12:300–314.
NELSON, K. (1986). *Event Knowledge: Structure and Function in Development.* Hillsdale, N.J.: Erlbaum.
——— ed. (1989). *Narratives from the Crib.* Cambridge: Harvard Univ. Press.
OLDS, J. & MILNER, P. (1954). Positive reinforcement produced by electrical stimulation of septal area and other regions of rat brain. *J. Comp. Physiol. Psychol.,* 47:419–427.
PATTERSON, G. R. & DISHION, T. J. (1988). Multilevel family process models: Traits, interactions, and relationships. In *Relationships within Families: Mutual Influences,* ed. R. Hinde & J. Stevenson-Hinde. Oxford: Clarendon Press (Oxford Science Publications), pp. 283–310.
PENFIELD, W. & PEROT, P. (1963). The brain's record of auditory and visual experience: A final summary and discussion. *Brain,* 86:595–696.
PETERFREUND, E. (1971). Information systems and psychoanalysis: An evolutionary biological approach to psychoanalytic theory. *Psychol. Issues,* monogr. 25/26. New York: Int. Univ. Press.
PIAGET, J. (1932). *The Moral Judgment of the Child.* New York: Free Press, 1965.
——— (1936). *The Origins of Intelligence in Children.* New York: Int. Univ. Press, 1952.
PLOMIN, R. (1986). *Development, Genetics and Psychology.* Hillsdale: N.J.: Erlbaum.

POLAK, P. R., EMDE, R. N., & SPITZ, R. A. (1964a). The smiling response: I. Methodology, quantification and natural history. *J. Nerv. Ment. Dis.*, 139:103–109.

——— ——— ——— (1964b). The smiling response: II. Visual discrimination and the onset of depth perception. *J. Nerv. Ment. Dis.*, 139:407–415.

RADO, S. (1964). Hedonic self-regulation of the organism. In *The Role of Pleasure in Behavior,* ed. R. G. Heath. New York: Harper & Row.

RAPAPORT, D. (1953). On the psychoanalytic theory of affect. *Int. J. Psychoanal.*, 34:177–198.

——— (1959). The structure of psychoanalytic theory: A systematizing attempt. *Psychol. Issues,* monogr. 6. New York: Int. Univ. Press.

REIK, T. (1937). *Surprise and the Psychoanalyst: On the Conjecture and Comprehension of Unconscious Processes.* London: Kegan Paul.

SAMEROFF, A. J. & EMDE, R. N., eds. (1989). *Relationship Disturbances in Early Childhood: A Developmental Approach.* New York: Basic Books.

SANDLER, J. (1978). On the development of object relationships and affects. *Int. J. Psychoanal.*, 59:285–296.

——— & SANDLER, A.-M. (1987). The past unconscious, the present unconscious, and the vicissitudes of guilt. *Int. J. Psychoanal.*, 68:331–341.

SAUSSURE, R. DE (1959). The metapsychology of pleasure. *Int. J. Psychoanal.*, 15:81–93.

SEM-JACOBSEN, C. W. (1976). Electrical stimulation and self-stimulation in man with chronic implanted electrodes. In *Brain-Stimulation Reward,* ed. A. Wanquier & E. T. Rolls. Amsterdam: Elsevier, pp. 505–526.

SHANK, R. C. & ABELSON, R. (1977). *Scripts, Plans, Goals, and Understanding.* Hillsdale, N.J.: Erlbaum.

SHOR, J. (1990). *Work, Love, Play: Self Repair in the Psychoanalytic Dialogue.* Los Angeles: Double Helix Press.

SILBERMAN, E. K. & WEINGARTNER, H. (1986). Hemispheric lateralization of functions related to emotion. *Brain and Cognition,* 5:322–353.

SORCE, J. F. & EMDE, R. N. (1981). Mother's presence is not enough: The affect of emotional availability on infant exploration. *Develpm. Psychol.*, 17:737–745.

——— CAMPOS, J. J. & KLINNERT, M. D. (1985). Maternal emotional signaling: Its effect on the visual cliff behavior of 1-year-olds. *Develpm. Psychol.*, 21:195–200.

SPITZ, R. A. (1959). Some early prototypes of ego defenses. *J. Amer. Psychoanal. Assn.*, 9:626–251.

——— (1965). *The First Year of Life.* New York: Int. Univ. Press.

——— & WOLF, K. M. (1946). The smiling response. *Genet. Psychol. Monogr.*, 34:57–125.

SROUFE, L. & WUNSCH, J. P. (1972). The development of laughter in the first year of life. *Child Develpm.*, 43:1326–1344.

STERN, D. N., PARMELEE, A. H., AKIYAMA, Y., SCHULTZ, M. A., & WENNER, W. H. (1969). Sleep cycle characteristics in infants. *Pediatrics,* 43:65–70.

——— (1985). *The Interpersonal World of the Infant.* New York: Basic Books.

——— (1977). *The First Relationship: Mother and Infant.* Cambridge: Harvard Univ. Press.

TELLEGAN, A. (1984). Structures of mood and personality and their relevance to assessing anxiety, with an emphasis on self report. In *Anxiety and Anxiety Disorders,* ed. A. Tuma & J. Moser. Hillsdale, N.J.: Erlbaum, pp. 681-706.

TOMKINS, S. S. (1962). *Affect, Imagery and Consciousness:* vol. I. *The Positive Affects.* New York: Springer.

——— (1979). Script theory: Differential magnification of affects. In *Nebraska Symposium on Motivation,* vol. 26, ed. H. E. Howe, Jr. & R. A. Dienstbier. Lincoln: Univ. Nebraska Press.

TREVARTHEN, C. (1979). Communication and cooperation in early infancy: A description of primary intersubjectivity. In *Before Speech: The Beginning of Interpersonal Communication,* ed. M. Bullowa. Cambridge: Cambridge Univ. Press, pp. 321-347.

——— (1984). Hemisphere specialization. *The Handbook of Physiology. Section 1: The Nervous System*, 3.

TRONICK, E., ALS, H., ADAMSON, L., WISE, S., & BRAZELTON, T. B. (1978). The infant's response to entrapment between contradictory messages in face-to-face interaction. *J. Amer. Acad. Child Psychiat.,* 17:1-13.

——— & GIANINO, A. F., JR. (1986). The transmission of maternal disturbance to the infant. In *Maternal Depression and Infant Disturbance,* ed. E. Z. Tronick & T. Field. San Francisco: Jossey-Bass.

TULVING, E. (1972). Episodic and semantic memory. In *Organization of Memory,* ed. E. Tulving & W. Donaldson. New York: Academic Press.

WALDEN, T. A. & BAXTER, A. (1989). The effect of content and age on social referencing. *Child Develpm.,* 60:1511-1518.

WELLMAN, H. M., CROSS, D., & BARTSCH, K. (1986). Infant search and object permanence: A meta-analysis of the a-not-b error. *Monogr. Soc. Research Child Devel.,* 51(3), Serial No. 214.

WHITE, R. W. (1963). Ego and reality in psychoanalytic theory. *Psychol. Issues,* monogr. 11. New York: Int. Univ. Press.

WINNICOTT, D. W. (1971). *Playing and Reality.* New York: Basic Books.

WOLFF, P. (1959). Observations on newborn infants. *Psychosom. Med.,* 21:110-118.

ZAHN-WAXLER, C. & RADKE-YARROW, M. (1982). The development of altruism: Alternative research strategies. In *The Development of Prosocial Behavior,* ed. N. Eisenberg. New York: Academic Press.

University of Colorado Medical Center
Box C 268
4200 East Ninth Avenue
Denver, CO 80262

SELF-CONSCIOUS EMOTIONS AND THE DEVELOPMENT OF SELF

MICHAEL LEWIS, PH.D.

The study of self-conscious emotions, in particular shame, has received relatively little attention. In this paper, I propose a theory of shame which relies upon the interface between thought and feeling. I postulate that self-conscious emotions require that individuals possess two cognitive abilities: the ability to set standards and to evaluate them, and the ability to focus on different aspects of oneself. In attending to the self, individuals can focus either on a global self or on a specific self-action. Shame is not necessarily a consequence of any particular event; rather shame occurs when individuals evaluate themselves as failing and consider that the failure involves the total self. Viewing self-conscious emotions in this way allows us to observe their ontogenetic development as a function of cognitive changes as well as the parental socialization factors which lead to individual differences.

IN THE PAPER TO FOLLOW I wish to discuss the general topic of self-conscious emotions with specific focus on shame. In order to do so it will be necessary for me first to present a diverse set of examples of the phenomena under inquiry. Having done so, I will define what I mean by self-conscious emotions. The etiology of the development of self-conscious emotions is next considered, while the paper will finish with the discussion of the socialization characteristics likely to lead to individual differences.

In order to understand what is to follow I will focus our attention on the shame that surrounds us in everyday life. These examples occur in almost all settings in which we find human behavior. The first example is what I have called Angry Donald.

Professor of Pediatrics and Psychiatry, University of Medicine and Dentistry of New Jersey, Robert Wood Johnson Medical School, New Brunswick, New Jersey.

We are in one of the observation rooms of my laboratory watching a mother playing with her two-year-old child. We have asked her to teach the child how to play a particular game.

We observe her showing the child how to do the task. "Look," she says, "take this donut and move it from here to there." The child complies. "Very good. You are a good boy. Now," she says, "take the second donut and put it on this one." In this way, she slowly goes through how to solve the task. The child watches her intently as she both explains and shows the child how it is done. She occasionally smiles, but her face is serious. She often praises the child with such comments as "Good boy," "You are really clever," "Smart lad." Now she rearranges the problem, and presents it to the child. The child takes the first piece and puts it on the wrong shaft. The child smiles and looks up at the mother. The mother looks at the child and hollers, "No, no, no! What is wrong with you?" Our cameras close in on her face. The expression is one in which the nose is raised, nostrils flared, and we know that we will later score it as a contempt/disgust look. The child looks up at the mother confused and turns back to the task. However, his body is now hunched over, his smile is gone, and he no longer appears interested in what is happening. The mother insists that the child go on. The child reaches for the ring and, rather than placing it on the shaft, throws it across the room.

The mother's disgusted face has shamed the child, and the child, ashamed, responds with what Helen Block Lewis (1971) calls humiliating fury; the child throws the quoit across the room. The second example also comes from an observation of a child.

Rebecca is four. She comes into the playroom and sits down with her mother at a table. Rebecca's mother hands her a doll. Unbeknownst to Rebecca, the doll has been designed to fall apart soon after she starts playing with it. She starts to play, showing the mother various pieces, pointing out the interesting aspects of the toy (it is a toy that was purchased in China, and so is dressed in unusual fashion). After about three minutes of play, the leg of the doll falls off. Our camera zooms in on Rebecca. Her mother looks at her and asks, "What is wrong?" Rebecca does not answer. Her face is turned away; her shoulders are raised; and she sits slumped over her chair. She will not look at her mother, although her mother asks her again what is wrong. Rebecca produces a faint smile, but still she will not look up. After a short time, she puts the doll with its broken leg back on the shelf where she got it and sits quietly in front of the toy cabinet, appearing to be aimlessly staring into space.

Rebecca has been shamed. She thinks she has broken the toy, and even though her mother has not said anything to her about the toy being broken, she has withdrawn from the situation, sits quietly alone, not attending to any particular activity, and appears to be depressed. She will not speak, although her mother repeatedly asks her what is wrong. This behavior is in marked contrast to another four-year-old who, once the toy broke, brought it to her mother, and tried to get her mother to help her fix it. Suzy did not appear depresssed; she did not withdraw; and with her facial expression and demeanor she sought to repair the harm she thought she had done. How unlike Rebecca, whose withdrawal, body posture, lack of speech, all inform us of her shame over her action.

Because of the unique nature of shame as a self-conscious emotion it has the capacity to affect those around us. The example of Paul's public performance, a case I present next, demonstrates this.

I am sitting in a high school auditorium next to the parent of a friend of my daughter. They are both in the school orchestra. While my daughter plays the violin, her friend Paul plays the oboe. We both sit as proud parents, admiring our children's performance and skill. The friend of my daughter has a solo piece. As he rises and begins his passage, it is obvious to the audience that something is wrong, and that he seems to have forgotten the passage. After what appears to be an interminable few seconds, the child remembers and begins to play. Having finished the portion, he sits down. I turn to look at his father to congratulate him on his son's behavior, and I say, in a whisper, "Once he got it, he played it really well." As I turn toward his parent, I notice that he is blushing, and that the blush extends from his face to below his collar. He does not look back at me, but does manage a faint smile, staring straight ahead. At the end of the concert, he gets up and leaves. He cannot be found among the other parents, who sip juice and cookies to celebrate the end of the concert.

The father of the child has been shamed. As many of us, he has experienced shame not because of any action that he has caused directly, but because he is associated with someone who has failed and may be ashamed. How similar this is to all parents who feel, at one point or another, shamed by the action of their children, or like husbands and wives, shamed by the action of their mates.

Not only is shame an intrapsychic event, but it is an interpsychic event affecting couples and interpersonal relationships. In the description to follow, called Dyadic Shame Games, we see this happening in terms of couple difficulty.

A couple came to see me who had been married for some time and who appeared to be having a rough time in their marriage. After they were seated for a while, the wife turned to me and said, "Doctor, I don't think I can stand it any longer. He is always criticizing me. Everything I do is wrong. I don't feel there is anything I can do which will please him." She continued like this for a few moments. I turned to the husband to give him his turn to complain. "Doctor," he said, "I don't know what is wrong with her. Half the time she is depressed, the other half of the time she is furious with me. I don't know what it is that I am doing. Just last night, for example, I said to her, 'Why did you use this tablecloth? It has a big stain. Why don't we use another one?' " He was just barely able to finish what had happened when she turned on him and said, "There, you see, Doctor, he is always critical, he is always hostile, he is always dissatisfied with me." The husband turned quickly and said, "No, I simply suggested that we use another tablecloth."

Unbeknownst to the husband, his "suggestions" are statements of shame for his wife. She is aware only of his aggressive action. He is aware only of making suggestions. Her response to this shame is withdrawal, depression, and anger. He is unaware that his action may be causing this response. He sees her withdrawal as the withdrawal of love, and he, in turn, is shamed by it. They, like many couples, have created a shame environment in which, unbeknownst to either, they both shame each other.

Given the centrality of this emotion in our everyday lives, it is interesting that relatively little work on the topic has appeared, either in the psychoanalytic field or in the study of emotion. D. L. Nathanson (1987) most recently said, "In the 20 years I have stayed awake at case conferences, attended lectures, professional meetings, and symposia, I have never heard a single case in which embarrassment, ridicule, humiliation, mortification, or any other of the shame family of emotions, was discussed" (pp. vii–viii).

There are of course exceptions to this. First, there is the pioneering psychoanalytic work of H. B. Lewis (1971), and before her, Piers and Singer (1953). In the literature on emotion, Tomkins (1963), especially his second volume focuses on shame. More recently, there have been a series of new books, including those by H. B. Lewis (1987), Nathanson (1987), and Morrison (1989). In my discussion I shall be referring to normal rather than pathological issues. From my perspective, shame and the other self-conscious emotions are as species specific and natural as are the other emotions, such as fear, joy, or sadness. While all emotions are "natural," it is important to keep in mind that to feel shame is, by definition, not in itself pathological. The pathology is to be found in too much or too little shame and in the repression of shame and its resulting symptomatology.

The Definition of Some Self-Conscious Emotions

Self-conscious emotions might be defined by looking for a unique set of behaviors which might reflect them. However, unlike the primary emotions, the self-conscious emotions have no unique facial or postural index to reference them. Although this appears true, Darwin (1872) suggested that self-conscious emotions were characterized by the species-specific behavior of blushing. Unfortunately individual differences in blushing prevent its use as a reliable measure. Other measures may be possible and these have been discussed elsewhere (see M. Lewis, in press a; Zahn-Waxler and Kochanska, in press). Nevertheless, a definition of these emotions, resting simply on a behavioral manifestation, is not adequate. This feature of self-conscious emotions distinguishes them from primary emotions, for, as has been amply demonstrated, primary emotions bear some correspondence to specific facial configurations (Ekman et al., 1972; Izard, 1977). Thus, for example, anger and angry face bear some one-to-one correspondence. However, even here, the relationship between expression and the actual internal state is not perfect (see Campos et al., 1989; Scherer and Ekman, 1984; Lewis and Michalson, 1983, 1985).

Another possible approach to the measurement of self-conscious emotions might be in regarding a specific set of stimuli which are likely to elicit these emotions. The psychoanalytic approach in regard to self-conscious emotions, in particular shame, has suggested that specific situations, particularly those having to do with toilet or genital functions, are likely to elicit shame or guilt. While it may be that shame or guilt or both are elicited by such situations, their occurrence does not bear a one-to-one correspondence to these emotions.

It does not seem that either situations or specific behaviors bear a strong one-to-one correspondence with particular self-conscious emotions. It is important to look elsewhere to understand and study these emotions. In what follows, I will present a structural analysis which utilizes a phenomenological approach based upon a cognitive attributional theory (Weiner, 1986).

Figure 1 presents the structural model which I will use to define self-conscious emotions. The reader will notice that there are three subscripts, A, B, and C, which represent cognitive processes that serve as stimuli for these specific emotions.

Standards, Rules, and Goals

This first set of cognitive processes has to do with standards, rules, and goals, and the evaluation of one's behavior in terms of these standards, rules, and goals (SRGs). From the developmental perspective the child needs to acquire SRGs. Goals are established both out of biological imperatives, the drive quality of primary emotions, and from goals as articulated by the culture in which they are born. The development of SRGs comes about through the child's knowledge of the societal and family SRGs. This knowledge is acquired through both a passive process and an active one (M. Lewis and Feiring, 1981).

In the passive process the child is rewarded or punished for certain behaviors and actions, and it is in the reward or punishment of the culture and the family that the child comes to acquire knowledge about these SRGs. In the active process, the children themselves discover the SRGs that guide the actions, thoughts, and emotions of others. In the social cognitive literature, it has been understood, at least for the past 25 years, that children's behavior can be shaped both by the passive mode and by the children's active exploration of their environment and their active attempts to acquire information about the rules and motives governing the behavior of others (see, for example, M. Lewis, in press b; Mischel, 1966; Bandura, 1986). The acquisition of these SRGs is slow and occurs over the entire life-span. Nevertheless, it is reasonable to

SELF-CONSCIOUS EVALUATIVE EMOTIONS

A. STANDARDS AND RULES

B. EVALUATION

C. ATTRIBUTION OF SELF

SUCCESS	FAILURE	
HUBRIS	SHAME	GLOBAL
PRIDE	GUILT/ REGRET	SPECIFIC

Figure 1

assume that the acquisition of SRGs starts quite early and this can be seen in the child's behavior, certainly within the first year or two of life.

Evaluation of Actions, Thoughts, and Feelings

The evaluation of one's actions, thoughts, and feelings in terms of these standards is the second cognitive evaluative process which serves as a stimulus for self-conscious emotions. It seems reasonable to assume that as soon as children acquire SRGs, they need to evaluate their behavior in terms of whether or not these SRGs have been reached or failed. It is reasonable, therefore, to assume that evaluation of one's action is a necessary feature of the acquisition of SRGs themselves. The consequence of this evaluation of the self's behavior is the resulting knowledge that one has succeeded or failed vis-à-vis the SRGs. It is possible that in the evaluation one neither succeeds nor fails. Such cases make the model more complex. For the sake of parsimony, only the consequences of evaluation as resulting in success and failure vis-à-vis SRGs will be considered. As one might imagine, success or failure can occur around any SRG, be it related to direct action toward others or toward the self. Moreover, success and failure can be evaluated for actions, thoughts, or feelings.

It is important to note that the evaluation of the self relative to actions, thoughts, or feelings can reflect an accurate interpretation—another self also would reach the same conclusion—or can reflect an inaccurate interpretation. For example, I knew a student who received a grade of 90 on her paper. While you and I might think this constituted success, she saw this as a failure. Many factors may be involved in producing inaccurate evaluations of success or failure. We do not have time to go into the various possibilities, but some are briefly mentioned as we proceed. Inaccuracy can be a consequence of establishing too high or too low an SRG or can be a consequence of a misinterpretation of one's behavior vis-à-vis the SRG. It is clear that individuals differ in the establishment of SRGs and in the process of evaluating their own behavior. These individual differences need to be explored. In the literature on achievement and school performance there has been an attempt to explore some of the evaluative processes (see, for example, Dweck and Leggett, 1988). Of particular importance has been the finding that there are sex differences in both the establishment of SRGs and the evaluative process. A number of authors have found that females are more likely than males to make a global evaluation when they fail (Beck, 1967; Seligman, 1975; H. B. Lewis, 1976; Weiner, 1986).

Self-Focus

The third cognitive attributional process involved in self-conscious emotions has to do with how an individual focuses on the self, in particular global vs. specific self-evaluation (Weiner, 1986). Global evaluation makes reference to "total" self-evaluation. Some individuals, some of the time, are likely to focus on the totality of the self, using such evaluative-like phrases as "because I did this, I am bad." In this type of global evaluation the individual focuses on the totality of the self. This is in sharp contrast to specific self-evaluative processes. Specific self-evaluation has to do with the process of focusing on a specific quality or action of the self. This is associated with such evaluative-like phrases as "what I did was to do *X* in the wrong way." Notice that in such thought processes, the focus is not on the totality of the self but upon the specific behavior of the self in a specific situation.

In the paradigm discussed, it should be clear that the cognitive evaluative processes are not dependent on specific SRGs or specific evaluative processes in terms of success or failure or in terms of global versus specific self-attribution. This is a general model and cannot be used in a predictive sense. Only if an individual has a SRG and evaluates it and gives attributes to the self in a certain way can we talk about the emergence of a specific self-conscious emotion.[1] Given these sets of cognitive evaluative processes, it is possible to observe the set of self-conscious evaluative emotional states that are the center of our concern. As one can see from observing Figure 1, four self-conscious emotional states can be distinguished on the basis of cognitive evaluative process as articulated. Hubris (pridefulness) and shame are a consequence of global self-focus and the evaluation of success and failure. Pride and guilt are the consequence of specific self-focus and the evaluation of success or failure. Each emotional state will be discussed in turn.

Shame. Shame is the product of two sets of cognitive activities: the person's evaluation of his or her action, thought, or behavior as failure, and a global self-evaluation. The phenomenological experience of the person having shame is that of a wish to hide, disappear, or die. It is a highly negative and painful state (perhaps the most painful emotional state known), and subjects having such a state report extreme discomfort. Because of the intensity of this emotional state, the global attack on the self-system, all the subjects can do when presented with such a state is to attempt to rid themselves of it. However, since this is a global attack on the self, subjects have

[1]Whether or not there are specific situations which are more or less likely to cause specific cognitive attributional processes to occur remains of concern. Are there specific situations more likely to elicit global versus specific self-focus? I cannot go into detail here except to say that there are certain classes of situations that should be more likely than others to elicit these different self-focuses. Moreover, and perhaps even more important, there are likely to be individual differences. Some individuals may be more likely than others to focus on global rather than the specific self. Sex differences appear to exist (Dweck and Leggett, 1988), with females rather than males more likely to focus on the global self. Finally, there may be age differences with younger children more likely to focus on the global self. While such individual and group differences may exist, there is no reason to imagine that individuals do not use both cognitive attributions. Thus, the difference between individuals is relative rather than absolute. In general, this seems a reasonable posture. However, in any discussion of personality types, for example, the narcissistic individual, the likelihood of using one type of focus, in this case, global, becomes relevant. Moreover, the literature on depression/helplessness also suggests that some personalities utilize a global self-focus strategy.

great difficulty in dissipating this emotion. I have proposed a variety of strategies for dealing with the emotion of shame (M. Lewis, in press a); however, I have space only to mention some of them. These include denial, laughter, displacement, confession, and, in more pathological situations, depression and rage.

Some evaluations of failure are more likely to produce more of a global evaluation than others. Two different causes for this exist, both having to do with the centrality of the failure. For example, it is important that I do not fail in a research project, but less important that I fail to drive a car properly. Likewise, some failures are more likely to deal with total self than others; for example, failures around the body—the prototype for women is being ugly; and for men, being impotent. These failures may invoke global evaluation because they are more self-centered (H. B. Lewis, 1971, 1987).

Embarrassment. It is important to mention the issue of intensity of shame. The reported intensity of shame appears to vary. Some situations evoke more shame than others. Differences in the intensity of shame have been used to discuss the emotion of embarrassment, and there are some who would argue that embarrassment is a mild form of shame (Izard, 1977). This seems reasonable, and one type of embarrassment does have to do with negative evaluation of the self. Nevertheless, phenomenological observation and inquiry reveal that the emotion "embarrassment" for the most part is quite different phenomenologically from shame. Shame may have more to do with the failure of standards, rules, and goals that are central to the core definition of the self. Embarrassment may have more to do with failures associated with less important features of the self. Thus, if I fail at being a good driver (not a core aspect of myself), I am embarrassed, whereas if I fail as a teacher (core), I am shamed.

Some embarrassment also may have to do with the exposure of the self rather than with the evaluation of the self (Buss, 1980). Perhaps the best example is the case of being complimented. The phenomenological experience of those who appear before audiences is that of embarrassment caused by the positive comments of the introduction. Compliments seem to produce embarrassment. *Since compliments cannot readily lead to an evaluation of failure, it is likely that embarrassment due to compliments has more to do with the exposure of the self than with evaluation.* At the moment, my best guess is that there are two different aspects of embarrassment, one having to do with exposure and with shyness (Buss, 1980), while the other has more to do with self-evaluation. This second feature is more related to shame. This issue remains unclear and in need of more study. It is clear, however, that embarrassment is not merely a less intense form of shame.

Guilt. If any self-conscious emotion has been discussed in detail, it is that of guilt. Both the psychoanalytic and the psychological literature have considered this concept in some detail. In fact, Hoffman (1970) sees shame as a subtype of guilt, and Zahn-Waxler and Kochanska (in press), in their review of the origins of guilt, often use guilt to mean both shame and guilt. An even greater problem is the diverse meanings given to guilt and shame. While the definition offered here cannot resolve these differences, it does allow us a starting point for empirical study.

The emotional state of guilt or regret is produced when an individual evaluates his or her behavior as failure but focuses on the specific features of the self or on the self's action which led to the failure. Unlike shame, where the focus is on the global self, here the individual focuses on the self's actions and behaviors which are likely to repair the failure. From a phenomenological point of view, the individual is pained by the failure, but this pained feeling is directed to the cause of the failure or the object of harm. Because the cognitive attributional process focuses on the action of the self rather than on the totality of the self, the feeling that is produced, guilt, is not as intensely negative as shame and does not lead to confusion and to the loss of action. In fact, the emotion of guilt often has associated with it a corrective action, which the individual can do, but does not necessarily do, to repair the failure. Rectification of the failure or preventing it from occurring again are two possible corrective paths. Whereas in shame we see the body hunched over itself in an attempt to hide and disappear, in guilt we see the individual moving in space as if trying to repair action. The postural differences which accompany guilt and shame are marked and are helpful in distinguishing these emotions and in measuring individual differences. We might point to blushing as a measure also distinguishing guilt from shame; because of the variability in an individual's likelihood to blush, however, the use of blushing is not an accurate index.

Because in guilt the focus is on the specific, individuals are capable of ridding themselves of this emotional state through action. The corrective action can be directed toward the self as well as toward the other; guilt has the self differentiated from the object; thus, the emotion is less intense and more capable of dissipation.

There are levels of this negative state, having to do with the ease or availability of corrective action. In some cases, corrective action may not be as readily available as in others. Should the corrective action not be forthcoming, either in thought, feeling, or deed, it is possible that a guilt experience can be converted into one of shame. Here, then, is another difference between shame and guilt. We can be ashamed of our guilty action, but we cannot be guilty over being ashamed, suggesting a levels difference and a directional difference in experiencing these emotions. The emotion of guilt lacks the negative intensity of shame and as such can be viewed as a more useful emotion in motivating specific and corrective action. However, because it is less intense, it may not convey the motivation necessary for change or correction.

This definition of shame and guilt is not consistent with that currently being used in the psychoanalytic literature. Nevertheless, the distinction made here is receiving more attention (Nathanson, 1987; Morrison, 1989). Moreover, such a definition allows us empirically to explore its possibility. Recall that in my earlier example, Rebecca was shamed, but Suzy was not. I claim this difference was based on the behavioral differences seen. Rebecca showed body collapse, she could not act coherently, she could not speak, all markers of shame (H. B. Lewis, 1971). Suzy, on the other hand, could act and she tried to rectify her failure. These differences mark the distinction between shame and guilt and can be seen in young children.[2]

Hubris and Pride. Language usage is a problem when discussing the self-conscious emotions. We have difficulty not only with "shame" and "guilt" but also with "pride." We do not have two terms to characterize "pride," although we do have two meanings for the term. The first meaning refers to the idea of "prideful"; that is, the negative type of pride. For this idea, I use the Greek term, "hubris." For the pride that comes with the success of a specific action, I use the term "pride."

Such a distinction immediately informs us about the relation of these two types of successful self-evaluation. In the first

[2]Such differences between shame and guilt lead us to a possible methodology for a behavioral examination of these emotions. In particular, under conditions of failure we should find some children or adults who move away from the source of failure while others try to rectify it. I would hypothesize that in the former case individuals are experiencing shame, and in the latter case, guilt. Recently, there have been several studies which have looked at children's behavior when confronted with a failure. Barnett and Zahn-Waxler (1987) and Zahn-Waxler and Kochanska (in press) have reported that when children are given toys which fall apart and break, some children attempt to repair the toy while others seem to move away. The use of reparation may be a valuable measure in differentiating shame and guilt. Moreover, H. B. Lewis (1971), Tomkins (1963), and Darwin (1872) have suggested that during shame there is a collapse of the body posture and inability to communicate and think clearly. This postural as well as cognitive collapse appears to support the difference between shame and guilt in terms of reparation. If we think of shame as an attack on the self, we would expect a collapsing of the self; therefore, the self's ability to act is unlikely, at least for a moment. This should take the form of body posture of collapsing, thought-pattern disruption, and, obviously, an unhappy, sad face. On the other hand, guilt, being associated with action, should not have those particular body features, specifically the collapsed body action.

hubris is a consequence of success vis-à-vis SRGs where the focus is on the global self. In this emotion, the individual focuses on the total self as successful. It is often associated, especially in extreme cases, with grandiosity or with narcissism. Because of the global nature of the emotion of hubris, it is likely to be transient and in order to be able to maintain this state, the individual must either alter standards or reevaluate what constitutes success. Like shame, it is unrelated to specific action; unlike shame, however, it is highly positive and therefore emotionally rewarding.

The prohibition against hubris is well-known and suggests that it needs to be avoided since it can be a potentially dangerous emotion. This danger comes from both internal process distortion and external interpsychic conflict. The internal problem is that the person focuses on self, not action. Because of this, the state is not readily reproducible except by altering the evaluative process, that is, by faulty reasoning. Interpsychic conflict is likely since hubris produces rancor and upset to those around the individual. Others view an individual's hubris as an attack on themselves and their worth.

Pride, on the other hand, is the consequence of a successful evaluation of a specific action. The phenomenological experience is "joy over an action well done." Here, again, the focus of pleasure is specific and related to specific behavior, thought, or feeling. One might think that this feeling is associated with achievement, and Heckhausen (1984) has discussed the acquisition of this type of pride. Its association with achievement motivation seems particularly apt. Because this positive state is associated with a particular action, individuals have available to themselves the means by which they can produce this state; thus the accent on achievement. Notice that unlike hubris, pride's specific focus allows for action.

The cognitive evaluative process that I have suggested allows us to consider the role of self throughout our understanding of this evaluative attributional process. Such a scheme not only is useful from a definitional point of view, but it has usefulness in articulating the processes which underlie the production of these emotions. Because this scheme is heavily dependent upon the emergence of consciousness, it has interesting developmental features.

Development of Self-Consciousness

Before presenting a developmental sequence, a discussion of several critical issues is necessary. The question that I will address is the development of consciousness. However, it is important that we first answer what we mean by human consciousness. In order to do this, it will be necessary to make use of a variety of terms which appear in the literature. These include self-schema, self-awareness, or self-consciouness. For the purpose here I will use self-schema to refer to the total knowledge that one has pertaining to the self. Self-awareness or self-consciousness will refer only to the final cognitive level associated with self-schema. To anticipate some of the detail to follow, self-schema and self-awareness or consciousness are not the same. Some knowledge pertaining to the self is known by the self; some is not known, but can be known; and some is not known and may not be known.

Levels of Self-Schema

When organisms are preverbal, it is not possible to explore the issue of awareness, because the organism cannot be easily questioned and because the self, as a phenomenological event, is not easily studied without access to the internal processes of the organism. Because of this, we must make inferences about self-knowledge; although we can study self-knowledge, we cannot explore, at least in infancy, the epistemological issue of knowledge of the knowledge of self (what I call consciousness). Moreover, self-knowledge can precede the knowledge of self-knowledge. For example, by eight months infants know something about objects—that is, will search for a hidden object—but cannot tell us if they have awareness of their knowledge of object permanence. We can accept their behavior as demonstrating knowledge, but do not ask about knowledge of knowledge. In the same way, we may speak of a cat's knowledge of spatial properties when it goes around an object rather than trying to go through it. Although we have no idea as to the form this knowledge takes (what is the nature of thought in the young infant or cat), we do infer that their knowledge exists.

In our discussion of consciousness, we have a similar problem; consciousness is equivalent to knowledge of the knowledge of self. By referring to adult behavior in this regard, we may be able to discuss this issue more clearly. We agree that adults have self-knowledge, citing as evidence their ability to engage in complex interactions involving the self and others—others including people and objects. Although adults have self-knowledge, they do not *always* have consciousness. Many thoughts and actions do not involve consciousness. For example, much adult behavior occurs rapidly, with little or no reflective thought. During times of decision-making, when action does not have to be carried out quickly, when we have made an error and need to rethink an action, or when we socially transgress some rule that makes us feel guilty or embarrassed, consciousness occurs (M. Lewis and Brooks-Gunn, 1979a).

Lack of consciousness does not reflect the absence of self-involvement in ongoing behavior, but suggests that the self has no executive role, leaving for other processes the mechanics of action. The self sets goals, has intentions, and evaluates, but specific behaviors are executed through simpler processes of associations, and learned or overlearned response patterns. Abelson (1976) has linked these lower level processes to scripts that guide behavior. Scripts, as a metaphor, are useful because they assume the organization and maintenance of complex behavior without evoking such executive functions as awareness, thinking, or planning. Recently, there has been a renewed interest in goals. Goals are like scripts because they are action plans as well as mental representations (Pervin, 1989). In brief, self-schema and self-awareness may be considered as somewhat separate.

Elsewhere, we have presented a description of the development of consciousness and the general development of self-schema (M. Lewis and Brooks-Gunn, 1979b). It is interesting to note that Sander (1964, 1980), using a more clinical approach, arrived at a similar sequence (see also Spitz, 1957). Most recently, Emde (1983, 1988) and Stern (1985) also have tried to articulate the levels or stages of development of the sense of self. Stern, for example, describes the final level of self-development as the verbal self which appears at around 15 to 18 months. This verbal self, if not the others, is clearly a cognitive milestone. It marks the emergence of language, but more since it makes reference to the self's ability to consider itself. Emde's (1983) analysis is even more cognitively based as he makes a distinction between a prerepresentational and a representational self. Again a representational self has to have features associated with language, representation, and reference. It is what I have called objective self-awareness or consciousness (M. Lewis, in press b). In general, then, there is some agreement as to the levels involved and what cognitive features are necessary when we speak of objective self-awareness or consciousness.

While we recognize that some aspects of self-schema exist at an early age, it is not until objective self-awareness evolves that we can speak of the human infant as acquiring consciousness. For us it is very important to differentiate the skill levels of identity. For humans the highest level of self-schema is achieved with the appearance of objective self-awareness. For example, although an infant may be able to differentiate itself from others or have knowledge of its location in space vis-à-vis other objects, and thus be able to reach for and obtain objects, these features do not constitute the equivalence of what we mean by objective self-awareness. The skill of uniquely human self-schema can be said to exist only when objective awareness of the self occurs (Duval and Wicklund, 1972). This is a meta cognition, it is knowledge of knowledge (Harre, 1984). Until such time the child certainly has a level of self-schema. However, we would maintain that this level of self-schema is in no way different from that level found in any living organism capable of interactive behavior. It is not the consciousness that characterizes our species.

Developmental Models

The developmental model I propose takes the general form that feeling gives rise to thinking about feeling, which gives rise to new feelings. The model has been presented before (M. Lewis et al., 1989); therefore, I will only present the highlights here. The first set of emotions that have been observed have been called primary emotions. These are fear, sadness, anger, joy, disgust, interest, and surprise (Izard, 1977). These are not self-conscious emotions. Their occurrence is not dependent on self-comparison (for a similar analysis of the difference between primary and secondary emotions, see Plutchik, 1980). These emotions emerge within the first six months of life (Bridges, 1932; Sroufe, 1979). As I have shown, the emergence of consciousness occurs in the second half of the second year of life. The emergence of consciousness itself gives rise to the first set of self-conscious emotions, called "the exposed emotions." These include embarrassment, empathy, and envy. The important feature in regard to these self-conscious emotions is that they are not evaluative in nature. Let us consider the case of embarrassment. Earlier I have suggested that embarrassment is the consequence of exposure. Using the case of being complimented as an example, I hope to have made clear that simple exposure, the self referring to the self, or others referring to the self, even in a positive way, leads to self-consciousness and the emotions associated with it. I would argue, therefore, that the emergence of these simple non-evaluative self-conscious emotions is the consequence of the acquisition of this cognitive capacity. In a series of studies, my colleagues and I have been able to demonstrate an association between the emergence of self-referential behavior and the emergence of embarrassment. In almost all cases (one subject did not show this) children who showed embarrassment also showed self-referential behavior. Moreover, differences in the age of self-referential behavior is related to the emergence of embarrassment; one subject showed self-referential behavior and embarrassment at 19 months, while another showed self-referential behavior and embarrassment at 22 months. In similar fashion, Halperin (1989) also has suggested that empathic behavior, specifically the combination of both appropriate facial response and appropriate action does not emerge until the emergence of self-referential behavior (for a similar point see Zahn-Waxler and Radke-Yarrow, 1982). At this time there is too little work on envy to see if this same relationship applies.

A second set of cognitive processes is necessary for the emergence of the evaluative self-conscious emotions, the knowledge of SRGs. Because two sets of cognitive processes are necessary, consciousness and SRGs, evaluative self-conscious emotions occur somewhat later than the simple self-conscious emotions (Heckhausen, 1984; Kagan, 1981). Such a scheme allows us to place the development of consciousness and self-conscious emotions within the first two to three years of life. It is reasonable to assume that the primary emotions emerge at least by six months of age, consciousness somewhere between 18 and 24 months and with it the emergence of the simple self-conscious emotions. The evaluative emotions appear later, somewhere between 24 and 36 months. Thus it would appear that the self-schema and those emotions most associated with it occur within the first three years of the child's life.

The Socialization of Shame

In discussing the cognitive-attributional model, I made reference to specific features which might be socialized in different ways. I will consider each of the features. Individual differences in shame may be produced by too high a set of standards and goals and/or the use of global vs. specific attribution. These two features are reflected in our model, but there are two other foci for the socialization of shame that need to be taken into account. These consist of shame through humiliation and disgust, and shame through love withdrawal.

Shame through Elevated Standards

Some adults appear to set very high standards for their behavior and therefore are unable to succeed. Failure relative to these standards leads to shame. Individual differences in the level of standard should affect individual differences in experiencing shame, all other variables being held constant. Consider the student who receives a B grade. If he hopes for and expects an A, the B grade will result in failure, while the student who sees a B as a measure of success will not respond to such a grade as a failure. Following a psychoanalytic perspective, we could say that such differences may have to do with a problematic ego ideal or superego. Although there have been attempts at exploring harsh socialization as related to strong superego, there have been only mixed results; for example, severity of toilet training (Zahn-Waxler and Kochanska, in press). Nevertheless, it seems reasonable to assume that early socialization vis-à-vis SRGs plays some role.

Individual differences in shame can be brought about by the differential socialization of SRGs. The child who is criticized for receiving a B in a test is likely to set high standards. It may be true that it is not only the demand of a high standard itself but the punishment inflicted once the standard is not achieved. Consider two families who each demands high standards. In the case of one, the parent's response to the child for failure is punitive. Thus, it is not the failure but the punishment for failure. Contrast such a family with a family equally insistent on high standards, who does not show punitive behavior but reasons with the child. The important feature may not be the imposition of high standards but rather the response to the violation of them.

Internal vs. External Attributions

Setting SRGs is one aspect of the attributional system which involves the self and which leads to self-conscious emotions. The second feature of the self has to do with the subject's evaluation of the self. It is possible that they could make an external evaluation, that is, attribute the failure to someone else or to chance. Individual differences exist. Likewise, for blame, individual differences exist. The best examples are either people whose family member has had a serious illness or people who have survived some holocaust.

The work on children of depressed parents has bearing on our consideration of the socialization of internal attributions. There is evidence to indicate that very young children of sick parents are more apt to internalize blame. They feel they are responsible for their parents' illness or, if they misbehave, they are responsible for it getting worse or continuing. This can come about in several ways. First, these children may feel, unrealistically, that there must be something they could do to help their parents. After all, parents are able to help children, why not children help their parents. Since realistically they cannot help, the child may assume some of the blame. Alternatively, the sick parent may lead the child to believe it is his or her fault (Zahn-Waxler et al., 1979).

Young children appear to be more susceptible to internalization than older children. Given instances of marked failure, children are likely to become shame susceptible. For example, the death of a parent early in the child's life may lead to internal attribution in these children, more so than a death of a parent when the child is older, since children are more apt to blame themselves and are more susceptible to shame. Individual differences in the socialization of this attribute have received only minimal attention. Children of depressed parents appear to internalize the blame for their parent's illness (Zahn-Waxler and Kochanska, in press). Whether one internalizes the blame or externalizes, it will be important in determining whether an individual is shamed by a failure. If one can blame an external source at all, then self-conscious emotions are unlikely to occur. Socialization appears to be one way in which the child learns internal or external self-attributions.

Specific vs. Global Attribution

The second attributional feature of the model involves the global vs. specific self-orientation. We can see that global and specific interacts with internal and external, thus giving us four cells. It seems logical that all four cells are possible. Global vs. specific attribution has been called by a variety of terms, including self-characteristic vs. self-action, entity vs. incremental, or self-focus on performance vs. focus on learning (Dweck and Leggett, 1988). In all cases, the difference is the focus on the total self vs. focus on the action of the self.

The acquisition of global vs. specific self-attribution and individual differences is of interest, but there is relatively little work in this area to guide us. As I search for studies of socialization, I have repeatedly come across achievement literature and school performance as possible sources of information. Wilkinson and Marrett (1985) have been able to show that teachers are likely to differentially use global vs. specific attribution toward children's success and failure within the educational framework (see also Dweck and Leggett, 1988; Minuchun and Shapiro, 1983). Findings from several studies of achievement behavior provide evidence for differences in global vs. specific attribution associated with success or failure. Some children tend to attribute their failures to factors such as lack of ability, while others tend to attribute failure to specific factors including teachers' attitudes (Dweck and Leggett, 1988; Nicholls, 1984). Moreover, some children avoid situations in which failure is likely, whereas others approach such a challenge, indicating that failure differentially affects self-esteem. Females, for example, who fail are likely to think that they are generally no good, a global attribution, and are likely to experience a loss of self-esteem (Dweck and Leggett, 1988). Males are likely not to think they are the cause of their own failures and therefore are not likely to suffer loss of self-esteem. In our terms they do not make an internal attribution, "It's not my fault that the failure occurred." Because experiences with teachers occur later, we looked at some data collected on mothers and fathers and their three-year-old children playing with toys. We scored parents' statements for a global attribution which had to do with statements pertaining to some aspect of the children themselves; for example, "You are so talented," or "You are handsome." We also scored specific self-attributions. These were statements in which parents commented on the child's particular action around the task; for example, "Very good" or "That's wrong." Both positive and negative global and specific attributions were scored. We found that parents have a wide range of attributional styles, and mothers and fathers showed only moderate consistency; that is, some mothers used more specific attribution than global, while some used more global than specific. The same held true for fathers. In general, we found large parental differences in self-attribution to the children. While we could not obtain attribution scores for the children themselves, we were able to score pride and shame responses to the success and failure in the task. We found a relation between the use of global and specific attribution by the parents and the amount of shame the children exhibited when they failed the task; more global attribution resulted in more shame.

In the model that we have been discussing, the causes of shame and other self-conscious emotions can be located in the evaluation of SRGs and in global vs. specific attributions. As we have seen, individual differences in both these aspects are likely to stem from individual differences in these processes.

The data on socialization reveal that how parents (and teachers) treat the child contributes to the differences in these attributions. Up until now we have looked at socialization experiences which operate on these attributions by direct action. While this is true, there are other factors which are likely to play a role in the creation of these attributes. The humiliation and shame children receive, or even the withdrawal of love, may contribute to these attributions.

Summary

In this paper I have touched upon three aspects of the study of shame. I have tried to articulate a model of self-conscious evaluative emotions, arguing that cognitive attributional processes provide the eliciting agents for these emotions. Second, I have attempted to provide a developmental model which relates consciousness with self-conscious emotions. Here we are on more sturdy ground since the research literature supports this general model. This model provides a framework in which to observe the development of consciousness and the development of emotions dependent upon this ability. In this regard, it should come as no surprise that I adhere to a strong form of the argument which suggests that self-conscious emotions do not evolve until a mature self-schema or self-consciousness have emerged.

Finally, I have touched upon the need to consider socialization factors which impact on individual differences in self-conscious evaluative emotions. In particular, I have suggested that self-conscious evaluative emotions might be impacted upon by parenting styles which affect the evaluation of success and failure as well as the creation of global and specific and self-attributional styles.

I have not had the opportunity to discuss in detail how such a theory might prove useful for treating individual differences that are pathological in nature. My comments suggest the consideration of cognitive therapeutic techniques once shame-causing events are revealed and understood. Patients can be helped either to reevaluate their success or failure criteria or to reevaluate global or specific attributions.

REFERENCES

ABELSON, P. (1976). Script processing in attitude formation and decision making. In *Cognition and Social Behavior,* ed. J. S. Carrol & J. Payne. Hillsdale, N.J.: Erlbaum.

BANDURA, A. (1986). *Social Foundations of Thought and Action.* Englewood Cliffs, N.J.: Prentice Hall.

BARNETT, K. C. & ZAHN-WAXLER, C. (1987). *Do Toddlers Express Guilt?* Society for Research in Child Development abstracts.

BECK, A. T. (1967). *Depression: Clinical, Experimental and Theoretical Aspects.* New York: Harper & Row.

BRIDGES, K. M. B. (1932). Emotional development in early infancy. *Child Develpm.,* 3:324–334.

BUSS, A. H. (1980). *Self-Consciousness and Social Anxiety.* San Francisco: W. H. Freeman.

CAMPOS, J., CAMPOS, R. M., & BARNETT, K. (1989). Emergent themes in the study of emotional development and emotion regulation. *Develpm. Psychol.,* 25(3):394–402.

DARWIN, C. R. (1872). *The Expression of Emotions in Man and Animals.* Chicago: Univ. Chicago Press.

DUVAL, S. & WICKLUND, R. A. (1972). *A Theory of Objective Self Awareness.* New York: Academic Press.

DWECK, C. S. & LEGGETT, E. L. (1988). A social-cognitive approach to motivation and personality. *Psychol. Rev.,* 95:256–273.

EKMAN, P., FRIESEN, W. V., & ELLSWORTH, P. (1972). *Emotion in the Human Face.* New York: Pergamon Press.

EMDE, R.N. (1983). The prerepresentational self and its affective core. *Psychoanal. Study Child,* 38:165–192.

——— (1988). Development terminable and interminable II: Recent psychoanalytic theory and therapeutic considerations. *Int. J. Psychoanal.,* 69:283–296.

HALPERIN, M. (1989). Sympathy and self awareness. Presented at the meeting of the Society for Research on Child Development, Kansas City.

HARRE, R. (1984). *Personal Being.* Cambridge, Mass.: Harvard Univ. Press.

HECKHAUSEN, H. (1984). Emergent achievement behavior: Some early developments. In *The Development of Achievement Motivation,* ed. J. Nicholls. Greenwich, Conn.: JAI Press, pp. 1–32.

HOFFMAN, M. (1970). Moral development. In *Handbook of Child Psychology,* 3rd ed., (Vol. II), ed. P. H. Mussen. New York: Wiley.

IZARD, C. E. (1977). *Human Emotions.* New York: Plenum.

KAGAN, J. (1981). *The Second Year.* Cambridge, Mass.: Harvard Univ. Press.

LEWIS, H. B. (1971). *Shame and Guilt in Neurosis.* New York: Int. Univ. Press.

——— (1976). *Psychic War in Men and Women.* New York: New York Univ. Press.

——— Ed. (1987). *The Role of Shame in Symptom Formation.* Hillsdale, N.J.: Erlbaum.

LEWIS, M. (in press a). *The Exposed Self.* New York: Free Press.

——— (in press b). Self knowledge and social influences. In *Social Influences,* ed. M. Lewis & S. Feinman. New York: Plenum.

——— & BROOKS-GUNN, J. (1979a). *Social Cognition and the Acquisition of Self.* New York: Plenum.

——— ——— (1979b). Toward a theory of social cognition: The development of self. In *New Directions in Child Development: Social Interaction and Communication during Infancy,* ed. I. Uzgiris. San Francisco: Jossey-Bass, pp. 1–20.

——— & FEIRING, C. (1981). Direct and indirect interactions in social relationships. In *Advances in Infancy Research,* 1, ed. L. Lipsitt. New York: Ablex.

——— & MICHALSON, L. (1983). *Children's Emotions and Moods: Developmental Theory and Measurement.* New York: Plenum.

——— ——— (1985). Faces as signs and symbols. In *Development of Expressive Behavior Biology-Environmental Interaction,* ed. G. Zivin. New York: Academic Press, pp. 153–182.

——— SULLIVAN, M. W., STANGER, C., & WEISS, M. (1989). Self-development and self-conscious emotions. *Child Develpm.,* 60:146–156.

MINUCHUN, P. P. & SHAPIRO, E. K. (1983). The school as a context for social development. In *Handbook of Child Psychology,* 4th ed. (Vol. 4), ed. P. Mussen & E. M. Hetherington. New York: Wiley, pp. 197–274.

MISCHEL, W. (1966). A social-learning view of sex differences in behavior. In *The Development of Sex Differences,* ed. E. E. Maccoby. Stanford: Stanford Univ. Press, pp. 56–81.

MORRISON, A. P. (1989). *Shame, the Underside of Narcissism.* Hillsdale, N.J.: Analytic Press.

NATHANSON, D. L., Ed. (1987). *The Many Faces of Shame.* New York: Guilford Press.

NICHOLLS, J. G. (1984). Achievement motivation: Conception of ability, subjective experience, task choice, and performance. *Psychol. Rev.,* 91:328–348.

PERVIN, L., Ed. (1989). *Goals and Concepts in Personality and Social Psychology.* Hillsdale, N.J.: Erlbaum.

PIERS, G. & SINGER, M. B. (1953). *Shame and Guilt.* New York: Norton.

PLUTCHIK, R. (1980). *Emotion: A Psychoevolutionary Synthesis.* New York: Harper & Row.

SANDER, L. W. (1964). Adaptive relationships in early mother-child interactions. *J. Amer. Acad. Child Psychiat.,* 3:231–264.

——— (1980). New knowledge about the infant from current research: Implications for psychoanalysis. *J. Amer. Psychoanal. Assn.,* 28:181–198.

SCHERER, K. R. & EKMAN, P., Eds. (1984). *Approaches to Emotion.* Hillsdale, N.J.: Erlbaum.

SELIGMAN, M. E. P. (1975). *Helplessness: On Depression, Development and Death.* San Francisco: Freeman.

SPITZ, R. A. (1957). *No and Yes: On the Genesis of Human Communication.* New York: Int. Univ. Press.

SROUFE, A. (1979). Socioemotional development. In *Handbook of Infant Development,* ed. J. Osofsky. New York: Wiley, pp. 462–516.

STERN, D. N. (1985). *The Interpersonal World of the Infant.* New York: Basic Books.

TOMKINS, S. S. (1963). *Affect, Imagery and Consciousness:* Vol. 2, *The Negative Affects.* New York: Springer.

WEINER, B. (1986). *An Attributional Theory of Motivation and Emotions.* New York: Springer.

WILKINSON, L. C. & MARRETT, C. B., Eds. (1985). *Gender Influences in Classroom Interaction.* New York: Academic Press.

ZAHN-WAXLER, C. & KOCHANSKA, G. (in press). The origins of guilt. In *The 36th Nebraska Symposium on Motivation: Socioemotional Development,* ed. R. Thompson.

——— & RADKE-YARROW, M. (1982). The development of altruism: Alternative research strategies. In *The Development of Prosocial Behavior,* ed. N. Eisenberg-Berg. New York: Academic Press.

——— ——— & KING, R. A. (1979). Child-rearing and children's prosocial imitations toward victims of distress. *Child Develpm.,* 50:319–330.

University of Medicine and Dentistry of New Jersey
Robert Wood Johnson Medical School
97 Paterson Street
New Brunswick, NJ 08903

A VIEW OF THE DEVELOPMENT OF HOSTILITY IN EARLY LIFE

HENRI PARENS, M.D.

Hostile destructive affects, from irritability to anger, hostility, hate, and rage, develop progressively during the first three years of life. Whereas pleasurable experiences are core determiners of the degree to which positive emotions develop, excessive unpleasure experiences are the central determiner and ingredient of the negative emotions. The progressive evolving of positively and negatively valenced emotions organizes into ambivalence which develops in two sequential basic conflicts of ambivalence during the early years of life. A critical relationship suggested from empirical research is that "excessive unpleasure experiences generate hostile destructiveness." This hypothesis suggests the crucial part played by such affective experiences in the generation and intensification of hostile destructiveness in humans. The generation of this trend in the aggressive drive and the affects that will now flow from it stabilize in the psyche, have continuity in development like the positive emotions and libidinal drive, and wield their influence on ego functioning and development, superego formation, personality development, and object relations.

FEELINGS OF HOSTILITY and hate and feelings of love stand out uniquely among the feelings most determining of the quality of human experience. Psychoanalysts from Freud to the present have shared the view that this is so as well for the development of self, psychic conflict, psychic structure formation, and human relationships. Freud (1913, 1926) emphasized that the core oedipal conflict is a conflict due to ambivalence. In the clinical situation, we know only too well the interaction of coexisting love and hate feelings to us in the transference. Psychoanalysts have emphasized the centrality of positive (good) and negative (bad) experiencing in the

Training and Supervising Analyst, Philadelphia Psychoanalytic Institute; Research Professor of Psychiatry, The Medical College of Pennsylvania.

mother-child relationship and their consequent internalizations and representations as central to all these developments (M. Klein, 1939; Jacobson, 1964; Mahler, 1965; with Pine and Bergman, 1975; Kernberg, 1966, 1976). Mahler pointed to the centrality of positive emotional interaction to the development of libidinal object constancy. Following a long list of earlier analytic writers, Emde recently underscored that "positive emotions play an important adaptive role" (1989a, p. 48). He proposes that "there is an affective core to self experience, [which provides] . . . a sense of continuity during times of developmental change" (p. 44). I will emphasize here, as is known in psychoanalysis, that although hostility and its related affects contribute importantly to ego development and adaptation, when hostility affects are excessive, on the other hand, they play an important role in maladaptation and, like positive emotions, contribute to the affective core of self experience which has continuity during development. I will here explore a composite ego psychological view (integrating structural, psychosexual, and separation-individuation concepts) of the influence exerted by this cluster of negative emotions in development during the early years of life.

Psychoanalytic theory places hostility and its related affects within the domain of aggression and drive theory. Our own studies in aggression (Parens, 1973, 1979a,1984a, 1989a) were compelled by an unexpected finding in the course of direct infant observational research: 15 children were observed since birth for from 1 year 4 months to 5 years 6 months (average 4.4 years; median = 4.10 years) for 1 to 4 hours weekly (average = 79 percent attendance). When they were under 4 to 6 months of age, we found manifestations of aggression in their behaviors, which challenged the classical psychoanalytic view that aggression is in origin inherently only destructive. For instance, during feeding, 3½-month-old Jane seemed to try to control the spoon mother put into her mouth, making quite vigorous efforts to feed herself. Then, for 25 minutes after napping she was continually busy, mouthing, pulling, and pushing a set of plastic rings on a string. A narrative of this activity states that "the sensorimotor effort is visible on her face, and one soon hears vocal concomitants of that effort, . . . a good deal of pressure can be inferred from the way she seems to be working. . . . Notable is the intense, worklike affect, . . . the inner drivenness of that activity. Much energy seems to be invested [in it]; indeed, her entire body is involved in her effort." It is on this kind of affective-behavioral evidence that Hendrick (1942), much like Winnicott (1950) and Spitz (1965), doubted a primary antagonism between drive and ego and, going further than Winnicott and Spitz, suggested an instinct to master (1943a, 1943b) which was widely argued in psychoanalysis. We reported that we found this type of pressured, driven activity in our subjects from the ages of 8 to 16 weeks. And we proposed that "What calls for classification are the inner-drivenness and constancy of this sensorimotor activity, . . . the pressure, . . . and attention cathexis commanded by this inner drivenness" (Parens, 1979a, pp. 24-25; Parens and Prall, 1974).

Finding affective behaviors suggestive of aggression which is neither hostile nor destructive prior to the structuring of the ego as an agency was in disharmony with existing theory. In 1970, when we first came upon these behaviors, what we inferred from them (that these appeared to the clinical eye of that day as if fueled by "neutralized" aggression) challenged the then prevailing psychoanalytic theory of aggression which had its origins in Freud's second instinctual drive theory. According to Freud's second drive theory, which now held the instinctual drives to consist of the sexual (life) and aggressive (death instinct) drives, during infancy self-destructiveness (death-instinct-derived) is turned toward the outside by virtue of primary adaptive mechanisms (primary narcissism and primary autonomous ego functioning). I have discussed how Freud came to the death-instinct-based theory of aggression, how the role of aggression as part of a self-preservative instinctual drive (Freud's first drive theory) was in better agreement with our findings, but how the problem Freud's (1914) study on narcissism created for libido theory compelled a revision of drive theory to which he eventually arrived in 1920 (see Parens, 1979a, chap. 2). How much for Freud, who according to Schur (1972) was preoccupied with death from early on in his life, the destructiveness of World War I influenced this 1920 revision is not clear.

Following principally from Hartmann et al.'s work (1949), this classical theory held that the modification of aggression becomes operative when the ego begins to be structured as an agency. Evidence for such structuring is manifest in the infant's becoming capable of experiencing anxiety (Freud, 1926), wishes (Schur, 1966), and intentionality of action (Hartmann, 1952). Observation leads me to believe that this level of adaptive ego functioning begins at about 6 months of age (Spitz et al., 1970; Weil, 1976; McDevitt, 1983). This coincides with Piaget's (1936) conceptualizing the infant's beginning capacity to experience means-ends relationships, his stage four of sensorimotor development. At this time the infant becomes attached emotionally to the mother (or other primary caregivers) and this attachment to a libidinal object is specific and relatively stable (Spitz, 1965; Mahler, 1965; Mahler et al., 1975; Bowlby, 1969; Bretherton and Waters, 1985). More recent reports on the beginning capacity for intersubjectivity at this age further support the assumption of the beginning structuralization of the ego as an agency (Kaye, 1982; Stern, 1985; Greenspan, 1989). In line with this, one might expect to find an ego function capable of modifying aggression to begin no earlier than about 6 months of age.

We found evidence in children under 6 months of age of an inner-drivenness, a pressured internal thrust to explore, to assert the infantile self upon the environment by means of sensorimotor functioning (Parens, 1973, 1979a; Parens and Prall, 1974). Influenced by clinical judgment, from its appearance I (1970) initially inferred that this pressured behavior was driven by "neutralized" aggression, an inference at odds with the theoretical assumptions just stated. Thus, finding this activity in infants under 6 months of age presented us with a challenge to resolve the disharmony between observable behaviors and elements of our (structural and drive) theories, the challenge Hartmann (1950) predicted might come from empirical study.

To investigate this challenge we explored the children's behaviors for manifestations of aggression. Our initially bewildering pool of observational data resolved satisfactorily into four categories of behavioral manifestations of aggression: (1) *unpleasure-related destructiveness*, the paradigm for which is the rage reaction of infancy; (2) *nonaffective destructiveness*, the paradigm for which is chewing and feeding activity; (3) *nondestructive aggression*, the paradigm for which is the inner-drivenness of pressured exploratory activity; and (4) *pleasure-related destructiveness*, the paradigm for which is teasing and taunting.

From these behavioral manifestations of aggression we first hypothesized that all of these behaviors comprise several trends in aggression, that is, that there are several types of aggression (Parens, 1979a, 1984a). Finding clinically that hostility and hate in relatedness (in the transference) can be modified to far more benign levels of intensity by means of analytic work, and that such modification is often linked among other things with the reduction of inhibitions and symptoms and an increase in work effectiveness and creativity—these findings support the psychoanalytic historical linking of nondestructive and destructive aggression. For such reasons I find the hypothesis that all these behaviors pertain to aggression more cogent than the long-established academic psychology dichotomy of *assertiveness* (for nondestructive aggression) and *aggression* (for destructiveness, hostile and nonhostile), which suggests these to be inherently unrelated categories of behavior. Therefore, because I continue to find dual instinctual drive theory better capable than other models available to date of explaining the nature and action of these inner forces operative in human adaptation, conflict, and relationships, I have attempted to revise aggression as instinctual drive (Parens, 1979a, 1989a). (See Lichtenberg [1989] for another proposed model.) We, therefore, conceptualized three trends in aggression which become inferable from behavior in the early months of life as follows:

1. *Nondestructive aggression* is manifest from the first months of life, challenging the classical view that destructiveness is the primary aim of aggression (indeed, *self*-destructiveness, according to the much criticized death instinct). This led us to hypothesize that: (a) there is an inherent nondestructive trend in aggression, evident within a few months of birth, well before the ego is capable of modifying it; and (b) that aggression, therefore, is not inherently only destructive.

2. *Nonaffective destructiveness* is manifest in behaviors like feeding (Eissler, 1971), evidencing destructiveness without being hostile. This is amply evident in animals in prey aggression. This destructiveness of animate structure is for the sake of self-preservation (alimentation). We err to equate this type of destructiveness with hostility.

3. *Hostile destructiveness* most clearly manifests from neonatal life on in rage reactions. This is the trend in aggression which during the latter part of the first year of life will, when associated with the wish to inflict pain or destroy an object, constitute the affects which concern us here, namely, anger, hostility, hate, and rage.

Hostile destructiveness subsumes the behaviors included in the two observational categories: "unpleasure-related destructiveness" and "pleasure-related destructiveness." Elsewhere I have stated the rationale for including these two categories under the trend *hostile destructiveness* (Parens, 1979a, chap. 3; 1989a).

As I understand them, a specific series or spectrum of negatively valenced affects—from *irritability* to *anger, hostility, hate,* and *rage*—constitute the affects that pertain to hostile destructiveness. Like the other trends in aggression, hostile de-

a continuum

structiveness has as its basic aim to act upon, assert oneself over, and control (Parens, 1979a, p. 115; see also Buie et al., 1982; McDevitt, 1983). Under the influence of *excessive unpleasure*, aggression is modified into hostility; the aim of hostile destructiveness then becomes the inflicting of pain or harm upon, and thus effecting the hostile destruction of, the object being controlled (Parens, 1979a, pp. 111-115; Parens, 1984a; Gunther, 1980; McDevitt, 1983).

A striking consensus has developed over decades of psychoanalytic study (see Parens, 1979a, chaps. 2 and 3, for one view of this evolving understanding of aggression theory) regarding the nature of what I am referring to as hostile destructiveness. Among more recent psychoanalytic investigators this consensus is found in the work of Storr (1972), Bowlby (1973), Rochlin (1973), Parens (1973, 1979a), Kernberg (1976), Saul (1976), and Kohut (1977). Each of them, working without cross-reference to another and using different psychoanalytic approaches and different conceptual contexts, came to the similar conclusion that hostile destructiveness is not inborn; rather, it is provoked in the self by experience. Rochlin (1973) ascribed the emergence of hostile destructiveness to the defense of the self, against and in reaction to narcissistic injury. Kohut (1977) and Gunther (1980) also proposed that it arises in reaction to narcissistic injury, as a by-product of the threat or the experience of disintegration of the self. Bowlby (1973) drew attention to its emergence in reaction to the pain of object loss as part of the adaptive process it activates. Storr (1972), leaning on Schilder (1964), ascribed it to experiences of unpleasure, especially to frustration (much like Buie et al. [1982] propose from clinical study). Saul (1976) ascribed it especially to painful and abusive, object-related experiencing from early childhood on. Parens (1973, 1979a), as already noted, proposes its emergence and generation to be activated by experiences of excessive unpleasure of whatever kind. Lichtenberg (1989) too ascribes hostility to such experiences, proposing it as a reactive affective component of an aversive adaptive system. And, from direct observation, that hostile destructiveness is reactive to excessive unpleasure experiencing is furthermore supported by McDevitt (1983) and Settlage (1990). Therewith, some of the above authors propose that aggression *develops* over time, under the influence of experience as it impacts on differentiating psychic organization (Parens, 1989a, 1989b).

Affect and Drive

Both concepts "affect" and "instinctual drives" are heuristically valuable explanatory models of critical constituents of psychological life. The interplay between and linking of affect and drive theory has a long history beginning in the writings of Freud. In my observational investigations as well as clinical work, and specifically pertaining to the topic of this paper, I have found a remarkable interrelation of affect and drive which I have stated in the hypothesis that "excessive unpleasure generates hostile destructiveness" (1979a), a hypothesis which subsumes the frustration-aggression hypothesis of Dollard et al. (1939) and which more specifically underscores the part played by affective experience in shaping especially the hostile destructive trend in human aggression.

I have found the "excessive unpleasure generates hostile destructiveness" hypothesis to be advantageous over the oft-criticized "frustration-aggression" hypothesis of Dollard et al. Among other things, the frustration-aggression hypothesis failed to account for the many instances when aggression is not provoked because the frustration does not reach the level necessary to generate hostility or, when sufficient to do so, was not discharged externally and therefore behaviorally not apparent. Psychoanalysts especially will have no difficulty accepting the inference for which we found empirical evidence that hostile destructiveness need not be immediately discharged outwardly upon its intrapsychic generation (see Parens, 1979a, pp. 118-119, for observational examples). In addition, we found that frustration is but one of several types of experience capable of generating hostile destructive feelings and that these, including frustration, have a lower common denominator: what is experienced as *excessively unpleasurable.* Thus, I have proposed that *excessive* unpleasure of any source, not only frustration, generates hostile destructiveness even in earliest childhood (Parens, 1979a, pp. 106-116, 158-161, 168-169; 1984, pp. 103-104).This is so whether the unpleasure results from painful somatic stimuli (e.g., illness or injury), emotional pain (e.g., parental abuse or explicit narcissistic injury), the frustration of libidinal needs, or of autonomy strivings (1979a, pp. 202-208). If these are experienced by the self as *excessive*, a subjective experience, each will generate hostile destructiveness. We shall elaborate below that several variables codetermine whether the unpleasure becomes experienced as excessive. The *meaning* to the self of the experience is a crucial variable. For instance, an event the child perceives as intentionally abusive (even if objectively it is not) will facilitate the unpleasure experience becoming felt as excessive. By contrast, an 18-month-old's earache is less likely to be experienced as *excessively* painful when mother (or father) ably and lovingly tries to comfort the child, even when that pain seems quite substantial. We infer that the child's perception of the parent's efforts to decrease the pain often somehow seems to keep the level of unpleasure experienced below the threshold of its being felt as excessive. Of course, there are times when the pain exceeds this remarkable capacity of parental care (or TLC) to raise the threshold of pain tolerance. More on this below.

Some psychoanalysts argue in favor of discarding drive theory because of the problems created by the concept "psychic energy," the "discharge" conceptualizations based on the pleasure principle, the hydrodynamic metaphor, and the energy transformation into anxiety theory, all of which were part of early drive theory. Some who call for discarding drive theory do so on the basis of the last two component concepts—

concepts which Freud himself abandoned during his lifetime. Our work compels us to call for a reformulation of instinctual drive theory which can be integrated with affect theory and disengaged from some of the component encumberments which were part of instinctual drive theory's early formulations. Drives need *not* be defined according to their "source," although their "aim" and "object" can be usefully—indeed, are of necessity—retained (Freud, 1915); nor is "discharge" invariably accompanied by pleasure, nor is drive solely a biological force compelling gratification, nor need we concern ourselves with the problematic concept of psychic energy elaborated to account for the remarkable characteristic of "peremptoriness," inner-drivenness, and inner pressure characteristic of drive (G. S. Klein, 1976). Perhaps most critical, following a hypothesis proposed by Loewald (1971, 1972) with respect to the libidinal drive, I have proposed that aggression *develops,* a too long insufficiently appreciated feature of instinctual drives (Parens, 1979a, 1989a). Rochlin (1973), Kohut (1977), Parens (1979a, 1989a, 1989b), Gunther (1980), Brenner (1982), McDevitt (1983), and others have proposed—and Freud implied in 1915—that *experience* influences the development of aggression (both nondestructive aggression as well as hostile destructiveness). This raises doubt about the assumption made by many that *only innate factors* are determinants of the nature and aims of instinctual drives.

Returning briefly to the hypothesis that excessive unpleasure generates hostile destructiveness and the question of its role in the domain of negative affects, I want especially to acknowledge Kernberg's proposition pertaining to this issue. Following on his model that experience is internalized in units of "self-object-affect" (1966, 1976), Kernberg has proposed that affects are "building blocks" of drives (1982, p. 908). More recently Kernberg proposed that "libido originates in primitive affect states" and that these are "integrated into libido strivings" or that such affect state "enters as a crucial component of libido as drive" (1989, mss. p. 15). That affective experience influences drives is a reversal of the assumption which views affects solely as reflective of drive activity. Whether the affect is a building block (Kernberg), or whether excessive unpleasure affect generates hostile destructiveness (Parens), or the drives are progressively structured by experience in the context of differentiating psychic organization (Brenner, Kernberg, Loewald, Parens, and others), these argue against Freud's hypothesis that affects are only manifestations of drive. Indeed, we want to underscore Spitz's (1959) proposition that affects are themselves organizers of experience, a hypothesis carried forward empirically by Emde et al. (1976).

Furthermore, the core experiences which determine the character of drive can be conceptualized along the axis: pleasure versus unpleasure. Pleasure is the central determiner and ingredient of positive emotions; and unpleasure is the core determiner and ingredient of negative emotions. I think there is an intermediate range of pleasure-unpleasure experiencing which does not yield positive or negative emotions; for instance, the benign unpleasure associated with a sustained effort in solving a problem does not itself yield positive or negative emotions, although success or failure in the effort will. Along this line, according to Jones (1935, p. 345), in 1896 Freud wrote that he found "a moderate amount of discomfort necessary for intensive work" (Akhtar, 1989). Outside of this intermediate range, pleasure and unpleasure experience-determined affects (emotions) influence the sexual and aggressive drives, shaping them as the individual develops.

All in all then, many analysts from Freud on—who in 1915 drew attention to the drives' "plasticity"—agree that emotional experience influences the development of drives. With regard to their relation to affects, our thinking is close to Kernberg's: that affective experience codetermines the development of libidinal and aggressive drives. We do not feel, though, that "building blocks" is an apt metaphor, and have elaborated elsewhere how *excessive unpleasure generates hostile destructiveness* and how its early cumulative history especially accounts for this current of the aggressive drive (Parens, 1979a, pp. 106-117).

Of course, outside of psychoanalysis affect theory has been conceptualized independent of drive theory. Some psychoanalysts are conceptualizing affect theory so as well (Basch, 1976, 1984; Emde, 1980a, 1980b; Stechler and Halton, 1983). Each phenomenon, affect and drive, can be explored at manifest and inferential levels in the psychoanalytic observational as well as clinical situations or at higher levels of abstraction, e.g., metapsychologically. Here I will address hostile destructiveness and its range of affective manifestations at the clinical-observational level. I emphasize that by the "psychoanalytic observational level" I am referring to what Hartmann (1950) identified as depth-psychological observation, which in its search targets motivations and psychodynamics underlying behavior (Kris, 1950; Anna Freud, 1958, 1965; Lustman, 1963; Spitz, 1946, 1965; Mahler, 1965, 1968; Mahler et al., 1975; Parens, 1979a, 1979b; Parens et al., 1976; Roiphe and Galenson, 1981; McDevitt, 1983; Settlage et al., 1985).

The Spectrum of Hostility and Its Related Affects

Hostile destructive affects observable in behavior consist of a range of negatively valenced affects of varying complexity, from its lowest level of feeling intensity manifest in *irritability*, increasing to *anger* and then to the hostile destructive affects proper, namely, *hostility, hate,* and *rage.* As I shall detail below, these affects differentiate over time, irritability and rage being evident from birth on, anger and hostility emerging in the second half of the first year, and hate organizing during the second half of the second year. As already emphasized, the core experience determining of these negative emotions is unpleasure. The hostile destructive affects proper are activated when unpleasure becomes excessive. The full range of hostile destructive affects are key determiners of the quality and intensity of ambivalence and give quality to psychodynamic constructs like sadism and masochism, envy, prejudice, and revenge.

Like their positive counterparts, the negative emotions are codetermined by inborn (biogenetic) reactivity characteristics like rapidity of reaction to rage (some infants reacting very rapidly, others being much slower to get there), thresholds of irritability (some infants reacting irritably to minimally disturbing stimuli as noise and light, others seeming undisturbed by even a milling environment), and aggressive drive endowment (Alpert et al., 1956; Parens, 1979a, pp. 193-200, pp. 224-227 for case illustrations) on the one hand, and the intensity, duration, and frequency of unpleasure experienced (frustration of needs, traumatizing caregiving, etc.) on the other (Escalona, 1963).

The spectrum of hostile and related affects may be conceptualized as follows. At the lowest intensity levels of unpleasure, the affective experience is expressed in *irritability*, manifest in fussiness, whimpering, annoyance, etc., even from the first months of life on. The affective experience of irritability is embedded in the biophysiological experience of unpleasure and leads to an organized, adaptive reaction, however archaic (primitive). In addition to its adaptive value simply as an emotive discharge phenomenon, it is highly adaptive in signaling distress to the environment (when the environment is responsive).

From about 6 months on (see below), when the ego's organizing, intersubjectivity, intentionality, and cognitive (means-ends) functions are beginning to develop, *anger* is elicited when an event-incited unpleasure experience occurs which is of moderate but greater intensity than that level which induces irritability. As I understand it, anger has beginning ideational (means-ends) and representational content, being an organized affective reaction to unpleasure experienced in an object-related context which is experienced below the level of being *excessively* painful to the child (and the ego). Because the unpleasure is not felt as excessive, the stress on the child (and ego) is moderate, and the ego is in an operationally good-enough state for age-adequate adaptive function. Anger mobilizes the child to deal with the source (and object) of unpleasure, and neither overloads nor disorganizes ego functioning, as can the hostility affects.

The hostile destructive affects proper, *hostility, hate,* and *rage,* are generated by unpleasure-inducing events, in early childhood invariably object-related, *which are experienced as excessively painful by the child* (and ego). Hostility, hate, and rage are the primary hostile emotions which differ from anger foremost by virtue of the unpleasure being felt as excessive to the child. Hostility, hate, and rage are distinguishable from one another as follows. *Hostility* is the most immediate affective reaction experienced when unpleasure becomes excessive and overtaxes the ego. Early in childhood, once the unpleasure experience ceases, the hostility is no longer activated and will cease after a lag period of variable duration during which it decreases to extinction. Early in life, hostility is triggered by an actual, invariably object-attached, experiential event. Like anger, though, the psychic registration of the experience of hostility requires ego-functional capacities that do not emerge before about six months; from that time on, hostility becomes internalized invariably in an object-related context. This factor makes it possible for an excessive unpleasure experience schema to become structured. The more frequent and intense such experiences, the more these become internalized, shaping the hostile destructive trend in aggression and stabilizing hostility-imbued self-object-experiential representational schemas. These in turn facilitate the activation of hostility by an external or internal (fantasy) event which resonates with these schemas (Parens, 1979a, pp. 115-117; Parens et al., 1989; Stern, 1985; Settlage et al., 1985; Slap, 1987).

Hate is the affective experience of hostility which has two cardinal features that distinguish it from hostility proper. First, hate is an enduring and stable (or stabilizing) affective experience (McDevitt, 1983), persists as an affect when it is activated, and seems more independent than hostility proper from the continuation of the event which triggered its emergence. Second, hate even more than hostility is the stable experiencing of hostile destructive affect attached to internalized representations of self-object-experiential events (Kernberg, 1966; Parens, 1979a; Stern, 1985; Settlage et al., 1985; Parens et al., 1989). These various features of hate—namely, its enduring and continuing character, its preeminent attachment to internalized representations of self, object and event (experience)—make for the capacity for hate to be present only when these functional capacities exist (see below).

Rage, by contrast to hostility and hate, is the physiologically based affective reaction of experiencing high levels of excessive unpleasure; it is the component affective-physiological reactivity of extreme unpleasure (Rochlin, 1973). Rage then, as the affect produced by the physiological reactivity to high-intensity excessive unpleasure, does not require postneonatal development of ego functioning, being the neonate's organismic ridding reaction (primary autonomous ego activity [Hartmann, 1939]) to the experience of a noxious life-threatening agent (Parens, 1979a, pp. 110-111).

Given that these varied unpleasure-determined negative affects and emotions are development-dependent, let us look at their emergence and vicissitudes in early life.

The Development of Hostile Destructive Affects and Their Influence on Psychic Development

In what follows an ego psychological developmental frame will be implemented based on the interplay of structural, psychosexual, and separation-individuation theories. Specifically, the developmental model implements a sequence and confluence of separation-individuation and oedipus complex theories (Parens, 1980). The role of hostility in psychic development is especially organized by the part it plays, in conjunction with core experiences of pleasure, in the development of ambivalence (Parens, 1979b). Ambivalence is the stabilizing patterning (intrapsychic structuring) of complementing positive emotions and negative emotions in the relationships of self to objects. Although there is no direct negative correlation between the experiential generations of negative and positive emotions (Emde, 1989b), the respective experiential generation of each is determining of the internalizing and developing ambivalence.

The First Two Months: The Neonatal Period Irritability & Rage

In the early weeks, we find that during states of alert wakefulness (Wolff, 1965; Wolff and White, 1965) infants attend visually to their environment, during nursing especially at their mothers' eyes-forehead. Bernie at 12 days of age stared at his mother's face minutes on end with no attention-holding distraction to other external events (Fantz, 1961; Wolff and White, 1965). Much developmental research during the last two decades informs us about the infant's already structured primary autonomous ego apparatuses and their functioning (Hartmann, 1939; Haith and Campos, 1983; Emde, 1988). "Normal autism" seems not adequately descriptive of some of the neonate's experiencing, a view expressed by a number of colleagues who value Mahler's separation-individuation theory. I prefer the classical concept of "primary narcissism" and that identified by Sander (1985, p. 30) as the "state ego"—the self, however archaic and not yet organized intrapsychically into a self image, capable of experiencing its inner states—a long-existing psychoanalytic concept Stern (1985) has elaborated upon in his idea of "the sense of an emergent self."

During these early weeks, unpleasure-related affects include among them elements of "distress-anguish" and "anger-rage" as catalogued by Tomkins (1962-63). That is, the negatively valenced affects include a range of "distress" affect which I prefer to identify as "irritability," staying closer to the predominantly physiological reactivity evidenced in fussiness, whimpering, moderate crying associated mostly with mounting hunger, caregiver interruption of sucking, rough handling, G.I. tract dysfunction, etc. And, we have observed "rage" reactions, as we define it (see Rochlin, 1973, p. 239), in some of our infants during this period, varying according to infant as well as caregiver intervention (Spitz, 1965).

We have proposed that rage reactions of infancy are affect states (storms) which manifest *the most primitive form* of (nonideational) hostile destructiveness (Parens, 1979a). One might equally reasonably hold that neither "hostile" nor "destructiveness" can be aptly applied to an affective experience with no ego-dependent ideational content. We prefer to do otherwise. First, we assume (contrary to Loewald, 1971) that hostile destructiveness owes a large debt to the soma, that drive cannot be construed to be only a psychological phenomenon. We propose, rather, that an underlying biophysiological mechanism is "built-in," exists at birth, ready to function, which when activated by the experience of excessive unpleasure during the neonatal period elicits a reaction of rage (Rochlin, 1973, p. 239). When ego functioning differentiates and psychological functioning to the point of ideation is possible (see below), reactivity to excessive unpleasure will differentiate into hostility (at lesser levels of activation) and rage reactions with murderous ideational content (at intense levels of activation). In this sense, the dominantly physiological rage reaction of infancy is paradigmatic for the earliest form of hostile destructiveness (Parens, 1979a, 1984a). Thus I propose that the primitive affective states of irritability and rage are physiologically based emotional reactivities which arise from that biopsychological substrate from which the hostile destructive affects and trend in aggression differentiate, hand in hand with other components of psychic organization.

Neonates whose immature or otherwise disordered biology and physiology make for greater difficulty in adaptive functioning, be it in organizing sleep (Sander, 1985; Sander et al., 1979), in experience/stimuli processing (Greenspan and

Porges, 1984), or feeding-digestion (Emde, 1989a), by virtue of their more frequent experiences of excessive unpleasure are more at risk for irritability and rage affects patterning within their emergent basic (self) core (Weil, 1970, 1976; Emde, 1983; Sander, 1985; Stern, 1985). And to be sure, the quality of experience, pleasurable and unpleasurable, will be powerfully codetermined by the quality of primary caregiving and object relatedness.

From 2 to About 8 Months

Propelled by the first biopsychological organizational shift (Benjamin, 1963; Spitz, 1946; Mahler, 1952, 1965; Weil, 1976; Emde, 1980b; Emde et al., 1976; Zeanah et al., 1989), affective experiencing develops apace, to some degree by virtue of differentiations in affective experiencing best exemplified in the emerging exogenous social smiling response (Spitz, 1946; Emde and Harmon, 1972; Emde et al., 1976), and also of experience especially in object relations.

Psychosexual theory, separation-individuation theory, and ego psychology provide us with models of infantile experience and development critical to our understanding, treatment, and prevention of many mental health problems. In terms of the activation of negatively valenced affects and therewith the generation and development of hostile destructiveness, primary caregivers (love objects) play a large role in the degree to which such negatively valenced, affective activation occurs. Interacting with the child's biological endowment and temperamental dispositions, the degree to which primary caregivers have failed to protect the infant against excessive pain of all sorts, to this degree the child's basic, negatively valenced, affective core becomes structured and hostile destructive development engendered (Weil, 1970; Kohut, 1977; Sander et al., 1979; Parens, 1979a, 1989a; Gunther, 1980; Main and Stadtman, 1981; Emde, 1983; Stern, 1985; Settlage et al., 1985; Parens et al., 1989).

From about the third month on, from behavior we infer progressive differentiation of primary autonomous ego functioning with the organization during the 5- to 8-months period of the ego as an emerging agency (Provence and Lipton, 1962; Weil, 1976; Parens, 1979a). The 7- to 8-month-old becomes capable of intentionality (Hartmann, 1952), recognitive memory (Piaget, 1937; Fraiberg, 1969), initiative (Sander, 1962), wishing (Schur, 1966), and the sufficient intrapsychic structuring of a libidinal object (Spitz, 1950, 1965; Mahler, 1965, 1968; Mahler et al., 1975).

These emergent ego capabilities integrate dramatically at about 6 to 8 months of age by a second biopsychological organizational shift (Emde, 1980b; Zeanah et al., 1989) and negatively valenced affective experiencing seems to undergo a crucial development. From about 5 to 6 months of age, excessive unpleasure leads progressively to *anger,* then as unpleasure mounts to *hostility*, and if unpleasure persists, to *rage*; now each of these levels of negatively valenced emotions becomes object-aimed and intrapsychically object-attached. In addition to these emerging ego capabilities, two major determiners to the development of hostility differentiate and develop at this time: (1) the structuring of the libidinal object, as already noted; and (2) what I have described as a biological upsurge of aggression (Parens, 1979a, pp. 192–202, 283–289).

From About 9 to 16 Months

With the sufficient structuring of the libidinal object, caregivers so emotionally invested play a unique part in the development of positively as well as negatively valenced emotions. For instance, prior to this time the experience of rage manifests in a comparatively simple pattern: as excessive unpleasure mounts, hostile emotion is progressively activated and culminates in a rage reaction with more or less rapidity and intensity, depending on the individual child's already patterning reactivity. If the source of unpleasure is not mitigated or stopped, the rage reaction will run its course to exhaustion (Parens et al., 1987).

With the structuring of the libidinal object, the reaction of negatively valenced emotions to excessive unpleasure becomes more complex. As unpleasure intensifies, the infant turns to the caregiver with the expectancy of being freed of pain (Parens, 1979a; Main and Stadtman, 1981). When the unpleasure is stopped, little more can be seen of the child's hostile reaction. Where unpleasure is protracted, however, we see evidence of hostile feelings experienced toward the object (Ainsworth et al., 1978). For example, during this period of development, observable separation anxiety—under optimal environmental conditions probably the most common and among the earliest sources of excessive unpleasure experiencing—seems more often than not to lead to the activation of some degree of hostile feelings toward the caregiver (Spitz, 1953; Benjamin, 1961, 1963; Bowlby, 1973; Ainsworth et al., 1978; McDevitt, 1983). This we assume, along with Freud (1926), results from the experienced threat of loss of the already observably emotionally valued caregiver, an experience instigated by her leaving the child which creates unpleasure in the form of anxiety; when the unpleasure is excessive, it generates hostility toward the separating caregiver.

Equally inevitable with a child 7 to 9 months of age, the libidinal object instigates the infant's unpleasure by imposing prohibitions against various forms of gratification such as taking a toy from another child, or touching items that are breakable. I will elaborate below how by these unavoidable unpleasure-producing experiences the libidinal object becomes the first object to whom the infant's hostile and hateful feelings become attached (Parens, 1979a, p. 278).

We have reported evidence of an upsurge in aggression in most of our subjects at about 9 months of age (also see Stechler and Halton, 1983).We assume it to be a primary differentiation in aggression which occurs during the second half of the first year of life (Parens, 1979a, 1989a; see also Benjamin, 1961, 1963; McDevitt, 1983). This upsurge of aggression, which powerfully enhances sthe child's narcissism and sense of omnipotence, is part and parcel of the second biopsychological shift in psychic organization. At about 9 months, major shifts have been observed and reported in the various developmental theories proposed by psychoanalysts: in their psychosexual theory Freud and Abraham proposed entry into an *oral-sadistic phase*; in her separation-individuation theory Mahler proposed the beginning of the *practicing subphase*; in his adaptive systems conceptualization of development Sander (1962, 1985) proposes the infant's beginning *initiation of activities* with mother; in his developmental structuralist theory Greenspan (1981) proposes the beginning of the level of organization he identifies as that of *behavioral organization, initiative, and internalization.* This is also the time when most analysts assume the ego to begin to function as an agency. Although a sense of autonomy begins to be structured during the second year as Erikson (1959) proposes, the thrust to autonomy which propels the child into the separation-individuation phase (Mahler, 1965; Mahler et al., 1975) emerges now, again variations depending on the structuring psychobiological core and adaptive-affective states experienced by the child.

The First Conflict of Ambivalence

From about 9 months on, some of the children in our study showed an impressive mounting of strivings toward autonomy: pressured exploratory activity, increasing assertiveness in self-initiated activities, and efforts to control and master self and environment (Parens, 1979a, 1979b; McDevitt, 1983; Stechler and Halton, 1983). At times of pleasure, these autonomy strivings take on the quality Greenacre (1960) aptly called the child's "love affair with the world." When, for instance, to protect a child from injury or to prevent socially undesirable behavior, these strivings are thwarted by the caregiver, one sees evidence of mounting unpleasure. Often then, when the child's inner-drivenness is high and the caregiver's persistence equal to it, an upsurge of hostile feelings becomes evident in the child's behavior (and often in the mother's as well) (Spitz, 1953; Parens, 1979a, 1979b; McDevitt, 1983; and Stechler and Halton, 1983). Since in the service of protecting her child the mother is the most frequent limit-setter, the hostile feelings generated in the child unavoidably become directed toward her. The interpersonal conflict which ensues takes on the character of a battle of wills. In children in whom the pressure activating these initiatives and the now-generated hostile feelings are especially large, this confict may create an acutely difficult situation for both child and mother. We inferred and elsewhere detailed how with subjects 9 to 16 months old, this conflict between child and mother leads to the emergence of an intrapsychic conflict within the child, a conflict of ambivalence (Parens, 1979a, pp. 202–210; 1979b).

Although positively valenced emotions modify the influence of negatively valenced emotions, in reaction to the anxiety associated with battles of wills and feelings of ambivalence the ego too functions autonomously in coping with object-directed hostility. I have detailed and illustrated elsewhere that from about 9 months of age on we see behavior from which we can infer inhibition (e.g., the child arrests the motion of his raised arm, pulls back, and does not follow through to strike); displacement of hostile feelings (e.g., threatening mother with a wood block, the child rotates and strikes a woman near her mother); denial, reaction formations, as well as behavior suggestive of splitting object representations which, in the context of behavior, suggests the child's efforts to cope with the hostile destructive feelings experienced toward the libidinal object (Parens, 1979a, pp. 212–220, 291–299; 1979b).

Important as well during the latter part of the first year, we find the earliest behavioral signs of beginning internalization of maternal dictates (Parens, 1979a, pp. 179, 298–299). We assume these to become the earliest precursors of superego formation (Spitz, 1958, 1965; Parens, 1979a, 1989a). When children, some even as young as 7 months of age, encounter the mother's first prohibitions against their strong inner-pressured autonomy strivings, they respond variably to this challenge. We have found that at this stage, the prohibition by the libidinal object begins to become internalized. The child at times now acts as if expecting a prohibition from mother when he repeats an act mother prohibited before. For example, the child turns to look at mother who may not even be looking at him, just as he is about to do something she prohibited earlier. Soon, about to do something forbidden, the child stops himself with head-shaking. Such episodes, repeated many times, suggest the progressive internalization of parental dictates and that these begin to have an influence on the child, however weak and object-dependent (Spitz, 1953, 1958, 1965; Parens, 1979a; McDevitt, 1983). These observations support the psychoanalytic assumption that the vicissitudes of hostile destructive feelings in love relationships (Freud, 1913) influence even beginning superego formation. That is to say, Freud's (1913) earliest conceptualization of superego formation held that hostile destructive wishes toward the loved parent lead to remorse, and he noted (1926) that the conflict contained in the oedipus complex is a conflict created by ambivalence; the wish to destroy the beloved parent of the same sex. May not ambivalence also be a major dynamic contributor to the development of superego precursors? That is, the battles of wills with mother, which generate much hostility toward her, create not only the fear of loss of love out of her disapproval, but also critically, by the fear of the child's own rage destroying her, threatening loss of the beloved mother herself. Even if guilt is not yet operative, we see the young child relinquish autonomy strivings, yield to mother in the battle of wills, and comply with her dictate which the child takes on as part of himself. *He* shakes his head "No" to himself, a component identification which if it stabilizes becomes a superego precursor. Thus not only does the even less than 16-month-old comply with the mother's dictate out of love for her and the need for her approval, but also due to the conflict of ambivalence which emerges out of the battles of wills, due to the anxiety the child experiences in the face of his rage toward the mother he or she loves, does the dictate become internalized, a superego precursor (see also Blum and Blum, 1989).

The Two Basic Conflicts of Ambivalence

The influence of the child's own hostility on his or her own psychic development is especially organized by the part it plays in the development of ambivalence. Hartmann et al. (1949) in their classic paper emphasized the part played by aggression in the development of psychic structure and conceptualized especially in the relations of the ego and aggression. I emphasize here that in the transference, that arena we find ourselves delved into in our work with patients, is powerfully determined by the patient's (and at times our own) ambivalence. Over the decades to the present, child psychoanalysts have uniformly stressed, using one model or another, that positively valenced and negatively valenced emotions are cardinal codeterminers of the quality of experience. By internalization, these experiences influence the character of psychic structure formation and the development of self and object relations. Pleasure experiences determine positive emotions and excessive unpleasure experiences determine the hostile destructive emotions.

Ambivalence as I have used the concept is restricted to the experience of coexisting feelings of love and hate toward an object (Parens, 1979b). In the course of development it is the stabilizing patterning (intrapsychic structuring) of complementing positive and negative emotions in relationships, each making its independent and interactive contribution to the quality of ambivalence.

Looking at ambivalence developmentally, I have proposed that there are two basic conflicts of ambivalence in early childhood (Parens, 1979a, 1979b). The first conflict is the progressively emerging and stabilizing balance of love and hate feelings toward the libidinal object during the preoedipal period. The second, which essentially pertains to the oedipus complex, arises in and from specific object relations of a specific triadic nature.

The first conflict of ambivalence, partly detailed in psychosexual theory as the "anal conflict," has its roots in the latter part of the first year, emerging especially in association with autonomy strivings and the battles of wills these engender (see Parens, 1979a, pp. 202-210; 1979b; 1989b), and undergoes change during the rapprochement subphase when two factors particularly play a part in the activation of hostile emotions; (1) the continuation, with modifications, of the preexisting autonomy conflict (manifest in battles of wills), and (2) the rapprochement crisis as conceptualized by Mahler and her co-workers.

From 16 to 24 Months

There is consensus among psychoanalytic child observers and development theorists that a major biopsychologic reorganization occurs at midpoint during the second year of life. We find support for this assumption in the Freud-Abraham formulations of the emergence of *the anal phase,* Spitz's (1957) proposition of the emergence of the "no," Mahler's (1965, 1968; Mahler et al., 1975) emerging *rapprochement subphase* and *crisis*, Greenspan's (1981) formulation of the emergence of the *capacity for organizing internal representations,* Sander's (1962, 1985) formulations on the emerging *recognition of the infant's own state, intentions, and thoughts,* and Stern's suggestion of an emergent *sense of a verbal self* (1985).

These newly emerging capabilities give new meaning to experience, now, to the task of the rapprochement subphase—that of resolving ambitendent wishes both to remain one with the symbiotic partner and to separate and individuate from her—and to the experience of self.

Prior to this era, negatively valenced affects could pervade experience with irritability and depressive affect, facilitate episodic reactive anger and hostility, and transiently motivate acts of hostility (Parens, 1979a, 1984a). Now the newly emergent capacities make possible the experience of *hate*, that uniquely human, further differentiated, stable hostile destructive affect, which attaches to self-object experience and becomes internalized (Novey, 1958; Kernberg, 1966; Parens, 1970; Stern, 1985; Settlage et al., 1985; Parens et al., 1989). On the side of positively valenced experiences, *love* too emerges now, with its enduring, stabilizing self-object attachments, intrapsychic representation and meaning. During this era then, the differentiation in ambivalence stabilizes into feelings of love and hate, as compared to less differentiated positively valenced and negatively valenced affects which constitute the earliest form of ambivalence (Parens, 1979b).

When the ambitendent wishes of the rapprochement task peak and create an intrapsychic crisis, to the degree that the child's unpleasure becomes experienced as excessive, to this degree will hostile destructive affects be activated, which then heighten the already internalized experience of hostility. This, side by side with the continuing influence of battles of wills, may lead to further intensification of hostile destructive affects and heightening of ambivalence (Blum and Blum, 1989).

The child's reactions to this heightening ambivalence, by virtue of its greater ego functional capacity, effect remarkable changes in the psyche such as a heightened capacity for shame reactions, a beginning capacity for humor, empathy, and altruism (Parens, 1979a). Consequent too upon these developments, from observation we infer a further level of preoedipal superego formation (Parens, 1979a, 1989a; Blum and Blum, 1989).

Not all of the child's efforts to cope with increased hostile destructive affects, however, are salutary. For example, displacement of hostility and hate from ambivalently loved objects onto the self leads to self-hurt and masochism; and when displaced onto weakly valued objects, for instance, onto peers, these may later lead to scapegoating, prejudice, and sadism (Parens, 1979a, p. 258; 1984a, pp. 104–105).

From 24 to 36 Months and Beyond

During this period from 24 to about 36 months of age, we have found observational evidence of the resolution of the rapprochement subphase in what Mahler and McDevitt have described as the subphase "On the Way to Self and Object Constancy," which occurs in confluence with the emergence of Oedipus complex activity (Mahler et al., 1975; McDevitt and Mahler, 1980). Soon after our subjects entered their third year, we found emerging manifestations of one or more of the three behavioral categories of oedipal activity (Parens et al., 1976); curiosity and preoccupation with their own genitals and those of others (with castration anxieties in both boys and girls), triadic rivalrous heterosexual activity, and such gender-differing patterns of reactivity as we found in the child's wish to have a baby (Parens and Pollock, 1979).

The Second Conflict of Ambivalence

Direct child observation during the third year of life amply supports the psychoanalytically reconstructed hypothesis that a marked increase in hostility and hate become generated in rivalrous heterosexual activity which constitutes the triadic relatedness of the oedipus complex. In both boys and girls a marked heightening of hostility and hate compels yet another developmental organization of ambivalence, which makes for a striking distinction between boys and girls. The girl experiences her first conflict of ambivalence (her earliest autonomy conflict and then her rapprochement crisis) with her mother, and experiences her second conflict of ambivalence, her oedipal conflict, again with her mother. The boy, on the other hand, experiences his first conflict of ambivalence with his mother, but his second conflict of ambivalence is experienced mostly with his father. Elsewhere, I have proposed that this model of the girl's heightened experience of ambivalence toward her mother, which is a powerful determiner of conscience formation, provides a better explanation of her often encountered heightened guilt and her ample and often harsh superego, a model better accommodating to clinical experience than the castration-complex-dependent model originally proposed for the girl by Freud (Parens, 1989c).

Conclusion

Hostile destructive affects, from irritability to anger, hostility, hate, and rage, develop progressively during the first three years of life. These beginnings are determined by the confluence of innate dispositions in interaction with experiences in the earliest relationships. Experiences of pleasure are core determiners of the degree to which positive emotions are activated and develop; whereas excessive unpleasure experiences are the central determiner and ingredient of the negative emotions. The progressive evolving of the positively valenced and negatively valenced emotions organize into ambivalence which can be understood to develop in two sequential and interdigiting basic conflicts of ambivalence that all children experience during the early years of life.

The question of drives and affects has been briefly addressed, especially in terms of the hostile destructive affects, hostility, hate and rage, and the aggressive drive. A critical relationship suggested from empirical observational research is that "excessive unpleasure" experiences of any type, including frustration and injury to narcissism, "generate hostile destructiveness." This hypothesis reveals the critical part played by such affective experience not only in the activation of hostility, hate, and rage, but especially in the generation and intensification of hostile destructiveness in humans. The generation of this trend in aggression and the affects that will now flow from it stabilize in the psyche and have continuity in development, as do the positive emotions and libidinal drive: they then wield an influence on ego functioning and development (e.g., defenses), superego formation, personality development, and object relations. The implications of such conceptualization for treatment, prevention, and theory are far-reaching.

REFERENCES

AINSWORTH, M. D., BLEHAR, M. C., WATERS, E., & WALL, S. (1978). *Patterns of Attachment.* Hillsdale, N.J.:Erlbaum.

AKHTAR, S. (1989). Review of *Freud without Hindsight,* ed. N. Kiell. *Int. J. Psychoanal.* (in press).

ALPERT, A., NEUBAUER, P. B., & WEIL, A. P. (1956), Unusual variations in drive endowment. *Psychoanal. Study Child,* 11:125–163.

BASCH, M. (1976). The concept of affects. *J. Amer. Psychoanal. Assn.,* 24:759–778.

——— (1984). Response to Dr. Freedman. In *Psychoanalysis: The Vital Issues,* Vol. 1, ed. J. Gedo & G. Pollock. New York: Int. Univ. Press.

BENJAMIN, J. (1961). Some developmental observations relating to the theory of anxiety. *J. Amer. Psychoanal. Assn.,* 9:652–668.

——— (1963). Further comments on some developmental aspects of anxiety. In *Counterpoint: Libidinal Object and Subject,* ed. H. S. Gaskill. New York: Int. Univ. Press, pp. 121–153.

BLUM, H. P. & BLUM, E. (1989). The development of autonomy and superego precursors. Read at the Twentieth Margaret S. Mahler Symposium, Philadelphia.

BOWLBY, J. (1969). *Attachment and Loss: Vol. 1, Attachment.* New York: Basic Books.

——— (1973). *Attachment and Loss: Vol. 2, Separation, Anxiety and Anger.* New York: Basic Books.

BRAZELTON, T. B. (1981). The first four developmental stages in attachment of parent and infant. Presented at the 12th Margaret S. Mahler Symposium Child Development, Philadelphia.

BRENNER, C. (1982). *The Mind in Conflict.* New York: Int. Univ. Press.

BRETHERTON, I. & WATERS, E., Eds. (1985). Growing points in attachment theory and research. *Monogr. Soc. Res. Child Develp.,* Vol. 49, No. 6, Serial No. 209.

BUIE, D. H., MEISSNER, W. W., RIZZUTO, A. M., & SABSHIN, J. I. (1982). Aggression in the psychoanalytic situation. *Int. Rev. Psychoanal.,* 10:159–170.

DOLLARD, J., DOOB, L. W., MILLER, N. E., MOWNER, O. H., & SEARS, R. R. (1939). *Frustration and Aggression.* New Haven: Yale Univ. Press.

EISSLER, K. R. (1971). Death drive, ambivalence, narcissism. *Psychoanal. Study Child,* 26:25–78.
EMDE, R. N. (1980a). Toward a psychoanalytic theory of affect: I. The organizational model and its propositions. In *The Course of Life: Vol. 1, Infancy and Early Childhood,* ed. S. I. Greenspan & G. H. Pollock. Washington, D.C.: Government Printing Office, pp. 63–83.
——— (1980b). Toward a psychoanalytic theory of affect: II. Emerging models of emotional development in infancy. In *The Course of Life: Vol. 1, Infancy and Early Childhood,* ed. S. I. Greenspan & G. H. Pollock. Washington, D.C.: Government Printing Office, pp. 85–112.
——— (1983). The prerepresentational self and its affective core. *Psychoanal. Study Child,* 38:165–192.
——— (1988). Development terminable and interminable: 1. Innate and motivational factors from infancy. *Int. J. Psychoanal.,* 69:23–42.
——— (1989a). The infant's relationship experience: Developmental and affective aspects. In *Relationship Disturbances in Early Childhood,* ed. A. J. Sameroff & R. N. Emde. New York: Basic Books, pp. 33–51.
——— (1989b). Emotional availability and developmental transitions. Presented at the Twentieth Margaret S. Mahler Symposium on Child Development, Philadelphia.
——— GAENSBAUER, T., & HARMON, R. (1976). Emotional expression in infancy: A biobehavioral study. *Psychol. Issues,* Monogr. 37. New York: Int. Univ. Press.
——— & HARMON, R. (1972). Endogenous and exogenous smiling systems in early infancy. *J. Amer. Acad. Child Psychiat.,* 11:177–200.
ERIKSON, E. H. (1959). Identity and the life cycle. *Psychol. Issues,* Monogr. 1. New York: Int. Univ. Press.
ESCALONA, S. K. (1963). Patterns of infantile experience and the developmental process. *Psychoanal. Study Child,* 18:197–244.
FANTZ, R. L. (1961). The origin of form perception. *Sci. American,* 204:66–84.
FRAIBERG, S. (1969). Libidinal object constancy and mental representation. *Psychoanal. Study Child,* 24:9–47.
FREUD, A. (1958). Child observation and prediction of development: A memorial lecture in honor of Ernst Kris. *Psychoanal. Study Child,* 13:245–265.
——— (1965). *Normality and Pathology in Childhood: Asssessments of Development.* New York: Int. Univ. Press.
FREUD, S. (1913). Totem and taboo. *S. E.,* 13:1–162.
——— (1915). Instincts and their vicissitudes. *S. E.,* 14:111–140.
——— (1926). Inhibitions, symptoms and anxiety. *S. E.,* 20:77–174.
GREENACRE, P. (1960). Considerations regarding the parent-infant relationship. *Int. J. Psychoanal.,* 41:571–584.
GREENSPAN, S. I. (1981). *Psychopathology and Adaptation in Infancy and Early Childhood.* New York: Int. Univ. Press.
——— (1989). *The Development of the Ego.* New York: Int. Univ. Press.
——— & PORGES, S. W. (1984). Psychopathology in infancy and early childhood: Clinical perspectives on the organization of sensory and affective-thematic experience. *Child Devel.,* 55:49–70.
GUNTHER, M. (1980). Aggression, self psychology, and the concept of health. In *Advances in Self Psychology,* ed. A. Goldberg. New York: Int. Univ. Press, pp. 167–192.
HAITH, M. M. & CAMPOS, J. J. (1983). Infancy and developmental psychobiol-

ogy. In *Handbook of Child Psychology,* Vol. II, ed. M. M. Haith & J. J. Campos. New York: Wiley.
HARTMANN, H. (1939). *Ego Psychology and the Problem of Adaptation.* New York: Int. Univ. Press, 1958.
——— (1950). Psychoanalysis and developmental psychology. *Psychoanal. Study Child,* 5:7–17.
——— (1952). The mutual influences in the development of the ego and the id. In *Essays on Ego Psychology.* New York: Int. Univ. Press, 1964, pp. 155–181.
——— KRIS, E., & LOWENSTEIN, R. M. (1949). Notes on the theory of aggression. *Psychoanal. Study Child,* 3/4:9-36.
HENDRICK, I. (1942). Instinct and the ego during infancy. *Psychoanal. Q.,* 11:33–58.
——— (1943a). The discussion of the "instinct to master." *Psychoanal. Q.,* 12:561–565.
——— (1943b). Work and the pleasure principle. *Psychoanal. Q.* 12:311–329.
JACOBSON, E. (1964). *The Self and the Object World.* New York: Int. Univ. Press.
JONES, E. (1935). Psychoanalysis and the instincts. In *Paper on Psycho-Analysis.* London: Baillière, Tindall & Cox, 1948, pp. 153–169.
KAYE, K. (1982). *The Mental and Social Life of Babies: How Parents Create Persons.* Chicago: Chicago Univ. Press.
KERNBERG, O. F. (1966). Structural derivatives of object relationships. *Int. J. Psychoanal.,* 47:236–253.
——— (1976). *Object Relations Theory and Clinical Psychoanalysis.* New York: Aronson.
——— (1982). Self, ego, affects and drives. *J. Amer Psychoanal. Assn.,* 30:893–917.
——— (1989). Sadomasochism, sexual excitement, and perversion. *J. Amer. Psychoanal Assn.* (in press).
KLEIN, G. S. (1976). *Psychoanalytic Theory.* New York: Int. Univ. Press.
KLEIN, M. (1939). *The Psychoanalysis of Children.* New York: Grove Press, 1960.
KOHUT, H. (1977). *The Restoration of the Self.* New York: Int. Univ. Press.
KRIS, E. (1950). Notes on the development and on some current problems of psychoanalytic child psychology. *Psychoanal. Study Child,* 5:24–46.
LICHTENBERG, J. D. (1989). *Psychoanalysis and Motivation.* Hillsdale, N.J.: Analytic Press.
LOEWALD, H. W. (1971). On motivation and instinct theory. *Psychoanal. Study Child,* 26:91–128.
——— (1972). Freud's conception of the negative therapeutic reaction with comments on instinct theory. *J. Amer. Psychoanal. Assn.,* 20:235–245.
LUSTMAN, S. L. (1963). Some issues in contemporary psychoanalytic research. *Psychoanal. Study Child,* 18:51–74.
MCDEVITT, J. D. (1983). The emergence of hostile aggression and its defensive and adaptive modifications during the separation-individuation process. *J. Amer. Psychoanal. Assn.,* 31:273–300.
——— & MAHLER, M. S. (1980). Object constancy, individuality, and internalization. In *The Course of Life: Vol. 1, Infancy and Early Childhood,* ed. S. I. Greenspan & G. H. Pollock. Washington: National Institute of Mental Health, pp. 407–423.
MAHLER, M. S. (1952). On child psychosis and schizophrenia: Autistic and

symbiotic infantile psychosis. *Psychoanal. Study Child,* 7:286–305.
——— (1965). On the significance of the normal separation-individuation phase. In *Drives, Affects, Behavior,* Vol. 2, ed. M. Schur. New York: Int. Univ. Press, pp. 161–169.
——— (1968). *On Human Symbiosis and the Vicissitudes of Individuation.* With M. Furer. New York: Int. Univ. Press.
——— McDevitt, J. B., Bergman, A., & Smith, J. R. (1982). *On the Emergence of the Self.* A film produced by the Margaret S. Mahler Psychiatric Research Foundation.
——— Pine, F., & Bergman, A. (1975). *The Psychological Birth of the Human Infant.* New York: Basic Books.
Main, M. & Stadtman, J. (1981). Infant response to rejection of physical contact by the mother. *J. Amer. Acad. Child Psychiat.,* 20:292–307.
Novey, S. (1958). The meaning of the concept of mental representation of objects. *Psychoanal. Q.,* 27:57–79.
Parens, H. (1970). Inner sustainment: Metapsychological considerations. *Psychoanal. Q.,* 39:223–239.
——— (1971). A contribution of separation-individuation to the development of psychic structure. In *Separation-Individuation: Essays in Honor of Margaret S. Mahler,* ed. J. B. McDevitt & C. F. Settlage. New York: Int. Univ. Press.
——— (1973). Aggression: A reconsideration. *J. Amer. Psychoanal. Assn.,* 21:34–60.
——— (1979a). *The Development of Aggression in Early Childhood.* New York: Aronson.
——— (1979b). Developmental considerations of ambivalence. *Psychoanal. Study Child,* 34:385–420.
——— (1980). An exploration of the relations of instinctual drives and the symbiosis-separation-individuation process: Part 1. Drive motivation and psychic development with special reference to aggression and beginning separation-individuation. *J. Amer. Psychoanal. Assn.,* 28:89–114.
——— (1984a). Toward a reformulation of the theory of aggression and its implications for primary prevention. In *Psychoanalysis: The Vital Issues,* Vol. 1, ed. J. E. Gedo & G. H. Pollock. New York: Int. Univ. Press.
——— (1984b). What is the first conflict of ambivalence? Presented to the Regional Council of Child Psychiatry, Philadelphia.
——— (1989a). Toward a reformulation of the psychoanalytic theory of aggression. In *The Course of Life: Vol. 2, Early Childhood,* S. I. Greenspan & G. H. Pollock. New York: Int. Univ. Press, 2nd ed., pp. 643–687.
——— (1989b). Toward an epigenesis of aggression in early childhood. In *The Course of Life: Vol. 2, Early Childhood,* ed. S. I. Greenspan & G. H. Pollock. New York: Int. Univ. Press, 2nd ed., pp. 689–721.
——— (1989c). On the girl's psychosexual development: Reconsiderations suggested from direct observation. *J. Amer. Psychoanal. Assn.* (in press).
——— & Pollock, L. (1979). Film #4 (a & b): *The Child's Wish to Have a Baby,* Parts (Reels) I and II. Audio-Visual Media Section, Eastern Pennsylvania Psychiatric Institute (MCP), Philadelphia.
——— ——— Stern, J., & Kramer, S. (1976). On the girl's entry into the oedipus complex. *J. Amer. Psychoanal. Assn.,* 24:79–107.
——— & Prall, R. C. (1974). *Film #2: Toward an Epigenesis of Aggression in Early*

Childhood. Philadelphia Audio-Visual Media, Eastern Pennsylvania Psychiatric Institute (MCP).
——— SCATTERGOOD, E., SINGLETARY, W., & DUFF, A. (1987). *Aggression in Our Children: Coping with It Constructively.* Northvale, N.J.: Aronson.
——— SINGLETARY, W., SKIVONE, L., & JESSAR, G. (1989). Toward preventing the development of excessive hostility in children: evolving methodology (unpublished ms.).
PIAGET, J. (1936). *The Origins of Intelligence in Children.* New York: Int. Univ. Press, 1952.
——— (1937). *The Construction of Reality in the Child.* New York: Basic Books, 1954.
PROVENCE, S. & LIPTON, R. (1962). *Infants in Institutions.* New York: Int. Univ. Press.
ROCHLIN, G. (1973). *Man's Aggression: The Defense of the Self.* Boston: Gambit.
ROIPHE, H. & GALENSON, E. (1981). *Infantile Origins of Sexual Identity.* New York: Int. Univ. Press.
SANDER, L. W. (1962). Issues in early mother-child interaction. *J. Amer. Acad. Child Psychiat.,* 1:141-166.
——— (1985). Toward a logic of organization in psychobiological development. In *Biologic Response Styles: Clinical Implications,* ed. H. Klar & L. Siever. Washington: American Psychiatric Press, pp. 20-35.
——— STECHLER, G., & BURNS, P. (1979). Change in infant and caregiver variables over the first two months of life. In *Origins of the Infant's Social Responsiveness,* ed. E. Thomas. Hillsdale, N.J.: Erlbaum, pp. 349-407.
SAUL, L. J. (1976). *The Psychodynamics of Hostility.* New York: Aronson.
SCHILDER, P. (1964). *Contributions to Developmental Neuro-Psychiatry.* New York: Int. Univ. Press.
SCHUR, M. (1966). *The Id and the Regulatory Principles of Mental Functioning.* New York: Int. Univ. Press.
——— (1972). *Freud: Living and Dying.* New York: Int. Univ. Press.
SETTLAGE, C. F. (1990). The regulation of aggression in the parent-child relationship. Presented at the Meetings of the American Psychoanalytic Association, New York.
——— AFTERMAN, J., & BEMESDORFER, S. (1985). The appeal cycle phenomenon in early mother-child interaction. Presented at Winter Meetings of the American Psychoanalytic Association, New York.
SLAP, J. W. (1987). Implications for the structural model of Freud's assumptions about perception. *J. Amer. Psychoanal. Assn.,* 35:629-645.
SPITZ, R. A. (1946). Anaclitic depression: An inquiry into the genesis of psychiatric conditions in early childhood. *Psychoanal. Study Child,* 2:313-342.
——— (1950). Anxiety in infancy: A study of its manifestations in the first year of life. *Int. J. Psychoanal.,* 31:138-143.
——— (1953). Aggression. In *Drives, Affects, Behavior,* Vol. 1, ed. R. M. Loewenstein. New York: Int. Univ. Press, pp. 126-138.
——— (1957). *No and Yes: On the Genesis of Human Communication.* New York: Int. Univ. Press.
——— (1958). On the genesis of superego components. *Psychoanal. Study Child,* 13:375-404.
——— (1959). *A Genetic Field Theory of Ego Formation.* New York: Int. Univ. Press.

——— (1965). *The First Year of Life.* New York: Int. Univ. Press.

——— Emde, R. N., & Metcalf, D. R. (1970). Further prototypes of ego formation. *Psychoanal. Study Child,* 25:417–441.

Stechler, G. & Halton, A. (1983). Assertion and aggression: Emergence during infancy. Presented at Winter Meetings of the American Psychoanalytic Association, New York.

Stern, D. N. (1985). *The Interpersonal World of the Infant.* New York: Basic Books.

Storr, A. (1972). *Human Destructiveness.* New York: Atheneum.

Tomkins, S. S. (1962–63). *Affect, Imagery, Consciousness,* 2 Vols. New York: Springer.

Weil, A. (1970). The basic core. *Psychoanal. Study Child,* 25:442–460.

——— (1976). The first year: Metapsychological inferences of infant observation. In *The Process of Child Development,* ed. P. B. Neubauer. New York: Aronson, pp. 1–20.

Winnicott, D. W. (1950). Aggression in relation to emotional development. In *Collected Papers.* New York: Basic Books, 1975, pp. 204–218.

Wolff, P. (1965). The development of attention in young infants. *Ann. N.Y. Acad. Sci.,* 118:815–830.

——— & White, B. L. (1965). Visual pursuit and attention in young infants. *J. Amer. Acad. Child Psychiat.,* 4:473–484.

Zeanah, C. H., Anders, T. F., Seifer, R., & Stern, D. N. (1989). Implications of research on infant development for psychodynamic theory and practice. *J. Amer. Acad. Child & Adol. Psychiat.,* 28:657–668.

D. 118 Presidential Apts.
Presidential Blvd.
Philadelphia, PA 19131

A CONCEPTUAL ANALYSIS OF THE AFFECTS

JEROME KAGAN, PH. D.

It is suggested that affects are defined conjunctively by physiological events, cognitive structures, and behavioral programs linked to specific classes of incentives. Further, distinctions must be made between affect states that are and those that are not detected by consciousness and, in addition, between affect states in the subjective frame of the experiencing agent contrasted with the objective frame of an observer.

It is also likely that several different neural circuits participate in the family of affect states called fear or anxiety. Finally, it is argued that scholars should use different constructs for states that represent (1) acute temporary changes in behavior and physiology to an incentive event; (2) chronic states that are the products of experience; and (3) temperamentally based vulnerabilities to specific affective states. Support for this last argument comes from research on the temperamental categories of inhibited and uninhibited children. The children in these two categories maintained their respective profiles over time and differed from each other in reactivity in limbic sites. It is suggested that inhibited children are at special risk for the development of panic disorder and agoraphobia.

THREE DEVELOPMENTS in the human sciences have been accompanied by a renascence of scientific concern with human emotions. The first, and perhaps most significant, originates in the physiological research on the relation of neural activity in selected limbic sites to changes in mood and behavior. The empirical work of Davis (1986, 1987), Mishkin and Aggleton (1981), and Adamec and Adamec (1986), along with many others, has taught us that the amygdala and hypothalamus and their projections to the frontal cortex and autonomic nervous system participate in a major way in the states philosophers, psychiatrists, and psychologists have called pas-

Professor of Psychology, Harvard University, Cambridge, Mass.

Preparation of this paper was supported, in part, by a grant from the John D. and Catherine T. MacArthur Foundation.

sion, surprise, fear, sadness, joy, anger, disgust, and, at a much more abstract level, pleasure and displeasure. When these structures are compromised, through surgery or chemicals, the action sequences normally linked to these states are absent or seriously different from their usual form.

A second development is derived from the studies of human affects. One line of inquiry, traceable to Paul Ekman (1980) and Carroll Izard (1977), focuses on the universality of a small number of discrete affect states, each associated with a facial expression. A related and relevant theme originates in the theoretical essays of John Bowlby (1969) on the emotional attachments of children to their caretakers.

The third development is the recent revival of empirical inquiry into infant temperamental types. The investigators in this domain regard variation in chronic mood and receptivity to specific affect states as due, in part, to inherited variations in susceptibility to specific profiles of limbic arousal (Kagan et al., 1988). This paper examines these new developments from two perspectives. One is derived from the research of developmental psychologists on the temperamental categories of inhibited and uninhibited children. This work suggests that some children are born with a preparedness to experience the related affects of uncertainty, anxiety, and fear. The second is Freud's prescient hypothesis that central nervous system activity is the foundation of the construct of the id. Although Freud could not have anticipated the discoveries of the last 20 years, I believe he would have smiled at these empirical victories.

The Concept of Affect

I approach the idea of affect in a nonpragmatic, Baconian frame which resists positing, a priori, a definitive set of emotional categories, like joy, sadness, or anger. My reason for this skepticism is that most of the popular affect categories in scientific discourse are derived from the language citizens use to name their subjectively experienced states. One serious problem with this strategy is that it ignores affective processes that are not experienced consciously and states for which familiar names are not available in the language of conversation.

The histories of physics, chemistry, and biology teach us that the first terms used to label natural phenomena, which also came from everyday language, were eventually replaced with technical words that were not part of the parole. I also believe that the popular affect terms in the West are too general and do not accommodate sufficiently to important features of context. Even Freud (1933), in the *New Introductory Lectures,* differentiated among objective, neurotic, and moral anxiety, implying different origins and, by inference, different states.

I am friendly to the idea of distinctive families of affect states. Each member of a family is defined conjunctively by a combination of physiological events, cognitive structures, and reflex or intentional motor actions, including facial expressions. Although some affect states are associated with distinctive facial expressions which function as information signals to others, other affect states are not so clearly tied to unambiguous facial expressions—guilt over violating a standard, anticipation of criticism, sexual arousal, and anxiety while lying to a friend are obvious examples. Distinct postures and facial expressions can be part of an affective process, but I view them neither as origins nor as necessary components of an affect. This claim rests on the assumption that elimination of the motor outputs to the facial muscles would not be accompanied by absence of an affective experience. The importance of facial expressions lies with the fact that when an expression occurs in the presence of another, the behavior of the other can produce changes in the affect state of the subject.

Each of these trios of biology, cognition, and motor response defines an affect and each trio is linked to a specific set of incentives. Consider as an example the family of states provoked by unfamiliar events that are not immediately assimilable which produces (a) activation of the central nucleus of the amygdala and its projections to the hypothalamus and sympathetic nervous system; (b) a cognitive inference of uncertainty as how to act; and (c) activation of motor patterns that lead to withdrawal or distress vocalizations. This family of events defines an affect that most Western scholars would call "anxiety to the unfamiliar." I suspect separation distress is a member of this category. However, I believe there is a related trio that includes the same state of the amygdala linked to a cognitive anticipation of criticism and a disposition to become quiet when the person believes his or her behavior is being evaluated by someone in a position of authority. This family of events defines an affect scholars might call "anxiety over evaluation." I also suspect there is a third trio that includes a similar state of the amygdala but a cognitive inference of physical danger and the disposition to flee, which might occur to dangerous animals. This trio defines an affect scholars might call "anxiety over harm." The distinctions among these three anxiety states are not trivial.

It is also necessary to differentiate between those affect states in which changes in internal physiology are experienced consciously and those states in which no conscious awareness occurs. In the former, psychological processes will be generated that impose an interpretation on the felt state. The subsequent emotional state will have a special quality and, as a result, behaviors might be initiated and thoughts generated that would not have been implemented if the change in internal state had remained undetected or unconscious. A person who detects a rise in heart rate and increased muscle tension in an unfamiliar social situation will interpret that information and, as a result, be in an altered state. At a minimum, we need a special term or a suffix to append to an affect construct that specifies whether or not an emotional state is a product of conscious awareness of changes in biology and intention.

In addition, we must acknowledge the distinction between an affective state in the subjective frame of the person in contrast to the objective frame of an observer. Freud, who sought unity and parsimony, wanted all discussion of affects to be in the objective frame; that is, events in the mind/brain whose characteristics were independent of how they were assessed. On this theme he was in close agreement with Albert Einstein. However, I side with Niels Bohr who argued that the source of evidence for a scientific construct determines its meaning.

When an analyst applies the term "anxious" to describe an obsessive-compulsive patient, the meaning of the concept is different from the meaning the patient understands when she says she is experiencing anxiety. The analyst's use of the diagnostic word is in the objective frame and is intended to imply both an emotional state and a hypothetical set of structures acquired over time (and perhaps locatable in brain circuits) of which the patient is unaware. The patient intends only to label her current feeling tone.

Consider a laboratory example of the differences in meaning that accompany subjective or objective frames. Although prosopagnosics report verbally that they do not recognize photographs of familiar persons, they nonetheless show a galvanic skin response when they look at familiar photographs, but not at unfamiliar ones (Tranel and Damasio, 1985).

This distinction is important in current research because a large number of psychologists study affects by using questionnaires which ask individuals about the frequency and intensity of their subjective awareness of states of anxiety, depression, and anger. Many of these psychologists assume that the meaning of the terms they use to describe this source of evidence is similar to, or identical with, the meaning understood by physiologists and analysts who use very different evidence when they write about these same states.

The distinction between subjective and objective frames is relevant also to consideration of the meanings of the terms "pleasure" and "displeasure." It is a truism in Western philosophy—from Hume and Locke to Freud and Thorndike—that humans and animals seek states of pleasure and avoid states of displeasure. But conceptual difficulties arise whenever one tries to define these hypothetical states in an objective frame. Similar difficulties apply to the term "reinforcement" as it is used by behaviorists. Although a person can say whether he or she is feeling pleasure, it is often the case that a context that generates pleasure in one person (sport parachuting or tending a sick parent) leads to displeasure in another. Therefore, it is not possible to define pleasure (or displeasure) in terms of a universal set of human activities or physiological events. The fact that there are sites in the brains of rats which, when stimulated, lead animals to work for electrical stimulation does not mean that the animals experience pleasure when these neurons are activated. I make this suggestion because in humans all pleasures habituate, at least temporarily, while rats who are pressing a bar in order to receive electrical stimulation of a pleasure center in the brain never habituate. They will press for an indefinite period of time (Liebman, 1989). This fact suggests that the state of an animal stimulated is not like that of a human who is reporting a feeling of pleasure. Liebman (1989) notes, "It has become clear that intracranial self stimulation may not always give rise to hedonic pleasure, thus prompting a call for the de-hedonization of intracranial self stimulation" (p. 10).

The conceptual difficulty can be put in concrete terms. Consider a compulsive adult who consistently cleans her kitchen a dozen times a day. When asked why, she says that it gives her pleasure to know that the room is always spotless and adds that she experiences displeasure whenever she sees any dirt. The psychiatrist, by contrast, assumes from the evidence of her behavior that she is anxious and therefore experiencing displeasure as she scrubs the floor. The psychiatrist's frame is objective, while the patient's is subjective. That is why we must differentiate between subjective and objective definitions of pleasure and displeasure—as we do for all affects—and why I am uncertain pleasure and displeasure will turn out to be theoretically useful ideas.

Neural Circuits and Emotion

Recent research by physiologists has led Joseph LeDoux (1989) to suggest that at least four different neural circuits can participate in the affective state that is often called fear. The most basic circuit, triggered by novel events, innate releasers, and conditioned stimuli, involves a set of connections among the thalamus, hippocampus, amygdala, and sensory cortex. (The hippocampus also sends projections to the amygdala, and the amygdala projects reciprocally to the thalamus and cortex.) Arousal of this complex circuit might represent the foundation of an affect or be regarded as a "state of preparedness" for an emotional state. For example, when an unexpected sound occurs while a person is reading in a moderately quiet room, the auditory signal, after processing by the cochlea and the colliculus, arrives at the medial geniculate of the thalamus. Three separate circuits leave the thalamus simultaneously—one to the hippocampus to evaluate familiarity (or unfamiliarity) of the sound in that particular context; one to the amygdala to prepare for motor and autonomic reactions; and, finally, one to the sensory cortex to perform a detailed analysis of the sound. The result of the cortical analysis is relayed to the amygdala to supplement the message that arrived about 50 to 100 msec. earlier.

If the result of the processing is the perception of an airplane overhead, there will probably be no further affective consequences. If, however, such assimilation is not possible, and the source or the meaning of the sound remains unclear, further mental work will be performed. Although many theorists might call this emotional state "alert attention," it can be part of the early phase of an emotional state of anxiety or fear, especially if the person cannot assimilate the sound.

An example is seen when a young infant is exposed to a series of taped sentences spoken by an adult but with no visual support for the human voice. The first sentence usually provokes alerting but not a wary face or crying. After the second or third sentence the infant's face often becomes wary and he or she may cry, presumably as a result of an analysis by the cortex and the recognition of a discrepancy.

A second circuit involves projections from the amygdala and hippocampus to the frontal cortex, where a further evaluation of the information in the context is performed and a more serious attempt at assimilation occurs. If assimilation is still not possible, that state is relayed back to the amygdala. The resulting state might be called "the anxiety of premonition" because of an expectation of potentially dangerous future events.

A third set of circuits adds motor and/or visceral reactions. The motor circuit involves projections from the amygdala to the corpus striatum and the central gray and from those sites to skeletal muscles. The visceral circuit refers to projections from the amygdala to the hypothalamus (especially the lateral and ventromedial hypothalamus), and from there to the autonomic nervous system. Activation of these circuits is accompanied by changes in motor tension, posture, speech, as well as heart rate, blood pressure, epinephrine and norepinephrine and, as the result of stimulation of the pituitary, increased cortisol.

The motor and autonomic changes engage a fourth circuit which serves afferent feedback from the peripheral target sites to the nucleus tractus solitarius, which projects back to the amygdala which, in turn, sends projections to the prefrontal cortex. It is presumed that the prefrontal cortex mediates action plans and subjective interpretations of physiological tone. The conscious perception of visceral arousal will, of course, change the person's emotional state.

I do not suggest that these four circuits are independent,

or easily separable; only that it is not necessary that all circuits be activated when a particular incentive occurs. An unexpected sound in a quiet room might arouse only the first circuit, without producing activation of motor or autonomic components. But that state of alerting is an affect state, different from the state that would be generated if our reader in a quiet room reacted with a ten beat rise in heart rate to the same auditory stimulus and guessed that there might be a small animal in the room. And once aroused by that idea the person would now be sensitized to a variety of subsequent unfamiliar events. Thus, the term "affect," as used popularly, may involve different neural circuits. Additionally, I do not suppose there is any simple correspondence between activation of any of these circuits and conscious psychological states. Rather, the situation resembles the relation between the physiological states of cells in tissues or organs and the psychological state of feeling fatigued.

The Place of Affect Constructs in Theory

One task facing scientists is to discover the core families of affects. Even if fear, anger, joy, sadness, and disgust turn out to be in that set, I believe they do not exhaust it. Further, I suspect that the discovery of the core families is not possible, at least at the present time, through a priori theorizing alone. Extensive empirical data will be necessary. I offer this conclusion with some confidence because it is unlikely any naturalist prior to 1800 could have inferred, through reflection on available evidence, the constituents and functions of living cells. The human mind does not like, and therefore is not likely to invent, categories that are as asymmetric, complex, or contextually constrained as those we now believe characterize living cells. Similarly, I suspect that when we finally understand human emotions, they, too, will be more complex, less discrete, and more closely linked to contexts than we now believe. The mind in quiet contemplation is attracted to logical, neat, mutually exclusive categories that are symmetrical around a deep idea. Nature, however, has different preferences.

A major difference between biologists and students of human nature is that the former more often invent constructs a posteriori to explain lawful empirical relations that have been discovered. Biologists are less likely to start with a priori, idealized concepts and seek to find them in nature. They prefer to start with robust phenomena and invent names after functional relations have been verified. Thus, we should ask what reliable phenomena are to be explained with affect concepts.

First, there are the acute changes in physiology and action that occur to novelty, challenge, loss, or frustration. These changes are sudden, often temporary, and come close in meaning to some of the discrete emotions posited by Ekman and Izard.

A second set of phenomena refers to the longer lasting states created by experiences that have occurred over many years. These are the chronic moods that can result, for example, from membership in a particular social class or minority group or a decade of academic failure or social rejection. These chronic moods bias a person's reaction to incentives in particular ways. Folk theory as well as psychodynamic propositions make the distinction between acute states and chronic moods. When we say, "Paul is angry because he was pushed," we understand that Paul's state is different from the one implied by the sentence, "Paul is angry because of his chronic life of poverty," even though the same word—"angry"—is used in both sentences. Moreover, because the physiological states and cognitions are different in the acute and chronic states, it seems reasonable to apply different names to them.

Finally, there is individual variation in the biologically based biases to react to certain events. These biases are called temperamental. Neither folk belief nor contemporary psychodynamic theory makes a distinction between chronic emotional moods and temperamental biases, even though nineteenth-century writers did.

Thus, I suggest that there should be at least three different terms for three different states that belong to the family of anxiety; a similar conclusion would hold for the other affect families.

1. A person is given a challenging problem and an investigator observes changes in heart rate and pupillary dilation, as well as a loss in the quality of recall memory. Most scientists would call this profile "acute anxiety," which is accompanied by sudden changes in the sympathetic and skeletal motor systems elicited by challenge or a novel event with which the subject cannot cope. We say, "when adults are in a novel or challenging situation and have no coping response, they become anxious."

2. A person who grew up in poverty and left school early fails to persist when cognitive tasks are presented to him, but does not show any change in physiological functioning in a test situation. Investigators are likely to call this profile "chronic anxiety," meaning the stable profile of behaviors and biological characteristics possessed by a select group of persons as a result of a prolonged history of specific experiences. Chronic anxiety is often indexed by self-effacing behavior, reluctance to accept challenge, and timidity in an unfamiliar social situation. We say, "Adults who set high academic standards but have consistently failed to meet them are anxious."

3. A person who was a temperamentally irritable infant and a fearful child has a chronically high and stable heart rate and a high cortisol level in all social situations. Scholars are apt to call this person "temperamentally anxious." We say, "Temperamentally inhibited adults are anxious in unfamiliar social situations," implying that such persons began life with a distinct physiology and, as a result of experience, became especially vulnerable to uncertainty in social situations.

The source of evidence for the term "anxiety" is different in the three instances described above, and theoretical statements using the concept of anxiety do not have the same meaning in the three instances.

Acute states are more characteristic of infants and young children for there has not been sufficient time for the young child to establish chronic moods. The contemporary investigators who study attachment, following Bowlby (1969) and Ainsworth et al. (1978) imply, sometimes directly, that the categories of a secure and insecure attachment are chronic emotional states that predispose infants to experience acute anxiety as a threat. These investigators recognize the difference between acute and chronic states but have been reluctant to acknowledge the role of temperamental biases. Indeed, many have insisted that the chronic state that biases a one-year-old to become acutely anxious to separation is the product of experience alone and is not influenced by temperament. It is appropriate now to consider the idea of temperament in more detail.

Temperament

The word "temperament" is used by most, but not all, behavioral scientists to refer to those psychological qualities that display considerable variation among infants and, in addition, have a relatively but not indefinitely stable biological basis in the organism's genotype, even though the inherited physiological processes mediate different phenotypic displays as the child grows. It is not unreasonable to suggest that some of the temperamental differences among children are analogous to the biobehavioral differences among closely related strains of dogs, cats, or monkeys. The temperamental qualities that are most obvious to contemporary parents, and investigated most often by psychologists and psychiatrists, include irritability, smiling, motor activity, sociability, and adaptability to new situations. It is not clear at the moment how many temperamental qualities will be discovered. I suspect it will be more than 6 but hopefully less than 60. We will have to wait for history's answer.

Steven Reznick, Nancy Snidman, and I, together with many students, have been studying two members of the larger set of temperamental qualities. The primary behavioral referent for each of these categories is the response profile of two-year-old children when they are in unfamiliar situations. Some children consistently become quiet, vigilant, and restrained while they assess the situation and their resources before acting. We call such children "inhibited." Others act with spontaneity in the same situations, and we call these children "uninhibited." The situations that best reveal these two temperamental qualities in young children are encounters with unfamiliar children or adults, perhaps because other people are the most frequent basis for categorizing a setting as unfamiliar. It is rare to find a large number of children who are consistently shy and emotionally restrained or spontaneous regardless of the context. We have discovered, however, that there is a small group of children, we estimate it to be about 10 to 15 percent, who usually bring one or the other of these behavioral styles to unfamiliar situations. Over the last 10 years we have found that there is modest, but significant, preservation of the inhibited and uninhibited behavioral styles from 21 to 31 months of age through 8 years of age (Kagan et al., 1988). About three-fourths of the children retain their expected classification, based on whether their standard score on an aggregate index at 7½ years of age was positive or negative. Although one-half of the original group of inhibited children no longer displayed an extreme degree of timidity and shyness at 7½ years, about three-quarters had not yet acquired the unusually spontaneous demeanor characteristic of the typical uninhibited child. A smaller number of uninhibited youngsters became shy; 10 percent of the original group had become very timid at 7½ years of age.

It is important to note that these results were found for

children who had been selected originally to be extreme on inhibited and uninhibited behavior. We do not believe that these two groups of children lie on a continuum of sociability, but rather represent two qualitative types. That is, the concept of temperament raises an epistemological issue; namely, whether some temperamental concepts are qualitative categories or refer to continuous dimensions. Freud wrote as if he believed that libido and anxiety were continuous processes that did not change their essential qualities, only their magnitudes. This is true of the physical concept of energy. Many theorists using the idea of self also posit a continuous construct; self-esteem or coherence of self, for example, are presumed to be continuous processes. But biology teaches us that discrete categories are often theoretically useful. For example, biologists who write about different strategies of reproduction regard them as types rather than continua. Similarly, classes of diseases, viruses, and pharmacological cures are conceptualized as qualitative categories. Among infectious diseases tuberculosis is not on a continuum with malaria or measles; it is a qualitatively distinct disease.

Inhibited and uninhibited temperamental types are analogous to biological strains. Each type refers to a class of children who share a genotype and environmental history and a set of correlated behavioral and physiological characteristics. Support for this claim comes from a study of a third longitudinal cohort of Caucasian, middle and working class children of both sexes who were not selected originally to be extreme on either of the two behavioral profiles (Kagan et al., 1989). The 100 children in this third cohort were observed initially at 14 and 20 months and followed up at 4 and 5½ years of age. The original variation in the continuous index of inhibited behavior at 14 and 20 months for the entire group did not predict inhibition at 4 years. Only when we restricted the analysis to those children who fell at the top and bottom 20 percent of the distribution of behavioral inhibition at 14 and 20 months did we find significant differences in behavior between the two extreme groups at age 4. These differences were preserved to 5½ years, with about three-fourths of the children retaining their category, whether it be inhibited or uninhibited. These results imply that the terms inhibited and uninhibited do not refer to a phenotypic continuum ranging from extreme shyness to extreme sociability in an unselected sample of children, even though such a phenotypic continuum exists and can be measured.

A second reason why we believe the two groups of children are qualitatively different is that they vary in physical and physiological characteristics which imply that the inhibited children have a low threshold of reactivity in the limbic system, especially the amygdala and hypothalamus, due to an inherited neurochemical profile. The uninhibited children have a higher threshold which is the result of a different neurochemical profile. Support for this idea comes from the fact that, compared with uninhibited children, the inhibited children show cardiac acceleration under mild cognitive stress, higher levels of cortisol early in the morning, greater muscle tension, and a cerebral asymmetry characterized by greater suppression of alpha in the right than the left frontal pole (Davidson and Finman, personal communication).

In addition, it appears that distinct profiles of behavior to visual and auditory stimuli in 16-week-old infants predict inhibited or uninhibited behavior in the second year. One group of infants is characterized by extreme degrees of motor arousal to the presentation of mobiles and human speech. These highly aroused infants arch their back and pump and extend their arms and legs frequently, often with vigor. In addition, on several occasions during a period of high motor arousal they will fret or cry. About two-thirds of these high motor arousal infants are also very irritable.

Over 70 percent of the infants with this pair of qualities show above average degrees of fear to unfamiliar events in the laboratory at 14 months of age, while only 4 percent (one child) are minimally fearful. Among the contrast group of infants who display low levels of motor arousal and no fretting to the same events, two-thirds are minimally fearful and only

10 percent show high levels of fear. It is possible that the highly aroused infants who show high levels of fear at 14 months are at risk for what Freud called hysterical symptoms. If so, his intuition that hysterics had a constitution that rendered them vulnerable to anxiety attacks was prescient.

It is important to note that it is the profile of characteristics at 4 months that predicts inhibited or uninhibited behavior in the second year. Motor arousal or crying considered alone is far less predictive of fear in the second year. That is, the profile of high motor arousal combined with no fretting does not predict inhibited, fearful behavior.

One possible interpretation of these findings emphasizes the excitability of the amygdala and its projections to the hypothalamus, sympathetic chain, and the motor system. We suggest that the high motor arousal, high cry, high heart rate infants inherit a low threshold of excitability, while the complementary group of infants inherit a high threshold. We suspect, however, that the neurochemical foundations of each of these two behavioral categories are qualitatively different. Future research will have to evaluate the fruitfulness of this suggestion.

Relation to Psychoanalytic Theory

How do these ideas on affects relate to early statements by psychoanalytic theorists, as well as more recent writings by psychiatrists and analysts? It is reasonable to suggest that, at least in his early writings, Freud believed that brain structures were the origins of the excitation that produced the prepared response programs associated with eating, sexual arousal, and aggression. That is why I suggested that Freud would have been pleased with the last two decades of work in the neurosciences. This research indicates that limbic structures are important origins of these affect states and their associated behavioral programs. However, he may have been less happy with the discoveries of developmental scientists who have found a maturational time table for the phenomena of smiling to a face, distress to strangers and to separation, symbolic language, a moral sense, and self-consciousness, each of which occurs in a regular sequence during the first two years of life (Emde and Harmon, 1972; Kagan, 1984). These psychological competences are not obvious derivatives of the ego's attempt to monitor the id, but develop under all conditions of gratification of hunger and relief from pain, excepting, of course, extreme deprivation of any contact with others. Experience is always necessary to actualize an affect. This hypothesis implies that some affects cannot appear until growth of the brain permits particular cognitive competences to mature—guilt being a prime example. Affects are as much dependent upon the maturation of cognitive abilities as on the physiological processes Freud believed were the primary foundation of the id.

It is, of course, unfair to fault Freud for suggesting that the ego's growth depended upon conflict. Scientists can never be completely free of the deep premises that dominate their historical era. The new discoveries in sensory physiology, Darwinian theory, and Helmholtz's principle of conservation of energy were so influential at the turn of the century it would have been impossible for any mind, no matter how creative or bold, to construct a theoretical system that was indifferent to or seriously inconsistent with these three ideas. It is to Freud's credit that he did posit a hypothesis, original at the time, that early childhood experiences determined the variations in affective development.

The most significant modern transformation of Freudian views involves the idea of anxiety. In Freud's original formulation, anxiety was a consequence of the flooding of the brain with stimulation and a subsequent inhibition on actions in order to reduce the excitation originating in the libido. In the *New Introductory Lectures,* where Freud tried to integrate recent insights with his earlier ideas, he suggested that anxiety occurred when the ego recognized that satisfaction of an instinct might lead to danger—the two prototypic dangers being fear of castration for boys and loss of love for girls. Hence, there was repression of the feared wish and inhibition of relevant actions. Freud acknowledged, as I indicated earlier, three classes of anxiety—objective, neurotic, and moral—and gave emphasis to the second, treating hysteria (characterized today by the panic patient) as a prototype.

In a panic attack the patient undergoes a sudden, unexpected, discharge of limbic structures that leads to visceral reactions whose feedback pierces consciousness demanding an interpretation. The victim usually interprets these feelings as fear. But it is not clear, as Eagle (1987) notes, that what the panic patient fears is an id impulse. It is more likely that the root cause of the attack is the temperamental vulnerability to limbic discharge, rather than the patient's past experiences and extensive reliance on repression as a defense. The psychological processes which Freud insisted were primary have been partially replaced in modern writings with the notion of an inherently excitable limbic system. Jung (1924) would have been pleased with this development.

Freud's category of moral anxiety is, of course, still relevant, for contemporary scholars continue to hold that shame, guilt, and anxiety occur to the contemplation or execution of violations of personal standards. And objective anxiety—fear of tarantulas—remains real. However, research points to a fourth source of anxiety which Freud seemed to ignore because, I suspect, it did not fit well with his conception of the mechanisms of anxiety. Therefore, he probably placed it in another category. I refer to the state produced by novel or unfamiliar events which cannot be assimilated or coped with immediately. This state is most obvious in infants. A 4-month-old alert baby resting quietly in a seat suddenly hears a tape recording of human speech. After a few seconds the infant's face becomes wary, and a few seconds later the infant begins to cry. I assume that the inability to assimilate the speech sounds without any visual support from a human face produced a special state which is a member of the family we call anxiety.

The Idea of Self. Some analytic theorists, accommodating to the discoveries and new attitudes of post-World War II science and associated changes in Western society, have tried to mute Freud's early physiological determinism and promote psychological functions over brain states, especially mental constructions, to a position of origin. This strategy worked well for Skinner and Piaget, as well as for cultural anthropologists like Kluckhohn, Whiting, and Geertz. It is not surprising that when contemporary psychoanalytic theorists, Erikson (1963) and Kohut (1984) are good examples, looked for psychological constructs, they decided to make a construct of self both origin and monitor of physiological processes. This idea has intuitive appeal because each of us has a compelling intuition that we possess a self which determines our actions, reflects on our wishes and intentions, and evaluates our feelings. But there is some danger in this new view.

The most powerful constructs in biology and chemistry are not intuitively obvious to human consciousness. Richard Feynman has urged that we must accept the fact that, at times, nature appears to our intuitions as absurd. Imagine assuming the state of consciousness of a 5-year-old child. Most psychiatrists and psychologists believe, in the objective frame, that the major processes controlling the child's behavior are identification with parents, temperamental biases, and socialized habits and values. However, none of these processes is salient in the child's phenomenological awareness. The experiential elements that dominate the child's consciousness usually refer to events and persons that are feared, including the threat of physical harm, punishment, or rejection, and the joys of play and sensory delights. For these reasons I am not certain that the self-system is as central as Kohut and Erikson have argued.

Although Freud may have awarded too much power to physiology, Kohut has awarded too much power to self. Kohut sees self as the captain of a ship; I see it as a team of anchor men in a TV newsroom trying to decipher the many complex events that are about to change an individual's actions and mood. Biological processes, unavailable to conscious awareness, are altering and are being altered by events in mind/brain. One of the self's tasks is to decipher these events and to impose a coherent meaning upon them. However, it is often difficult for self to transform or to gain complete control over these forces. Sylvia Plath could not master her chronically dysphoric feeling tone. To claim that Ms. Plath had a weak or incoherent self does not explain her mood, it simply describes it. This is not to say that the idea of self or selves is without utility. But the characteristics of the self-concept are not as malleable to experience nor as potent an origin of action as some writers imply. Further, one can argue that each person has several self-concepts, one for each major dimension of living. There is a concept of self with respect to moral virtue, one for technical competences, and another for social skills—some may have additional selves. The profile of self-concepts can be as uneven as the profile of competences needed to perform well on a battery of cognitive and motor performance tests. As with the cognitive profile, it does not seem theoretically useful to talk of an average self-concept. Local contexts determine the particular self that will be ascendant, and therefore which mood and behaviors are appropriate for particular moments.

REFERENCES

Adamec, R. E. & Stark-Adamec, C. (1986). Limbic hyperfunction and limbic epilepsy in interictal behavior. In *The Limbic System,* ed. B. K. Doane & K. E. Livingston. New York: Raven, pp. 129–145.

Ainsworth, M. D. S., et al. (1978). *Patterns of Attachment.* Hillsdale, N.J.: Erlbaum.

Bowlby, J. (1969). *Attachment.* New York: Basic Books.

Davis, M. (1986). Pharmacological and anatomical analyses of fear conditioning using the fear potentiated startle paradigm. *Behav. Neurosci.,* 100:814–824.

——— HITCHCOCK, J. M., & ROSEN, J. B. (1987). Anxiety and the amygdala: Pharmacological and anatomical analysis of the fear potentiated startle paradigm. In *Psychobiology of Learning and Motivation,* 21:263–305. New York: Academic Press.

EAGLE, M. N. (1987). *Recent Developments in Psychoanalysis.* Cambridge: Harvard Univ. Press.

EKMAN, P. (1980). Biological and cultural contributions to body and facial movement in the expression of emotions. In *Explaining Emotions,* ed. A. O. Rorty. Berkeley: Univ. California Press, pp. 73–102.

EMDE, R. N. & HARMON, R. J. (1972). Endogeneous and exogeneous smiling systems in early infancy. *J. Amer. Acad. Child Psychiat.,* 11:177–200.

ERIKSON, E. H. (1963). *Childhood and Society.* New York: W. W. Norton.

FREUD, S. (1933). New introductory lectures on psycho-analysis. *S. E.,* 22.

IZARD, C. E. (1977). *Human Emotions.* New York: Plenum Press.

JUNG, C. G. (1924). *Psychological Types.* New York: Harcourt Brace.

KAGAN, J. (1984). *The Nature of the Child.* New York: Basic Books.

——— REZNICK, J. S., & GIBBONS, J. (1989). Inhibited and uninhibited types of children. *Child Developm.,* 60:838–845.

——— ——— & SNIDMAN, N. (1988). Biological bases of childhood shyness. *Science,* 240:167–171.

KOHUT, H. (1984). Introspection, empathy, and the semicircle of mental health. *Emotions and Behavior Monographs,* Monogr. 3:347–375.

LEDOUX, J. E. (1989). Cognitive emotional interactions in the brain. In *Cognition and Emotion,* ed. C. Izard. Hillsdale, N.J.: Erlbaum, pp. 267–289.

LIEBMAN, J. M. (1989). Introduction. *The Neuropharmacological Bases of Reward,* ed. J. M. Liebman & S. J. Cooper. Oxford: Clarendon Press, pp. 1–13.

MISHKIN, M. & AGGLETON, J. (1981). Multiple functional contributions of the amygdala in the monkey. In *The Amygdaloid Complex,* ed. Y. Ben-Ari. Elsevier, North Holland Biomedical Press, pp. 409–420.

TRANEL, D. & DAMASIO, A. R. (1985). Knowledge without awareness. *Science,* 228:1453–1454.

Department of Psychology
Harvard University
33 Kirkland Street
Cambridge, MA 02138

THE DEVELOPMENT AND EXPERIENCE OF AFFECT IN ADOLESCENCE

STUART T. HAUSER, M.D., PH.D.
AND HENRY F. SMITH, M.D.

In reviewing theoretical and empirical contributions from psychoanalysis and developmental psychology, we begin to chart several converging themes and pose two fundamental questions: (1) How does adolescent development influence affective experience and expression; and (2) Are there affective currents, unique in their intensity and configuration, that influence adolescent development? The first question leads to a detailed consideration of adolescent ego development; the second question touches upon the impact on adolescence of earlier developmental periods, such as infancy, the influence of the emergent biological events of puberty, and the organizing function of adolescent affects and moods. In the concluding sections we discuss some implications for clinical work.

AFFECTS AND THEIR STUNNING vicissitudes are the centerpiece of most clinical descriptions and theories about adolescent development. It is especially striking, then, that our theoretical understanding of adolescent emotional development and experience is so sparse, representing "almost wholly uncharted territory" (Thompson, 1986, p. 169), a point echoed by Petersen and Craighead (1986), and referred to several decades ago by Ausubel (1954). In this essay, drawing upon contemporary contributions from psychoanalysis and developmental psychology, we begin to chart this territory,

Dr. Hauser is Professor of Psychiatry, Harvard Medical School, and on the faculty of Psychoanalytic Institute of New England East and the Boston Psychoanalytic Institute. Dr. Smith is Assistant Clinical Professor of Psychiatry, Harvard Medical School, and on the faculty of Psychoanalytic Institute of New England East.

Preparation of this paper was supported in part by an NIMH Research Scientist Award (K-05 70178-07).

pointing to important convergences from both fields and to newly crystallized questions.

Two overarching questions frame our inquiry and reflections about affect within adolescence. The first involves how adolescent development influences affective experience and expression. With this in mind we will look in some detail at diverse paths of adolescent ego development. The second question is whether there are affective currents, unique in their intensity and configurations, that influence adolescent development. This question, drawing attention to the impact of affective experience on adolescence, is implicit in many clinical formulations about emotional development occurring during this period; discussions touch on such topics as impacts of earlier developmental epochs (e.g., infancy), influences of the emergent biological events of puberty, and organizing functions of affect in adolescence.

Models of Adolescent Development

One understanding of adolescence, articulated at the turn of the century by G. Stanley Hall (1904), perpetuated by many clinical studies, magnified by the media, and often assumed by the public, is that a healthy adolescent will appear to have a mild case of mental illness. Adolescents are expected to be extremely moody, depressed one day and excitedly "high" the next. Intensely charged conflict with family, friends, and authorities is thought of as commonplace. The theoretical work of the psychoanalytic community in the 1950s and early 1960s was consistent with this view (Blos, 1962; Erikson, 1959, 1964a, 1964b, 1968; A. Freud, 1936, 1958). Clinicians and theorists described adolescence as necessarily a time of profound inner turmoil and outward conflict, based on their observations of patient populations. Emotional crisis and upheaval were viewed as appropriate responses by the adolescent to the major psychological and societal tasks accompanying this phase of life: dramatically reducing psychological dependency on parents, separating from the family, and forming an adult identity. Turmoil was considered necessary for subsequent normal personality integration.

The "storm and stress" model of adolescent development underscored the array of physical, social, and psychological changes experienced by adolescents in this culture. The model accorded dignity to the stressfulness of managing these concurrent changes. In addition, this perspective invigorated the scholarly community in the mid-1960s and prompted important new research (Bandura, 1964; Douvan and Adelson, 1966; Offer, 1969; Offer and Offer, 1975). Data from study after study were analyzed to determine whether the majority of adolescents were in serious psychological turmoil. Although many observers agree that adolescence is a period of development requiring multiple changes (in fact, significant programs of research have been focused on each major area of change—biological, social, and psychological), the current consensus is that adolescence cannot simply be described as a time of major dysfunction or vulnerability (Powers et al., 1989). For instance, epidemiological studies indicate that about 10 to 20 percent of adolescents exhibit some type of severe emotional disturbance (as defined by descriptive diagnostic criteria)—approximately the same percentage as reported in similar surveys of the adult population (Offer et al., 1981; Petersen, 1988).

Within the field of developmental psychology, contemporary studies of adolescent development are strongly grounded in theoretically guided, empirically derived, profiles of adolescent adaptation and growth (e.g., Brooks-Gunn et al., 1989; Collins and Gunnar, 1989; Petersen, 1988). This attention to individual differences—describing a spectrum of adolescent behaviors and developmental patterns—is pertinent to our thinking about emotional development during adolescence. A central focus of theoretical and empirical studies has been the role of pubertal changes in adolescent development (Paikoff and Brooks-Gunn, 1991). Earlier research assumed that pubertal changes created or triggered various psychological states, with puberty conceived of as a single, and major, discrete event (e.g., growth spurt, menarche; Faust, 1983). In contrast, investigators now explore "pubertal changes as multiple overlapping events with important dimensions, such as the rate, tempo and salience of pubertal events affecting adolescent outcomes" (Paikoff and Brooks-Gunn, 1991, p. 47; cf. also Brooks-Gunn et al., 1985). Accumulating evidence supports the view that pubertal changes are associated, in complex ways, with transformations in family relationships and shifting affective experience in these and other relationships. Moreover, the impact of pubertal events upon adolescent affects, close relationships, and associated behaviors is likely influenced by contextual factors, such as gender of adolescent and parent, family structure and ethnicity, as well as by intrapsychic processes (Paikoff and Brooks-Gunn, 1991). Although in the remainder of this paper we concentrate on intrapsychic (e.g., cognitive processes, ego development) and interpersonal dimensions, this emphasis is not meant to minimize the multifold influences of pubertal events upon affective development and experience during adolescence. Indeed, an important task for future theoretcal and empirical work will be to more precisely understand how biological (pubertal) and psychological processes, separately and in combination, underlie affect development and experience during adolescence.

Other works especially relevant for considering affective development and adolescence are the studies that conceptualize *pathways* of adolescent development (Block, 1971; Hauser et al., 1988, 1990; Powers et al., 1985; Powers, in press a, b; Offer and Offer, 1975). More specifically, an examination of the multiple paths of ego development during the adolescent years suggests how these trajectories shape affective experience within this era. But before exploring adolescent ego development and affect development, we must first briefly turn to the basic question of how cognitive and emotional development are related during adolescence.

Intersections of Cognitive and Affective Development in Adolescence

The relation between emotion and cognition has interested man from the beginning of recorded self-reflection. Cowan (1982) notes that historical accounts of the study of emotion and cognition in Western thinking usually begin with Aristotle's *De Animus,* and until recently the two have traditionally been seen to represent clear and separate domains. Contemporary theoretical analyses explicitly oppose this conceptual isolation, as well as any assumption of linear relationships between cognition and affect (e.g., that emotions are consequences of cognitive processes). Instead, theories now persuasively advance a more complex view, one emphasizing that "affect and cognition are inseparable, two aspects of the same process" (Sroufe, 1979, p. 491), and citing the continuous interplay between the two domains (Lewis et al., 1984; Piaget and Inhelder, 1969).

In the psychoanalytic literature, affect has been seen as closely related to cognitive or ideational components. Brenner (1982) is the clearest spokesman for this position. Basing his conceptualization on data derived from the psychoanalytic situation, he notes that "any affect includes (a) sensations of pleasure, of unpleasure, or of a mixture of the two plus (b) thoughts, memories, wishes, fears—in a word ideas. *Ideas and sensation together constitute an affect* as a psychological phenomenon" (p. 41). On the other hand, when considering the development of affects, Brenner returns to the familiar emphasis on the fundamental importance of cognition: "Pleasure and unpleasure have no developmental history, as far as is known at present. . . . Thus, as far as present knowledge goes, the development of affects from infancy to adult life means the development of the ideas which are a part of the affects" (p. 42).

As a number of excellent integrative reviews have observed and demonstrated, there is a recent surge of interest in conceptualizing and studying affective development within the fields of psychoanalysis and developmental psychology (Campos et al., 1983, 1989; Collins and Gunnar, 1989; Emde, 1990; Izard and Maletesta, 1987; Sroufe, 1979). Attempts to detail—conceptually and empirically—more specific ways that emotion and cognition are interwoven now characterize many contributions (cf. Fischer et al., 1989b; Harter, 1980; Izard et al., 1984; Lewis et al., 1984). Four significant areas of investigation are emphasized in these active research programs: (1) the infant's expressions of and responses to emotions; (2) socialization of emotions after infancy; (3) the child and adolescent's understanding of emotions; and (4) the role of emotions in organizing behaviors, cognitions, perceptions, and personality development (Collins and Gunnar, 1989). Unsettled questions that are especially of interest for our considerations of affect in adolescence involve the third and fourth areas of work—the adolescent's understanding of emotions and the role of emotions in adolescent development.

Among the more comprehensive investigations of the impact of adolescence on affective development and the role of affect in adolescence are those of Fischer and colleagues (1989a, 1989b; in press). Consistent with other recent contributions about affect development, they too argue that cognition and emotion are complexly intertwined: "In development what changes is the *organization* of behavior, whether that behavior fits under the rubric of cognition, emotion, or social interaction" (Fischer et al., in press). Nonetheless, their analysis of the developmental aspects of affect, like Brenner's, strongly emphasizes cognitive components.

Viewing emotional behavior as in part a learned "skill," Fischer et al. (in press) note that the adolescent has entered a "new developmental tier," characterized by cognitive advances in abstract thinking. The expression and appreciation of affect begins to take on a more complex meaning. Beyond the basic emotions of anger, sadness, fear, joy, and love, for example, adolescents can appreciate more complex, adultlike "scripts" for emotions, such as jealousy and resentment as well as the concept of deeply hidden or repressed emotions (see also Harris et al., 1986; Harris and Gross, 1988).

Like any skill, in Fischer's view, the level of a child's or adolescent's emotional behavior at any given moment is characteristic of a "person-in-a-context." Behavioral levels are highly dependent on environmental contexts. Adolescents are particularly vulnerable to contextual factors because of their newly acquired cognitive capacity for abstraction, which, like any newly attained foothold, is tenuously held and quickly reversed by environmental failure, reversing at the same time previous attainments established during the more stable childhood period. Hence, cognitive change, which we from the outside may view as advance, might be considered as much a destabilizer as are the hormonal vicissitudes of adolescence (Susman et al., 1987; Brooks-Gunn et al., 1989).

Fischer's idea of what might be called the *contextual responsiveness* of the adolescent is consistent with the work of Isberg and colleagues (1989), who describe family contexts of adolescent self-esteem. Of particular interest is their conclusion. In linking their work with the findings of others (Gecas and Schwalbe, 1986; Holmbeck and Hill, 1986), they write: "Children's *perceptions* of parent behaviors are more likely to coincide with self-evaluation than are a neutral observer's perceptions of these same behaviors. Our *observations* of parents do not have as strong a relationship with children's self-esteem as do children's own perceptions of parental behavior" (p. 19). Noteworthy is the emphasis on the importance of the individual adolescent's perception of his or her context as opposed to any so-called "objective" assessment of it, a crucial point for psychoanalytic work, to which we will return.

Two aspects of Fischer's work are especially pertinent for our thinking about affect in adolescence. First, there is the view that skill development may change the experience and expression of affect, a point that is strongly convergent with the way we consider ego development paths as influencing adolescent affective development. In addition, affect may modify the organization of behavior, and hence the *direction of development itself.* This intriguing second point, well known to clinical observers and theorists considering affect development during infancy (Campos et al., 1983, 1989; Sroufe, 1979), has not yet been systematically extended to adolescent development.

A second germane theoretical perspective is provided by Thompson (1985, 1986), who draws upon cognitive (Piagetian) and psychoanalytic considerations. Of central importance in Thompson's sequential model is the concept of "reversibility," a notion embedded in analyses of preoperational thought. An affect is termed "irreversible" when "while in one affective state, the child cannot conceptualize his or her relationship to other affective states or to other evaluations of the object . . . a hated object is a hateful object, and cannot be evaluated independent of that feeling" (1985, p. 161). These affect states, termed "eventlike affects," usually occur early in development, are rigid yet ephemeral; and are not clearly attributed to the self or directly to an object.

In the early development of affects, then, there is a tendency toward *externalization* of affect; "good" or "bad" qualities are tied to the objects rather than to the internal state of the individual. A further limitation imposed by irreversibility of affect is the inability of the child (or developmentally delayed adolescent) to appreciate the possibility of "mixed," "contradictory," or ambivalently held emotions: "the introduction of a new feeling represents a new irreversible affect event" (Thompson, 1985, p. 162). Between six years and early adolescence reversibility of affect becomes possible, paralleling the reversibility inherent in the cognitive realm of concrete operations. This advance leads to distinctions among "self," "inner experience," and "external reality," *and* experiences of mixed and contradictory emotions toward the same object.

The basic sequence leading from eventlike affects to reversibility of affects describes a modal course of emotional development during the childhood years. There is likely continued affective development during the preadolescent and adolescent years. Yet it is here that our knowledge dramatically dwindles. We have little understanding of how certain situations in adolescence (for example, new heterosexual relationships or intensified same sex relationships) may impinge on emotional development in adolescence with respect to stability of affects, reversibility, and other possibly emergent features. Nor do we know—except through clinical observations—what happens under "the pressure of strong affects" or how "different objects affect the nature and structure of the affect elicited" (Thompson, 1985, p. 164).

There are a number of questions even more directly pertinent to adolescence. Are the attainments of the latency and preadolescent period with respect to reversibility of affect so crucial that variations in this capacity will strongly shape individual differences in adolescent affect development? It is possible that during adolescence the greater ability to think hypothetically will extend the capacity for reversibility of affects (Greenspan, 1979). Moreover, widening time perspectives and the development of a greater capacity for reflectiveness—"thoughts about thoughts" (Flavell, 1979)—can enable the developing adolescent to "step back" from his or her feelings, monitoring himself and others as "affect experiencers," appreciating individual differences in how people react to others' feelings, *and* express their own (Thompson, 1985, p. 165). But at this point in our understanding, we do not know about the specific steps during adolescence through which eventlike affects are further transformed into mature reversible affects.

We find some leads in new empirical studies of the child and adolescent's understanding of his or her affective experience and the affective experience of others. Harris et al. (1986; Harris and Gross, 1988) discuss the seeming delays between the child's or adolescent's experiencing conflicting or simultaneous emotions and their awareness of these states. Harter (1980) describes sequences in the individual's developing "theory" of emotional experience, particularly his or her recognizing the coexistence of simultaneous or conflicting emotions directed toward the same object. Normatively, this recognition has been found to occur in early adolescence, but there is wide individual variation as to the timing of this awareness. The contributions of Harter and Harris, underscoring *differing sequences* in the understanding of emotions, lead directly to the topic of individual differences among adolescents and paths of adolescent ego development.

Paths of Adolescent Ego Development and Affective Experience

Explorations of ego development take different forms in the psychoanalytic and psychological literatures, yet there is a shared interest across different frames of reference. From the perspective of psychoanalytic studies, Blos's view of ego development in the main concentrates on vicissitudes of individuation during this period. Loevinger and Wessler's (1970) model of ego development includes considerations of separation, individuation, and reversibility of emotion in its delineation of the evolving *framework of meaning* that the individual imposes upon inner experience and perceptions of people and events (Hauser, 1976; Loevinger, 1976, 1979). This conception of ego development assumes that each person has a customary orientation to himself and to the world, and that there is a continuum (ego development) along which these frames of reference can be arrayed. "In general, ego development is marked by a more differentiated perception of one's self, of the social world, and of the relations of one's feelings and thoughts to those of others" (Candee, 1974). It is the sequence of steps along this continuum of complexity and differentiation that Loevinger and her co-workers have described as stages of ego development (Hauser, 1976).

Using this model of ego development, and a well-constructed linked projective assessment of it, Hauser and colleagues have described *paths* of ego development, as they unfold during the adolescent years (Hauser et al., 1988, 1990, 1991; Powers et al., 1985; Powers, in press a, b). In a large ongoing longitudinal project, boys and girls from a normal high school population and an inpatient psychiatric hospital are followed from their early adolescence through later adolescent years and into young adulthood with respect to their ego development and familial interactions.

In order to study a wide range of developmental trajectories, the two groups are closely observed through annual clinical research interviews and psychological assessments. Our clinical experience suggested that many of the hospitalized adolescents would show early developmental arrests, functioning at low levels of ego development, and not progressing to appreciably higher levels over the four years of the study. Although the hospitalized adolescents were not psychotic, there were strong reasons to expect that most of them would be developmentally impaired in terms of their perceptions of others, interpersonal styles, understanding of their surroundings, and impulse control (e.g., Blos, 1962; Weiner, 1970; Stierlin, 1974). In contrast, we expected that the high school freshmen, with no apparent psychiatric problems, would include many teenagers with progressing or accelerated ego development.

The psychiatrically hospitalized adolescents included consecutive admissions to the children's unit of a private university teaching hospital between autumn 1978 and winter 1980 who agreed to participate in the study. Their diagnoses, formulated 30 days after admission by the senior clinician responsible for them, divided evenly between adjustment disorder, personality disorder, and conduct disorder, using the DSM II diagnostic system then in place (Beardslee et al., 1990). The average age was 14.6 for the patient group and 14.3 for the high school group. Members of both adolescent groups were predominantly from upper-middle-class and middle-class families (Hollingshead, 1957). Despite the demands of our procedures, all of the adolescents and their families completed the various tests, interviews, and family discussion tasks after first joining the project. The total number of adolescents and families longitudinally studied with respect to paths of development was 133 (70 high school students and 63 patients).

Shortly after agreeing to participate, each of the adolescents responded to the well-known sentence completion measure of ego development directly linked with Loevinger's ego development model (Hauser, 1976; Loevinger and Wessler, 1970; Loevinger et al., 1970). On a second visit, within one month of the first, each adolescent met with one of the clinical interviewers for his or her annual exploratory semistructured interview, during which several topics were always covered, in whatever order seemed most natural. These topics included school experience, peer relationships, family history, illness experience, and wishes and fantasies about the future. Our examples of variations in adolescents' affective life are drawn from these transcribed interviews.

To determine initial ego development levels, and ultimately paths of ego development, adolescents were asked to respond to 36 incomplete sentences, or stems, such as *"When they talked about sex, I ____,"* or *"A mother is ____."* Each response was segregated from the subject's whole test to avoid halo effect and then rated by a trained coder, along with other subjects' responses to the same stem. The responses were then reassembled and stage scores determined for each subject, based on the pattern of scores for his or her 36 responses (Loevinger and Wessler, 1970). All of our references to "ego development'' are based on perceptions, attitudes, and emotions expressed by the adolescents in their, often lengthy, completions to these sentence fragments. Besides helping us gauge ego development stages, the individual sets of sentence completions provide the equivalent of a rich written interview, as the adolescents describe varied and often poignant emotional experiences alone and in close relationships with parents and friends.

Early stages of ego development are marked by a sense of external control, an egocentric view of the environment, and a limited ability to relate to others. Later stages represent a progression toward internal control, an appreciation of subtle differences among people, objects, and events; and an ability to establish intimate, collaborative relationships (Swensen, 1980, 1985). Each stage is more complex than the last. Adolescents (and adults) who do not advance beyond a particular early or intermediate stage represent forms of developmental arrest. At the very lowest stages of ego development individuals are described as symbiotic and impulsive. Directly following are the *self-protective* stages, where morality is purely pragmatic: Avoid what is bad or you will be caught. Conscious concerns focus on control and domination, leading to little interest in or curiosity about others' feelings. Taken together, these first stages and the transition to the conformist stage refer to the ''preconformist'' level of development.

In the *conformist* stage, morality is partly internalized. The affect of shame—for transgressions against rules—becomes especially meaningful at this time. An understanding of mutuality begins to emerge, although relationships are seen along the lines of concrete events and actions, more than feelings or motives. Most people eventually advance to a transitional phase, marked by a growing realization that the ''right ways'' of living are relative to situations. Although many stereotypes continue to be held, there is now less absolute conviction than in previous stages. As self-awareness grows, so too does the adolescent's access to a broader, more complex repertoire of emotions and understandings of others' emotions. This transition and the conformist stage itself form the "conformist" level of ego development.

In the next, *conscientious,* stage there is a consolidation of the changes begun during this last transition. Rigid stereotypes begin to fade, replaced by an abiding interest in differences among people. Relationships are understood along the lines of feelings, rather than only actions and events. Inner standards and a keener sense of inner feelings guide behavior, rather than the external rules so characteristic of the earlier stages. Adolescents who reach this stage engage in meaningful self-criticism, as they think about ideals, achievements, and obligations. In the later stages (*autonomous* and *integrated*) there is increasing respect for individuality and inner experience. Noteworthy, and relevant to adolescent emotional development, is the greater value placed on relationships with others. A growing recognition of emotional interdependence accompanies a decreasing emphasis on striving for independence. Adolescents grasp the need for others to be independent, to have their own feelings, and to learn from their own mistakes. This most advanced set of stages (beginning with conscientious) represents the "postconformist" level of ego development. These are but telegraphic descriptions of complex stages of development. While as we discuss below, these stages are not "things" through which all adolescents must mechanically pass, they do provide a useful way of characterizing subtle and dramatic differences in cognitive and interpersonal styles that may provide a scaffolding or template for the recognition and expression of emotions. Table 1 presents more expanded definitions and delineates the sequences of development for each aspect of ego development.

Adolescents can be grouped with respect to their varied *ego development paths,* based on our longitudinal observations of the stages of development outlined above (Hauser et al., 1990; 1991). Before describing these trajectories in greater detail, an important cautionary point is in order. It is ever tempting, and

Table 1

Loevinger's Stages of Ego Development •

Table 1.—Milestones of Ego Development*

Stage	Impulse Control "Moral" Style	Interpersonal Style	Conscious Preoccupations	Cognitive Style
Preconformist				
Presocial (I-1)	. . .	Autistic	Self vs nonself	. . .
Symbiotic (I-1)	. . .	Symbiotic	Self vs nonself	. . .
Impulsive (I-2)	Impulsive, fear	Receiving dependent, exploitive	Bodily feelings, especially sexual and aggressive	Stereotypy, conceptual confusion
Self-protective Δ	Fear of being caught, externalizing blame, opportunistic	Wary, manipulative, exploitive	Self-protection, wishes, things, advantages, control	. . .
Transition from self-protective to conformist (Δ/3)	Obedience and conformity to social norms are simple and absolute rules	Manipulative, obedient	Conrete aspects of traditional sex roles, physical causation as opposed to psychological causation	Conceptual simplicity, stereotypes
Conformist				
Conformist (I-3)	Conformity to external rules, shame, guilt for breaking rules	Belonging, helping, superficial niceness	Appearance, social acceptability, banal feelings, behavior	Conceptual simplicity, stereotypes, clichés
Transition from conformist to conscientious; self-consciousness (I-3/4)	Dawning realization of standards, contingencies, self-criticism	Being helpful, deepened interest in interpersonal relations	Consciousness of the self as separate from the group, recognition of psychological causation	Awareness of individual differences in attitudes, interests and abilities; mentioned in global and broad terms
Postconformist				
Conscientious (I-4)	Self-evaluated standards, self-criticism	Intensive, responsible, mutual, concern for communication	Differentiated feelings, motives for behavior, self-respect, achievements, traits, expression	Conceptual complexity, idea of patterning
Transition from conscientious to autonomous	Individuality, coping with inner conflict	Cherishing of interpersonal relations	Communicating, expressing ideas and feelings, process and change	Toleration for paradox and contradiction
Autonomous (I-5)	Add: Coping with conflicting inner needs†	Add: Respect for autonomy	Vividly conveyed feelings, integration of physiological and psychological causation of behavior, development, role conception, self-fulfillment, self in social context	Increased conceptual complexity; complex patterns, toleration for ambiguity, broad scope, objectivity
Integrated (I-6)	Add: Reconciling inner conflicts, renunciation of unattainable	Add: Cherishing of individuality	Add: Identity	. . .

• From Loevinger and Wessler, 1970

* From Hauser et al., 1983

† "Add" means in addition to description applying to previous level.

mistaken, to categorize an adolescent as being at one or another ego development stage, and thereby imply that this "explains" him or her. The stages do not capture all of the individual's thoughts, feelings, or behaviors. They represent predominant features of the person, his or her "core" perspectives and styles. Moreover, the stages are not concrete things; they are concepts that meaningfully characterize how the person generally functions with respect to thinking, perceiving, and feeling. To assume that these stages, or the following developmental paths, fully capture how the individual experiences and acts in the world violates the meaning of this view of development and grossly underestimates individual complexity. Rather, we might think of these stages as one way of viewing how the adolescent deals with certain tasks that are open over the life-span, tasks that fit into a richly detailed and complex tapestry of development, much like the one Stern (1985) has begun to describe for infancy.

Although we have alluded to affective experience in describing the ego development stages, it is with respect to paths of development, adolescent "growth curves," that we can most clearly identify links between emotional life and adolescent development. The eight paths we identify represent a spectrum of possibilities. At one extreme are those adolescents whose development appears to be profoundly interrupted. Year after year they experience the world, and other people, in conflicted and restricted ways. At the other extreme are those boys and girls who began our study with unusually complex perceptions and thoughts about themselves and others. These remarkable adolescents continue to see and understand themselves and their surroundings in subtle and complex ways over several years. Between these extremes are less profound arrests in development and clear cut progressions.

Profound Arrests in Development

Profoundly arrested teenagers remain at one of the *preconformist* stages throughout their adolescence. They have a limited range of emotional responses to other people and key events. They are restricted in their perceptions and expectations—often framing their experience of themselves and the world in either/or terms. They rely on powerful stereotypes and have interpersonal styles that emphasize giving *or* taking, one-up *or* one-down. An understanding of themselves or other people as complex and multifaceted is not within their reach. Abstract principles or reflections about their own or others' feelings—conscious or unconscious—are simply not relevant. Besides having a limited range of experienced emotions, individuals so arrested in their development perceive feelings as residing in the *other* person, as they consistently project wishes, impulses, and conflicts. Forty-one adolescents (25 boys and 16 girls) remained arrested at this early point in their development.

Steady Conformists

Adolescents who reach, and remain at, the *conformist stages* are the most familiar and least worrisome for adults as well as their peers. They express socially acceptable feelings, and respond appropriately to the feelings of others. To be sure, they participate in group activities, have friends, are usually not puzzling to others, and, by and large, are "team players." Group norms and other regulations do not pose a problem for these adolescents. For the most part, they see the importance of cooperating, going along with standards set within the school, within their families, and within the larger social setting. Steady conformist adolescents are aware of inner feelings, but they usually express them in nonoffensive bland general terms, or as clichés. These cooperative and superficially adjusted teenagers do not advance beyond their preoccupations with acceptance and achievement of group-defined goals, and thus represent a milder, socially acceptable, form of developmental arrest. Their conscious affective experience is strongly colored by standards of acceptable feelings: modulated intensity, without extremes of tenderness or aggression. Lou, one of the steady conformist adolescents, actively worries about the dangers of erupting when upset by others: "Most of the time I'm just cool. I don't like to get annoyed. I don't like to get very emotional, 'cause you sort of make a fool of yourself when you're very emotional." There is no room for sudden, novel, or surprisingly paradoxical emotions. Twenty-four adolescents entered the study at the conformist level and did not move beyond it.

Three Paths of Progression

Another group of adolescents clearly progress in their ego development as they begin at either very low (preconformist) or intermediate (conformist) stages, and within subsequent years are functioning at unmistakably higher stages. There is a "family" of progressions. Characteristic of adolescents following these paths is noteworthy *change;* transformations in understandings of self, friends, and parents leading to recognition and expression of a greater range of feelings. Teenagers following early progression paths advance from more concrete, often one-dimensional ("either-or") views to socially acceptable, yet less simplified ones. Or, teenagers following later progression paths move from conventional views to more complex ones, based on inner principles, and with greater appreciation of individual differences.

Progressive ego development was the most prevalent developmental path among the many adolescents we followed from 14 to 17 years of age, occurring for close to one third of the high school students and patients (Hauser et al., 1991). Since there are such clear qualitative differences among the kinds of progression, we consider them separately in terms of their affective experience.

Early Progression. The adolescent following this path changes from viewing the world and himself or herself in terms of concrete and immediate satisfactions. Feelings and their expression become more restrained, since there are social rules to be followed, closely linked with belonging to prized social groups. Concerns about acceptance and rejection now govern behavior. Meeting others' expectations, having "acceptable"—not only self-satisfying—expressions of feelings (e.g., letting out anger when frustrated) is the order of the day. Disturbing feelings, when recognized, are no longer seen as the other person's fault. Thirty-four adolescents (15 boys and 19 girls) traversed this first path of progression.

Advanced Progression. Along this path, the adolescent moves from attentively organizing perceptions and expressions of feelings in response to others' standards to concentrating on his or her *own* inner standards, on complexity, and on individual differences. Conscience and integrity are now the watchwords, rather than acceptance and belonging. A small number of the adolescents that we studied, 2 boys and 4 girls, followed this path. All were high school students. The outstanding change is from a restrained range of experienced and expressed feelings toward enhanced awareness and expression of them in relation to others, and richer appreciation of them within oneself. Lois, a high school student with unusually high self-esteem and intense awareness of the importance of her relationships with friends and family, tells of her strong feelings when she was left out of a party, and her connectedness to her mother around these feelings: "I was very depressed. A lot of crying. I did a lot of yelling at my mother, but she knew why. I told her . . . so I talked to her for awhile and told her that I was going to be real crabby because I was in a bad mood and she said she understood." Besides this level of awareness, empathy, new relationships, and paradoxical and conflicting feelings now characterize the adolescent's experience.

Dramatic Progressions. The change from perceiving the world as dichotomous to recognizing multiple groups, many social norms, and the cherishing of individual differences among people represents a dramatic personal transformation (or "paradigm shift"). Three teenagers, all patients, underwent this stunning change within one or two years of entering our study (Hauser et al., 1991). Possibly these teenagers were functioning at higher levels of development before becoming hospitalized. This dramatic progression would then represent a return to previous functioning. Even so, the dramatic change in affective experience is striking. These adolescents, within a brief span of time, leap from their wary perceptions of feelings (many unacceptable and attributed to others) and impulsive expressions of feelings to an awareness of subtle emotional states in themselves and in others. Close relationships—not possible in the past—are now envisioned and sought.

Accelerated Development

Unusually mature adolescents often evoke delighted and, at times, perplexed reactions from adults, as they express unexpectedly insightful perceptions about themselves and their surroundings, and are surprisingly attuned to others' feelings. Far earlier than most of their peers (and many adults), they comprehend complex personal relationships and can articulate subtle aspects of their inner lives. Only 6 teenagers began at these stages and remained at them over the next years. While representing a small proportion of our sample, these adolescents are nonetheless important exceptions. They may be considered "gifted," but not in the ordinary sense of academically gifted children. Rather, their strengths lie in their ability to see and convey "shades of gray," contradictory ideas, paradoxes, and novel perspectives. They are aware of many, often inconsistent, feelings. Differences among friends are welcomed, not simply "tolerated" or rejected in favor of more palatable stereotypes. The affective life of these adolescents is highly differentiated, sensitively responsive to different settings, different relationships. Their feelings vary greatly in kind and intensity, reactive to subtle cues emanating from internal meanings and aspects of the context.

At age 15, Sarah describes her thoughts about closeness with her mother and separation: "I think I have become a little closer, especially to my mother [long pause]. And that's funny, because at the same time that I say we're not that close, I'd like to be a little more close. I'm also feeling that I'm ready to, you know [laugh] to let . . . leave home."

There is also the *regressive ego development* path, where an adolescent shifts downward in his or her level of develoment (e.g., from conformist to preconformist) over the years. These 9 adolescents (3 boys and 6 girls) changed from recognizing complex affects within themselves and others to having simpler perceptions, giving great emphasis, usually through their projections, to the disquieting and threatening feelings that they see as residing in the other person. Finally, there is a trajectory that we term (after Erikson, 1959) *psychosocial moratorium,* where the adolescent at first decreases and then increases levels of ego development. Accompanying these often precipitous swings are striking changes in the adolescent's understandings of others' affective states and expressions of his or her own feelings. Such oscillations are sometimes considered to reflect "experimentation" by an adolescent, as he or she tries out new roles and/or enacts conflicting yet personally prized ideals and wishes (Erikson, 1959). Ten adolescents (4 boys and 6 girls) expressed these fluctuations.

Viewing adolescent development with respect to multiple pathways of perception and cognition provides one entry to understanding how affective development is intertwined with varied types of intrapsychic organization during adolescence. In saying this we are not, however, returning to the argument that cognitive development, in the final analysis, underlies and structures affective development. Rather, we view affective development and experience as representing significant aspects of these several complex developmental paths. A second way to view affect in adolescence is in terms of the special properties of emotions, and their special influences during the adolescent years. In taking this vantage point, we depart from concentrating on individual differences to considering affect as the central player, now reversing figure and ground.

Affects and Moods in Adolescence as Organizers

The question of "storm and stress," emotionality, during adolescence can be reframed along the lines of whether there are particular qualities or functions of affect reflecting the special conditions of this era. In an attempt to gather empirical data about conscious emotional experience during adolescence, Larson and Lampman-Patraitis (1989) examined hour-by-hour emotional states, reported by children and adolescents. A total of 437 children and early adolescents in the fifth to ninth grades (ages 9 to 15) from four suburban neighborhoods in the Midwestern United States was randomly selected. The neighborhoods ranged from lower middle class to upper middle class, and were composed almost exclusively of people with European ancestry. The participants carrying electronic pagers responded, for one week, to signals at random intervals, reporting their emotional states or moods on scales whose items dealt with pleasure-displeasure (e.g., happy-unhappy-bored). A total of 17,752 signals were responded to. Two noteworthy conclusions emerged from these many observations. First, early adolescents do not show any greater variability of emotional states during daily life than the children. Second, "the adolescent's conscious experience includes many fewer occasions when the individual feels on top of the world and more occasions of feeling mildly negative" (p. 1258).

Our interpretation, based on empirical studies of nonclinical samples (Csikszentmihalyi and Larson, 1984, 1987; Larson et al., 1990) and on clinical observations, is that compared to children and adults, adolescents do not necessarily experience greater variability in emotional states. However, their mood swings may be sharp, highly significant, and often dysphoric.

An important point to keep in mind is that adolescent mood swings do not simply disrupt and disorganize. These experiences can also serve as *touchstones,* which adolescents then use to orient, organize, and structure themselves. A most evocative illustration of this notion, drawn from another literature altogether, is James Joyce's narrative of Stephen Daedalus's adolescence in *A Portrait of the Artist as a Young Man*:

> But when he had sung his song and withdrawn into a snug corner of the room he began to taste the joy of his loneliness. The mirth, which in the beginning of the evening had

> seemed to him false and trivial, was like a soothing air to him, passing gaily by his senses, hiding from other eyes the feverish agitation of his blood [Joyce, 1916, p. 68].

This vivid description is Joyce's evocation of the affect-seeking behavior, which Blos (1967) finds characteristic of adolescent relationships and solitude. For Blos, the adolescent seeks "not the personal bond but the sharpness of affect and the emotional agitation evoked by it . . . the solitude and splendid isolation where he conjures up in his mind affective states of extraordinary intensity" (pp. 158–159). Blos explores in detail the significance of these intense emotional states, arguing that they may reflect adaptive regressive experiences of adolescence, representing the recapitulation of tasks of separation and individuation in the service of further growth and development.

The idea that in adolescence certain affects may powerfully organize perceptions, actions, and personality patterns represents a specific instance of a more general organizational approach in affect theory (Collins and Gunnar, 1989; Emde, 1990; Sroufe, 1983). Studies of children and adults support the common clinical observation that perceptions and cognitions are powerfully influenced by the individual's emotional state. Positive feelings appear to enhance learning and reasoning, while dysphoric feelings, particularly sadness, appear to disrupt cognitions and perceptions (Collins and Gunnar, 1989; Harris and Gross, 1988).

In addition, while there are accumulating studies in children suggesting the role of emotions in regulating relationships, these perspectives have not yet been applied in studies of adolescents (for a recent review of this area in affect theory, see Campos et al., 1989). Thus, there remain basic questions about the importance of emotions in the immediate regulation of adolescent behaviors, in maintaining continuities in relationships, and in underlying the emergence of new close relationships during this period.

Affects and Attachments: Relations between Infancy and Adolescence

There are intriguing suggestions in several theoretical and clinical contributions of links between infancy and adolescence. Here again, there is a symmetry in the psychoanalytic and psychological literatures, bridging two separate frames of reference. Blos (1967), for example, investigates adolescent regression in the service of the ego, and considers ties between adolescence and infantile states. The notion of connections between adolescence and infancy is, in fact, a time-honored one in psychoanalysis. From Hall's (1904) characterization of adolescence as a "second birth" through Jones's (1922) notion of a recapitulation of infancy in adolescence and Anna Freud's (1958) position that "in adolescence impulses from all pregenital phases rise to the surface and defense mechanisms from all levels of crudity or complexity come into use" (pp. 267–268), we have now come to a more complex view of basic developmental processes that begin in infancy and continue with recapitulations of specific patterns in particular developmental and environmental contexts.

In the psychological literature, cognitive and attachment theorists have also considered associations between adolescence and infancy. Fischer and colleagues (1989a, 1989b), for example, suggest that there may be a similarity between the emotional experience of infancy and adolescence due to the fact that adolescents, like infants, are on the first tier of a new cognitive domain, hence vulnerable in similar ways. The infant is at the beginning stage of representation and the adolescent at the beginning stage of abstraction. As Fischer et al. see it, to be at the beginning of *any* new cognitive tier implies a common ground in terms of vulnerability and emotional experience.

One extremely important consequence of the many theoretical and empirical studies of infant attachment has been a new generation of work following attachment relationships and affective experiences in adolescence, considering ways these relationships may be closely involved with the regulation of responses to affect. Kobak and Sceery (1988) examined the relation between "working models of attachment" and adjustment during the first year of college, and found that those who fell into a "secure" attachment group were more ego-resilient and less anxious than either those in groups labeled "dismissing" or "preoccupied" with "attachment-relevant information." Furthermore, the "dismissing" group showed more hostility than either of the other two groups. Kobak and Sceery concluded that secure individuals have an ability to tolerate and integrate negative affect and to maintain adaptive functioning. On the other hand, individuals expressing the two types of insecure attachments showed impaired affect regulation; with anger predominating in those classified as dismissing of attachment, and anxiety predominating in those classified as preoccupied with attachment. Although it is highly speculative in the absence of longitudinal data, Kobak and Sceery imply that there may be a similarity between affective styles in infancy and adulthood, and—speculating even further—suggest that even in the face of known reorganizations during the course of cognitive and social development the patterns of affective organization may remain descriptively similar across the life-span.

Along similar lines, Salzman (1988) studied attachment relationships in female adolescents, finding preoccupied attachment relationships to be clearly associated with affective experience. For instance, in her sample of college-aged female adolescents those with preoccupied attachments described high levels of emotional distress, poor-quality peer relations, and a high incidence of eating disorders.

In the ego development path studies described earlier (Hauser et al., 1991), we found certain groups of adolescents—those showing progressive and accelerated development—dealing with parents in more individuated ways, while at the same time maintaining strong affective connections with them. Thus, here too we find suggestions of ties between specific styles and affective experience. Follow-up studies of these same adolescents, now in progress, should illuminate the extent to which these aspects of adolescent development predict adult affect experience and the maintaining of secure attachment relationships.

It is likely that the constructs referring to variations in attachment relationships will receive increasing attention in studies of adolescent affective experience, with respect to regulation of affective expression, subjective states, and influences of affect on development. Based on these approaches and concepts, impressive advances have already taken place in understanding affective development in infancy and childhood (Hartup, 1989; Hartup et al., 1988; Sameroff and Emde, 1989). Application of these generative constructs and paradigms to investigating adolescent and early adult affective development represents the next frontier (Allen et al., 1990; Kobak and Sceery, 1988; Hazen and Shaver, 1990), bearing in mind that attachment relationships in these later developmental eras cannot simply be seen as having exactly the same meaning as these concepts do when referring to phenomena of infancy and childhood (Gilligan, 1987).

Implications for Psychoanalytic Understandings and Technique

In 1958 Anna Freud noted, "how seldom in the treatment of my adult cases I succeed in reviving their adolescent experiences in full force." She went on to describe a failure to recover in analysis the atmosphere of adolescence and, in particular, the adolescent's experience, the elations, despairs, preoccupations, loneliness, rages and suicidal fantasies and erotic urges. "Unlike the affective states of infancy and early childhood," she wrote, those of adolescence "seem disinclined to reemerge and be relived in connection with the person of the analyst" (p. 259).

In the earlier sections of this paper we followed the affective experience of adolescence as seen through the lenses of a number of different investigative approaches, some of which argue that the tumult Anna Freud portrays is not characteristic of adolescence in the first place. Can the understandings drawn from these disparate frames of reference shed any light on the puzzling difficulty of "recovery" described by Anna Freud? Do we fail to recover the affective states of adolescence because for one reason or another they are unrecoverable, or because we do not know *how* to recover them, how and where to look for their traces?

Could it be that the adolescent period as it appears in adult analysis has a peculiarly ephemeral or transparent quality, such that the patient passes quickly through to some earlier infantile reflection of the same or similar experiential states? Analysts might inadvertently encourage this passage because of a theoretical preference that earlier is better or more fundamental, a form of developmental reductionism and neglecting the adolescent component of what appears to be a preoedipal issue. We might even expect such neglect to reenact earlier parental neglect of a patient's adolescent experience, thereby contributing to analytic stalemate.

Could it be that we place too little emphasis on the analytic context (Gill, 1982; Schwaber, 1983, 1985; Smith, 1990a) and that were we to examine more systematically the patient's "perception of the external," the specific intrapsychic examination Schwaber (1985) has advocated, we might more consistently recover the adult analysand's adolescent experience? As we have already noted, adolescent experience is particularly responsive to the external or environmental context, something that Blos (1967) suggests in describing the "reality-bound" (p. 158) quality of adolescent experience. Erikson (1964a), discussing Freud's treatment of Dora, also touches on this theme. Adolescence would seem to be a time when the "reality considerations" (Boesky, 1989; Smith, 1990b) of compromise formation are particularly important.

Perhaps it is then no coincidence that it was an adolescent, Dora, who led Freud to inquire about the importance of the patient's perception of the analytic context at the time of his discovery of the centrality of the transference, and his first recommendation for its analysis:

> I ought to have said to her, '. . . Have you noticed anything that leads you to suspect me of evil intentions similar (whether openly or in some sublimated form) to Herr K.'s? Or have you been struck by anything about me which has caught your fancy, as happened previously with Herr K.?' Her attention would then have been turned to some detail in our relations, or in my person or circumstances, behind which there lay concealed something analogous but immeasurably more important concerning Herr K. [Freud, 1905, p. 118].

It was an adolescent who led Freud to this particular aspect of transference analysis, with its emphasis on "the perception of the external."

Our impression, in short, is that there are qualities unique to the affective experience of adolescence which, if defined and described more prescisely, might more accurately be observed in the analytic situation, rather than passed through en route to earlier developmental moments. Further, just as it has been difficult to observe with confidence the reflections of infancy in the adult analytic situation, adolescence, too, may escape our notice because we do not know precisely what to look for, the unique cognitive and affective strands of adolescence as they reappear in analysis. The stages and paths of ego development, as they begin to define the varieties of cognitive and affective experience in adolescence, may serve as useful signposts for observing those reflections of adolescence as they appear in the analysis of adults.

In a recent address, Gardner (1987) described the entire psychoanalytic enterprise as a kind of "second adolescence" for the adult patient, replete with various re-created forms of the language, gestures, affective states, and modes of inquiry of that individual's first adolescence. His position stands in sharp contrast to Anna Freud's observations on the dearth of recoverable adolescent experience. Gardner writes, "I believe that as analysis deepens (the analysis of an adult), it involves more and more re-creations of adolescent psychological events . . . that what we commonly call regression in the service of the ego . . . is usually a regression to the passions, turmoils, modes of inquiry, and thrust toward development of adolescence."

Gardner is looking here at analysis as a whole. In our experience, the analyst may encounter the reemergence of adolescent memories, affects, and cognitive styles during the termination phase of analysis in particular. If adolescence is a "second individuation process" (Blos, 1967), patients near the end of analysis may be impelled by the pressure of separation into a kind of third "individuation phase" of termination. Terminating patients may feel that they are being returned, however changed, to a sort of preanalytic state wherein they must begin to rely again on old as well as new modes of "self-inquiry" (Gardner, 1983). Thus, the modes of inquiry that served them in that most self-inquiring period of adolescence may be pressed into service once again in the termination phase of analysis.

Concluding Comments

We have explored and reflected upon varied approaches to affective experience in adolescence and to the development of affect during adolescence. Each investigative approach represents a unique frame of reference, some distinct from the psychoanalytic frame of reference. Our aim is not to encourage a new or eclectic metapsychology, nor do we assume that any direct bridge can be built from one investigative domain to another. In fact, we particularly caution against attempts to use information derived from other investigative channels to construct more or less direct interpretive approaches in the psychoanalytic situation.

We have had two sets of goals in mind with respect to the value of the constructs and data drawn from these other investigative approaches: first, to shed as much light as possible on the adolescent experience, the sights and sounds that Gardner describes, in order to sharpen the analyst's observations; second, to link, however slowly and carefully, theoretical formulations derived from psychoanalysis with those derived from other related scientific endeavors. If such links are ever to be discovered, and constructed, it would seem that the realm of adolescent affect, with roots in so many different developmental domains, might be the place to begin.

REFERENCES

Allen, J. P., Aber, J. L., & Leadbetter, B. J. (1990). Adolescent problem behaviors: The influence of attachments and autonomy. *Psychiat. Clin. No. Amer.,* 13:455–468.

Ausubel, D. P. (1954). *Theory and Problems of Adolescent Development.* New York: Grune & Stratton.

Bandura, A. (1964). The stormy decade: Fact or fiction? *Psychology in the Schools,* 1:224–231.

Beardslee, W., Powers, S., Hauser, S. T., Jacobson, A. M., Noam, G. G., Macias, E., & Hopfenbeck, J. (1990). Adaptation in adolescence: The influence of time and severe psychiatric disorder. *J. Amer. Acad. Child & Adol. Psychiat.,* 29:429–439.

Block, J. (1971). *Lives Through Time.* Berkeley, Calif.: Bancroft Books.

Blos, P. (1962). *On Adolescence.* New York: Free Press.

——— (1967). The second individuation process of adolescence. In *The Adolescent Passage.* New York: Free Press, 1979.

——— (1979). *The Adolescent Passage.* New York: Free Press.

Boesky, D. (1989). Enactment, acting out, and considerations of reality. Presented at the Annual Meeting of the American Psychoanalytic Association, San Francisco.

Brenner, C. (1982). *The Mind in Conflict.* New York: Int. Univ. Press.

Brooks-Gunn, J. & Petersen, A. C., Eds. (1983). *Girls at Puberty: Biological and Psychosocial Perspectives.* New York: Plenum.

——— ——— & Eichorn, D., Eds. (1985). Time of maturation and psychosocial functioning in adolescence. *J. Youth & Adol.,* 14:149–264.

——— Rock, D., & Warren, M. (1989). Comparability of constructs across the adolescent years. *Develpm. Psychol.,* 25:51–60.

——— & Warren, M. P. (1987). Biological contributions to affective expression in young adolescent girls. Presented at the Biennial Meetings of the Society for Research in Child Development, Baltimore.

——— ——— (1989). Biological and social contributions to negative affect in young adolescent girls. *Child Develpm.,* 60:40–55.
CAMPOS, J. J., CAMPOS, R. G., & BARRETT, K. C. (1989). Emergent themes in the study of emotional development and emotional regulation. *Develpm. Psychol.,* 25:394–402.
——— BARRETT, K. C., LAMB, M. E., GOLDSMITH, H. H., & STENBERG, C. (1983). Socioemotional development. In *Handbook of Child Psychology:* Vol. 2, ed. P. Mussen, J. J. Campos, & M. H. Haith. New York: Wiley.
CANDEE, D. (1974). Ego development aspects of new left ideology. *J. Pers. & Soc. Psychol.,* 30:620–630.
COLLINS, W. A. (1990). Parent-child relationships in the transition to adolescence. In *From Childhood to Adolescence: A Transitional Period,* ed. R. Montemayor, G. Adams, & T. Gullata. Newbury Park, Calif.: Sage Publications.
——— & GUNNAR, M. (1989). Social and personality development. *Annu. Rev. Psychol.,* 41:387–416.
COWAN, P. A. (1982). The relationship between emotional and cognitive development. In *New Directions for Child Development,* no. 16, ed. D. Cicchetti & P. Hesse. San Francisco: Jossey-Bass.
CSIKSZENTMIHALYI, M. & LARSON, R. (1984). *Being Adolescent.* New York: Basic Books.
——— &——— (1987). The experience sampling method. *J. Nerv. Ment. Dis.,* 175:526–536.
DEMOS, E. V. (1982). Affect in early infancy. *Psychoanal. Inq.,* 1:533–574.
DEUTSCH, H. (1944). *The Psychology of Women,* Vol. 1. New York: Grune & Stratton.
DOUVAN, E. & ADELSON, J. (1966). *The Adolescent Experience.* New York: Wiley.
DOWLING, S. (1989). Epilogue. In *The Significance of Infant Observation Research for Clinical Work with Children, Adolescents, and Adults,* ed. S. Dowling & A. Rothstein. Madison, Conn.: Int. Univ. Press.
EKMAN, P. & OSTER, J. (1979). Facial expression of emotion. *Annu. Rev. Psychol.,* 30:527–554.
EMDE, R. N. (1988). Development terminable and interminable: I. Innate and motivational factors from infancy. *Int. J. Psychoanal.,* 69:23–42.
——— (1990). Toward a psychoanalytic theory of affect: I. The organizational model and its properties. In *The Course of Life: Psychoanalytic Contributions towards Understanding Personality Development,* ed. S. I. Greenspan & G. H. Pollock. Madison, Conn.: Int. Univ. Press.
ERIKSON, E. H. (1956). The problem of ego identity. *J. Amer. Psychoanal. Assn.,* 4:56–121.
——— (1959). Identity and the life cycle. *Psychol. Issues,* Monogr. 1. New York: Int. Univ. Press.
——— (1964a). Psychological reality and historical actuality. In *Insight and Responsibility.* New York: Norton.
——— (1964b). *The Challenge of Youth.* New York: Anchor paperback.
——— (1968). *Identity: Youth and Crisis.* New York: Norton.
FAUST, M. S. (1983). Alternate constructions of adolescent growth. In *Girls at Puberty: Biological and Psychosocial Perspectives,* ed. J. Brooks-Gunn & A. Petersen. New York: Plenum.
FISCHER, K. W., CARNOCHAN, P., & SHAVER, P. R. (1990). How emotions develop

and how they organize development. *Cognition and Emotion,* 4:81–121.

——— & LAMBORN, S. D. (1989a). Mechanisms of variation in developmental levels: Cognitive and emotional transitions during adolescence. In *Transitional Mechanisms in Emotional Child Development,* ed. A. de Ribaupierre. Cambridge (U. K.): Cambridge Univ. Press.

——— SHAVER, P. R. & CARNOCHAN, P. (1989b). A skill approach to emotional development. In *Child Development Today and Tomorrow,* ed. W. Damon. San Francisco: Jossey-Bass, pp. 107–136.

FLAVELL, J. (1963). *The Developmental Psychology of Jean Piaget.* Princeton, N.J.: Van Nostrand.

——— (1979). Metacognition and cognitive meaning. *Amer. Psychologist,* 84:906–911.

FREUD, A. (1936). *The Ego and the Mechanisms of Defense.* New York: Int. Univ. Press, 1966.

——— (1958). Adolescence. *Psychoanal. Study Child,* 13:225–273.

FREUD, S. (1905). Fragment of an analysis of a case of hysteria. *S. E.,* 7.

GARDNER, M. R. (1983). *Self-Inquiry.* Boston: Little-Brown.

——— (1987). Sexuality, neurosis, and analysis. Presented at the Annual Meeting of the American Psychoanalytic Association, Chicago.

GECAS, V. & SCHWALBE, M. L. (1986). Parental behavior and adolescent self-esteem. *J. Marriage & Family,* 48:37–46.

GILL, M. M. (1982). *Analysis of Transference.* New York: Int. Univ. Press.

GILLIGAN, C. (1987). Adolescent development reconsidered. In *New Directions in Child Development,* no. 37, ed. C. E. Irwin. San Francisco: Jossey-Bass.

GREENSPAN, S. I. (1979). *Intelligence and Adaptation.* New York: Int. Univ. Press.

HALL, G. S. (1904). *Adolescence,* 2 Vols. New York: Appleton.

HARRIS, P. L. (1989). Developmental change in children's understanding of mixed and masked emotions. In *Transitional Mechanisms in Child Development,* ed. E. de Ribaupierre. Cambridge (England): Cambridge Univ. Press.

——— DONNELLY, K., GUZ, G. R. & PITT-WATSON, R. (1986). Children's understanding of the distinction between real and apparent emotion. *Child Develpm.,* 57:895–909.

——— & GROSS, D. (1988). Real and apparent emotion. In *Developing Theories of Mind,* ed. J. W. Astington, P. L. Harris, & D. R. Olson. Cambridge (England): Cambridge Univ. Press.

HARTER, S. (1980). A cognitive-developmental approach to children's understanding of affect and trait labels. In *Social Cognition in Context,* ed. F. Serafica. New York: Guilford.

HARTUP, W. W. (1989). Social relationships and their developmental significance. *Amer. Psychologist,* 44:120–126.

——— LAURSEN, B., STEWART, M. I., & EASTENSON, A. (1988). Conflict and the friendship relations of young children. *Child Develpm.,* 59:1590–1600.

HAUSER, S. T. (1976). Loevinger's model and measure of ego development. *Psychol. Bull.,* 83:928–955.

——— BORMAN, E. H., POWERS, S. I., NOAM, G. G., & JACOBSON, A. M. (1990). Paths of ego development. *Psychiat. Clin. No. Amer.,* 13:489–510.

——— POWERS, S., BOWLDS, M., & NOAM, G. (1988). Family interiors of adolescent ego development. *Family Perspective,* 21:263–282.

——— ——— & NOAM, G. G. (1991). *Adolescents and Their Families.* New York: Free Press.

——— ——— ——— JACOBSON, A., WEISS, B., & FOLLANSBEE, D. (1984). Familial contexts of adolescent ego development. *Child Develpm.,* 55:195–213.

HAZAN, C. & SHAVER, P. (1990). Love and work: An attachment-theoretical perspective. *J. Pers. Soc. Psychol.,* 59:270–280.

HOLLINGSHEAD, A. B. (1957). *Two-Factor Index of Social Position.* Mimeographed. New Haven, Conn.: Yale Univ.

HOLMBECK, G. N. & HILL, J. P (1986). A path-analytic approach to the relations between parental traits and acceptance and adolescent adjustment. *Sex Roles,* 14:315-334.

INHOFF-GERMAIN, G., ARNOLD, G., NOTTLEMAN, E., SUSMAN, E., CUTLER, G., & CHROUSOS, G. (1988). Relations between hormone levels and observational measures of aggressive behavior of adolescents in family interactions. *Develpm. Psychol.,* 24:129–149.

ISBERG, R., HAUSER, S. T., JACOBSON, A. M., POWERS, S. I., NOAM, G. G., WEISS-PERRY, B., & FOLLANSBEE, D. (1989). Parental contexts of adolescent self-esteem. *J. Youth & Adol.,* 18:1–23.

IZARD, C. E. (1977). *Human Emotions.* New York: Plenum.

——— KAGAN, J., & ZAJONC, R. B., Eds. (1984). *Emotions, Cognition, and Behavior.* Cambridge (England): Cambridge Univ. Press.

——— & MALETESTA, C. W. (1987). Perspectives on emotional development; I. Differential emotions theory of early emotional development. In *Handbook of Infant Development,* 2nd ed., ed. J. Osofsky. New York: Wiley.

JONES, E. (1922). Some problems of adolescence. In *Papers on Psycho-Analysis.* London: Baillière, Tindall & Cox, 1948.

JOYCE, J. (1916). *Portrait of the Artist as a Young Man.* London: Penguin Books, 1988.

KOBAK, R. R. & SCEERY, A. (1985). The transition to college. Unpublished MS.

——— &——— (1988). Attachment in late adolescence: Working models, affect regulation and representations of self and others. *Child Develpm.,* 59:135–146.

LARSON, R. W., CSIKSZENTMIHALYI, M., & GRAFF, R. (1980). Mood variability and the psychosocial adjustment of adolescents. *J. Youth & Adol.,* 9:468–490.

——— & LAMPMAN-PETRAITIS, C. (1989). Daily emotional states as reported by children and adolescents. *Child Develpm.,* 60:1250–1260.

——— RAFFAELLI, M., RICHARDS, M. H., HAM, M., & JEWELL, L. (1990). Ecology of depression in late childhood and early adolescence: A profile of daily states and activities. *J. Abn. Psychol.,* 99:92–102.

LEWIS, M. & MICHALSON, L. (1983). *Children's Emotions and Moods.* New York: Plenum.

——— SULLIVAN, M. W., & MICHALSON, L. (1984). The cognitive-emotional fugue. In *Emotions, Cognition, and Behavior,* ed. C. E. Izard, J. Kagan, & R. B. Zajonc. Cambridge (England): Cambridge Univ. Press.

LOEVINGER, J. (1976). *Ego Development.* San Francisco: Jossey-Bass.

——— (1979). Construct validity of the sentence completion test of ego development. *Appl. Psychol. Measurement,* 3:281–311.

——— & WESSLER, R. (1970). *Measuring Ego Development,* Vol. I. San Francisco: Jossey-Bass.

——— ——— & REDMORE, C. (1970). *Measuring Ego Development,* Vol. 2. San Francisco: Jossey-Bass.

MAHLER, M. S., PINE, F. & BERGMAN, A. (1975). *The Psychological Birth of the Human Infant.* New York: Basic Books.

MALATESTA, C. Z. (1990). The role of emotions in the development and organization of personality. In *Socioemotional Development: Nebraska Symposium on Motivation,* 36, ed. R. A. Thompson & R. A. Dientsbier. Lincoln, Nebr.: Univ. Nebraska Press.

——— & IZARD, C. E., Eds. (1984). *Emotion in Adult Development.* Beverly Hills: Sage Publications.

OFFER, D. (1969). *The Psychological World of the Teenager: A Study of Normal Adolescent Boys.* New York: Basic Books.

——— & OFFER, J. (1975). *From Teenage to Young Manhood: A Psychological Study.* New York: Basic Books.

——— OSTROV, E., & HOWARD, I. (1981). *The Adolescent: A Psychological Self-Portrait.* New York: Basic Books.

——— & SABSHIN, M. (1984). *Normality and the Life Cycle.* New York: Basic Books.

PAIKOFF, R. L. & BROOKS-GUNN, J. (1991). Do parent-child relationships change during puberty? *Psychol. Bull.*, 10:47–66.

PETERSEN, A. C. (1988). Adolescent development. *Annu. Rev. Psychol.,* 39:583–607.

——— & CRAIGHEAD, W. E. (1986). Emotion and personality development in normal adolescents and young adults. In *Suicide and Depression among Adolescents and Young Adults,* ed. G. Klerman. Washington, D.C.: APA Press.

PIAGET, J. (1954). *Intelligence and Affectivity.* Palo Alto, Calif.: Annual Reviews, 1981.

——— & INHELDER, B. (1969). *The Psychology of the Child.* New York: Basic Books.

POWERS, S. I. (in press, a). Individual development through the lifespan. In *Family Systems Throughout the Lifespan,* ed. K. Kreppner & R. M. Lerner. Hillsdale, N.J.: Erlbaum.

——— (in press, b). Moral judgment development in the family. *J. Moral Educ.*

——— HAUSER, S. T., & JACOBSON, A. (1985). Parent and adolescent longitudinal trajectories of ego development. Presented at the meetings of the Society for Research in Child Development.

——— ——— & KILNER, L. (1989). Adolescent mental health. *Amer. Psychologist,* 44:200–208.

RICHARDS, A. D. (1990). The future of psychoanalysis. *Psychoanal. Q.,* 59:347–369.

RUTTER, M., GRAHAM, P., CHADWICK, O., & YULE, W. (1976). Adolescent turmoil: Fact of fiction? *J. Child Psychol. & Psychiat.,* 17:35–56.

SALZMAN, J. (1988). Primary attachment at adolescence and female identity: An extension of Bowlby's perspective. Unpublished MS.

SAMEROFF, A. J. & EMDE, R. N., Eds. (1989). *Relationship Disturbances in Early Childhood: A Developmental Approach.* New York: Basic Books.

SCHWABER, E. (1983). A particular perspective on analytic listening. *Psychoanal. Study Child,* 38:519–546.

——— Ed. (1985). *The Transference in Psychotherapy: Clinical Management.* New York: Int. Univ. Press.

SIMMONS, R. G., ROSENBERG, F., & ROSENBERG, M. (1973). Disturbance in self-image at adolescence. *Amer. Sociol. Rev.,* 38:553–568.

SMITH, H. F. (1990a). Cues: The perceptual edge of the transference. *Int. J. Psychoanal.,* 71:219–228.

——— (1990b). Presentation to the panel on "The Analytic Surface." Annual Meeting, American Psychoanalytic Association, New York.

SROUFE, L. A. (1979). Socioemotional development. In *Handbook of Infant Development,* ed. J. Osofsky. New York: Wiley.

——— (1983). Infant-caregiver attachment and patterns of attachment in preschool: The roots of maladaptation and competence. In *Minnesota Symposium on Child Psychology,* 16:41–81, ed. M. Perlmutter. Hillsdale, N.J.: Erlbaum.

STERN, D. N. (1985). *The Interpersonal World of the Infant.* New York: Basic Books.

STIERLIN, H. (1974). *Separating Parents and Adolescents.* New York: Quadrangle.

STRAYER, J. (1986). Current research in affective development. *J. Children in Contemp. Soc.,* 17:37–55.

SUSMAN, E., INHOFF-GERMAIN, G., NOTTELMAN, E. D., LORIAUX, D. L., CUTLER, G. B., & CHROUSOS, G. P. (1987). Hormones, emotional dispositions, and aggressive attributes in young adolescents. *Child Develpm.,* 58:1114–1134.

SWENSON, C. H. (1980). Ego development as a general model for counseling and psychotherapy. *Personnel & Guidance J.,* 6:382–388.

——— (1985). Personality development in the family. In *The Handbook of Family Psychology and Therapy,* Vol. I, ed. L. L. Abate. Homewood, Ill.: Dorsey Press.

THOMPSON, A. E. (1985). The nature of emotion and its development. In *Event Theory: An Integration of Piaget and Freud,* ed. I. Fast. Hillsdale, N.J.: Erlbaum.

——— (1986). An object relational theory of affect maturity: applications to the thematic apperception test. In *Assessing Object Relations Phenomena,* ed. M. Kissen. Madison, Conn.: Int. Univ. Press.

TOMKINS, S. S. (1962). *Affect, Imagery, Consciousness,* Vol. 1: *The Positive Affects.* New York: Springer.

——— (1963). *Affect, Imagery, Consciousness,* Vol. 2. New York: Springer.

WEINER, I. (1970). *Psychological Disturbance in Adolescence.* New York: Wiley.

Harvard Medical School
Massachusetts Mental Health Center
74 Fenwood Road
Boston, MA 02115

II. CLINICAL PERSPECTIVES

INTRODUCTION

THEODORE SHAPIRO AND ROBERT N. EMDE

The theory and practice of psychoanalysis are inextricably interwoven. They are complementary aspects of how we work and learn about our science and about our patients. It is difficult to approach a patient without a model of how he or she behaves and how his or her mind operates. At the same time that we are encouraged to listen empathically and sensitively to our patients, we also are asked to be enmeshed in a dyadic arrangement observing not only them, but ourselves. These are the models that have arisen during the last decades; they have changed psychoanalysis from a singular natural science vantage point, employing observer and subject to an observer within a dyadic field. Nonetheless, we have a central model we call classical that involves the notion of a psychic apparatus with its varying compartments, and we attempt to decipher how the patient's behavior and report can be reduced to common themes or derivative variations of universal fantasy. The defenses and resistive operations our patients use within the transference and the enactments that somehow permit us to understand what organizations dictate the patients' behavior are our data base.

This series of papers approaches the patient from these varying vantage points—that is, looking at theory and how it influences our practice, and looking at the practice of psychoanalysis for what it shows that is unique about our theories and also what it tells us about how to revise our theories. The language of each of the authors varies. Some authors cast their models in the classical language of Freud's structural theory. They also modify that theory omitting the concept of defense mechanism, espousing the idea that any behavior can be employed defensively. Signal affects other than anxiety are also postulated in a new theory of neurosogenesis that still bears the stamp of the structural model. Other authors argue that affects may be unconscious, an idea that Freud struggled with and never satisfactorily resolved. Still others work with the idea of potential affects or of unconscious organizations that may give rise to affective expressions brought to consciousness as ideas and as affective discharges. Some authors take a long look at the historical origins of Freud's concepts of affectivity, while others start from a vantage point that makes new demands on our curiosity. We are asked to look at what has gone on in cognitive science and consider language such as internalized object schemas, person schemas, or examine the cognitive and personality organizations that subsume the experience of affect. Affective experience and display embedded in elaborate mental structures are introduced to account for the form and expression of a variety of experiences that can be observed clinically. How is hatred involved in object-centered themes, and finally expressed in the transference?

How does the pathology of the patient determine the expression of hatred or love? These are questions that can only be answered from the vantage of clinical observation.

Regardless of theoretical position, all of our clinicians are interested in how emotions are organized around themes which have meaning, and how the analytic process illuminates those themes and whether the focus is two person, one person, or triadic. Authors use structural theory, topographic theory, and new models of selfhood, person schemas, or object relations to portray how the working analyst uses theory to inform clinical work and uses his or her work to elaborate new theories.

Arlow's notion that moods are structured affective states perpetuated by the continuing influence of unconscious fantasies is the theoretical lynch pin of most of the ideas presented in this section. The linkages between unconscious fantasies and conscious experience are the stuff that analysts tease apart in their work. Their use of transference and anamnesis and verbalization for plumbing such mysteries are elaborated in each of the clinical presentations. This middle section functions as a bridge between the vantage point of affect development in the first section and the vantage point of integrative and applied sciences in the last section.

PERSON SCHEMAS AND EMOTION

MARDI HOROWITZ, M.D., BRAM FRIDHANDLER, PH.D.,
AND CHARLES STINSON, M.D.

A relational theory of emotion allows one to understand complex feelings toward and about self and others. By use of state theory, schemas theory, and control process theory, emotionality can be understood in terms of sequences of experienced and expressed affects, actions, and internal thoughts, reactions, and reappraisals. This paper presents a relational theory that includes unconscious processes that anticipate conscious feelings and regulate affect expression in thought or action. A case example of pathological grief provides a concrete illustration of what is meant at each level of theoretical discussion.

PSYCHOANALYSIS INVOLVES knowing one's own feelings, empathically understanding the emotional expressions of another person, and interpreting the often obscure and complex layers of affective meaning detected in serial thoughts and actions that may at first seem mysteriously motivated. These tasks of developing clinical knowledge of emotionality are not easy, and they are not made easier by using only a few elemental emotions such as fear, anger, joy, and surprise as theoretical building blocks. Instead, an integrated, cognitive, affective, dynamic relational theory is necessary, one that can contain the formation and expression of emotions in a model that posits unconscious impulsive and defensive conflicts. We aim to present our version of such a relational theoroy of conscious

---

Mardi Horowitz is Professor of Psychiatry, UCSF; Director, Program on Conscious and Unconscious Mental Processes of John D. and Catherine MacArthur Foundation. Bram Fridhandler is Assistant Clinical Professor, Department of Psychiatry, UCSF. Charles Stinson is Adjunct Assistant Professor, UCSF.

Research on which this contribution is based was supported by The Program on Conscious and Unconscious Mental Processes of the John D. and Catherine T. MacArthur Foundation.

emotional experience, interpersonal emotional action, and unconscious formative processes.

Background

Freud (1915a, 1915b, 1926, 1933; Breuer and Freud, 1895) defined emotions as conscious felt experiences, and potentials for emotion as unconscious templates with a relational quality. For example, some criminal acts might be compulsively carried out in order to be caught and punished to appease "an unconscious sense of guilt." This formulation of "guilt" does not refer to emotion so much as to dynamically active dispositions to enter a state of feeling guilty, with defenses against such entry. "Guilt" is a shorthand for a mental set of relationship views that involve self, others, and scripts of transaction and emotional expression. The person, one infers, has an internal script or schema involving a memory or fantasy of breaking rules, acting the role of an aggressor, harming others, expecting others to have anger at the rule-breaking, expecting fear of others' anger, and anticipating self-disgust, shame, and sadness over loss of honor. Such aspects of an "unconscious sense of guilt," might be consciously experienced in various ways, all organized around the general theme of crime and punishment.

Emotional States of Mind

Even the "basic" emotions, such as guilt, anger, and sadness, are not well characterized as fundamental entities (Mandler, 1979). They are more usefully viewed as *sets of states of mind that together might be labeled* as "sadness," "rage," "shame," or "guilt." Of course, the affective phenomena we encounter clinically—"agitated fearful sadness," "mixed fear, rage, and guilt," and so on—are generally more complex than the so-called "pure" emotions and thus are even more difficult to capture in elemental emotion theories. The concept of states of mind assists our clinical and theoretical grasp of simple and complex emotions alike (Horowitz, 1987). To discuss such emotional sequences and colorations, we will provide as a concrete example a patient with a pathological grief reaction. Using that example we will present a theory about emotional states of mind, the schematic relationship models that lead to such states, and the processes of control that lead to state transitions by effecting changes in these schemas.

In taking our relational or person-schematic point of view and stressing observation in terms of states of mind, we are emphasizing *patterns* of features that may occur in many verbal and nonverbal channels of expression, and many modes for conscious representation of emotional concepts. No component feature is regarded as primary. We use schemas as the "wholes" that contain the patterning of components, and we emphasize self and others, relationships and roles, as the most important components for a psychoanalytic theory of affects (Arlow, 1969, 1977; Bowlby, 1969; Dahl, 1978; Emde, 1988a, 1988b; Fridhandler, 1986; Horowitz, 1979, 1987, 1988a, 1988b; Kernberg, 1976; Schafer, 1964; Stern, 1985).

In taking this theoretical stance we stand on different ground than those who attempt to construct a theory of components of emotion (as reviewed by Emde, 1980; Izard, 1977; Mandler, 1979; Plutchik, 1980). We are also on somewhat different ground than those who seek an object relations theory of affect (e.g., Dahl, 1978; de Rivera, 1977; Kernberg, 1976) that links to an elemental set of names for emotion. We wish to emphasize that we do not see emotions as separate or intervening "entities." Rather, we see emotion as contained within the meaning structures we will describe. The potential for emotion is within memories, fantasies, and schemas.

A Case Example

A young man, Mr. B, was describing his brother's suicide to his psychotherapist. At the time of this session it was over three years after the suicide. In a pensive state of mind, Mr. B was talking to the therapist about his brother.

When Mr. B spoke of how much he had once enjoyed weekends with his brother, his pensive state deepened: tears welled in his eyes, he looked sad, his voice choked, he paused and stared fixedly into the distance as he fell silent. Then his face showed a micro-momentary expression of disgust. Mr. B next began speaking in an animated way about a different topic. This sequence of starting the focal topic and then avoiding it occurred again and again with the same displays and stifling of emotion. When aspects of this repetitive pattern were called to Mr. B's attention, he reported that he felt the sadness but did not know what to make of the observed facial expression of apparent disgust.

Mr. B felt shame about the suicide of his brother but not, he said, any guilt. He was able to push the shame from his mind by not revealing to people that his brother was dead. He also tried to push sadness from his subjective experience, but this emotion sometimes intruded upon his conscious awareness when something he perceived reminded him of his brother.

The vignette describes a state with complex cues and hues of emotion, labeled as Mr. B's "pensive state of mind," which "deepens" into one with more intense emotion, that of "deep and sorrowful pining." These experiences and expressions are not "simple" or "pure" emotions, although all relate to "being sad." They imply a relational emotionality, with self as agent and other as a target of feeling (e.g., the self pines for the return of the lost other) (Dahl, 1978; de Rivera, 1977). For clinical work, we need a theory that can give us explanations for such complex hues and relational aspects of emotion.

We hope the person-schematic approach we discuss in this paper can lead to a differentiated relational view of emotional thoughts and actions. This approach should show itself capable of describing how a patient such as Mr. B can unconsciously have a "guilt potential" while consciously not experiencing and socially disavowing guilt, and unconsciously "leaking" a momentary facial display of what may have been disgust with self. The approach we outline integrates three related domains of theory, including states of mind, person schemas, and control process theories. Although we present these three sectors of theory in sequence, we conceptualize them as dynamically interactive—all three are important in the formation and experience of emotions.

States of Mind Theory

The concepts of state of mind, states of consciousness, and mood are similar, yet distinct. States of consciousness range from ordinary consciousness to hallucinatory, dreaming, sleeping, intoxicated, or otherwise altered states of consciousness. A state of mind refers to a finer-grained typology of *types* of consciousness. A state of mind differs from a mood because it is more than a set of time-extended emotional colorations. A state of mind includes manifest signs of cognitive operations as well. And there are states of mind that are characterized by few, if any, felt emotions.

A state of mind is a coherent set of features. This pattern of verbal, nonverbal, and experiential cues can be recognized by an observer or the self as observing the self. Such features of a state include the form and content of recurrent ideas, emotions, and actions. Styles of communication and action may also differentiate states. So too may patterns of apparent modulation in how ideational and affective signals are represented in consciousness or communicated to others (Horowitz, 1987, 1988b).

In other words, the features of a specifiable state of mind tend to occur together. Human beings preconsciously assess all, or at least many, channels of expression to recognize their own state of mind or that of a companion. Features that are repeated together and that change together allow one to discriminate a point of transition from one state of mind to another.

Less emotional states are as important to describe as "moody" states if one is to include issues of motivation and self-regulation in descriptions of states, transitions, and repeated cycles. Consider as one example how multiple states of mind might express the same type of emotion. An angry woman may have a state cycle beginning with a *stony indifference* that seems rigid and overcontrolled to an observer. This state of mind may usually contain little manifest emotion. Then she may have a transition into a state of *explosive, undermodulated rage.* Next there may be a transition to a well-modulated state of expressing her *anger.* This woman may wish to assert her feelings of irritation yet she may dread experiencing herself or being seen as being out of control of her hostility.

The state of stony indifference may be a compromise, a defensive maneuver that is neither what she desires (controlled expression of her anger to another with reference to changing some specific situation) nor what she fears (a blind, impulsive rage that destroys a relationship).

A state description may include the emotional, relational, ideational, and stylistic patterns noted in posture, facial expression, tone and inflection of voice, flow of speech and images, dialect, gestures, deployment of gaze, and other signs. From the subject's verbal reports, we may include the specific thought contents and felt emotions as labeled in words, metaphors, and descriptions of bodily sensations.

Control of state is important: can persons enter *desired* states? Are they able or unable to prevent entry into *dreaded* states? Do they defend against dreaded states in such a way as to enter instead a *problematic* state? Are they able to stabilize themselves in *compromise* states, ones in which both wishes and fears of the consequences of wishes are warded off from conscious experience or interpersonal action? The discrepancy or harmony across channels of expression gives an observer a sense of the subject's degree of control.

State theory leads to description of how emotions, moods, ideas, and styles of action interrelate. The style of action is an important cue to intrapsychic views of a current interpersonal situation and to self-appraisal. State theory also leads to regarding personality as a repertoire of states and of the schemas that lead to the formation of states. In other words, each state in the repertoire of an individual is organized by particular schemas.

Before going on to consider person schemas, we want to examine the vignette about Mr. B in terms of desired, dreaded, problematic, and compromise states of mind.

Mr. B's pensive state of mind, in which he pined for his brother, was followed by a momentary emotional expression, the facial expression of disgust (drawing back the corners of his mouth, wrinkling up his nose, and squinting his eyes). This transient sign of disgust may have been an intrusion of one feature of a multifeatured but warded-off state. We think we observed his passage through a repetitive cycle of states and state transitions: first a *problematic* state of deep pining that we called *distraught sadness,* then partial emergence of an even more *dreaded* and warded-off state of mixed guilt, shame, and fear. The "partial emergence" or brief "shimmer" of this state was the facial expression of disgust (disgust with self, we infer). From this dreaded state of mixed guilt, shame, and fear we called *shameful sorrow* there was a quick shift to a *compromise* state of *assertive animation.* We also inferred a *desired* state of mind: to feel *calm and safe,* perhaps by imagining restoration of a good relationship with his brother.

Person Schemas Theory

State theory asserts that whenever a particular state recurs, its patterns of recognizable features will be relatively similar to its previous occurrences. Again, by examining many instances of the same state, one can draw inferences about the coherence of the patterns that the state comprises. The explanation of such coherent patterns is then the task of person schemas theory, which describes the views of self and objects that organize perceptions, ideas, emotions, memories, and actions into coherent experiences and patterned sequences of expression.

The concept of schemas has in recent years received widespread attention as part of the interdisciplinary field of "cognitive science." Bartlett (1932) did classical work on memory schemata. He observed that in the presence of partial, ambiguous, or ill-structured information, people perceive and remember in ways that "fill in" compatible information from prior experiences. Perception and meaning seem to be organized in chunks, clusters, or outlines rather than in isolated particles (Paul, 1967; Piaget, 1970). The concept of schemas has been applied to knowledge in general (Rumelhart and Ortony, 1977) and, most broadly, to all mental phenomena (Mandler, 1984). It covers several kinds of frameworks or skeletal organizations which bring order and integration among elements. Most uses of the concept assume that schemas may be viewed in both static and active aspects. They are spoken of as being "stored," but also as doing various things once they are "activated."

Rumelhart (1980) has offered an introduction to the uses of the concept of schema in cognitive science. He provides no single definition of schema, but instead gives a series of analogies. He first likens schemas to plays. The chief parallel here is that both schemas and plays have component parts that have stable general definitions but which, on given occasions, can be filled by different specific items. In a play, the general definitions are the roles and the specific items are the actors. In a schema, these are commonly termed the "variables" and their "values." Rumelhart gives the example of the schema for purchasing something. We all know that a purchase involves a buyer, a seller, some medium of exchange, and merchandise. These are the variables. On any given occasion, they can be filled by any of a large set of items. Almost anyone can be a buyer or seller and almost anything can be bought. The medium of exchange is typically money but may be goods or services.

Rumelhart's second analogy for a schema is a theory. In scientific inquiry, the predictions of a theory are tested against observations of reality. In a similar way, the features of a schema are compared with the current situation. When a sufficient number of a theory's predictions are confirmed, it is accepted by the scientific community. Similarly, when the features of a schema fit a situation sufficiently well, that schema is activated, and the newly adopted schema (which, following Bowlby [1969], we call the "working model") guides further perceptions of the situation.

"Once we have accepted a configuration of schemata, the schemata themselves provide a richness that goes far beyond our observations. On deciding that we have seen an automobile, we assume that it has an engine, headlights, and all of the standard characteristics of an automobile. We do this without the slightest hesitation. We have complete confidence in our little theory" (Rumelhart, 1980, p. 38). This phenomenon is known as *schematic completion.* In complex schemas such as *person schemas,* the completion can include expectations of *roles* and *transactions* that are likely to take place.

A schema not only provides assumptions about what further observations will reveal, it also provides a course of *action.* This feature leads to Rumelhart's third comparison, namely, to the procedures in computer programs. Like such procedures, schemas are sets of instructions that, once activated, provide a sequence of actions. (Rumelhart need not have turned to computer programs for this analogy, since the script of a play also prescribes sequences of action.)

In short, schemas have the following features: they are mental *organizations* of elements; they fit situations more or less well; and once they are activated, they organize perception and guide action.

Schema theory in psychoanalysis is recognizable in

Freud's (1915a) discovery of transference as a kind of template that stamps its form on new perceptual experiences (Knapp, 1991; Luborsky et al., 1991). That is, transferences lie latent until a situation is encountered to which they have some relevance. Once activated, they bring perceptions of the situation into accord. Latent transferences are part of the individual's repertoire of schemas, and "here-and-now" transferences are activated schemas or "working models" (Lichtenberg, 1975; Slap and Saykin, 1983).

Other theoretical work on such large-scale information structures as schemas of persons has used such terms as "frames" (Minsky, 1975), enduring attitudes (Horowitz and Becker, 1972), "schemas" (Horowitz, 1976; Paul, 1967; Rumelhart, 1975), and "scripts" (Abelson, 1976). Until recently, cognitive science models of such information structures (which we will unify under the term *schema*) required unwieldy *sequential symbolic processing* of the sort associated with usual computer programming. For reasons discussed in detail elsewhere (Rumelhart and McClelland, 1986; Stinson and Palmer, 1991), this was not a satisfactory way to represent the information processing of the human mind. Simultaneous parallel processing theories have a better fit to observations of mental processes.

Recent schema theory, including that of person schemas, fits more readily with emerging neuroscience theory of network organization of information and parallel distributed processing (PDP) in the brain (for a review see Stinson and Palmer, 1991). Although the brain has specialized modules, it seems that network encoding of anything but the simplest information is probably distributed across broad areas. On large and small scales, and in a variety of ways, the differently specialized brain areas are connected with each other. Important information is associated with related information by means of the connections among neurons and their activation patterns.

No central agency needs to select which of several schemas within a repertoire might be activated during the recognition of a stimulus situation. The selection of a schema occurs as a network relaxes into the best fitting activation pattern available given the current memory state of the net (Rumelhart and McClelland, 1986; Stinson and Palmer, 1991). The activation of a schema is thus a natural and automatic response to a stimulus. This response progresses automatically unless some regulating factors such as control processes intervene, in which case, as we will describe later, the appropriate representation may fail to activate.

When schemas include mainly roles and characteristics of self or others, we call these *person schemas.* When these models include self *interacting* with other people, we call these *role-relationship models* (Horowitz, 1979, 1987, 1988a, 1988b, 1991; Horowitz et al., 1984). A diagram representing such a role-relationship model is shown in Figure 1. The first action of a role-relationship model can be a wish, the next the response of other, then the reaction of the self to that response. The concept is that such intrapsychic schematizations direct wishes into particular forms that include expected consequences which may link fears to wishes, or compromises to both fears and wishes (Luborsky et al., 1991).

To reiterate, a *person schema* is a special type of schema about self or other. A *role-relationship model* (RRM) is a schematized representation of an interpersonal interaction, each person represented by individual person schemas. It is a plan or format for sequences of transaction. These transactions include emotional expressions and conscious experiences. Thus the RRM includes the potential for organizing, forming, and releasing specific forms of emotional transaction.

Throughout life an individual develops a large number of schemas of many sorts, including person schemas and role-relationship models. This repertoire of possible schemas offers different (and sometimes competing) alternative mean-

Figure 1
A Role-Relationship Model

The actions and traits depicted are a mental schema of what form real events *might* take. The patterned expected sequence of the events is labled with the successsive numbers. Actions include emotional expressions and consicous experiences. Self-estimation may include pride, guilt, bolstering of self, attacks on self.

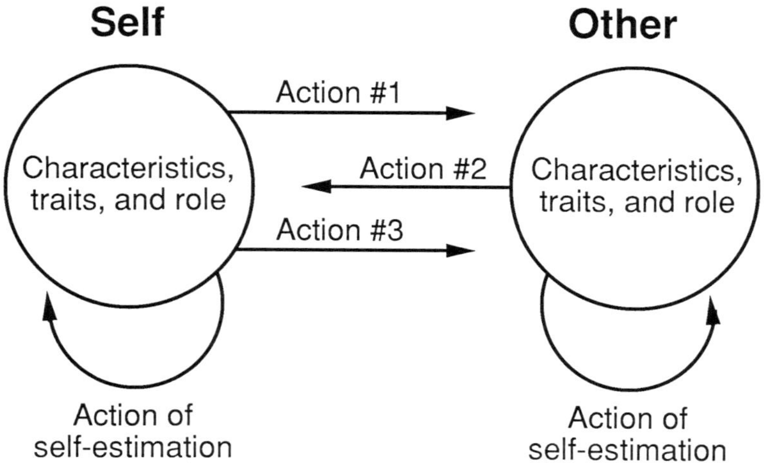

From Horowitz, M. J., Ed. (1991). *Person Schemas and Maladaptive Patterns*. Chicago: Univ. Chicago Press.

ing representations for the same situation. The theory presumes that any individual (not just one with a multiple personality disorder) has multiple self schemas, schemas of others, and RRMs (Horowitz, 1979, 1987, 1988a, 1988b, 1991). The different schemas are characterized by different constellations of features. When activated, these features may lead to some of the coherent patterns recognized as a state of mind.

Person schemas and RRMs permit recognition of various features of self and other, including affect, as signals of the progress of an interpersonal situation. In addition to recognition, such schemas can also trigger expressions, including emotional arousal, as associated features of the fully activated schema. Schemas thus organize perception, thought, emotion, and action.

Depending on the circumstances, the mind may tend predictably toward monofocal schema activation; at other times it may proceed along a predictable scriptlike sequence of schemas; at still other times it may oscillate between or among two or more predominating schemas. The latter would underlie "shimmering" states of mind in which features of two or more schemas seem to coexist. For example, signs of an intensely emotional state may intermittently pierce through a dominant state characterized by suppression of affective features. Phenomenally, the individual would seem in an overmodulated state, but telltale leakage would reveal competing states supported by schemas with powerful emotional features.

Schemas are a special form of knowledge that, in general, change slowly (Piaget, 1952, 1970). Schemas, including RRMs, endure, but new schemas can develop and existing schematic potentials can change as memories of new experience are continually being encoded. These alterations may lead to fresh perceptions of prior situations, contributing to the revision of schemas.

If a schematized working model does not accurately represent or predict objects and ongoing events, the ill-fitting features provide novel stimuli that must eventually be dealt with in some way: either ignored (as in misperceptions or overgeneralizations) or used in revising the predominant schema into a more apt working model that may become part of the schematic repertoire. If a familiar object or situation suddenly and unpleasantly changes, important features may not be recognized: one may deny key aspects of stressful events because they are incongruent with available schemas, and thus avoid entry into emotionally overwhelmed states.

Mental contents of strongly activated ("instantiated" is the more correct term in this context) schemas—the state's ideational and emotional features—may distort the perceived features of ongoing experience and, therefore, any new memory laid down (Kernberg, 1976, 1982). Similarly, mental contents of a state may distort the features of an old memory or recollection. If strongly incongruent, it may suppress the recollection altogether. One's recollection of a traumatic event may be frightening, poignantly tragic, or even humorous, depending on the current state of mind and instantiated schemas.

Certain potent, well-organized, and durable schemas support particularly important states of mind. The activation of dreaded, desired, or compromise RRMs results in dreaded, desired, or compromise states of mind. A memory, an unconscious fantasy, or representation of a current interpersonal situation might be perceived and dealt with differently depending on which RRM was concurrently active. Important repetitive patterns noted in processing of memories, fantasies, or situations while in different states can be noted in a format containing several RRM diagrams, a format we call a Role-Relationship Models Configuration (RRMC), as illustrated in Figure 2.

Figure 2
Role-Relationship Models Configuration Format

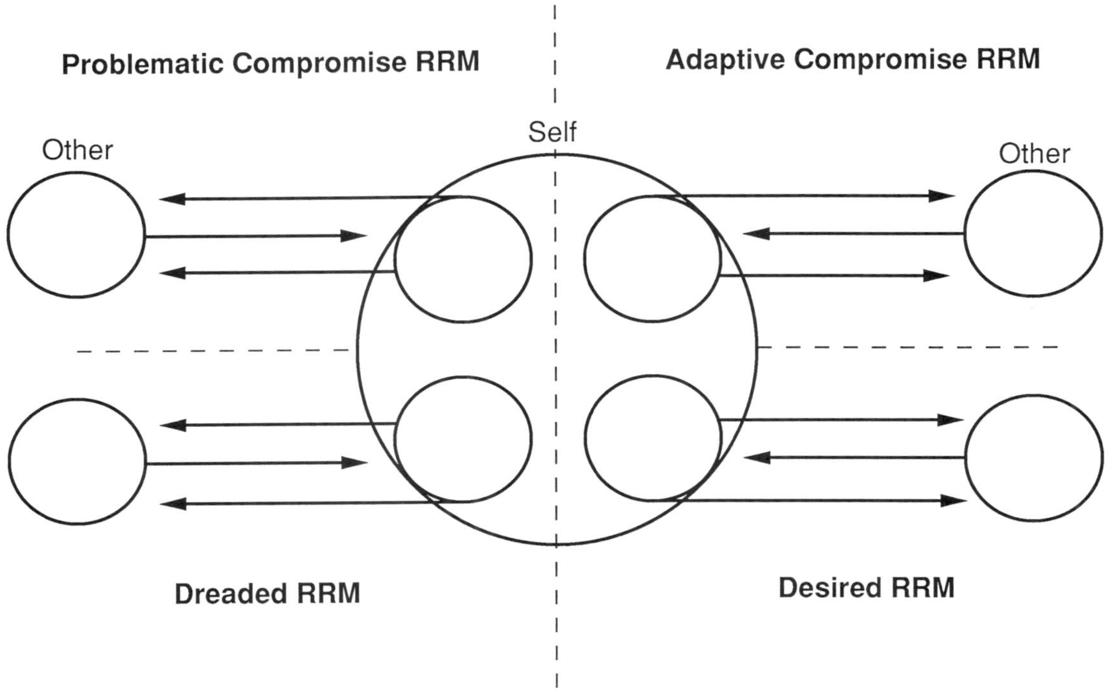

From Horowitz, M. J., Ed. (1991). *Person Schemas and Maladaptive Patterns*. Chicago: Univ. Chicago Press.

Emotions are not identical with states, yet an understanding of states and person schemas such as RRMs is a key to emotions. States of mind are integrated patterns of subjective experience, expressive behavior, trends of thought, and physiological changes. These are the major features of emotions as well; in fact, this description of states might serve equally well as a definition of emotions. Yet the reader may object that the state descriptions we have given do not seem to be *emotions* per se. These states appear more complex than emotions, as the latter are depicted in everyday language and in many scientific theories. But states are closer to what we deal with clinically, closer to the way emotional phenomena actually make their appearance in interpersonal interaction. If the question is asked, "What is the relationship between emotions and states?" we answer that in many instances it is only necessary to deal theoretically with states. "Emotions," in these cases, are abstractions from the observed states—important for some purposes, but not essential to pinpoint as a "singular entity" in clinical work.

Like other states, emotional states often reflect person schemas, especially RRMs. In organizing the interpretation of an interpersonal situation, the person schema activates tightly associated thoughts, feelings, images, speech, and behavioral patterns, which thereby pervade current experience. In other words, specific stable states are supported by the activation of potent schemas. As the RRMs are successively activated, a succession of emotional states may appear.

We will return to the subject of Mr. B to illustrate some of the ways in which an emotional theme, such as the memory of his brother's death, may be schematically encoded and variously reexperienced and/or revised during contemplation in different episodes of remembrance.

Mr. B had intrusive images of his brother coming into his room, as the brother actually had done in regular visits before his death. Mr. B would then have the idea, expressed in words, "but he is dead," and feel a pang of grief and perhaps shed tears. He would then push the topic from his mind to ward off staying in or deepening into a painfully emotional state. This patterned sequence, repeated over and over, was similar to his initial response to his brother's death: On hearing of the suicide, he felt an initial horror but quickly told himself that he would immediately get on with the agendas of his own life. He emphasized to himself that he had important and pressing goals requiring his full undivided attention for success, and that he had no time or energy for extended grief.

A similarly patterned sequence also occurred before the death. His brother had asked Mr. B to come to his city the weekend of the suicide. Mr. B declined; he was busy with his own time-pressured goals and deadlines. He knew his brother felt troubled periodically but he knew as well that other family members were there to provide support if needed; he did not, of course, anticipate the suicide.

Years after the traumatic event, however, Mr. B still felt vulnerable to self-accusations that he should have visited his brother on that weekend. He yearned to restore a sense of closeness with his brother, experienced sadness at the loss, and then felt a pang of disgust with both his brother and himself at the suicide and its irrevocability. Closeness could not be reestablished in reality. And it could not be established in memory because any reminder led to a repetition of intrusive, painful, conscious experience that, in a schematized fashion, Mr. B felt he had to ward off.

Person schema theory allows a plausible explanation for these phenomena of Mr. B's varied states of mind in contemplating his attachment to his brother and his brother's death. Figure 3 fills in the blank format of an RRMC as viewed in Figure 2. Several RRM schemas for understanding his relationship with his brother are placed in the desired, dreaded, and two types of compromise quadrants of the configuration. The stereotypical, scriptlike interactions of several possible self schemas with relevant schemas of the brother are shown in the diagram by connecting lines between each self-other pair.

The RRMs of Figure 3's RRMC were drawn from recur-

Figure 3
RRMC for the Brother Theme

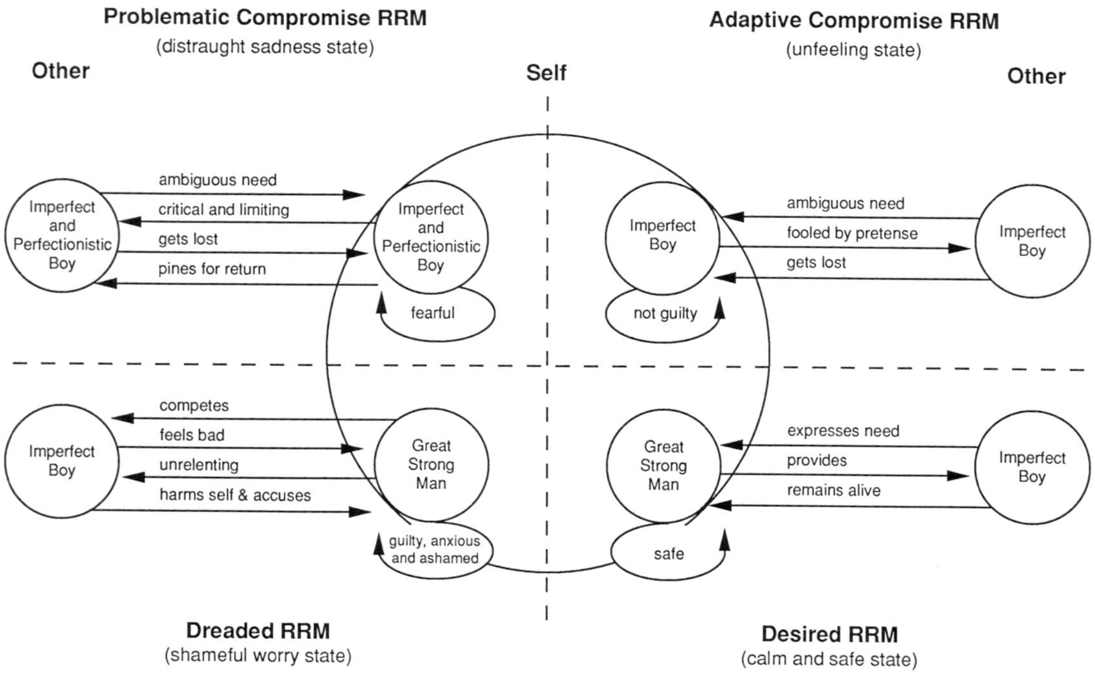

ring themes reviewed in recordings of therapy and research-exploration sessions with Mr. B, including his past relationship with his brother, mourning the loss of this brother, and assessing the correctness of his own actions.

In Figure 3, the desired RRM in the lower right quadrant contains a self schema as a great strong man. This is an ideal self-image, and the RRM shown with it represents Mr. B's wish that the brother would still be alive, and that Mr. B would have provided enough restoration for his turbulence that the suicide would have been unnecessary, and that it would not, in reality, have occurred. Having a fantasy organized by the desired RRM could not stabilize Mr. B in the desired calm and safe state, however, because that schema sequence ended with incongruence to actual fact. The memory of the death activated and was organized by the dreaded RRM shown in the lower left hand quadrant of Figure 3. Mr. B's self-schema in that RRM is still that of being a great and strong man, but the scripts of emotion and action stemming from that role are different: there he sees himself as a person who has competed in order to be better than his brother, and as a person who will, as a consequence, be criticized by others (leading to shame and worry) or feel guilty. To ward off the experience of a shameful worried state organized by this dreaded RRM, Mr. B attempted to stabilize either an unfeeling state or one that was less infused with shame, worry, and guilt.

The unfeeling state is organized by an adaptive compromise RRM shown in the upper right quadrant of Figure 3. Mr. B hoped that in an unfeeling state he might be able to pursue his work. The RRM that organizes this state is one in which he has a self schema as an imperfect boy who cannot be expected to have recognized the ambiguous signals from his brother. He is alright except that he was fooled by pretense, so he does not now feel guilty.

A more problematic RRM is shown in the upper left RRM of Figure 3. Here brother is represented as being lost because there is the expectation that he might yet return, and there is pining for that return. There is fear for the self if the brother does not return, because he has criticized his brother and offered him limited support. Thus this has some ingredients of the dreaded RRM, but the problematic RRM is less emotionally intense and painful. The dreaded RRM subsumes the dreaded state of shameful worry. The problematic RRM subsumes the problematic state containing Mr. B's chief complaint, that of distraught sadness.

Because various person schemas might organize the reconstruction of a memory or dialogue on the meaning to the self of an event such as the suicide of a relative, the state of mind during reminiscence or communication can be changed by shifts in which schema from a repertoire is dominant. The activation of a given schema could be affected by inhibitions or facilitations, that is, by the processes of control.

Control Process Theory

A purpose for controls of mental processes and schemas is to prevent entry into undermodulated states, ones in which emotional intensity is so high that disorganization may occur, as well as ones that are anticipated to be too painful or distressing to tolerate. These anticipations of "too much" are often unconscious, leading to unconscious defensive or coping operations. We will first consider control processes in terms of how they might affect selection of schemas and so might affect shifts in state of mind. In so doing, we will attempt a bridge between "brain" and "mind," between neural information processing and systems of meaning.

Current neural net theory holds that schematized memory information is distributed among the neurons composing the brain's networks. One does not (nor does a homunculus) select the schema to be activated: the net relaxes into the best fitting activation pattern available given the current memory state of the net. The locus of control for general mechanisms of schema activation, then, is distributed.

This assumption about control of schemas does not relegate human mental activity to an endless chain of predictable responses devoid of purposes for and choices about control. There is plenty of room for volitional conscious control and automatic, anticipatory, unconscious control. Because distributed control is within the person, it is highly personal: it is forged from enormous personalized, self-integrated, or self-labeled experience. Schemas for control operations themselves evolve as part of a developmental construction and continuing evolution of processes with emergent characteristics.

We alluded to such additional levels of schema control when, in the section on person schemas, we referred to schematized scriptlike sequences. In a scriptlike sequence the activation of one schema serves as a triggering stimulus feature for activation of the next. These might be tightly ordered, as in a well-defined set of expected perceptions or a sequence of ensuing actions. A sequence of schemas may lead to processes that are adaptive, providing accurate modeling, prediction, and preparation for unfolding interpersonal and emotional events. The schematic sequence might also unfold in a way that was disruptive and maladaptive: a sequence may lead to composing an inner working model and set of actions with features entirely incompatible with the environmental reality or even inconsistent with the views of self and other contained in the initial part of the schematic sequence. For example, an early RRM in a script sequence of schemas may involve identification of the self as benevolent protector of a weaker other; the scriptlike sequence may involve mutual approach and expressions of fondness, followed by arousal of sexually aggressive feelings and views of sexually harming the other incompatible with the original role of protector. This unfolding sequence might lead to the activation of an alternative RRM, with the self viewed as a shameful and disgusting sadist and the other as a harmed innocent victim, or perhaps (with role reversal) of the self as righteous and innocent and the other as a sexually wanton and disgusting person. Such *obligatory scripts,* followed in one maladaptive interpersonal relationship after another, are common in neurotic character pathology.

Schemas *about* schemas are also possible. If well-developed as symbol structures, these could permit states of conscious contemplation that have in the past been called "the observing ego." These schemas about schemas allow reflective self-awareness (Schafer, 1968), as in reconstruction of memories and observing one's own pattern of emotional, relational, and defensive processes. These schemas about schemas are, in effect, schematized processes that can control other schemas (including still other schematized control processes). Thus conscious control purposes can override some unconscious control purposes and automatic tendencies. That is why conscious reflection can serve as a special tool for adaptation, as when one attempts to contrast two constructs which were previously contradictory or confused. One may then consciously create two variants of one schema, adding distinguishing features to the separate cases. One may learn to counteract previously "obligatory" or automatic scripts and transferences.

Conversely, another possibility for control might be the development of unifying abstraction classes from separate schemas: simultaneous or rapidly successive activation of separate schemas would elicit a class schema containing the common features. This process creates a new synthesis or supraordinate schematization, perhaps counteracting unconsciously automatic splitting or dissociation.

Still another means of schematized control might involve stimulating or inhibiting bias of activation of specific schemas or classes of schemas. Schematized inhibition of certain features (e.g., painful emotionality) may suppress, neutralize, or dramatically modify entire classes of other schemas: the activation of an RRM entailing an "intolerable" emotion might be rendered almost inaccessibly unstable.

As another possible conscious or unconscious control process, the activation of schemas could be facilitated or inhibited in a way that could be called "automasking." This could distort prior perception in a manner analogous to the way in which a subsequent perceptual stimulus may obscure conscious representation of a prior one through an effect known as "backward-masking." The activation of a schematized percept (e.g., anger or sexual feelings toward a specified kind of object) may trigger activation of a prohibiting schema (e.g., extremely strong moral beliefs opposing such feelings or objects). The prohibiting schema may lead mechanically to activation of a powerful alternative schema of sufficient strength as to make unavailable to consciousness any awareness of the prior perception of the stimulus (e.g., ritualistic behavior, ideational preoccupation, or contrary emotional feelings such as disgust instead of "unacceptable" eroticism).

Controls that can inhibit or facilitate activation of schemas are additions to the usual view of controls that inhibit or facilitate conscious representation of a particular drive, wish, memory, idea, or emotion. This theory permits an articulation of psychoanalytic defense mechanisms theory with object relations theories, self psychology (multiple selves, especially), cognitive theory, and neural net theory.

Purpose, Process, and Outcome of Control

There are different purposes for activating control processes, some conscious and some unconscious. Some purposes are wishfully impulsive and may stem from biological drives such as sexual ones. Other purposes aim at mastery by resolving, coping with, or defending against contradictions, dilemmas, threats and problems. Still other purposes are to maintain values, rules, and social systems. These id, ego, and superego aims may conflict, and they all occupy the same mind, brain, and body. Diverse purposes affect how the processes of control influence emotionality. To examine this confluence and these effects, we turn once again to the clinical illustration, Mr. B's traumatic memory about his brother's suicide.

Confronting a painful memory of losing a loved one for the purpose of mastering it (i.e., to establish new schemas) may lead to intensely emotional trains of conscious thought. A conflicting purpose may be to avoid intense negative emotions in order to avoid states of distress, flooding, and confusion. The intensity of each purpose, the current capabilities of the inhibitions and facilitations that constitute control processes, and the outcome of efforts at self-regulation may vary from state to state in Mr. B. The many cognitive, emotional, relational, and schematic levels at which control processes may operate have been discussed elsewhere (Horowitz, 1988a, 1988b, 1991). Controls may, by inhibition or facilitation of mental activities, influence which topics will gain the focus of attention, which sequencing rules and logic (e.g., primary and secondary processes) will organize thought, and which modes of representation (e.g., images, words, enactions) or action (e.g., declarative plans, procedural knowledge) might predominate. Our concern here will be on control of relative activation within repertoires of person schemas.

These control processes can lead to the use of reality-inappropriate schemas, as in transference phenomena and image-distorting defenses such as externalization, internalization, reaction formation, role-reversal, splitting and dissociation (Perry and Cooper, 1989; Vaillant et al.,1986). Such control processes will result in experienced fluctuations in intensity of emotionality, and in sequences of what emotions are felt and expressed.

To illustrate this, reconsider now the vignette involving Mr. B's contemplation of the "unfinished business" around his brother's suicide. Mr. B might contemplate the memory sequence; indeed he might reconstruct it variably according to different person schemas and RRMs, and so have different emotional states of mind in different periods of contemplation of this topic.

If the dreaded RRM, containing a relatively too-strong, bad self schema were facilitated, guilt would be more likely as a felt emotional experience. If an RRM with a too-weak, vulnerable self schema were facilitated, and a too-strong self schema inhibited, the resultant emotion might be fear or horror. The dreaded state of shameful worry contains mixed emotions, including fear, guilt, shame, and hate because there may be a defensive shift back and forth between self schemas within a general RRM such as that depicted in the left lower quadrant of Figure 3. This becomes a version of what was earlier called a "shimmering" state.

This type of theory will strike the reader as complex; this complexity is desirable because emotional states in neurotic patients are often so complex that both patient and clinician are quite unclear for a long time just how to accurately label feelings. We may too soon say and repeat simplified emotion labels such as "angry" or "guilty." States are recurrent, and so, gradually, the mixed emotional colorations can be analyzed as a part of script sequences and changing, conflicting, and contradictory views. Clear emotional metaphors may have more power as labels than simple emotion words. This process of labeling emotionality can lead to conscious override of automatic schematic assumptions, change in working models, development of new schemas, progress in a mourning process, and so to new emotional responses to which is superficially the same memory, as, for example, Mr. B's memory about his brother's suicide, and its meaning.

Emotional states have a motivational property. The desire to reexperience a positive state of mind makes one seek the acts, beliefs, memories, fantasies, ideas, and sensations that infuse it. Increasing intensity of negative emotions and painful sensations within a state makes one wish to change the state of mind within which one experiences situations.

As Mr. B talked about the loss of his brother he reenacted parts of his memory. Not only recalling, he also was creating a new situation; in working through, he was aware he was telling the therapist something and anticipating his own and the therapist's ensuing reactions to that tale. If he were to have a working model in which he said his brother should not have killed himself, that it was stupid to do such an imperfect and bad act, then he would at some point experience and express anger. When Mr. B talked about how much he wished his brother were back with him, alive again, he would feel sadness. When he talked about wishing he had gone to his brother's assistance, he would feel self-disgust, shame, or guilt. Or when he talked about his own idea that he would not like to get into a state of low self-esteem, the kind of state he believed may have led to his brother's suicide, then Mr. B might feel fearful for his own life.

These emotions of anger, sadness, self-disgust, and fear occur as part of a conceptual sequence. That sequence is organized by scripts and roles contained in a person schema such as an RRM. *The potential for the recurrent patterns of emotion is contained in the particular model that is active.* Control processes can affect which model is active. In addition, the potential for spontaneous "new" aspects of emotion is contained partly in the current situation and partly in how that situation is modeled currently in the activity of the mind.

Emotionality from Concept-to-Concept and Schema-to-Schema Mismatches

In the preceding paragraphs we covered the unfolding sequential aspect of how emotion is felt during the contemplation of memories, perceptions, ideas, and actions. Another aspect of the occurrence of specific, consciously felt, or action-expressed emotions is derived from parallel processes and schemas that, arriving at some comparison point, do not accord. One source of emotional activation is such a mismatch between a situation as *perceived* or remembered and a situation as *expected* (according to inner schemas).

In the first discussion of Mr. B, we noted a brief facial expression of disgust. This disgust, which functions as a *signal,* was inferred to be the result of a mismatch between value schemas about what a person *ought to do* when someone else reaches out for help and what he remembered *having done* in response to his brother's request for him to visit. The affective signal led to an interruption of Mr. B's train of thought about his brother's suicide and provided a motivation for controls that could facilitate some other topic for conscious representation and communication while inhibiting the topic that was leading toward more guilt, shame, or disgust with self. The disgust in this example is like anxiety in that it signals a threat were consciousness to flow unaltered.

Other types of concept-to-concept and schema-to-schema mismatches can be postulated. For example, there may be an enduring schema that, as a template of how situations "ought" to be, indicates a need for the brother as a *selfobject,* as suggested by Kohut (1971). This schema would "say," in effect, "I have to have my brother in order to feel good about us as a pair of people, protectively joined together, facing the world. Without my brother, I am a very weak and vulnerable person." That template of a situation perceived as necessary for the safety and coherence of the self would be matched to the working model of the situation that says there is no brother in the world anymore. As Mr. B contemplated the suicide, this mismatch could lead to an intense alarm emotion such as anxiety about the safety of the self (Sandler, 1960).

Integration of States, Schemas, and Control Theories

We can now look at the case vignette in a way that shows how state, schemas, and controls can influence short-order (i.e., a few seconds) complex emotional experience. First, we will consider Mr. B's contemplation of his brother's suicide according to the *problematic RRM* already shown in the RRMC of Figure 3. The *problematic RRM* is a way of modeling the schemas organizing the emotional state of pining sadness that Mr. B gave as his chief complaint when he sought help.

In the state of pining that we called *distraught sadness,* Mr. B experienced intrusive images of his brother as alive and returning. He also felt himself to be an imperfect and perfectionistic boy and attributed these traits to his brother. Neither of them could tolerate existence as imperfect. The brother wanted to erase imperfection. In an ambiguous way he expressed this need to Mr. B who, in turn, was critical; this expressed need, he felt, might have been mere whining, not serious. To avoid contamination by imperfection and depletion of his time, he himself should limit his involvement.

As Mr. B experienced this state he schematized his brother as lost, not dead, the separation too long but nonetheless temporary. That is one reason why, in the intrusive imagery that came to Mr. B, the brother was not depicted as dead but, rather, about to come into Mr. B's room at any time. Mr. B was in a painful period of waiting and yearning for the brother. These ideas and feelings were all recurrent elements during the distressing state of pining sadness.

As the therapeutic relationship provided support and safety, another state that increased in frequency was governed by a slightly different role-relationship model shown as the *adaptive compromise* in the upper right quadrant of Figure 3. The roles were: brother as an imperfect boy who had expressed an ambiguous need, and Mr. B also as an imperfect boy. The brother's actions were the same as in the problematic role-relationship model, but Mr. B had been fooled because the brother was pretending to be well. The brother sometimes said, in effect, "Oh, pay no attention to what I said last night. I was just in a slump, and I'm really fine. There is nothing to worry about." The brother then "got lost" from Mr. B.

Mr. B was not guilty of causing the loss because he had been fooled, and in this recurrent state of mind he emphasized his lack of guilty feelings to the therapist. Mr. B's self-appraisal was that he was neither remorseful nor exposed to recrimination by others (e.g., the brother) because he was fooled, and he felt safe as long as he could stabilize this schema. He was "better off" in this unfeeling state than in the state of pining sadness with its slight, shimmering hints of remorse for not being more helpful.

Both the *compromise* and *problematic role-relationship models* were preferable to the *dreaded role-relationship model* of the lower left quadrant of Figure 3. In that schema, Mr. B had the role and attributes of a great strong man and the brother was still an imperfect boy. Mr. B had been competing with and defeating the brother, who felt bad. Mr. B was unrelentingly looking after only himself, making himself better and better. The brother subsequently harmed himself and accused Mr. B of not helping. Then Mr. B felt guilty and anxious about recriminations. Were he to organize information by this RRM, Mr. B could enter a painful state that contained specific emotions of guilt, shame, fear (of retaliation), or expectation of criticism.

In the *desired role-relationship model* in the lower right quadrant of Figure 3, Mr. B was a great, strong man, and his brother an imperfect boy who expressed need to him. Mr. B provided for his brother, who remained alive, and Mr. B was then in a state in which he felt calm and safe with the brother. Even though the brother had died, there were memories that fulfilled this RRM. Recollecting them worked to restore Mr. B's well-being, his feeling whole and wholesome.

Active organization of information by use of a desired RRM may lead as well to activation of a dreaded one. The elements of the two schemas may be too similar, and both schemas might be simultaneously activated (parallel processing). The person must, in some way, avoid the desired model to avert the dreaded one, and thus also may fail to enter desired states because of the need to inhibit activation of a dreaded schema.

One way to do that is to have control processes effect a

shift to the use of problematic or compromise schemas. Thus, patients like Mr. B often present with affects that are not desired but that are also not as "bad" an experience as they might have. That is, they ward off states that would be even more distressing and affectively intense.

Other Relational Theories of Emotion

The views presented in this paper are like those of Dahl (1978) and of de Rivera (1977) in that emotions are considered to be often relational, and these authors have been influential in the development of our own position on the prominence of relationality in the structure of emotions. When some emotions are active, an interpersonal wish is present, and the experience of the emotion is due in part to a cognitive estimate of this wish and its fate. Moreover, our view that emotions can both reflect the activation of an internal relational model and signal an intrapsychic mismatch is similar to Dahl's basic distinction between "IT" emotions and "ME" emotions. The IT emotions center on internal relations of self and other, whereas the ME emotions monitor the status of the self's wishes.

Otto Kernberg has demonstrated the utility of analyzing internal relationships, for purposes of understanding affect and for many other purposes as well. His theory of affect (Kernberg, 1976, 1982) has influenced the one offered here. In his theory, inborn affects color all internal object relations and form the basis for drives. Moreover, once drives and object relations are developed, the presence of an affect signals the activation of a drive, and—most importantly for us—is inseparable from a corresponding self and object representation. These "self-object-affect units" have much in common with the RRM-state structures in our theory.

The view of emotion presented here also has close correspondences with that of Arlow (1977) because it is in part derived from study of his work. Arlow's central contention is that affects must be understood on the basis of *unconscious fan-*

tasies and that without a consideration of these fantasies the theoretical or clinical analysis of an affect must be incomplete, incorrect, or incoherent. As a consequence, he disputes those within and outside psychoanalysis who regard affects as products of biological evolution, essentially neurophysiological. He also rejects the related view that affects exist in some preset, limited number, each one with an identifiable essence—Arlow likens it to a "Platonic ideal"—which is the same from one person to another. Instead, he argues, underlying every instance of affect is a specific unconscious fantasy, and this fantasy is the key to grasping the nature of the affect and its "organic unity" of cognition, feeling tone, and physiology.

The unconscious fantasy of which Arlow (1977) speaks is similar to an RRM, both in its structure and in its effects on emotion and perception. Like RRMs, unconscious fantasies are thought to bring affects about and to constitute their essence. We have described above how the RRM gives rise to emotions appropriate to the various steps in its unfolding "script"; in a similar way, Arlow traces an affect to an unconscious fantasy in which it is natural and appropriate. The emotional function of an RRM is similar, for when these are activated, they give rise to appropriate emotions. Arlow also attributes to unconscious fantasies the property of influencing perception, tending to make perceptions conform to them; when one is gloomy, the world looks gloomy. RRMs, like all schemas, also have this property; as we have noted, the currently activated RRM—the "working model" of a situation—*assimilates* perceptions to itself, until it is replaced by a different working model. In distinction to Arlow, we would emphasize that the RRM underlying an emotion need not be a primitive scenario which is unacceptable to the person—i.e., a "dynamically unconscious" idea. Such scenarios may indeed underlie emotions. However, many other sorts of scenarios may play this role, including compromised ones which are perfectly acceptable to consciousness.

Brenner's (1974, 1982) theory of emotion is also an important milestone in developing a cognitive and relational affect theory. Brenner defines affects as "(a) sensations of pleasure, of unpleasure, or of a mixture of the two plus (b) thoughts, memories, wishes, fears—in a word, ideas" (1982, p. 41). The cognitive content (particularly, in our view, models of interpersonal interaction) is intrinsic to emotion. A central feature of Brenner's model is its assertion that, apart from the gross differentiation between pleasant and unpleasant, differences between emotions are a consequence of the specific "ideas" attached to them. Thus, emotions differ from one person to another, and the labels applied to them—joy, anger, embarrassment, guilt—are only approximations, often giving a false appearance of uniformity.

Lewin and Emde have particular relevance to a relational theory of affects. Lewin (1965) emphasized the intrinsic "structure" of affects and Emde (1980, 1988a) conceptualizes affects as complex organizations that may cross the border from "I" to "we." Bowlby's (1969) theory holds "emotion" to characterize a state of mind or being and does not posit emotions as causal entities (pp. 116–120). Tomkins (1979) and the philosopher de Sousa (1980) have both argued that relational models are central to emotion. Lazarus et al. (1970) and Averill (1982) have also given a prominent place to interpersonal transactions in their theories of emotion. Averill (in press), like Tomkins (1979) and Mandler (1984), gives a fundamental place to the concept of schemas in a theory of emotion.

Summary

The affect theory we have presented is a partial one. It emphasizes states, schemas, control of emotionality, and relational meaning. Its key points are as follows:

1. Considered as an aspect of mind, emotions are not separate from meaning systems. Emotionality often results from activation of self-other meanings (i.e., person schemas).

2. Meaning systems use schemas that contain potentials

for emotion as part of a sequence of concepts and/or actions. Emotionality occurs as the sequence unfolds.

3. The world and the self are examined unconsciously, and unconscious processing can lead to activation of schemas leading to affective arousal and emotional expressions. Parallel processing by diverse schemas can lead to competing or contradictory emotional arousals.

4. Recurrent patterns involving complex emotion can be modeled within a schema such as a role-relationship model.

5. Emotional activation can also occur as the result of a comparison or matching of one meaning with another meaning, one schema with another schema, with mismatches leading to emotional alarms or signals.

6. The processes of emotional activation are themselves meaning structures, and there are emotional responses to these meanings.

7. Parallel emotional responsivity patterns can be modeled as a configuration of schemas comprised of desired, dreaded, and compromise role-relationship models.

8. Role-relationship model configurations contain information pertinent to motives and defensive purposes, and so model emotional conflict in a relational manner useful to interpretive work.

9. Emotional experiences and expressions can be controlled by schematized purposive unconscious control processes that can affect concepts (e.g., meanings, memories) and schemas (e.g., role-relationship models). Conscious self-reflection can lead to new symbol structures and a chance to override unconscious habitual control processes and risk a trial of new emotional action and experience.

REFERENCES

Abelson, R. P. (1976). Script processing in attitude formation and decision making. In *Cognition and Social Behavior,* ed. J. S. Carrol & J. W. Payne. Hillsdale, N.J.: Erlbaum, pp. 33–45.

ARLOW, J. A. (1969). Unconscious fantasy and disturbance of conscious experience. *Psychoanal. Q.,* 38:1-27.

——— (1977). Affects and the psychoanalytic situation. *Int. J. Psychoanal.,* 58:157-170.

AVERILL, J. R. (1982). *Anger and Aggression: An Essay on Emotion.* New York: Springer.

——— (in press). Emotions as episodic dispositions, cognitive schemas, and transitory social roles. In *Perspectives in Personality,* ed. D. Ozer, J. M. Healy, & A. J. Stewart. Greenwich, Conn.: JAI Press.

BARTLETT, F. C. (1932). *Remembering.* Cambridge: Cambridge Univ. Press.

BOWLBY, J. (1969). *Attachment and Loss,* Vol. 1. New York: Basic Books.

BRENNER, C. (1974). On the nature and development of affects. *Psychoanal. Q.,* 43:532-556.

——— (1982). *The Mind in Conflict.* New York: Int. Univ. Press.

BREUER, J. & FREUD, S. (1895). Studies in hysteria. *S. E.,* 2.

DAHL, H. (1978). A new psychoanalytic model of motivation. *Psychoanal. & Contemp. Thought,* 3:373-408.

DE RIVERA, J. (1977). A structural theory of emotions. *Psychol. Issues,* Monogr. 40. New York: Int. Univ. Press.

DE SOUSA, R. (1980). The rationality of emotions. In *Explaining Emotions,* ed. A. O. Rorty. Berkeley: Univ. California Press, pp. 127-151.

EMDE, R. N. (1980). Toward a psychoanalytic theory of affect. In *The Course of Life,* ed. S. I. Greenspan & G. H. Pollock. Washington, D.C.: U. S. Government Printing Office, pp. 63-112.

——— (1988a). Development terminable and interminable: I. Innate and motivational factors from infancy. *Int. J. Psychoanal.,* 69:23-42.

——— (1988b). Development terminable and interminable: II. Recent psychoanalytic theory and therapeutic considerations. *Int. J. Psychoanal.,* 69:283-296.

FREUD, S. (1915a). Observations on transference-love. *S. E.,* 12.

——— (1915b). The unconscious. *S. E.,* 14.

——— (1926). Inhibition, symptoms and anxiety. *S. E.,* 20.

——— (1933). Anxiety and instinctual life. *S. E.,* 22.

FRIDHANDLER, B. M. (1986). Outline of a psychoanalytic theory of emotion. Unpublished doctoral dissertation, University of Massachusetts.

HOROWITZ, M. J. (1976). *Stress Response Syndromes.* Northvale, N.J.: Jason Aronson.

——— (1979). *States of Mind,* 1st ed. New York: Plenum.

——— (1987). *States of Mind,* 2nd ed. New York: Plenum.

——— (1988a). *Introduction to Psychodynamics.* New York: Basic Books.

——— Ed. (1988b). *Psychodynamics and Cognition.* Chicago: Univ. Chicago Press.

——— ed. (1991). *Person Schemas and Maladaptive Interpersonal Patterns.* Chicago: Univ. Chicago Press.

——— & BECKER, S. S. (1972). Cognitive response to stress. In *Psychoanalysis and Contemporary Science,* 1:285-305, ed. R. Holt & E. Peterfreund. New York: Macmillan.

——— MARMAR, C., KRUPNICK, J., WILNER, N., KALTREIDER, N., & WALLERSTEIN, R. (1984). *Personality Styles and Brief Psychotherapy.* New York: Basic Books.

IZARD, C. E. (1977). *Human Emotion.* New York: Plenum.
KERNBERG, O. F. (1976). *Object Relations Theory and Clinical Psychoanalysis.* New York: Aronson.
——— (1982). Self, ego, affects, and drives. *J. Amer. Psychoanal. Assn.,* 30:893-917.
KOHUT, H. (1971). *The Analysis of the Self.* New York: Int. Univ. Press.
KNAPP, P. H. (1991). Self-other schemas: Core organizers of human experience. In *Person Schemas and Maladaptive Interpersonal Patterns,* ed. M. J. Horowitz. Chicago: Univ. Chicago Press, pp. 81-102.
LAZARUS, R. S., AVERILL, J. R., & OPTON, E. M. (1970). Toward a cognitive theory of emotion. In *Feeling and Emotion,* ed. M. B. Arnold. New York: Academic Press, pp. 207-232.
LEWIN, B. D. (1965). Reflections on affect. In *Drives, Affects, Behavior,* Vol. 2, ed. M. Schur. New York: Int. Univ. Press, pp. 23-37.
LICHTENBERG, J. D. (1975). The development of the sense of self. *J. Amer. Psychoanal. Assn.,* 23:453-484.
LUBORSKY, L., CRITS-CHRISTOPH, P., FRIEDMAN, S., MARK, D., & SCHAFFLER, P. (1991). Freud's concept of a transference template and vicissitudes of the core conflictual relationship theme. In *Person Schemas and Maladaptive Interpersonal Patterns,* ed. M. J. Horowitz. Chicago: Univ. Chicago Press, pp. 167-196.
MANDLER, G. (1979). Emotion. In *The First Century of Experimental Psychology,* ed. E. Hearst. Hillsdale, N.J.: Erlbaum, pp. 275-322.
——— (1984). *Mind and Body: Psychology of Emotion and Stress.* New York: Norton.
MINSKY, M. (1975). A framework for representing knowledge. In *The Psychology of Computer Vision*, ed. P. H. Winston. New York: McGraw-Hill.
PAUL, I. H. (1967). The concept of schema in memory theory. In *Motives and Thought,* ed. R. R. Holt. New York: Int. Univ. Press, pp. 219-258.
PERRY, J. C. & COOPER, S. H. (1989). An empirical study of defense mechanisms: I. Clinical interview and life vignette ratings. *Arch. Gen. Psychiat.,* 46:444-452.
PIAGET, J. (1952). *The Origins of Intelligence in Children.* New York: Int. Univ. Press.
——— (1970). *Structuralism.* New York: Basic Books.
PLUTCHIK, R. (1980). *Emotion: A Psychoevolutionary Synthesis.* New York: Harper & Row.
PULVER, S. E. (1971). Can affects be unconscious? *Int. J. Psychoanal.,* 52:347-354.
RUMELHART, D. E. (1975). *Explorations in Cognition.* San Francisco: Freeman.
——— (1980). Schemata: The building blocks of cognition. In *Theoretical Issues in Reading Comprehension,* ed. R. Spiro, B. Bruce, & W. Brewer. Hillsdale, N.J.: Erlbaum, pp. 33-58.
——— & MCCLELLAND, J. L., Eds. (1986). *Parallel Distributed Processing,* 2 Vols. Cambridge, Mass.: MIT Press.
——— & ORTONY, A. (1977). The representation of knowledge in memory. In *Schooling and the Acquisition of Knowledge,* ed. R. C. Anderson, R. Spiro, & W. Montague. Hillsdale, N.J.: Erlbaum, pp. 99-135.
SANDLER, J. (1960). The background of safety. *Int. J. Psychoanal.,* 41:352-356.

SCHAFER, R. (1964). The clinical analysis of affects. *J. Amer. Psychoanal. Assn.,* 12:275–299.

——— (1968). *Aspects of Internalization.* New York: Int. Univ. Press.

SLAP, J. W. & SAYKIN, A. J. (1983). The schema: Basic concept in a nonmetapsychological model of the mind. *Psychoanal. & Contemp. Thought,* 6:305–325.

STERN, D. N. (1985). *The Interpersonal World of the Infant.* New York: Basic Books.

STINSON, C. & PALMER, S. (1991). Parallel distributed processing models of person schemas and psychopathologies. In *Person Schemas and Maladaptive Interpersonal Patterns,* ed. M. J. Horowitz. Chicago: Univ. Chicago Press, pp. 339–378.

TOMKINS, S. S. (1979). Script theory: Differential magnification of affects. In *Nebraska Symposium on Motivation,* Vol. 26, ed. H. E. Howe & R. A. Dienstbier. Lincoln: Univ. Nebraska Press, pp. 201–236.

VAILLANT, G. E., BOND, M., & VAILLANT, C. O. (1986). An empirically validated hierarchy of defense mechanisms. *Arch. Gen. Psychiat.,* 43:786–794.

Center for the Study of Neuroses
Langley Porter Psychiatric Institute
401 Parnassus Avenue
San Francisco, CA 94143

THE PSYCHOPATHOLOGY OF HATRED

Otto F. Kernberg, M.D.

The basic affect state characterizing the activation of aggression is that of rage. Hatred is a derived, complex, aggressive affect characterized by a chronic, stable, characterologically anchored, internalized object relation involving the self and a desperately needed and yet dreaded, persecutory object.

This paper describes a spectrum of severity of hatred in the transference, ranging from the need to destroy the object (or to destroy oneself in identifying with that object) at one extreme, through an intermediate zone in which what predominates is the need to make the object suffer physically or mentally while preserving it, to milder forms of hatred expressed in the need to exercise power over a submissive object.

Clinical examples illustrate this spectrum of hatred, ranging from aggressive psychopathy to neurotic, sadistic character traits. I explore the corresponding dynamics, and conclude with technical considerations in dealing with transference and countertransference developments when the patient's hatred is activated.

Affects and Drives

In this paper, I shall focus on hatred, a complex affect derived from rage, itself a primary affect at the core of the aggressive drive. Hatred, a universally present disposition, occupies a central role in severe personality disorders that are characterized by the psychopathology of aggression. In order to provide a background for the formulations regarding affects and drives that I present here, let me briefly recapitulate the ideas on which these formulations are based.

Associate Chairman and Medical Director, The New York Hospital-Cornell Medical Center, Westchester Division; Professor of Psychiatry, Cornell University Medical College; Training and Supervising Analyst, Columbia University Center for Psychoanalytic Training and Research.

Presented at the Symposium on "Rage, Power, and Aggression" sponsored by the Columbia University Center for Psychoanalytic Training and Research and the Association for Psychoanalytic Medicine, New York, October 14, 1989.

In earlier work (1984, chap. 14; 1990a, 1990b, 1990c) I proposed that libidinal and aggressive drives are a hierarchically supraordinate motivational system constituted by affects which are their "building blocks." Affects are behavior patterns that include a specific cognitive appraisal (basically, of perceived reality as "desirable" or "undesirable"), a specific expressive facial pattern, a subjective experience of pleasurable (rewarding), or painful (aversive) quality, and both muscular and neurovegetative components. The facial expression is part of a general communicative pattern that differentiates each affect.

Affects may be classified as primary and derived. The former make their appearance within the first two to three years of life; they have an intense, global quality, and their cognitive elements are diffuse and not well differentiated. Derived affects consist of cognitively elaborated combinations of the primary affects; unlike primary affects, they may not show all their original components with equal strength, and their experiential aspects gradually come to dominate the psychophysiological and facial communicative ones. For these derived affects I would reserve the terms *emotions* or *feelings.* This distinction derives from the clinical observations regarding primitive affect states and emotional developments in the psychoanalytic situation. I use the term *affect state* to refer to the temporary activation of a particular affect. The term "primitive" refers to affects that are either primal or early derived ones, characterized by a relatively full-fledged presentation of all their component features.

I also proposed that early affective development is based on the fixation of early, affectively invested object relations in the form of affective memory. The empirical research of Emde (1987; Emde et al., 1978), Izard (1978), and Stern (1985) points to the central function of object relations in the activation of the infant's affects. Contemporary affect theory emphasizes the signaling function of affects in the relationship of the infant to the caregiver. This connection of object relations with the activation of affects supports the proposal that early affect states fixed in memory always involve an object relation. The activation of different affect states toward the same object takes place as the infant or child performs different developmental tasks and under the influence of biologically determined instinctive behavior patterns. The variety of affect states directed to the same object may provide an economical explanation for how affects are linked with each other and are gradually integrated into a supraordinate motivational system that becomes the sexual or aggressive drive. Libido, or the sexual drive, results from the integration of positive or rewarding affect states such as elation and sexual excitement. Aggression as a drive results from the integration of negative or aversive affects, such as hatred, rage, and disgust. Rage may in fact be considered the central affect of aggression. It is under conditions of intense, peak affect states, both pleasurable and painful, that the infant's relationship to the caregiver is highlighted and powerfully reinforces the establishment of affective memory: here, generalized arousal and intensity of motivational state are maximal.

The unconscious integration of affectively invested early object relations requires assuming the existence of a higher level motivational system than that represented by affect states per se, a motivational system that is provided by the libidinal and aggressive drives. This concept of drives does justice to the complexity of the affective developments in relation to the parental objects. In summary, I proposed that affects are the link between their biologically determined ("wired in") components, on the one hand, and their intrapsychic organization into the overall drives, on the other. The correspondence of the series of pleasurable or rewarding and painful or aversive affect states with the dual lines of libido and aggression makes sense both clinically and theoretically.

Memory structures acquired during peak affect states will be very different from those acquired during quiescent or low-level affect states. When the infant is in a quiescent or low-level affect state, the memory structures established will be largely of a cognitive, discriminatory nature and contribute directly to ego development. Ordinary learning thus occurs under conditions in which alertness is focused on the immediate situation and tasks, with little distortion derived from affective arousal and no particular defensive mechanism interfering with it. These memory structures constitute the early precursors, we might say, of more specialized and adaptive ego functioning—the affective memory structures of early consciousness. Affect, in short, also guides and facilitates memory organization under conditions of low-level affect activation. Here, memory is apt to be continuous and schematic, procedural rather than declarative (Robert Emde, personal communication).

In contrast, peak affect experiences facilitate the internalization of primitive object relations organized along the axes of rewarding or all-good and aversive or all-bad objects. The experiences of self and object under the impact of extreme affect activation acquire an intensity that facilitates the laying down of affectively impregnated memory structures that have an episodic, declarative quality. These affective memory structures, constituted in essence of self and object representations in the context of a specific peak affect experience, represent the earliest intrapsychic structures of the symbiotic stage of development (Mahler and Furer, 1968). They mark the beginning of structure formation of internalized object relations, as well as the beginning of the organization of libidinal and aggressive drives. Peak affect states represent, by definition, extremely desirable (pleasurable) or undesirable (painful) experiences, which motivate wishes to repeat or avoid similar affective experiences. These wishes, gradually elaborated in unconscious fantasy, determine the motivational repertoire of what eventually constitutes the organized id.

I suggest that the concept of erotogenic zones as the source of libido be replaced by that of a peak-affect state that includes all physiologically activated functions and bodily zones which become involved in the affectively invested interactions of the infant and child with mother under condition of erotic, sensual arousal. Further, I suggest that the central affect around which clusters the affective constellation of libido as a drive is the affect of sexual excitement (Kernberg, 1990c). It is curious but perhaps not surprising that sexual excitement as an affect has received much less attention from empirical research on early affect development than the other affects. It may well be, however, that sexual excitement, in its maximum intensity and definite form, requires a more complex and lengthier development than other primary affects.

The affect of rage, in contrast, the early characteristics and development of which have been documented extensively by infant researchers, constitutes, in my view, the essential affect around which clusters the complex affective formation of aggression as a drive. In what follows, I focus for the most part on the developmental vicissitudes of rage that lead to the dominance, in certain patients with severe character pathology, of hatred, which emerges as an overriding affect in the transference. This emergence permits the psychoanalytic exploration of hatred, but also presents formidable challenges to the analyst's efforts to resolve the corresponding psychopathology in the transference. The basis for the formulations that follow includes, on the one hand, the relationship between the pathology of mother-infant relations in infants at high risk and the development of severe aggression in such infants (Massie, 1977; Gaensbauer and Sands, 1979; Call, 1980; Roiphe and Galenson, 1981; Fraiberg, 1982; Galenson, 1986; Osofsky, 1987) and, on the other hand, the psychopathology of severe aggression in the transference in patients with borderline personality organization and narcissistic and antisocial personality disorders (Winnicott, 1949; Bion, 1957, 1959, 1970; Green, 1977; Moser, 1978; Ogden, 1979; Krause, 1988; Krause and Lutolf, 1988; Grossman, 1989; Kernberg, 1989, 1990a). The observations of severe regression in patients who show predominance of hatred in the transference constitute the principal source for the formulations that follow.

Rage

Clinically, the basic affect state characterizing the activation of aggression in the transference is that of rage. Other aggressive affects include anger and irritation. Irritation is a mild aggressive affect that, in the form of a chronic mood, takes the form of irritability. Anger is a more intense affect than irritation, usually more differentiated regarding its cognitive content and the nature of the object relationship that is activated. A full-fledged rage reaction, its overwhelming nature, diffuseness, "blurring" of specific cognitive contents and corresponding object relations, may erroneously convey the idea that it is a "pure" primitive affect. Clinically, however, the analysis of rage reaction—as is true also for other intense affect states—always reveals an underlying conscious or unconscious fantasy involving a specific relation between an aspect of the self and an aspect of a significant other.

Infant research documents the early appearance of rage as an affect, and its primordial function to eliminate a source of pain or irritation. As the infant's cognitive appraisal of his environment expands, rage no longer functions in this limited way, and now includes the desire to eliminate an obstacle or barrier to gratification. At this stage, the originally biological function of rage, namely, signaling a state of pain to the caregiver to facilitate the elimination of the irritant, becomes a more focused appeal to the caretaker to restore a desired state of gratification. In the unconscious fantasies that develop around rage reactions, rage comes to signify both the activation of an all-bad object relationship and the wish to eliminate it and restore an all-good one. At a later developmental stage, rage reactions may function as last-ditch efforts to restore a sense of autonomy in the face of severely frustrating situations unconsciously perceived as the threatening activation of all-bad, persecutory object relationships. A state of narcissistic equilibrium may be restored by a violent assertion of one's will, representing an unconscious identification with an idealized—all-good—object.

Clinically, the intensity of the aggressive affects—whether irritation (mild), anger (moderate), or rage (maximal)—correlates roughly with the psychological function of the affects: to assert one's autonomy, to eliminate an obstacle or barrier to a desired degree of satisfaction, or to eliminate or destroy a source of profound pain or frustration. But the psychopathology of aggression is not limited to intensity and frequency of rage attacks: the most severe and dominant of the affects that jointly come to constitute aggression as a drive is the complex or elaborated affect of hatred. As we move from the transference developments of patients with neurotic personality organization to those of borderline personality organization, particularly those with severe narcissistic pathology and antisocial features, we are increasingly faced not only with rage attacks in the transference, but with the development of hatred, which emerges along with certain typical secondary characterological expressions and defenses against the awareness of this affect.

Hatred

a) *Clinical Characteristics.* Hatred is a complex aggressive affect: in contrast to the acuteness of rage reactions, and the easily varying cognitive aspects of anger and rage, the cognitive aspect of hatred is chronic and stable. Hatred also presents with characterological anchoring that includes powerful rationalizations and corresponding distortions of ego and superego functioning. The primary aim of one consumed by hatred is to destroy the object (a specific object of unconscious fantasy and this object's conscious derivatives), an object who at bottom is both needed and desired and the destruction of whom is equally needed and desired. The understanding of this paradox is at the center of the psychoanalytic investigation of hatred. Hatred is not always pathological: as a response to an objective, real danger of physical or pathological destruction, a threat to the survival of oneself and those one loves, hatred is a normal elaboration of rage aimed to eliminate that danger. But unconscious motivations usually enter and intensify hatred, as in the search for revenge. As a chronic, characterological predisposition, hatred always reflects the psychopathology of aggression.

b) *Extreme Forms of Hatred.* An extreme form of hatred demands the physical elimination of the object, and may be expressed in murder, or in a radical devaluation of the object that may generalize in the form of a symbolic destruction of all objects, that is, all potential relationships with significant others, as clinically observable in antisocial personality structures. This extreme form of hatred may also sometimes be expressed in suicide, where the self is identified with the hated object and self-elimination is the only way to destroy the object as well.

Clinically, some patients with the syndrome of malignant narcissism (narcissistic personality, ego-syntonic aggression, paranoid and antisocial tendencies [Kernberg, 1989]) and "psychopathic" transferences (deceptiveness as a dominant transference feature) may consistently and ruthlessly attempt to exploit, destroy, symbolically castrate, or dehumanize significant others, including the therapist, to an extent that defies the therapist's efforts to protect or recapture some "island" of an idealized primitive, all-good object relationship. At the same time, the transference may apparently be remarkably free from overt aggression; chronic deceptiveness, the search for a primitive all-good self state that eliminates all objects—such as by means of alcohol or drugs, and unconscious and conscious efforts to coopt the therapist in the exploitation or destruction of others—may dominate the scene. The therapist's efforts to stand up against this diffuse, generalized destruction or corruption of everything valuable may be experienced by the patient (by projective mechanisms) as a brutal attack. This leads to the emergence of direct rage and hatred in the transference: we witness the transformation of a "psychopathic" into a "paranoid" transference. Paradoxically, this transformation is a frail hope for these patients. The following case illustrates all these issues.

Mrs. A, a housewife with borderline personality organization, a narcissistic personality disorder displaying the syndrome of malignant narcissism, was in intensive, long-term, psychoanalytic psychotherapy. She had a history, from early childhood, of an intense relationship with her father, a prominent public figure whose private life was in striking contrast to his public display of puritanical and moralistic convictions, and who encouraged and colluded with her in deceiving her mother. Abuse of hypnotics, sedatives, and analgesics was rampant in the home: the patient and her siblings as well as her mother swallowed pills casually at times of frustration or unhappiness. Mrs. A's self-mutilating symptoms had brought her close to death several times, and she had managed to burn herself with cigarettes to the extent of suffering from third-degree burns in various parts of her body. Serious suicidal attempts punctuated her life throughout late adolescence and into her 20s, when she started her treatment.

At a certain point of her psychotherapy, she managed to obtain anxiolytic and analgesic medications from several physicians by providing them with false information. She also became engaged in several sexual relationships while professing concern over her husband's serious illness and his failure to be appropriately concerned about this illness. She had married shortly before starting this psychotherapy. She had also joined a social group active in proselytizing against the use of drugs; Mrs. A gave speeches protesting against drug abuse while abusing them herself. In the psychotherapy, she evinced an attitude of provocative indifference toward what the therapist was communicating to her, alternating with paranoid suspiciousness to any change of routine in the sessions.

Mrs. A showed an inordinate talent for finding the weaknesses of others that would then justify her exploitation or mistreatment of them. Her dreams reflected extremely sadistic fantasies, such as her participation in mass murder of inmates of psychiatric hospitals, her being a member of the prison guard of Nazi concentration camps, and her throwing to their death couples from balconies of high-rise buildings. Although she gave no evidence of rage in her daily life or in the transference, she seemed aloof and indifferent.

Any efforts the therapist made to confront her with the emotional implications of her behavior brought about intense paranoid developments in the transference, micropsychotic episodes in the hours, with quasi-hallucinatory experiences during and in between the sessions, and suicidal behavior. In the case of Mrs. A, the predominance of "psychopathic" over "paranoid" transferences (her chronic deceptiveness in relation to her therapist) indicates the most severe kind of activation of the psychopathology of hatred in the treatment situation. The behavior that symbolically reflected the defensive dismantling of all object relationships protected her from activation in the transference of the intense hatred manifest in her dreams. Consistent clarification, confrontation, and interpretation of the deceptiveness toward the therapist, the other physicians, her husband, and the social organization in which she worked, shifted that psychopathic transference into a paranoid one. At first she projected her hatred onto the therapist and reacted with intense suspiciousness and even psychoticlike regression in the hours; only later on could she tolerate the direct awareness of the intense hatred that dominated all her object relationships, including her attitude toward the healthier aspects of her own personality. At one point, she became aware of how badly she had been treating an old friend of hers, felt genuinely regretful and remorseful over her own behavior toward her, and was able to recognize the displacement of similar feelings toward the therapist away from him and onto this friend. The sequence of psychopathic to paranoid to depressive transferences is typical for the transformation and resolution of severe hatred in the transference.

c) *Moderate Degrees of Hatred.* Hatred takes the form of sadistic tendencies and wishes in conditions of lesser severity. Here the patient's wish, unconscious or conscious, is to make the object suffer, with a sense of profound conscious or unconscious enjoyment of that suffering. This sadism may take the form of a sexual perversion with actual, physical damaging of the object, or of characterological sadism as part of the syndrome of malignant narcissism, or a sadomasochistic personality structure, or, sometimes, of a rationalized, intellectualized form of cruelty that includes powerful wishes to humiliate the object. In contrast to the earlier, more extreme form of hatred mentioned, here the wish is not to eliminate but to maintain the relationship with the hated object, in an enactment of an object relationship between a sadistic agent and a paralyzed victim. The desire and pleasure in inflicting pain are central here, representing an implicit condensation of aggression and libidinal excitement in inducing such suffering. The following case illustrates this level of psychopathology.

Miss B, in her early 30s, is a patient with a narcissistic personality functioning on an overt borderline level, severe suicidal tendencies without depression, failure in her intellectual pursuits in spite of high intelligence, but without antisocial features. Miss B, who had been subjected to severe physical abuse by her stepmother throughout her early childhood, had only a vague memory of her father, who died before she entered elementary school. She presented intense rage attacks in the early stages of her treatment, efforts to control the therpist's life by refusing to leave his office at the end of the sessions and by insistent telephone calls. But, with sufficient structuring of the treatment situation, she was able gradually to reduce the direct expression of violence in the hours and in her daily life outside the hours as well. At the same time, she used the hours to acquire knowledge from him that she would then elaborate herself to deal with her problems, while carefully avoiding any actual collaborative work with him. As a result, his interpretations seemed to be vaguely related to a gradual improvement she showed outside the hours, but were consistently rejected by her within the hours themselves.

In the fourth year of this psychotherapy, and with a marked reduction in the acting out outside and in the sessions, it was possible to explore a silent but consistent relationship she evinced in the hours with him, characterized by the combination of arrogance, curiosity (about him, not herself), and the "pseudostupidity" described by Bion (1957). The activation of a pathological grandiose self identified with an omnipotent, sadistic, and envious image of her stepmother finally clarified the nature of the unconscious, sadistic destruction of everything coming from the therapist silently occurring in the hours, and gradually led to the emergence of direct hatred, death wishes, and sadistic triumph over the therapist in the hours.

Only after consistent, painstaking analysis of the paranoid transferences that emerged as a consequence of the efforts to analyze the narcissistic resistances in the transference was this patient finally able to acknowledge the pleasurable aspect of her aggression, her intense hatred of the therapist's capacity to help her; she was then able to reduce the acting out of unconscious envy together with the reduction of the paranoid transference and the beginning capacity for guilt feelings in the hour, the initiation of "depressive" transferences. Miss B did not show psychopathic transferences; she started with paranoid ones that eventually changed into depressive ones.

d) *Mild Forms of Hatred.* An even milder form of hatred centers around the desire to dominate the object, a search for power over it that may include sadistic components, but tends to be self-limited in the attacks on the object by the object's submission and the implied reconfirmation of the subject's dominance, freedom and autonomy by this very submission to him. Here, anal-sadistic components dominate over the more primitive oral-aggressive ones in the more severe form of hatred. An individual's assertion of hierarchical superiority and "territoriality" in social interactions, and individuals in groups showing the aggressive aspects of regressive, small and large, group processes are the most frequent manifestations of this milder level of hatred. The following patient, although presenting a psychotic illness, illustrates this milder form of hatred.

Miss C, in her late 20s suffered from a chronic paranoid schizophrenic illness. Her relationship with her mother had been characterized by intense ambivalence from early childhood on, great dependency upon this dominating and overwhelming mother, and intense rebelliousness against her, which culminated during late adolescence in Miss C's abrupt departure from home. The father maintained a warm and somewhat erotized relationship with her, but avoided becoming involved in her conflictual interactions with her mother; she experienced him as pleasing her, and secretly on her side, but weak and overtly abandoning her in her fight with her mother.

After several unhappy love affairs, Miss C had entered psychotherapy in which she regressed and became overtly psychotic for the first time. She experienced acute depersonalization, ideas of reference, and unusual powers of perception. Impulsive moves from one part of the country to another helped her to keep her psychotic symptoms from destroying intimate relationships. She eventually developed multiple auditory and visual hallucinations, chronic delusions of bodily and thought control, and intense psychomotor agitation, which required hospitalization. Over a period of one year in the hospital, she gradually compensated with the help of moderate doses of neuroleptics, but without abandoning some basic psychotic convictions, particularly the idea that other people, especially women, were attempting to steal her "energy."

She entered psychoanalytic psychotherapy with me while psychopharmacological maintenance with low-dose neuroleptics permitted her to function outside the hospital and to resume a position in computer programming. The patient was aware that she had to control and keep to herself her convictions that women were stealing her energy, and in the sessions this symptom became a major transference pattern. Characteristically, at times when she treated me as the benign, impotent, yet seductive father, she became very suspicious in the hours, watched my every movement, and interpreted minor shifts in my position as an indication that I was now stealing energy from her, and therefore weakening her capacity to think—to the extent of blocking all her thought processes.

It gradually emerged that these developments occurred at times when she felt sexual feelings toward me, unconsciously implying sexual feelings to her father, and projected these feelings onto me with the fear that I would want to rape her. Then she experienced me as acquiring powerful hostile capabilities leading to my enriching myself at the cost of robbing her of her physical and mental energy. Simultaneously, it also became clear that she experienced herself to be in an intense rivalry with the secretaries of the office suite where I saw her, and she eventually experienced these secretaries as engaged in a conspiracy against her, making fun of her, and also attempting to steal her energy.

Still later, she was able to become aware of her intense hatred of these secretaries as representing maternal figures, and was able to tolerate fantasies of attacking and destroying them. She was also able to experience intense hatred against me because I had not protected her against the "sadistic" female nursing staff, as she saw it, who allegedly were trying to destroy her capacity to think and to become independent while she was in the hospital.

Miss C now became aware of a confusion in her feelings toward me, a shift between erotic feelings and hatred that was so intense that she could no longer recognize the very nature of her feelings, nor if she or I or both of us had these feelings.

At one point, in bringing all these elements together, I interpreted that confusion as derived from her fear of experiencing sexual fantasies and wishes toward me as a symbolic father because it would lead to her mother's immediate aggressive destruction of her mind, an aggression from mother that was particularly dangerous because, as she saw it, the mother was aware of the patient's own murderous rage against her. As the patient became less afraid to experience her feelings of hatred against the mother and motherly representatives in my office and at her work, the enactment of the delusion that I and other people stole her energy gradually subsided.

This case, in my view, illustrates severe hatred condensing preoedipal and oedipal issues under an overriding oedipal structure, projective identification of that hatred with a lack of differentiation between herself and her object, and the effort to deal with her hatred by psychotic projection onto threatening maternal objects. Miss C had been subject to severe rage attacks when she was in frank psychotic regression. As she became able to function more appropriately in reality and her psychotic symptoms became more circumscribed to the transference, the chronicity and intensity of her hatred of mother emerged as major sources of the regressive nature of her oedipal conflicts, the defensive refusion with an idealized but erotically threatening father image, and the return of the projected aggression in the form of delusions of bodily influence.

e) *Neurotic and Normal Integration of Hatred.* Finally, under conditions of relatively normal superego integration and within a neurotic personality organization with a well-differentiated tripartite structure, hatred may take the form of a rationalized identification with a strict and punitive superego, the aggressive assertion of perhaps idiosyncratic but well-rationalized systems of morality, justified indignation, and primitive levels of commitment to vindictive ideologies. Hatred at this level, of course, bridges over to the sublimatory function of courageous aggressive assertion at the service of commitment to ideals and ethical systems.

At this level of integration of hatred there is usually also a tendency toward self-directed hatred in the form of cruelty of the superego. Clinically, we see a potential for a transformation of transferences from the primitive "paranoid" into the more advanced "depressive" type. Masochistic and sadomasochistic personality structures and mixed neurotic constellations including paranoid, masochistic, and sadistic traits may experience relatively sudden shifts between depressive and paranoid transference regression. In contrast, at more severe levels of the psychopathology of hatred the transference is overwhelmingly paranoid, except when psychopathic transferences defend the patient against the paranoid ones. Here, what dominates is the "paranoid urge to betray" (Jacobson, 1971). The following patient illustrates the shifts between paranoid and depressive transferences in the context of activation of hatred.

Miss D had a depressive-masochistic personality structure with strong paranoid features, and a chronic, characterological depression that brought her to treatment. She was in standard psychoanalysis, four sessions per week. In the third year of her psychoanalysis, a severe depression developed related to the activation in the transference of the relationship with her deeply disturbed, drug-addicted mother. During Miss D's childhood, the mother, under the influence of drugs, would reject the patient and treat her in a sadistic and neglectful way, and, while engaged in severe conflicts with the equally drug-addicted father, let the patient in on all the sexual and nonsexual intimacies of the relationship between the parents. The development of this transference can be understood if we examine an important transition that took place in the transference after two years of treatment.

In the first two years of treatment the transference remained at an advanced oedipal level, with a nonsexualized idealization of the therapist as an ideal father and repression of underlying sexual feelings. After two years the transference changed, with the activation in Miss D of a sense of being misunderstood, mistreated, controlled, and brainwashed by the analyst. Her complaints of mistreatment on the part of the therapist alternated with angry, sarcastic outbursts in the sessions and abrupt storming out of his office. What is significant here is the "moralistic" tone in which hatred was expressed in the treatment situation, in the form of superego-determined, rationalized blaming of the analyst for not living up to the patient's expectations of perfection, oscillating with severe self-depreciation of the patient also reflecting cruel, exaggerated, and infantile superego attacks, all of them illustrating the absorption of hatred within her masochistic personality structure.

Now the sadomasochistic relationship with mother was enacted in the patient's alternation between masochistic complaints and sadistic attacks on the analyst in an escalating violence that, at times, made it practically impossible for the analyst to say anything without its triggering a rageful affect storm. Gradually the repeated interpretation that she was recreating in the hours the chaotic situation and the hateful relationship with her mother—in alternation of the enactment of the identification of the analyst with her mother while she became her infantile self, with the projection of her infantile self representation onto the analyst while she enacted her mother's image—permitted a clarification of this situation over a period of time. It became clear that the defensive activation of this relationship with her mother protected her against more deeply lying, positive, sexual feelings toward the analyst as oedipal father.

I return to the clinical characteristics of hatred. The entire spectrum of its corresponding affective and characterological components may be observed in patients of the second level of pathology mentioned before, who have at least a wish to preserve the hated object, and in whom the full range of characteristics of this affect may be observed in the transference. The chronicity, stability, and characterological anchoring of hatred is matched by the desire to inflict pain upon the object, characterological and sometimes sexual sadism, and cruelty.

Dynamics in the Transference

a) *Envy.* As I have pointed out in earlier work (1990a), primitive hatred often takes the form of an effort to destroy the potential for a gratifying human relationship and learning something of value in that human interaction. Underlying this need to destroy reality and communication in intimate relationships lies, I believe, unconscious and conscious envy of the object, particularly of the object not controlled from within by similar hatred. The cases of Mrs. A and Miss B presented these dynamics in dominant ways.

It was Melanie Klein (1957) who first pointed to the envy of the good object as a dominant characteristic of patients with severe narcissistic psychopathology. I believe that such envy is complicated by the patient's need to destroy his own awareness of this envy because it would expose the patient's terror over the savagery of his own hatred of what, *au fond,* he values in the object. Clinically, it is impressive how, under conditions of intense hatred, a patient's capacity for self-awareness is practically obliterated. Behind the envy of the object and the need to destroy and spoil anything good that might come from contacts with the object is also the terror of the unconscious identification with the originally hated—and needed—object. Envy may be considered both a source of a primitive form of hatred, intimately linked with oral aggression, greed, and voracity, and a complication of the hatred that derives from the fixation to trauma referred to below.

At the surface, the hatred of the unconsciously and consciously envied object is usually rationalized as the fear of the object's destructive potential. This destructive potential of the hated object derives from both actual aggression inflicted by essentially needed objects in the patient's past (in patients who have been severely traumatized) and the projection of their own rage and hatred upon that object.

Tendencies toward chronic and potentially severe self-mutilation and nondepressive suicidal behaviors frequently accompany the syndrome of malignant narcissism, where these manifestations of intense primitive hatred are dominant. Self-mutilation typically reflects unconscious identification with a hateful and hated object. Hatred and intolerance of communication with the object may protect the patient from what might otherwise emerge as a combination of cruel attacks on his part onto the object, paranoid fears of that object, and self-directed aggression in identification with the hated object.

Clinically, the transference characterized by a combination of arrogance, curiosity, and pseudostupidity (incapacity to reflect on what the therapist says), described by Bion (1957), illustrates the acting out of patients' envy of the therapist, destruction of meaning, and sadism.

b) *Fixation to the Trauma.* One of the most consistent features in transferences dominated by the acting out of severe hatred is the patient's intense involvement with the therapist, the extraordinary dependence manifest simultaneously with the aggression to the therapist, an impressive demonstration of the "fixation to the trauma." At the same time, in the patient's fantasies and fears, there is also the assumption that unless the patient consistently fights off the therapist, the patient will be subjected to a similar onslaught of hatred and sadistic exploitation and persecution by the therapist. Obviously, by means of projective identification, the patient is attributing to the therapist his own hatred and sadism, but, by the same token, the total situation illustrates the intimate link between the persecutor and the persecuted, master and slave, sadist and masochist; all referring in the last resort to the sadistic, frustrating, teasing mother and the helpless, paralyzed infant. The cases of Miss B, Miss C, and Miss D presented these dynamics at various levels of severity.

Basically, what the patient is enacting is an object relationship between persecutor and victim, with alternating identifications with these roles while projecting the reciprocal role onto the therapist. In the most severe cases, it is as if the only alternative to being victimized is to become a tyrant, and the repetitive assertion of hatred and sadism would appear to be the only form of survival and meaning, aside from murder, suicide, or psychopathy. In less severe cases, the psychopathology of envy of the good object emerges as an additional dynamic factor, the intolerance of the good object who escapes from that savagery and who is hated because of the willful withholding (as the patient fantasizes) of what could transform the object from a persecuting one into an ideal one. Here, the search for an ideal object, in the last resort an ideal mother, lies behind the unending, repetitive onslaught of hatred in the transference.

All these dynamics may emerge intimately condensed and combined in many cases, with differences in degree and proportion. What they have in common, however, is the intense motivation for maintaining the link with the hated object, a link that gratifies these various primitive transferences and is responsible for, in my view, the powerful fixation to this traumatic relationship.

c) *Pleasure in Pain.* In still less severe cases, where more sophisticated and elaborated types of sadomasochistic behaviors dominate within a neurotic personality organization, we discover the unconscious potential for pleasure in pain, the temptation to experience pain as a precondition for experiencing pleasure, in the context of castration anxiety, unconscious guilt over oedipal strivings, and as ultimate transformation of passively experienced pain into an active compromise solution of the corresponding unconscious conflicts. The case of Miss D illustrates these issues.

Etiology and Psychopathology

I believe that peak-affect states organize internalized object relationships not only under conditions of love, the elation that corresponds to a primitive idealized fusion between an all-good self and all-good object, but also under conditions of rage. Under this latter condition there evolves the internalization of originally undifferentiated, all-bad self and object representations, which are gradually sorted out into the typical object relationships under the domination of hatred. An extremely powerful link to the traumatizing object—under the dominance of hatred—has been observed in the study of battered children, of infants at high risk, and even in the fixation to extremely traumatic circumstances, such as the "Stockholm Syndrome" of hijacked airplane passengers who end up defending their captors. The Stockholm Syndrome illustrates the traumatic, total dependency on a bad, persecutory object. Research by Fraiberg (1982) and Galenson (1986) is particularly instructive regarding infants' internalization of aggressive behavior of mothers toward them, and these infants' replication of their mothers' behavior in relationships with her and with other objects.

The intense attachment to the frustrating mother is the primary origin of the transformation of rage into hatred. The ultimate cause of the transformation of rage into hatred is the fixation to a traumatic relationship with a fundamentally needed object that is experienced as all-bad, and as having destroyed or "swallowed up" the ideal, all-good object. The revengeful destruction of this bad object is intended magically to restore the all-good one, but, in the process, it leads to the destruction of the very capacity of the self to relate to the object. This transformation takes the form not of simply identifying with the object (mother), but with the *relationship* to her, so that the hatred of her as victimizer, with its painful, impotent, paralyzing implications, also is transformed into the identification with the mother as the cruel, omnipotent, contemptuously destructive object, while a search develops for other objects onto whom the attacked, depreciated, teased, and mistreated self can be projected. In identifying himself with both suffering self and sadistic object, the subject is himself "swallowed up" by the all-encompassing aggression in the relationship.

Hatred as a reversal of suffering is a basic type of revengeful triumph over the object, a triumph also over the terrifying self representation achieved by projective identification, and the symbolic revenge for past suffering condensed in the fixation to sadistic behavior patterns. Consequently, these patients mistreat others sadistically because they experience themselves as mistreated, once more, by sadistic objects; unconsciously, they become their persecutory objects while sadistically attacking their victims, the dissociated and projected victimized self. At the bottom, they cannot escape being victim and perpetrator at the same time. As victimizer, they cannot live without their victim—the projected, disowned persecuted self; as a victim, they remain attached to their victimizers internally and, sometimes in behavior shocking to an observer, to external persecutors as well.

Extremely contradictory, unreliable behaviors on the part of mother probably reinforce the "psychopathic" end of the spectrum of hatred: the infant and small child interprets mother's behavior as a betrayal by the potentially good object that becomes unpredictably and overwhelmingly bad. In identifying himself, in turn, with a betraying object, the child initiates the path to a revengeful destruction of all object relations. Here probably lies the ultimate source of Jacobson's (1971) paranoid urge to betray. The most severe psychopathology of attachment behavior has been described in infants with mothers whose behavior combined abandonment, violence, chaos, and a teasing overstimulation together with chronic frustration (Fraiberg, 1982; Galenson, 1986).

I have described (1990c) the aggressive implication of penetrating and being penetrated as a means to incorporate aggression at the service of love, utilizing the erotogenic potential of the experience of pain as a crucial contributor to the gratifying fusion with the other in sexual excitement and orgasm. This normal capability for transforming pain into erotic excitement miscarries under conditions of severe aggression in the mother-infant relationship, and is probably a crucial bridge to the erotic excitement with the induction of suffering in others that consolidates the pleasurable characteristics of sadistic hatred. Braunschweig and Fain (1971, 1975) have suggested that the alternatingly erotically stimulating and withdrawing attitudes of a mother toward her infant originate his unconscious identification with a teasing mother as well as with being teased, and activate, in the process, his own sexual excitement as a basic affect. In agreement with these authors, I suggest that severely traumatizing mothers, whose behavior includes exaggerated teasing of the infant, may orient his hatred particularly toward the more severe sadomasochistic perversions as an expression of this hatred.

More generally, the induction of severe pain in the infant and small child leads to rage first, and then, by the identificatory and transformational mechanisms mentioned, to the development of hatred. Thus, as Grossman (1989) has proposed, pain may lead, by a series of intrapsychic transformations, into the intensification and psychopathology of aggression as a major drive.

Consequences for Ego and Superego Integration

Excessive activation of aggression as a drive (to which characterologically fixated hatred contributes fundamentally) interferes with the normal integration of the mutually dissociated, all-good and all-bad internalized object relations at the conclusion of the developmental phase of separation-individuation, and, therefore, with the initiation of object constancy and the advanced stage of oedipal development. Excessive aggression, in disrupting these processes, leads to the fixation at a stage of lack of integration of all-good and all-bad internalized object relations, while self and object representations within each of these all-good and all-bad object relationships are differentiated from each other. These constitute the psychostructural conditions of borderline personality organization, characteristic of severe personality disorders where preoedipal and oedipal aggression are dominant.

Under more favorable circumstances, integration of all-good and all-bad internalized object relations may proceed, and object constancy may develop, which leads to the integration of the definite ego and superego structures and the establishment of repressive boundaries separating ego from id: the definite tripartite structure consolidates.

Here, the psychopathology of hatred is absorbed by the superego. The integration of early sadistic superego precursors with the preoedipal ego ideal, on the one hand, and of oedipal prohibitions and demands with those earlier superego structures, on the other, leads to sadistic superego demands, depressive-masochistic psychopathology, and secondarily rationalized, characterological sadism correlated with the integration of cruel and sadistic ethical systems. Or else, various sexual pathologies, including perversions at a neurotic level of personality organization, may contain hatred as a relatively harmless, erotized perverse symptom.

The induction of shame in, and the humiliation of, others as characterological traits are other manifestations of hatred potentially integrated into superego-mediated characterological features. Obsessive-compulsive patients need to control and dominate others to feel protected against threatening outbreaks of aggressive rebelliousness and chaos in others—thus enacting their identification with a hated object and their projection of unacceptable, repressed, and projected aspects of their self at a relatively high level of psychic functioning. Thus the intense fixation to specific hated objects may be seen along the entire spectrum of psychopathology, and illustrates, sometimes in almost caricaturesque ways, the attachment to the enemy or persecutor. It says something about the profound commonality of the basic affects of rage and sexual excitement, in their role of fixating object relationships, that it is under conditions of intense hatred and intense love that the highest tendency exists for sustained mutual gaze.

Technical and Countertransference Aspects of Intense Hatred

What follows are some general considerations regarding the treatment of patients with severe psychopathology of aggression, particularly intense hatred in the transference. In an earlier paper (1990a) I pointed to the importance of interpreting consistently and in depth the nature of the unconscious fantasies implied in the activation of rage in the transference, and particularly the importance of interpreting secondary defenses against acknowledging the pleasurable aspects of rage. Here, in broadening my focus and considering the entire spectrum of the psychopathology of hatred, I would stress first the countertransference consequences of this affect.

I have pointed out in earlier work (1975, 1984) that what the patient hates, particularly the narcissistic patient with antisocial features, is what he most needs to receive from the therapist, which is the therapist's unwavering dedication to him. The patient also hates, because he envies, the creativity involved in the therapist's efforts to gain understanding and to communicate this understanding to the patient. The therapist's creativity is an indication of his capacity to generate something essential and good and, therefore, not to be threatened by a basic sense of emptiness and need. The analyst's sense of being exhausted, of his efforts going to waste, of the enormity of the patient's lack of gratitude may bring about complications in the countertransference that tend to perpetuate or even obscure the patient's acting out of hatred and envy.

The therapist may attempt to escape from his discouragement by an emotional disconnection from the patient. The restoration of the therapist's tranquillity may be at the cost of an internal giving up that, not surprisingly, is often perceived by the patient but easily tolerated by him because it is rightly experienced as the therapist's defeat. An uneasy equilibrium may ensue, in which a surface friendliness obscures the "parasitic" (Bion, 1970) nature of the therapeutic relationship.

Or the therapist may enter into a collusion with the splitting process in the patient, facilitate the displacement of aggression elsewhere, and foster the creation of a pseudotherapeutic alliance that assures a friendly surface relationship in the transference while aggression is acted out outside the treatment sessions.

Another solution frequently adopted by the therapist may be that of absorbing the patient's aggression, with full awareness of what is going on, but without finding a way to transform this acting out into viable interpretations. This development amounts to a masochistic submission to "impossible" patients, sometimes quite consciously engaged in by a therapist who believes that with sufficient love most things can be cured. The counterpart to such a masochistic submission to the patient, however, is often the eventual acting out of aggression in the countertransference, with a sudden disruption of the treatment, dismissing the patient, or an enactment on the part of the therapist unconsciously geared to provoking the patient to leave the treatment.

Most frequently, however, it is likely that the therapist, even the experienced therapist, may shift in his internal stance from day to day, from session to session, oscillating between efforts to resolve analytically the activation of hatred in the transference and times of giving up or withdrawal. These natural oscillations may actually reflect a reasonable compromise formation, which permits the therapist to step back and evaluate the effects of his various interventions, gives him some breathing space to reevaluate the situation, and then return once more to an active interpretative stance.

In all cases, I think it is extremely important to diagnose secondary defenses against hatred at the most severe end of the spectrum of aggression in the transference, that is, the development of antisocial or psychopathic transferences referred to before. The patient's conscious or unconscious corruption of all relationships, particularly the therapeutic one, must be examined consistently, with the therapist fully aware that such an examination will probably shift the apparently "quiet," psychopathic transference relationship into a severely paranoid one with the activation of intensive hatred in the transference. The therapist's normal superego functions, his being moral but not moralistic (E. Ticho, personal communication), will be experienced by patients with antisocial tendencies as devastating attacks and criticism.

It is important to interpret the patient's paranoid reaction as part of the interpretation of the antisocial transferences. In other words, an interpretation might go as follows: "I am under the impression that, if I point out to you that I believe (such and such behavior) is an expression of your profound need to destroy (a certain relationship), you might interpret my comment as a savage attack on you, as if I were attacking you rather than trying to help you understand what I consider a very important aspect of your difficulties at this time."

Once the transferences have shifted from a dominantly antisocial into a paranoid mode, the following general technical approach to severe paranoid regression is indicated (Kernberg, 1984): it is important to acknowledge to the patient who is convinced of a paranoid distortion of reality that the therapist sees that reality in a completely different way, but respects the temporary incompatibility of the patient's and the therapist's perception of reality; in other words, a "psychotic nucleus" is identified, circumscribed, and tolerated in the transference before work on its interpretive resolution. It is usually only at advanced stages of the treatment of patients with severe psychopathology that integration of idealized and persecutory internalized object relations can take place, with a corresponding shift of paranoid into depressive transferences—that is, the emergence in the patient of guilt feelings, concern over the dangerous effects of aggression, and wishes to repair the psychotherapeutic relationship.

When the sadistic elements are particularly marked, it is important that the patient become aware of his pleasure in hatred (Kernberg, 1990b): this requires that the therapist be able to empathize with the pleasure implied in the patient's aggression. When power relations are the dominant issue in the transference and hatred is expressed as an inordinate need for assertion of power and autonomy, the analysis of this aspect of the transference is usually facilitated by the fact that ordinary anal-sadistic components are involved, and the therapist is dealing with the "healthier" end of the spectrum of psychopathology of aggression.

Again, the most difficult cases are those in whom extremely severe aggression goes hand and hand with extreme psychopathology of superego functioning, so that internal constraints against dangerous enactment of aggression are missing, and the therapist may be realistically afraid of unleashing destructive forces beyond the capacity of the treatment to contain them. This applies to some patients who present the syndrome of malignant narcissism, and is probably a major reason why the antisocial personality proper cannot be approached with psychoanalytic modalities of treatment. It is important that the therapist have a reasonable sense of security that the analysis of powerful aggressive forces will not create new risks for the patient or others, including the therapist. A realistic assessment of this possibility, and a realistic structuring of the treatment situation to protect patient, therapist, and others from inordinate and dangerous, potentially irreversible effects of the acting out of aggression is a precondition for successful work in this area.

REFERENCES

BION, W. R. (1957). On arrogance. In *Second Thoughts: Selected Papers on Psycho-Analysis.* New York: Aronson, 1967, pp. 86–92.

——— (1959). Attacks on linking. In *Second Thoughts: Selected Papers on Psycho-Analysis.* New York: Aronson, 1967, pp. 93–109.

——— (1970). *Attention and Interpretation.* London: Heinemann.

BRAUNSCHWEIG, D. & FAIN, M. (1971). *Eros et Anteros.* Paris: Payot.

——— ——— (1975). *Le Nuit, le jour: Essai psychanalytique sur le fonctionnement mental.* Paris: Payot.

CALL, J. D. (1980). Attachment disorders of infancy. In *Comprehensive Textbook of Psychiatry,* Vol. III, ed. H. I. Kaplan et al. Baltimore: Williams & Wilkins, pp. 2586–2592.

EMDE, R. N. (1987). Development terminable and interminable. Plenary Presentation at the 35th International Psycho-Analytical Congress, Montreal, Canada.

——— et al. (1978). Emotional expression in infancy: 1. Initial studies of social signaling and an emergent model. In *The Development of Affect,* ed. M. Lewis & L. Rosenblum. New York: Plenum, pp. 125–148.

FRAIBERG, S. (1982). Pathological defenses in infancy. *Psychoanal. Q.,* 51:612–635.

GAENSBAUER, T. & SANDS, K. (1979). Distorted affective communications in abused and neglected infants and their potential impact on caretakers. *J. Amer. Acad. Child Psychiat.,* 18:236–250.

GALENSON, E. (1986). Some thoughts about infant psychopathology and aggressive development. *Int. Rev. Psychoanal.,* 13:349–354.

GREEN, A. (1977). Conceptions of affect. In *On Private Madness.* London: Hogarth Press, 1986, pp. 174–213.

GROSSMAN, W. I. (1989). Pain, aggression, fantasy, and concepts of sadomasochism (unpublished).

IZARD, C. (1978). On the ontogenesis of emotions and emotion-cognition relationships in infancy. In *The Development of Affect,* ed. M. Lewis & L. Rosenblum. New York: Plenum, pp. 389–413.

JACOBSON, E. (1971). Acting out and the urge to betray in paranoid patients. In *Depression.* New York: Int. Univ. Press, pp. 302–318.

KERNBERG, O. F. (1975). *Borderline Conditions and Pathological Narcissism.* New York: Aronson.

——— (1984). *Severe Personality Disorders: Psychotherapeutic Strategies.* New Haven: Yale Univ. Press.

——— (1989). The narcissistic personality disorder and the differential diagnosis of antisocial behavior. In *Psychiatric Clinics of North America: Narcissistic Personality Disorder,* 12:553–570. Philadelphia: Saunders.

——— (1990a). Hatred as pleasure. In *Pleasure Beyond the Pleasure Principle:*

Developmental and Psychoanalytic Concept of Affect, ed. R. Glick & S. Bone. New Haven: Yale Univ. Press (in press).

——— (1990b). New perspectives in psychoanalytic affect theory. In *Emotion: Theory, Research and Experience,* ed. R. Plutchik & H. Kellerman. New York: Academic Press, pp. 115–130.

——— (1990c). Sadomasochism, sexual excitement, and perversion. *J. Amer. Psychoanal. Assn.* (in press).

KLEIN, M. (1957). *Envy and Gratitude.* New York: Basic Books.

KRAUSE, R. (1988). Eine Taxonomie der Affeckte und ihre Anwendung auf das Verständnis der frühen Störungen. *Psychotherapie und medizinische Psychologie,* 38:77–86.

——— & LUTOLF, P. (1988). Facial indicators of transference processes in psychoanalytical treatment. In *Psychoanalytic Process Research Strategies,* ed. H. Dahl & H. Kachele. Heidelberg: Springer, pp. 257–272.

MAHLER, M. S. & FURER, M. (1968). *On Human Symbiosis and the Vicissitudes of Individuation.* New York: Int. Univ. Press.

MASSIE, H. (1977). Patterns of mother-infant behavior and subsequent childhood psychoses. *Child Psychiat. & Hum. Develpm.,* 7:211–230.

MOSER, U. (1978). Affektsignale und aggressives Verhalten: Zwei verbal formulierte Modelle der Aggression. *Psyche,* 32:229–258.

OGDEN, T. (1979). On projective identification. *Int. J. Psychoanal.,* 60:357–373.

OSOFSKY, J. D. (1987). Affective exchanges between high risk mothers and infants. Presented at the 35th International Psycho-Analytical Congress, Montreal, Canada.

ROIPHE, H. & GALENSON, E. (1981). *Infantile Origins of Sexual Identity.* New York: Int. Univ. Press.

STERN, D. N. (1985). *The Interpersonal World of the Infant.* New York: Basic Books.

WINNICOTT, D. W. (1949). Hate in the countertransference. In *Collected Papers.* New York: Basic Books, 1958, pp. 194–203.

New York Hospital—Cornell Medical Center
Westchester Division
21 Bloomingdale Road
White Plains, NY 10605

EMOTION AND THE PSYCHOANALYTIC ENCOUNTER

PETER H. KNAPP, M.D.

Three overlapping aspects of emotion are important in the clinical psychoanalytic encounter: (1) Expressive-Communicative features comprise a transactional network of lexical, acoustic, kinesic, and visceral signals passing between the two participants. Some of the analyst's "freely hovering attention," ideally, includes empathic perception tuned to the stream of emotional information. Part of the force of the analytic approach derives from restricting feedback to patients, so that they generate their own. (2) Regulatory aspects of emotion are provided early in life by outer and later by internalized cues. Smooth regulation is a goal, dysregulation is a target, of psychoanalysis. In crises, psychopharmacologic intervention may be necessary. However, the most effective regulatory influences are the stabilizing analytic holding environment and the caring empathy of the analyst, mainly articulated in words. (3) Motivational aspects of emotion stem from their ingrained coupling with cognitive components in unconscious fantasies, especially self representations or schemas; these require multileveled integrative empathic grasp by the analyst, in a kind of trial identification. Such schemas organize and are organized by primitive emotions. They are influenced by psychoanalytic work, which combines cognitive learning with early modes of internalization and with slow patterns of extinction and reinforcement. These all coalesce in the symbolic activity of insight, which is part result, and part cause of emotional growth.

MR. C, 53 YEARS OLD, was brought to the emergency ward by a police ambulance because of one in a series of panic attacks in a metropolitan tunnel. His terror was so severe that he had gotten out of his car, bringing traffic to a standstill.

For many reasons, including his rejection of prolonged treatment, he was taken into time-limited psychoanalytic psychotherapy of the kind advocated by J. Mann (1973), confined to 12 weekly sessions.

Boston University, School of Medicine, Division of Psychiatry.

His history rapidly unfolded. He had been one of the youngest of a large Southern family, raised on his family's estate. Much of the childhood play of the siblings had centered around his father's stable, and in it the oat bin. His older brothers had been fond of seizing him and locking him there in pitch blackness for what seemed like hours, to his agony and their sadistic delight. In due course, as he grew older, he became a perpetrator, inflicting the same fate on his younger sister and relishing her terror.

He wondered, somewhat skeptically, whether these almost forgotten experiences could have anything to do with his panic now. Gradually he gave further details. Almost 30 years ago, on a honeymoon trip through a southern state, he had had a similar series of atttacks. The first came while visiting a mammoth cave with his bride. Subsequently, he had learned to keep away from enclosed spaces and soon he was symptom free.

His wife had died, and after several years he had married again and simultaneously moved to an area where it was necessary to make frequent business trips through a long tunnel. Shortly after these two changes his recurrent phobia had broken out with its present violence.

In response to some questioning, he also revealed that he had had occasional anxiety and interference with sexual function. He was reluctant to explore this aspect and seemed greatly relieved when it was handled reassuringly. In the next sessions, he reported dramatic improvement in both his minor sexual and his major claustrophobic concerns. In fact, he became eager to leave therapy; our final two sessions were devoted to talk about his job, on a rather pedestrian level. Any feelings, including those of impending loss, were uniformly and jovially minimized.

After treatment ended, I saw him several times at large social gatherings over a span of two decades. Both he and his wife, to whom he introduced me, were effusive in their gratitude for what to them had been a miraculous and lasting cure.

This anecdote can do little more than raise questions. What led to this "cure" in what can be such a stubborn symptom? Certainly not insight. Was it the therapeutic relationship? Flight from deeper probing? The suggestion implicit in the 12-session contract? Dynamic features surrounding the symptom bore a striking relationship to early psychoanalytic reports of claustrophobia (Lewin, 1935; Feldman, 1941), suggesting that fears of closed spaces might have their roots in fantasies of sexual penetration or fusion with a woman, self becoming confused with phallus, suffocation the peril. Did touching this deep constellation allusively facilitate some realignment of his fantasy organization, as F. Deutsch (1958) postulated in his technique of the associative anamnesis?

At a more comprehensive level, how do emotional reactions, innate and unlearned at the start of life, become modulated by learning? At the same time, what are their effects, negative and positive, on the processes of learning? What kind and degree of change results, or seems to, or fails to, in emotions as targets of psychoanalytic treatment and from emotions as key components of the psychoanalytic encounter?

As a form of treatment, psychoanalysis involves a number of simultaneous processes (Bibring, 1954; Lewin, 1954; Macalpine, 1950; Stone, 1961) some common to many forms of psychotherapy and relying heavily on the personal relationship to the therapist. These factors supplement distinctively psychoanalytic interpretation of unconscious attitudes and intentions.

I will use the term emotion broadly (and synonymously with affect) to refer to an array of processes shared with most of the animal kingdom, having clear physiologic and expressive components, linked to stereotyped ideational systems, and mobilizing significant adaptive behaviors. For simplification, I will focus on three emotional aspects. First is the communicative aspect—emotions as they are manifest in the dyadic interchange. Second is the regulatory aspect—how emotions become regulated by, and also regulate, other features of behavior. Third is the motivational aspect—the lasting participation of emotions in unconscious fantasy constellations, especially images, representations, or schemas involving the self and key others.

Emotional Expression and Communication in Psychoanalysis

Emotion is a continuous component of human experience; and in the psychoanalytic situation there is a constant interchange of messages about the emotions of both participants. Transmission comes over many channels, often simultaneously (Scheflen, 1963: Knapp, 1963).

"Nonverbal" communication is not exclusively emotional. Gestures may instruct, ask precise questions, or answer them: a finger pointed up or down, north or south; a look of deliberate puzzlement; a nod of assent—or, for that matter, the whole language of signing. And in everyday discourse, gestural information may be emblematically coded: an out-thrust arm, with the hand forming a vertical wall, signifying, "Stop." Nor is all emotional information nonlexical, that is, beyond what is captured by a written typescript. Narrative arrangement, timing, word selection, repetition, metaphor, are often designed for emotional effect, as rhetoric has taught for generations. Emotional effect likewise may be unintended, in blocking, incoherence, disruptions of syntax (Dahl et al., 1978), or common dysfluencies (Mahl, 1977).

Dysfluencies shade off into paralanguage, sobs, throat clearing, coughing, voiced hestitations. These merge into purely acoustic qualities: stress, loudness, timbre. Acoustic features, too, become codified and are used for strict cognitive guidance; but their variations can be rich in emotional significance, starting with the cry or cooing of the infant and its counterpart, quite uniform across cultures, namely, parental tones of soothing, warning, or admonition. We can often know a patient's mood, within seconds, as we can that of a friend over the telephone: the increased volume and harshness of anger, the muted, breaking, near sobbing voice of sadness; the constricted, tight voice of anxiety.

The importance of kinesics was heralded by Darwin (1872), elaborated by Tomkins (1962–63), and solidified by Ekman (1982), Izard (1971), Emde (1988), and others. These authors have demonstrated the pan-cultural, lifelong, regularity with which facial expressions convey the basic emotions of anger, fear, sadness, joy, and possibly several others, such as disgust and surprise (as efforts to extend the basic list increase, so does controversy). Clearly, the emotional variations we encounter daily consist of many blends, How soon in life these develop, and whether they are truly simultaneous or micromomentary oscillations, remain questions for the future. The emotions reflected on the face may be manifest, even rhetorically practiced, so as to underline or punctuate ongoing narration; on the other hand, they may represent "leakage" or warded-off feelings and attitudes. Ekman (1985) has called attention to the flickers of hidden emotions in subjects deliberately lying, and also the distortions that such individuals may show, such as the false smile in simulated cheerfulness.

Finally there are visceral signals, from a subject to an observer, usually slower and often more ambiguous. Pallor, trembling, blushing, or irritated skin, a sudden nasal congestion, or a well-timed rumble of borborygmi—all can be momentary events, or they may extend into psychosomatic exacerbation (the thesis of Groddeck, 1928; F. Deutsch, 1939; McDougall, 1989).

A young physician suffering from well-documented bronchial asthma was robbed of his night-off duty by a negligent colleague, who failed to show up for a rotation. My asthmatic patient was enraged. The next day, when he saw the offender, he was about to launch a verbal assault but instead found himself uttering pleasantries. At the same instant he was overtaken by one of his familiar bouts of paroxysmal coughing and wheezing, which progressed into a clear attack of asthma. Although we still have much to learn about the pathophysiologic mediation of such an episode, its meaning is clear: I am not dangerous, filled with murderous rage, but sick and suffering, needing pity and help.

Communication over all of these channels may reflect pervasive emotional style, in characterologic patterns such as smugness (Arlow, 1957), poise (Rangel, 1966), or pouting (Adatto, 1957). Again, the transition from momentary states to sustained character traits is a matter for future study. We do know, however, that they may combine together in broad personality types, for example, the inhibitory, mournful, chronically depressed individual.

Dr. D, a distinguished lawyer having many of those characteristics, though outwardly successful and admired, spoke almost inaudibly. Early in analysis we found out that at about the age of 8, when he was a loud, boisterous, troublemaking, physically big and energetic youngster, he had made a vow—the epitome of massive reaction formation—never to raise his voice again.

Needless to say, mere elucidation of the memory did not remove the inhibition. For example, after many more years of analysis, leading to considerable improvement in his assertiveness, he gave an invited keynote address at a national meeting. He rose to this considerable honor, and spoke without notes, fluently and also critically about organizational flaws as he saw them. After the talk, two women came forward and launched a violent attack of their own on what they saw as his flaws. He was paralyzed, unable to answer them. Instead of feeling flushed with success he was deeply depressed for two days. In reconstructing the emotional sequence, the school boy scene of renunciation was again clear, and also its origins—which we had worked on many times—in his dimly remembered helplessness when faced by verbal attack from his forceful mother.

He added an interesting postscript at this time. Insight, he thought, should be curative, a surgical removal. He still found it hard to realize he had to keep applying it, the way his analyst must do.

Nonlexical behavior may also encapsulate highly specific details of past emotional experience. Mahl (1977) describes an analytic patient who announced an important, emotion-laden fantasy by the simple motor act of removing the pillow from the analytic couch. Only several sessions later did he recall an episode from childhood: being discovered by his mother in the act of masturbating into his pillow. His involuntary enactment had tried to guard against a similar misfortune.

What are the clinical implications of this multichanneled emotional communication? First, we must be aware of its sheer volume. We must try to keep our receptive channels open. Such a recommendation is perhaps a contemporary addendum to Freud's prescription of freely hovering attention. We must be ready to detect, and help the patient to detect, the wide range of expressive and communicative cues studding our transactions. Our own nonlexical emotional behavior, along with other feelings and fantasies—as Beres and Arlow (1974) so eloquently show—can make an indispensable contribution to our empathic awareness of these clues in the analytic encounter.

Spence (1987), it should be noted, argues that such empathic awareness does not provide a privileged quasi-mystical access to psychoanalytic truth. I am not claiming that it does. Rather it maximizes awareness of *all* the data flooding us as clinicians—from which we try to select and reconstruct and pursue the most emotionally relevant themes.

Naturally, too, we must be aware that emotional communication is a two-way street. Our own nonlexical behavior, especially the tone, tempo, and choice of words, may be tinged with irritation or other unwanted emotion. We are wise—as in the case of other errors—to acknowledge the fact, and then to proceed with analyzing its meanings.

In view of the enormous amount of information about emotion conveyed visually, particularly by the face, what about the couch? Clearly it deserves more research attention than it has received. It deprives the analyst of some visual information, and at times helps the patient to withhold and conceal; but to a great extent these obstacles can be overcome. More important are the many other meanings of the couch. In the expressive-communicative arena it is part of a drastic reordering of our ingrained social rules. The analyst curtails customary emotional feedback. This act partly amplifies the responses that are given. At the same time its inevitable ambiguity allows patients to supply their own feedback, shaped by their specific inner experiences.

Here it may be useful to add a word about empathy. The term refers to different, intertwined, processes. Empathic perception, the aspect considered so far, denotes grasp of expressive cues about another person's emotional experience. Empathic acknowledgment—on which I have only touched—refers to reflecting one's awareness of experiences back to another person, largely, though not exclusively, by words. Finally, we may speak of empathic integration, a reconstruction based on information from many levels—expressive, contextual, tacit, narrational, fantasied, dreamed—leading to what has been called trial identification (Fliess, 1942; Greenson, 1960). This multileveled integrative empathy is stimulated by perceptual cues, and guides the timing, tact, and clarity of empathic acknowledgment. We shall refer more to those levels of empathy, as we look at other more long-lasting aspects of emotion and psychoanalysis.

Regulatory Aspects of Emotion

Communication of emotion—primarily the expressive interchange of signals, often from moment to moment—borders on another aspect. Emotions are partially regulated by cognitive and action systems, and in turn have regulatory influence on these. The regulation may be successful and harmonious; or it may be ineffective, chaotic, or rigid. Optimal regulation is a goal of maturation, including therapeutic maturation. Dysregulation is a therapeutic target.

Developmentally the major early influences on infants and their emotions come from the outside world and from the body. The environment, particularly mothering and caretaking figures, soothe and stimulate, and to the best of their ability, assist the developing inner regulatory resources of the infant toward the distant goal—never completely attained—of autonomous self-regulation (Stern, 1985; Emde, 1983). Gradually, as regulatory factors become internalized, memories or cognitive representations of key humans in the child's world elicit responses; pleasurable or stimulating images gradually counteract distress.

Emotions, in turn, have a regulatory influence on systems beyond their sphere. Initially the infant is, in part, buffeted by emotional storms that can destroy his or her cognitive-attentional abilities, and can also disrupt the smooth functioning of motor and bodily systems. Such storms have a powerful effect in eliciting response from caregivers, at times soothing, at times anxious or angry. As emotions become regulated, they in turn have positive and enriching effects, which further reverberate in the surrounding human milieu. Rewards, satisfaction, the search for, and provision of, more rewards inspire performance. As maturation proceeds, performance itself—athletic or academic, for example—flourishes on an optimum level of vigor, enthusiasm, and well-regulated arousal. Excitement alternates with relaxation. Love as well as ambition to work—using Freud's duality—make their indispensable contributions to well-being. The chain linking emotions to the outside, social world is never broken; but internalized processes of signaling, switching, blending develop into the subtle tapestry of adult emotional life.

Intricate machinery seldom functions flawlessly. Emotional dysregulation, acute or chronic, localized or massive, is maladaptive, and when severe or sustained results in major forms of psychopathology. The cycle of panic begetting more panic, augmented by unconscious fantasies, is illustrated by Mr. C's claustrophobia. Other core emotional processes may be exaggerated in similar fashion: the mixed array of depressive feeling states; uncontrollable elation; ungovernable rage or hostility; excessive eroticism and its opposites, shame and disgust; fatigue; disturbance of sleep and appetites. All of these in turn can contribute to more specific organ disorders, the vast range of psychosomatic syndromes. Let me comment on only a few features.

Emotional pathology is marked, in general, by dysregulated feedback. This may be positive feedback—peripheral emotional manifestations becoming a focus of conscious attention. We encounter the patient who wakes for a moment free of symptoms, only to find that he "needs" them. As circular build-up goes on, control weakens, intensifying both the original emotion and anxiety associated with its intensity.

Other forms of pathology may exemplify negative feedback. Emotional cues, including bodily responses, become isolated, sometimes intellectualized, sometimes totally disavowed. An extreme instance is the group of patients with so-called alexithymia. This is not the place to debate whether that term properly designates a fixed, organically based, barrier walling off all affective experience, or whether it represents a reversible constriction resulting from parental and cultural prohibitions against feeling and fantasy. When the latter case is true, primitive fantasy persists alongside potential explosive emotion, both features warded off by conscious diversion to affectless rationality. The pattern fits most patients I have seen answering to the alexithymic description. In fact, perhaps most common are individuals who have selective areas of emotional construction: a conventional surface, often genuinely friendly but bland and largely devoid of affect or imagination, pierced by bursts of intense feeling. Indeed that was the emotional picture presented by Mr. C.

I agree with McDougall who warns against the dangers of "categorizing people, with a consequent tendency to concretize our thinking. . . . Certain practitioners say 'this person is suffering from alexithymia,' as though it were a definable illness, rather than an observable but little understood phenomenon" (1989, p. 103). I agree also with Krystal (1979) that it is possible to educate such patients slowly into the existence and power of emotions.

Many emotional symptoms, both acute and prolonged, are marked by significant biological dysregulation. A persuasive argument has been made that many instances of addictive drug use can be seen as self-medication in an effort to restore regulation. At times dysregulation alone may merit auxiliary pharmacotherapy. The disadvantages of such an added intervention are clear: "addictive" dependence, in the widest sense of the term; the masking of gain from the symptoms, thus helping to perpetuate them; and transference complications, no matter who writes the actual prescription. Nevertheless, as is true of obviously disabled psychosomatic patients, medical intervention may preserve essential competencies or, at times, life. Even for psychoanalytic patients, the benefits of drug treatment can outweigh the risks, serving as a preferably time-limited, ancillary crisis intervention. Above all, the issue cries out for research. Psychoanalytic data, before, during, and after psychopharmacologic intervention, offer a rare opportunity to study the ebb and flow of emotional regulation over extended periods of time.

These fluctuations, of course, reflect not only pharmacologic effects, but also the multifarious vicissitudes of transference-inspired emotions. Throughout medical history, positive fluctuations have been recognized and labeled, if narrowly, "placebo" effects. Psychoanalysis has done much to deepen our knowledge of such personal and cultural phenomena.

Indeed, psychoanalysts have begun to ask about the lasting nature of these "nonspecific" effects in their own consulting rooms. The setting, the role, and the person of the analyst combine to make explicit therapeutic contributions (Lewin, 1954; Stone, 1961; Schlesinger, 1988). The frequency and regularity of sessions, the nonjudgmental atmosphere (imperfect as we have seen it to be), provide a holding environment: its regulatory, restorative influences are hard to measure.

Rogers (1957) and his followers (themselves coming from the tradition of Rank and Ferenczi) proposed an essential triad of therapeutic qualities: genuineness, nonpossessive warmth, and accurate empathy. Rogers meant not merely perception of emotional cues but empathic acknowledgment, which reflected back in words the feelings and attitudes of the patient. Independently Lindemann (1945) had reported that patients suffering from ulcerative colitis were severely disturbed, massively dependent on one or two key persons. He recommended that their psychotherapy should be supportive, essentially based on similar Rogerian principles. Kohut's elaboration (1977) of the personality deficits in narcissistic characters, and their need for continuing outer "selfobjects" to give them inner cohesion, can be seen as developing this theme of a reparative and sustaining personal therapeutic milieu.

Such personal factors are present tacitly in the spectrum of psychotherapeutic interventions that inevitably color the most classical of psychoanalyses. Bibring (1954) in particular pointed to these. They include suggestion and its still incompletely understood combination of wishes to believe and quasi surrender of critical ego functions—again a probable factor in Mr. C's "cure." Bibring also used the somewhat unfortunate term "manipulation" for the deliberate mobilization of desired responses and attitudes, often brought about by the inevitable emotional reinforcements of the close analytic relationship. Finally there is the necessary role of mentor, along with the frequent concomitant of idealization, perhaps valuable for some patients, but in others serving to obscure rebellious and destructive attitudes.

These unverbalized features recapitulate early, emotionally important forms of learning—the slow molding of expectations through experience, so that old fears and suspicions are relinquished and gradually replaced by security and trust, and the discovery of automatic ways of managing feelings in one's social environment and later in one's internal psychic world. We can see, in infants, steady acquisition of patterns from their caretakers. This process may start with restricted imitation of specific behaviors; it goes on to internalized and progressively more intricate patterns of identification.

In identification, seen as a major form of learning, emotions play a double role. Initially they are motives: the child's natural imitative urge is stimulated by affection, a wish to be close to the loved human exemplar. Later we see many variations. Admiration may still inspire identification, but it may be colored by wishes for envied strength; or it may be more perverse—learning to be a sadistic bully; or trying to be the feared aggressor not the victim; or to be the victim rather than the hated and unloved perpetrator. Thus identifications become objects of therapeutic scrutiny. Analysts must try to disentangle the threads that go into them; and the very inquiry, if successful, fosters wishes to identify with the observing and understanding component in therapy and therapist—the step so different for Mr. D and for many other patients.

Ms. I, a tall, attractive, extremely active woman executive in her late 30s came into analytic therapy because of chronic anxiety and depression, much of it centering around conflicting demands of career and marriage. Very early she revealed enormous ambivalence about all aspects of pregnancy and motherhood, going back to a troubled relationship to her own narcissistic, erotically restless mother, who finally abandoned home, husband, and two children when the patient was an adolescent.

Treatment was complicated by infertility, necessitating many diagnostic and therapeutic efforts seemingly as endless as they were unsuccessful. The result was a crescendo of increasing anxiety, difficulty in looking at her own profound characterological ambivalence, and increasing rage. The rage itself became more and more amplified. She raged at her physicians, her husband, herself, and at me. Gradually it was possible to show her that she had an almost addictive relationship to the rage itself. Anger energized her, warded off a sense of helplessness and total despair.

Mere expression of this emotion led to only temporary relief. It was difficult for her to step back and get any perspective on her anger, or on possible contributions of her ambivalence to the difficulties conceiving. After two years, as her fortieth birthday began to loom, her husband and family began insisting that she consider adoption. Her fury only intensified: she desperately wanted her own flesh and blood, she said, and the idea of raising an unknown, possibly defective child was anathema to her.

As the pressures of time mounted, several changes took place. It was possible to get her to a sensitive, skilled fertility team. She and her husband also agreed to see a skilled, dynamically oriented woman couples therapist, who reiterated the interpretation I had made about her basic ambivalence, and the way she lived it out in the present—furiously repudiating the idea of adoption, consciously longing for natural motherhood, but insisting that her body doomed that longing. For the first time she seemed able to listen, and for short periods think about herself, her feelings, and her body from the perspective I had been proposing. In this setting, just before a course of in vitro fertilization was about to begin, she became pregnant.

This sketch illustrates the defensive layering of emotions—her anger defending against her sense of helplessness. It also shows how a complex supportive ambience could promote self-observation, identification with the analyst, and an approach to the connections between emotions and buried, motivationally powerful fantasies.

Emotions, Motivation, and Unconscious Fantasy

Unconscious fantasies have been conceptualized classically as representations that emerge from the opposition of instinctual drives and defenses (Rapaport, 1953; Brenner, 1975). Alternative conceptual language describes them as symbolic constellations, organized by, and at the same time organizing, primitive emotions (Knapp, 1969, in press; see also Kernberg, 1971; Horowitz, 1988). Whatever theoretical terms are used, this hidden fantasy world is populated by pleasurable and painful wishes, fears, urges, and inhibitions, involving essential persons. Efforts to get these "schemactive" features, as I have called them, into awareness are accompanied by manifest emotions, sometimes excited and joyful, often fearful and turbulent.

We come to truly psychoanalytic terrain. The earliest approach to it was by frontal attack on buried memories and their affects—to induce catharsis. In its restricted sense the term is a metaphor for physical riddance. That, in turn, is part of the hydraulic model depicting emotion held in a container that swells until it is relieved by "discharge." Catharsis, as a concept, proved to have limitations; yet the notion hung on, corresponding in some way to clinical experience. Freud (1914) and others after him (Novey, 1962) continued to speak of cumulative discharge or abreaction of quanta of energy.

Can the clinical phenomena be accounted for in less cumbersome, more exact terms? Generally speaking, we, as humans, remember affectively intense moments. Expressing strong feelings entails at least some unspoken inclusion of the audience. It provides relief from the effort to keep them in one's private personal world. Further the channelization of emotion into language in the therapeutic theater, where it is observed and shared, not condemned, brings about what

Aristotle called more than twenty centuries ago catharsis in a wider sense. As Gifford (1973) has contended, the process is not mere confession, nor is it only sublimation. Revealing our own terrifying and haunting emotional universe is like witnessing Medea's final pyromanic revenge. Conflict is still tragic, but it is put in a wider social context, felt as part of our humanity, a struggle from which we gain some distance. Our emotional horizon is widened by the freedom of voicing passionate desire, or, still more—as Winnicott (1958) believes—by vicariously and by safely experiencing destructive rage. Not only are we forgiven, we forgive ourselves; and we begin to master ourselves through broadened understanding.

Understanding necessitates some cognitive framework. This is most solid when it is etched into memory by the vividness of immediate experience in the therapeutic encounter. The relative silence and invisibility of the analyst induce a controlled regression, a return toward the world of private fantasy and powerful early feelings (Macalpine, 1950; Lewin, 1954). The method of free association not only impels irrational thoughts and related emotions toward awareness; by necessity it makes the listening analyst their target. A third consequence is equally inevitable: the automatic, emotionally tenacious resistant fight against seeing and believing this course of events.

Convincing evidence comes best from emotionally vivid details, which increasingly cluster around the therapeutic relationship, in Strachey's (1934) mutative interpretation. To that end it is useful to heed the advice of his contemporary, Brierley (1937), who said we must "follow the Ariadne's thread of transference affects." Bibring (1954) later emphasized the gradual nature of interpretation: clarification of preconscious material; the frequent use of confrontation, drawing attention to the obvious that is being avoided; and finally, often in small increments, major elucidation of a truly repressed theme.

The question of how such understanding can be validated lies beyond the reach of this paper. Let me stay with insight and its intricate interactions with emotion. The term insight implies looking into things, discovering aspects of their arrangement or function, their language or logic. Familiar clinical parlance contrasts "intellectual" with "emotional" insight: verbalization that is somehow empty, versus moments of vivid feeling, the genuine therapeutic article. But what precisely is emotional insight?

Zilboorg (1954) complained that we do not really know what the term insight itself means, or even where it first originated. His provocative argument—elaborated later by Modell (1988)—was that insight may be "something that is a result (and therefore more lasting) rather than a cause (and therefore less reliable) of the process of integration" (Zilboorg, 1954, p. 23).

One step out of apparent paradox is to reiterate the gerund understanding; this applies to *both*—both process and outcome, both the grasping or gaining of knowledge, and the final fact of that knowledge. Richfield (1954) refined the argument. His starting point was Bertrand Russell's (1929) distinction between knowledge by description and knowledge by acquaintance. We can know things by hearing or reading about them, or even by knowledge of their properties; or we can know them by intimate personal experience. The latter form of knowledge—and, by extension, insight—Richfield called not "emotional" but ostensive, meaning directly demonstrable.

Where does that argument leave emotion? Squarely in the center of the process, if what is to be demonstrated is hidden personal experience with its inevitable tangible emotional components. Put more fully, psychoanalysis involves insight about emotions and also emotions along with insight. Insight is grasping the many threads in the emotional dimension of the experience and their sensory vividness, tangled with fantasy and urge. Insight leads also to feelings about what is grasped—about the opening of a specific, sensuous, private, and dangerous world. It stirs excitement, distress, shame, anger, relief, and at times gratitude.

Capturing emotional experience in words is not easy. Description is hard put to replace firsthand experience. Symbolic grasp and its expanded range come at a price. The cognitive map is necessary, but it is not the emotional territory. Seeing is still believing, and the experience of human contact, like a picture, may be worth a thousand words. Richfield's conclusion, that psychoanalysis needs both kinds of knowledge, was foreshadowed by Kant's dictum "Concepts without percepts are empty; percepts without concepts are blind."

Working Through: Some Questions about Psychoanalysis and Learning

The course of psychoanalytic learning is slow and tortuous. Flashes, including those of insight, illuminate but tend to fade. The term that tries to capture the key features of psychoanalytic learning is "working through." Unfortunately it is a term with a number of shades of meaning. Most often, starting with Freud (1914), it refers to continued grappling with resistances at all levels: resistance to the person of the analyst, to the external details of the contract, to the process of free association itself, to the assimilation of unconscious meanings, and finally to change.

It also refers to working down, through the various and progressively more alien layers of intrapersonal organization. Greenson (1965) illustrates this progression in his report of a young man whose final difficulty in changing turned on a primitive fear of taking in anything from his analyst, because that would mean a feeling of fusion, a terrifying sense of being powerless, no longer himself.

Finally the phrase may mean simply working over and over again at the acquisition and retention of a new vision and at skills in implementing it, at facing old errors under new guises, and at practicing new remedies until they become ingrained. It requires the attunement of a ballet teacher, at times the firmness of a fencing master, and the patience of a tennis coach.

None of these metaphors does full justice to the process. It is not linear, nor does progress often appear to result directly, much less solely, from interpretative insight. Indeed, the "work" of analysis does not center exclusively around interpretations. The whole relationship, especially, but not exclusively, its moments of peak emotion, are repetitively and cumulatively experienced.

Ms. I's crucial moment of truth when many things fell into place occurred at about the time of the interpretation: your ambivalence about adoption is largely a split to avoid experiencing your more long-standing ambivalence about being a mother at all. However, this conflict had been pointed out from virtually her first session. Its roots had been traced both to oedipal rivalry and guilt, and to early rage over her self-absorbed and abandoning mother, who left the patient with wishes to join forces with a man as an attempted solution to despair. In addition, she was in an auxiliary relationship to a thoughtful fertility team and to a perceptive woman couples therapist, who could tolerate her rage. By the time of the crucial reinterpretation, all of these elements were on stage; and, in fact, she was already pregnant!

The original aim of psychoanalysis, as formulated in Freud's successive topographic and structural aphorisms, was to descend through symbolic layers, defensively arrayed, and to lay bare the instinctive-affective roots of behavior. But, once exposed, those roots did not always wither away. Attachment to analysts and identification with their observational stance often still left only intellectual insight; islands of recalcitrant defense remained, peopled by stubborn emotional conflicts. The gloom in Freud's views (1937) of "psychical inertia" and "adhesiveness of the libido" has not yet been dispelled. The emotional sphere can be remarkably impervious to the talking cure.

It seems possible that some analogies drawn from experimental studies of learning might be helpful in this dilemma. Early observations in animals of approach-avoidance conflicts, stimulus generalization, and persistent maladaptive behaviors suggested such analogies (Dollard and Miller, 1950; Wolf, 1967); although the unfolding realization of human complexity made early learning theories seem not only simple but simplistic. Nonetheless, neuropsychological laboratories have continued to generate a sophisticated body of knowledge, much of it stemming from simple learning models, that bears directly on emotional bonds and emotional regulation.

Instrumental (Skinnerian or Thorndykian) learning, augmented by the techniques of brain self-stimulation, has studied reward and aversive central centers and the relation of these to appetitive, addictive, and other emotional states. Human biofeedback methods represent an effort to extend instrumental control of physiological and sometimes emotional processes. How successful they will be remains to be seen; but they suggest that under the right circumstances humans can learn to manipulate psychophysiologic processes that ordinarily lie out of awareness. Such inner manipulations may play an overlearned and automatic role in the gamut of human defense mechanisms.

Respondent (Pavlovian) sequences, reflecting environmental impact, were originally thought to be fragile and readily extinguished. However, they vary widely; and under appropriate conditions they may last virtually a lifetime, for instance, after painful shock—to the foot in dogs (Solomon, 1968), or to the tail in the sea snail, Aplysia, which shows not only long-standing conditioned aversion but changed cellular biochemistry (Kandel, 1979, 1983). Respondent learning may contribute to the enduring aftereffects of some traumatic events, and, on the positive side, they may play a part in attachment behavior (Schur, 1960).

Rescorla, attempting to shed the restrictive image of Pavlov's dog in harness, states that respondent learning "results from exposure to relations among events in the environment" (1988, p. 152); and he points out that it can result from a multitude of signals and signals of signals. Similarly Turkhan (1989) speaks of classical conditioning as "the new hegemony," an empire based on associative learning. Schwartz (1987) has also proposed that many, if not most, human emotional disturbances may result from associative learning gone awry. Particularly relevant to emotion is Bykov's notion of "viscero-visceral conditioning," in which one visceral response serves as stimulus for another—part of the "observable unconscious" (see Razran, 1961).

I am not suggesting that these are the only learning paradigms that may be pertinent to the study of emotions, and I am certainly not advocating direct transportation of simplified laboratory approaches into the clinic. Attempts in that direction have too often neglected the human emotional interactions that they inevitably entail.

I am, however, suggesting that we look carefully at the possible contribution of these and other mechanisms to the learning, past and present, in our patients, as well as to the unlearning and relearning that we try to foster. Instrumental and respondent sequences may be integral to what Kubie (1941) called the repetitive core of the neurosis. Instrumental and respondent devices, moreover, may be used intuitively and unwittingly by the skilled analytic practitioner. If so, we should ourselves learn which devices may assist our all too cumbersome enterprise, and which may, on the other hand, impede it.

Analogies can be misleading; but there is little doubt on two points. First, carefully guarded, automatic, defensive tactics and strategies of patients—like the split in Ms. I's affects about pregnancy—must be brought repeatedly into emotional awareness to be felt as real and slowly relinquished. Second, affective reactions echoing past environmental impact—like the paralysis of Mr. D under a barrage of female criticism—must be experienced again and again to be slowly moderated and mastered. Such is the work of working through.

Epilogue: The Search for Gold

Whether we like it or not, the psychoanalyst is part shaman, part mentor, part confessor, as well as helmsman on the psychoanalytic voyage of discovery. But still we are left with the question: what in those roles is truly curative?

Starting with Freud, there has been endless debate about the relationship of the "pure gold" of psychoanalytic interpretation, as against less valued, subordinate psychotherapeutic activities, and the personal influence that seemed so paramount in them (Schlesinger, 1988). Freud himself was wise enough, as early as 1915, to recognize the crucial motivational role of "transference love." Yet he himself, fresh from his years of neuropathology and still, we can suspect, ill at ease in the uncharted seas of therapeutic intimacy, sought scientific *terra firma*. After all, he gave his new discipline the name "analysis," carrying its connotations of laboratory and logic.

The first generation of psychoanalysts continued—with significant exceptions, such as Ferenzci (1923)—to view the "lesser" psychotherapeutic components, and the relationship in which they were embedded, as necessary dross, to be purified by the gemlike flame of interpretation. Now the pendulum has swung—possibly as psychoanalysts have tried to accomplish more and more in work with deeply ingrained disturbances. The role of the personal relationship to the analyst (Greenson, 1971; Zetzel, 1965), the reproduction of a nurturant holding environment (Winnicott, 1958), and the provision of empathic caring that can be internalized (Kohut, 1977), all have become currency that rivals interpretative exchange.

Perhaps we must forego allegiance to single, simple answers. True, psychoanalytic skill involves the capacity for empathy at what I have referred to as its several levels; but it also includes wider knowledge of dynamic and developmental principles, including accurate knowledge of affects in all their layers and guises, of the painful shock involved in discovering alien ones and the slow process entailed in rediscovering and relinquishing unwanted ones. Put more succinctly, a reasonable hypothesis is that psychoanalysis requires a caring empathic relationship and also accurate knowledge of a wide range of psychic functioning; both are necessary, and neither is sufficient, for growth and change in psychoanalysis.

The hypothesis is hardly revolutionary. If we accept as a premise that psychoanalysis repeats crucial aspects of early development, it becomes absurd to force a choice between interpretative accuracy and empathic caring. Parents impart wisdom that becomes solidified in maxims and precepts; these, however, are not their sole teaching vehicles. Parental influences—along with wider cultural ones—stem from myriad other, emotionally tinged, contacts. So it is inevitably with the analyst.

The real task ahead—as in the broader nature versus nurture controversy—is to sharpen both prongs of the hypothetical argument, and to find ways of assessing which apply to which patients under which circumstances. Several decades of research into psychodynamic areas (exemplified by Luborsky, 1984; Strupp and Binder, 1984; Weiss and Sampson, 1986; Dahl et al., 1978) have pointed the direction. Emotionally the task is formidable but exhilarating.

REFERENCES

Adatto, C. (1957). On pouting. *J. Amer. Psychoanal. Assn.,* 5:245–249.

Arlow, J. A. (1957). On smugness. *Int. J. Psychoanal.,* 38:1–8.

Beres, D. & Arlow, J. A. (1974). Fantasy and identification in empathy. *Psychoanal. Q.,* 43:4–25.

Brenner, C. (1975). Affects and psychic conflict. *Psychoanal. Q.,* 43:532–556.

Bibring, E. (1954). Psychoanalysis and the dynamic psychotherapies. *J. Amer. Psychoanal. Assn.,* 21:745–770.

Brierley, M. (1937). Affects in theory and practice. *Int. J. Psychoanal.,* 18:256–274.

DAHL, H., TELLER, V., MOSS, D. & TRUJILLO, M. (1978). Countertransference examples of the syntactic expression of warded-off contents. *Psychoanal. Q.,* 47:339–363.

DARWIN, C. (1872). *The Expression of Emotions in Man and Animals.* Chicago: Univ. Chicago Press, 1965.

DEUTSCH, F. (1939). The choice of organ in organ neurosis. *Int. J. Psychoanal.,* 20:252–262.

——— (1958). The associative anamnesis and sector therapy as a psychoanalytically oriented approach to patients. *Acta Psychother. Psychosom. Orthopaed.,* 6:289–306.

DOLLARD, J. & MILLER, N. E. (1950). *Personality and Psychotherapy.* New York: McGraw Hill.

EKMAN, P. (1982). *Emotions in the Human Face* (2nd ed.) New York: Cambridge Univ. Press.

——— (1985). *Telling Lies.* New York: Norton.

EMDE, R. N. (1983). Levels of meaning for infant emotions. In *Development of Cognition, Affect and Social Relations,* ed. W. A. Collins. Hillsdale, N.J.: Erlbaum.

——— (1988). Development terminable and interminable: I. *Int. J. Psychoanal.,* 69:23–42.

FELDMAN, S. S. (1941). On the fear of being buried alive. *Psychiat. Q.,* 16:641–645.

FERENCZI, S. (1923). *Sex in Psychoanalysis.* New York: Basic Books, 1950.

FLIESS, R. (1942). Metapsychology of the analyst. *Psychoanal. Q.,* 11:211–227.

FREUD, S. (1914). Remembering, repeating, and working-through. *S. E.,* 12.

——— (1915). Observations on transference. *S. E.,* 12.

——— (1937). Analysis terminable and interminable. *S. E.,* 23.

GIFFORD, S. (1973). Comments on Binstock's paper "Purgation through pity and terror." *Int. J. Psychoanal.,* 54:499–504.

GREENSON, R. R. (1960). Empathy and its vicissitudes. *Int. J. Psychoanal.,* 41:418–424.

——— (1965). The problem of working through. In *Drives, Affects, Behavior,* ed. M. Schur. New York: Int. Univ. Press.

——— (1971). The "real" relationship between the patient and the psychoanalyst. *Int. J. Psychoanal.,* 53:403–417.

GRODDECK, G. (1928). *The Book of the Id.* New York & Washington: Nervous and Mental Disease Publishing Co.

HOROWITZ, M. J. (1988). Unconsciously determined defensive strategies. In *Psychodynamics and Cognition,* ed. M. J. Horowitz. Chicago: Univ. Chicago Press, p. 49–88.

IZARD, C. (1971). *The Face of Human Emotion.* New York: Appleton-Century-Crofts.

KANDEL, E. R. (1979). Psychotherapy and the synapse. *New Eng. J. Med.,* 301:1028–1037.

——— (1983). From metapsychology to molecular biology. *Amer. J. Psychiat.,* 140:1277.

KERNBERG, O. F. (1971). *Object Relations Theory and Clinical Psychoanalysis.* New York: Aronson.

KNAPP, P. H., Ed. (1963). *Expression of the Emotions in Man.* New York: Int. Univ. Press.

——— (1969). Image, symbol and person. *Arch. Gen. Psychiat.,* 21:392–406.
——— (in press). Self-other schemas. In *Person Schemas and Maladaptive Interpersonal Behavior Patterns,* ed. M. J. Horowitz. Chicago: Univ. Chicago Press.
KOHUT, H. (1977). *The Restoration of the Self.* Madison, Ct.: Int. Univ. Press.
KRYSTAL, H. (1979). Alexithymia and psychoanalytic treatment. *Amer. J. Psychother.,* 33:17–31.
KUBIE, L. S. (1941). The repetitive core of neurosis. *Psychoanal. Q.,* 10:23–43.
LEWIN, B. D. (1935). Claustrophobia. *Psychoanal. Q.,* 4:227–233.
——— (1954). Sleep, narcissistic neurosis and the analytic situation. *Psychoanal. Q.,* 23:487–510.
LINDEMANN, E. (1945). Psychiatric problems in conservative treatment of ulcerative colitis. *Arch. Neurol. Psychiat.,* 53:322–325.
LUBORSKY, L. (1984). *Principles of Psychoanalytic Psychotherapy.* New York: Basic Books.
MACALPINE, I. (1950). The development of the transference. *Psychoanal. Q.,* 19:501–539.
MCDOUGALL, J. (1989). *Theatres of the Body.* New York: Norton.
MAHL, G. F. (1977). Body, movement, ideation and verbalization during psychoanalysis. In *Communicative Structures and Psychic Structures,* ed. N. Freedman & S. Grand. New York: Plenum.
MANN, J. (1973). *Time-Limited Psychotherapy.* Cambridge, Mass.: Harvard Univ. Press.
MODELL, A. H. (1988). On the protection and safety of the analytic setting. In *How Does Treatment Help?* ed. A. Rothstein. New York: Int. Univ. Press.
NOVEY, S. (1962). The principle of "working through" in psychoanalysis. *J. Amer. Psychoanal. Assn.,* 10:658–676.
RANGELL, L. (1966). The psychology of poise. *Int. J. Psychoanal.,* 35:313–332.
RAPAPORT, D. (1953). On the psychoanalytic theory of affects. *Int. J. Psychoanal.,* 34:177–198.
RAZRAN, G. (1961). The observable unconscious and the inferable conscious in current Soviet psychophysiology. *Psychol. Rev.,* 68:81–141.
RESCORLA, R. A. (1988). Pavlovian conditioning: it's not what you think it is. *Amer. Psychologist,* 43:151–160.
RICHFIELD, J. (1954). An analysis of the concept of insight. *Psychoanal. Q.,* 23:390–408.
ROGERS, C. R. (1957). The necessary and sufficient conditions of therapeutic personality change. *J. Consult. Counsel. Psychol.,* 21:91–103.
RUSSELL, B. (1929). *Mysticism and Logic.* New York: Norton, p. 209.
SCHEFLEN, A. (1963). Communication and regulation in psychotherapy. *Psychiatry,* 26:128–136.
SCHLESINGER, H. J. (1988). A historical overview of conceptions of the mode of therapeutic action of psychoanalytic psychotherapy. In *How Does Treatment Help?* ed. A. Rothstein. Madison, CT.: Int. Univ. Press.
SCHUR, M. (1960). Discussion of "Grief and mourning in infancy and early childhood" by J. Bowlby. *Psychoanal. Study Child,* 15:63–84.
SCHWARTZ, A. (1987). Drives, affects, behavior and learning. *J. Amer. Psychoanal. Assn.,* 35:467–506.
SOLOMON, R. L. (1968). Avoidance learning. In *Int. Encyl. Soc. Sci.,* 9:148–154, ed. E. Jills. New York: Macmillan.
SPENCE, D. P. (1987). *The Freudian Metaphor.* New York: Norton.

STERN, D. N. (1985). *The Interpersonal World of the Infant.* New York: Basic Books.
STONE, L. (1961). *The Psychoanalytic Situation.* New York: Int. Univ. Press.
STRACHEY, J. (1934). The nature of the therapeutic action of psychoanalysis. *Int. J. Psychoanal.,* 15:127–159 (revised, *Int. J. Psychoanal.,* 50:275–292, 1969).
STRUPP, H. & BINDER, J. (1984). *Psychotherapy in a New Key.* New York: Basic Books.
TOMKINS, S. S. (1962–63). *Affect, Imagery, Consciousness,* 2 Vols. New York: Springer.
TURKHAN, J. S. (1989). Classical conditioning: the new hegemony. *Behav. Brain Sci.,* 12:121–179.
WEISS, J. & SAMPSON, H. (1986). *The Psychoanalytic Process.* New York: Guilford Press.
WINNICOTT, D. W. (1958). *Collected Papers.* New York: Basic Books.
WOLF, E. (1967). Learning theory and psychoanalysis. *Int. J. Psychiat.,* 7:525–535.
ZETZEL, E. R. (1965). A developmental model and the theory of therapy. In *The Capacity for Emotional Growth.* New York: Int. Univ. Press, 1970, pp. 246–269.
ZILBOORG, G. (1954). The emotional problem and the therapeutic role of insight. *Psychoanal. Q.,* 21:1–24.

Boston University School of Medicine
Division of Psychiatry
83 East Newton Street
Suite 810
Boston, MA 02118-2393

AFFECT THEORY AND THE THEORY OF TECHNIQUE

HAROLD P. BLUM, M.D.

Affects are discussed from a psychoanalytic perspective; developmental, cultural, and genetic influences on affective expression and experience are also noted. Basic human affects evolve from innate potentials, species-specific with individual and cultural dimensions, increasing in complexity, and serving multiple functions in the course of development. The theory of psychoanalytic technique has always included consideration of affects, beginning with Freud's use of the cathartic method and later the relationship of affect to structural theory and defense. Communication of affect within the two-way field of the analytic process as well as particular problems in the analysis of patients who have specific difficulty in recognition, experience, communication, and regulation of affect are discussed. Unconscious trauma, elaborated in fantasy, may leave a permanent imprint on mood. The centrality of affects in psychoanalytic work is stressed. Affects are analyzed in the context of conflict, including the significance of defense against affect, affect as defense, and progressive as well as regressive modification. Affective disorders are multiply determined and cannot be isolated from intrapsychic conflict.

THOUGH AFFECTS HAVE always had a central role in both clinical psychoanalysis and recently in normal psychology, affect theory remains diffuse. Affects have been operationally defined and clinically utilized without a consensual definition and cohesive, unified formulation of the concept. The lack of adequate definition and the multiplicity of theories, in psychoanalysis and in academic psychology, may be related to both the subjective component and the complexity of affects. I shall focus upon psychoanalytic considerations while referring, where relevant, to academic and developmental psychological contributions. I will discuss the theoretical

---

Clinical Professor of Psychiatry and Training Analyst, New York University School of Medicine.

concepts of affect which continue to evolve, and will focus on the role of affects in clinical psychoanalytic work. Affect dispositions and their relationship to mood and to character traits will also be addressed.

The word "affect" is often used interchangeably with "feeling" and "emotion," but affect includes much more than subjective feelings. In addition to the experiential feeling or emotional dimension, affect encompasses activating or inhibiting, hedonic, adaptive, communicative, and neurophysiological aspects. Affects are related to motivation, cognition, and behavior. Although influenced by maturation, development, and life experience, by society and culture, affects also are innate and genetically determined. Based upon both phylogeny and ontogeny, the basic human affects evolve from innate potentials which are species-specific and cross-cultural. Developmentally basic affects have been categorized (Ekman et al., 1972) as happiness, sadness, surprise, interest, fear, disgust, contempt, and anger. These basic affects are "prewired" innate potentials, each with its own facial configuration and neurophysiology. These affects also are thought to have differentiated in the course of evolution from the more general affective states of pleasure and unpleasure and are important to ego development, object relations, and infant-caregiver communication.

In addition to the basic categorization of affects as pleasurable or unpleasurable and positive or negative, psychoanalytic writing has also more loosely categorized affects as single or multiple, primary or secondary, simple, complex, or compound, fixed or labile (Glover, 1939). Contemporary views of affect theory have led to varied models taking into account vast overdetermination and multiple function.

Freud's Formulations and Evolving Analytic Concepts of Affect

Initially, characterizing affects as discharge processes, Freud (1916–17) also noted the subtle complexities within the concept: "And what is an affect in the dynamic sense? It is in any case something highly composite. An affect includes in the first place particular motor innervations or discharges and secondly certain feelings; the latter are of two kinds—perceptions of the motor actions that have occurred and the direct feelings of pleasure and unpleasure which, as we say, give the affect its keynote. But I do not think that with this enumeration we have arrived at the essence of an affect . . . the core which holds the combination we have described together is the repetition of some particular significant experience. This experience could only be a very early impression of a very general nature, placed in the prehistory not of the individual but of the species" (pp. 395–396).

For Freud, the psychological and the biological aspects of affect and their interrelationship were all important. Probably early inferences about unconscious mental activity drawn from hypnosis led Freud to relate affect storms to hysterical attacks, and to assume that the repressed or blocked accumulated affect underlay the pathogenesis of hysterical symptoms (Breuer and Freud, 1895). The "dammed-up" state was relieved by abreaction, leading to the treatment method of catharsis. In this early "preanalytic" period, the dammed-up state, especially of anxiety, was a result of abnormal sexual behavior with either insufficient or incomplete sexual discharge, either diminished or excessive libidinal gratification (Freud, 1895). It should be noted that the biological basis of the dammed-up state of internal tension was related both to affect and to a primordial concept of drive. In early theory drive and affect were intricately related.

Anxiety neurosis was at that time seen as a syndrome separate from other conditions with mental content, since the anxiety was an indirect, as it were, toxic product of the repressed drive. This was historically related to the concept of "actual neurosis" in which the clinical picture was derived from an abnormal psychophysiological set of reactions in which libido had been converted into anxiety. Actual neurosis is related to current psychosomatic concepts in which repressed and suppressed affects are regarded as pathogenic.

The explicit prominence of affect theory may be discerned in remarks which are prescient of later drive theory. Using energic terms and a borderland concept interfacing the physical and psychological, Freud (1894) referred to the psyche operating with "a quota of affect or sum of excitation—which possesses all the characteristics of quantity . . . , which is capable of increase, diminution, displacement and discharge, and which is spread over the memory-traces of ideas somewhat as an electric charge is spread over the surface of the body" (p. 60). In the pleasure-unpleasure principle itself, the basic motivation was affective.

The cathartic method, developed to relieve the dammed-up affect associated with hysteria and anxiety neurosis, was also related to the evolving theory of psychic trauma. Ideas, and particularly memories connected with traumatic experience, were associated with strangulated affects. Recovery depended upon recapture of the traumatic memories or reconstruction of the traumatic situation with associated affects. Affective abreaction and reexperience were necessary in the current safe context of treatment and in the cognitive context which placed traumas in historical perspective and differentiated past and present. Thoughts were involved in the recognition, expression, and modification of traumatic anxiety and rage and in the understanding of pathogenesis. In clinical work, from Freud onward, affects were considered to be elicited by cognitive activity, for example, pleasure following winning an award, anxiety caused by separation or castration threats, guilt following a self-critical moral judgment, etc. Much of the affective-cognitive change sought in the prestructural, pioneer period of psychoanalysis has been incorporated into later analytic aims. In contemporary theory affects reciprocally influence thought, fantasy, action, and the internal ego system of self and object representations; affects influence cognition and learning as well.

For Freud, affects not only could be separated from all other mental content but could be sharply differentiated from ideas. Ideas had a different evolutionary, neurobiological substrate and were not subject to affect discharge patterns and displacement. Unlike affects, ideas could be transformed into plastic visual representations. Affects challenged total translation into equivalent language (Greene, 1977), and the relations between affect and ideation remain controversial. Affect and ideation may be conceptually linked (Brenner, 1974) or may become inseparable in the course of development. I believe that affect and cognition are different though interrelated processes, and affect may be conceptualized independently of intrinsic ideation.

Early psychoanalytic discussion of affect involved different domains of discourse, e.g., the biological, psychological, metapsychological, and psychosomatic. While Freud (1940) had tried to relate the rate, rhythm, and patterning of affect discharge to pleasure/unpleasure experiences, he finally returned to qualitative considerations. Jacobson (1953), among later analysts, continued to emphasize quantitative, energic processes of rate, rhythm, and discharge, but this did not determine the direction of investigation of affect in contemporary psychoanalysis. Furthermore, the emphasis upon the processes of discharge and economic theory would not prove to be convergent with more current concerns close to clinical experience (experience near). Clinicians have been aware of the relative inapplicability of metapsychological notions of affects to analytic work with patients. Arlow (1977) noted that within the psychoanalytic situation many of these remote, speculative, theoretical formulations tended to obscure clinical investigation.

Rapaport (1953) explicated the development of affect theory within the larger development of psychoanalytic theory. Following the initial cathartic phase, he described a second period, during which affects were regarded primarily as discharges into the interior, subjectively altering the subject's own body. Subjective feeling, perceived sensation, and neurophysiological response were interrelated but could be partially independent. Affects, along with ideas and actions, were then considered derivatives of the instinctual drives. Affects were related to topography, with inconsistent exposition of unconscious, preconscious, and conscious aspects of affect and emotions or feelings (Pulver, 1971). The locus of affect, though primarily a conscious experience, was in a topographic limbo.

Rapaport (1953) noted that after the introduction of the structural viewpoint in 1923 and the signal theory of anxiety (Freud, 1926), the ego became the "seat" of the affects, although all three psychic structures influenced the development of affects through life. In the course of both normal development and analytic progress, affects tend to become differentiated and identified, tamed and neutralized, controlled and modulated (Fenichel, 1941; Rangell, 1974). Freud (1926) delineated the transformation of traumatic anxiety into signal anxiety, and this became a model for the transformation and taming of affects, in general. Reduced to signals, affects were then continuous with cognition, with implicit emphasis upon regulatory functions. In later structural theory affects were also reciprocally influenced by the developing psychic structures as well as by external reality and object relations.

The relation of affects to defense, particularly anxiety, is a central issue in psychoanalysis. As a core affect, Freud (1926) gave anxiety a crucial position in both neurosis and normal psychic function. In the second theory of anxiety, there is always a possibility of a traumatic state brought about by the ego's recognition of danger. The transformation of traumatic anxiety into signal anxiety is a developmental achievement. As the signal of anticipated danger, anxiety is no longer the consequence of repression and damming up; anxiety is the cause of repression rather than a physiological consequence of repression. Anxiety is psychological, although it has biological roots and referents and psychosomatic ramifications. Anxiety may appear to be absent or may be overshadowed by other affects such as shame and guilt, but the analyst will be aware that there is always anxiety intrinsic to every form of symptomatic and character disturbance (Rangell, 1978). However, anxiety is not necessarily paradigmatic for other affects.

Anxiety, so closely linked to the motivation for defense, may also be the object of defense. In fact, the analytic situation is continuously complicated by the ego's use of affects as defense, with one affect sometimes defending against others. Elation may ward off depression through the denial of the emotional impact of loss, and anger may serve to mask anxiety. Affect patterns are expressions of or part of a person's self representation and identity, but the layering of the affects is exceedingly complex and serves multiple functions in the analytic situation and in life. The function of an affect or how it is used in the analytic situation is probably best understood in association with unconscious conflicts embedded in the unconscious transference fantasy (Arlow, 1977). Elucidating the difficulty in the clinical comprehension of affects, Schafer (1964) observed that affects may or may not be artificial and that surface affect expressions may be deceiving or misleading. There are also fused or blended affects, and it is the clinician's task to unmask and differentiate affects that are amalgamated and have become conglomerates or compound rather than simple affects.

Recognition of the importance of signal anxiety may be linked to the emergence of increasingly sophisticated concepts of affect, the danger situation, the mechanisms of defense, and ego psychology. Signal anxiety involved the transformation of traumatic anxiety to a thought-like communication within the psyche. The concept of signal anxiety introduced new regulatory and communicative dimensions of affect.

The concept of signal anxiety also has contributed to new paradigms for an enlarged view of affects in the theory of technique. Signal affects of unpleasure, in addition to anxiety, play an important role in psychic conflict and in the mobilization of defense (Schur, 1969; Rangell, 1974; Brenner, 1975). Signal anxiety can thus be associated with the entire gamut of the signals of unpleasure, elaborated by the ego in the face of danger. The danger situation itself is complicated by the influence of all three psychic structures as well as the ego's response to the external world. In this newer formulation, defense could be mobilized by shame and guilt as well as anxiety, although signal anxiety would occupy the exceptional position which Freud (1926) had noted in both pathogenesis and adaptation.

A further enlargement of the signal function of affects is related not only to unpleasure and defense, but to pleasure and gratification. Affects may serve "go" as well as "stop" functions and are involved in the motivational thrust toward the pleasurable experience as well as the pleasure itself. Analysts will be sensitive not only to the presence of anxiety and other affects of unpleasure but also to the presence or absence, the range and intensity, and conflicts associated with pleasurable affect. Anhedonic patients who are relatively incapable of pleasant, gratifying life experiences, in the course of progressive analytic work, will be able to recover and express positive affects. What has been called the "contagion of anxiety," the communication and evocation of affective responses and expressions of others, also applies to the shared pleasures of object relations. In the analytic situation, there is a sublimated pleasure in toleration and clarification of frightening thoughts and feelings, the achievement of insight, and the gradual attainment of mastery over unconscious conflict and trauma. The pleasure of mastery and achievement in analytic growth has often been underrated compared to the motivating power of anxiety. The satisfaction associated with understanding and insight also generates interest in maintaining and advancing the analytic process.

Developmental Considerations

Understanding of the role of affect expression and communication in analysis and in object relations has been greatly expanded in recent years (Sandler and Sandler, 1978). This has come from two different directions, inside and outside the analytic situation. From within the analytic situation, interest in affects has been associated with newer considerations of the importance of empathy and of the potential value as well as the impeding effect of countertransference. Outside of clinical psychoanalysis, neuropsychology, infant research, and developmental studies of affects have provided major influences. Affects are part of the bond between analyst and patient, but also part of all human attachment beginning with infant and caregiver.

Affective bonds promote development which, in turn, enriches the entire panoply of human affective states. Protoaffects or affect tendencies precede cognition and appear to be essential to primordial "attachment." Spitz (1965) noted the essential importance of the dialogue between caregiver and infant, an affective and socializing experience for the infant which propels ego development and the formation of more advanced object relations. As development and differentiation progress, the dialogue becomes more complex, as does the concomitant affective experience.

Infant research has shown that the communication of affect in earliest life—for example, through visual or tactile contact, through a host of affectomotor cues and clues, through appeal or aversion, starting/stopping and selectively reinforcing certain aspects of the infant-caregiver dialogue—has illuminated the complex role of affects in development. Building on the pioneer path of Spitz (1965) several analysts (Mahler et al., 1975; Emde, 1983; Stern, 1985) have contributed to our understanding of the genesis of affects and their interplay with other factors in the course of development.

The infant's affective experience of himself and the caregiver is coordinated and organized with maternal empathy and communication (Shapiro, 1974). Certain analytic functions are analogous to those of the caregiver, and the analyst will also recognize, validate, articulate, and help to reorganize affects in the analytic process. This occurs pari passu with interpretation of repressed and isolated affect, and the taming or modulation of affect with analytic insight. The observing, reflecting, discriminating, clarifying, and synthesizing aspects of analytic technique indicate that analysis is far more than interpretation alone. Some patients first identify some of their affects in the course of analytic work.

Constitutional factors, usually described as innate disposition and powerful influences stemming from earliest object relations, interact in development. Affective dimensions of the infant-caregiver relationship have been referred to as attachment, attunement, bonding, affectomotor communication, mutual cueing, etc. The infant will develop ambivalence as affects acquire increasing psychological meaning in the second year of life. As object constancy develops, there is greater tolerance and taming of negative affects and integration of affects within the emerging personality (Mahler et al., 1975; Kernberg, 1976). Parallel to the formation of intrapsychic conflict and of tripartite structure, affect responses accompany and reciprocally influence ego and superego functions. Guilt will emerge as an affective ingredient and gradient of superego function in oedipal and postoedipal development. Here identifications indirectly influence affects through ego and superego development and directly through identifications with the affects and moods of signficant objects and with their defenses against affects.

While affects are, in degree, genetically determined, cultural determinants also play a significant role. Affects are influenced by the customs and values of the particular cultural settings and backgrounds of the participants. Affects are not only species-specific, but person-specific, and though affects have always been considered part of the human condition in all of the world's languages and literature, what is experienced as anger or anxiety by the particular individual will not necessarily be the same for another individual. Furthermore, the differentiation and recognition of affects and the capacity to express affect are all subject to cultural influence and individual variations. The capacity to express (or to mask affect) in words also varies considerably, depending upon endowment and development. The recognition of different affects may be relatively independent of the expression of affects and affective phenomena. In contemporary psychoanalysis we are much more likely to focus not only upon individual, pertinent, and prominent affects, such as anxiety or guilt, but upon affective styles, patterns, and range of "affectivity." In general, we speak of affect as impoverished or excessive, inappropriate or inconsistent, masked or conspicuous, intrusive or restrained, and labile or fixed, etc. Affects in the transference-countertransference field are under constant analytic scrutiny, and in this connection, the transference was first divided according to positive or negative affect expression.

Families have special importance for affect development and style and for learning affect expression and modulation. Childhood is lived within a familial group process where affect dispositions, patterns, and styles are developed and shaped within the framework of object relationships and identifications. Later group processes may influence the activation and disposition of anxiety, shame, guilt, etc. Group process exerts a selective and regulatory effect, but affect reciprocally influences group formation and cohesion.

The emphasis upon affects in relation to ego, self representation, and object relations theory, rather than being viewed primarily as id derivatives or as phylogenetically determined, is coincident with contemporary appreciation of developmental complexity rather than simple schemas.

Affects and Analytic Process

Subtle affective exchanges, sometimes demonstrable only with the aid of specialized scientific equipment, doubtless also go on in the network of conscious and unconscious communication within the intimacy of the psychoanalytic situation. In the first consultation, affective relatedness and responsiveness have diagnostic and analytic significance. Affects continue to exert an important influence upon and within the transference, in the motivation for beginning treatment, and in the separation anxiety, sadness, and mourning associated with termination.

The analytic process favors uncensored affect recognition, response, and expression and identifies affects "for analytic scrutiny." From the point of view of technique, clinical psychoanalysis has moved away from a one-person or mirror psychology to a two-person psychology in which the analyst is both observer and participant. The analyst's responses to the patient occur in the context of a transference-countertransference field in which two-way affective/cognitive communications are part of the analytic process. In the two-person field, although affects are bilaterally scrutinized and assessed, considerable registration and response may remain outside of conscious awareness. Affects have the unusual capacity to become contagious and silently to involve the analytic partner. Silence may be a rich medium for experiencing affect and may arouse affects such as feeling soothed, isolated, blissful, etc. Patients may attempt to edit, dampen, mask, and monitor their emotional responses and feelings. Patients can more successfully mask facial and vocal affective expression than autonomic responses, such as tachycardia and sweating.

In terms of contemporary technique, the analyst continuously screens and scrutinizes his or her own feelings and emotional responses to the patient. I do not refer here only to countertransference impediments to the accurate understanding of the analyst's own emotional reactions. I also refer to the analyst's empathic awareness, increasing knowledge, and reasonable assumptions about the patient's feelings, defenses against affects, and attempts to induce emotional reactions in the analyst. Most of the muted, internal signals within the analyst's "work-ego" do not constitute countertransference interference. They are or may become part of the analyst's empathy and affective attunement to the patient, although they may often overlap with countertransference interference. For example, the analyst's own anger or guilt may lead to a regressive loss of neutrality to the point of obstructing the analytic process; but as analyzed signals, they may point to the patient's attempt to arouse the analyst's guilt and blame the analyst.

The analyst learns about the patient's affective life through the patient's verbal and nonverbal communication by combining analytic knowledge with direct observation and empathy. The empathic analyst is affectively attuned to the patient, feeling the "vibes," observing eye contact and facial expression, posture and gesture, and the patient's gait upon entering and leaving the session, as well as attending to the patient's verbal free association. The patient's central verbalization is analytically coordinated with the affective cues of pitch, pressure, and tone of voice. The analyst also affectively scans the scene through educated inferences and constructions of what the patient is feeling, and through analysis of irrational countertransference responses. If the analyst is anxious or angry with the patient, this may be based upon the analyst's own unconscious, irrational reactions to the patient's transference or something about whom or what the patient represents to the analyst, i.e., the analyst's transference to the patient (Blum, 1986). An accurate, empathic perception of the patient's feeling and mood, however, is in the long run essential for an appropriate analytic ambience and correct interpretation. Empathy, appropriately processed, informs and potentiates the analytic process.

In the intimacy and complexity of the analytic situation,

the analyst would also have to take into account the reciprocal communication of the analyst's affective experience and that of the patient. This could be conveyed through the analyst's and patient's tone of voice, pitch, pressure, and intensity of speech, frequency of respiration and movement as well as well-organized, calm, analytic linguistic communication. Language, of course, communicates and conveys affect, so important in object relations.

Language directly designates affects and implies affects in context or in metaphor such as "tickled pink" or "down in the dumps." But though language cannot fully articulate the ineffable, silent, subjective reactions that are part of affective experience and expression, language communicates and transforms affect. Verbalizing affects promotes ego discrimination, expression, and regulation of affects. The affective dimension of discourse is comprised of language as well as the metalinguistic contributions from tone, volume, etc. Parallel to language, then, are nonverbal sighs and cries, as well as the affectomotor communication of gesture, facial expression, posture, and gait. Analysis attempts to experience and reexperience affects, to identify, clarify, and communicate affect in words, and to reintegrate isolated affect through language and insight.

Persistent affective states and moods color the analytic relationship and are of central interest in analytic work. The transference relationship involves complex affective states of love and hate which, though related to libido and aggression, cannot be simply reduced to drive derivatives. From early infancy, object relationships encompass instinctual investments, affective bonds, and increasingly subtle and differentiated affectively laden cues and communications. Affects contribute to and are altered by structure formation. Representations of self and object probably include the experience of the relationship (Loewald, 1974). Transference is more than a distortion of the actual perception of the analyst, but always includes some effort to reinstate a wished-for relationship of the past; to defend against the forbidden and anxiety-laden aspects of the relationship; and an effort to induce, seduce, provoke, or otherwise elicit desired interactions with the object. Those wished (and feared) interactions may repeat in disguised form infantile object relationships. The patient is always attempting to elicit particular affective responses from the analyst and reacting to the analyst's affective style and response. What the patient evokes in the analyst in the form of signal affects and feeling states may be a very useful source of material for the analyst's further awareness of transference pressures. Affects are fundamental to subjective experience and to the meaning of experience. Here again, meaning is a function of both affect and cognition and probably of cognitive-affective systems reciprocally influenced by the totality of psychic structure. However, many affects follow upon cognitive evaluation, e.g., anxiety as response to danger, grief as a response to loss, etc. In extreme situations it is possible that we may approach states of pure affect or pure thought. Technically it is not necessarily correct or always desirable to give affect interpretation first priority; passive compliance may require clarification before underlying rage. Since affects are crucially related to conflict and compromise formation, to meaning, to conviction, to "genuine" insight, and to feelings of authenticity and self-continuity, it is clear that affects will influence every dimension of the psychoanalytic process and situation.

Patients with unstable object constancy often have very wide swings of ambivalence and tend to have unmodulated affect states and storms. Affect issues are then likely to be more prominent in the transference and countertransference. Countertransference signals help delineate transference configurations. If the patient is repeating in the transference subjective affective responses to a mother who was in a chronic state of agitated depression, is the affective response evoked in the analyst by the patient's communications necessary for the understanding of those communications? The analyst's signal affect may be carefully monitored and helpful, but the analyst does not depend upon countertransference signals as essential to understand the patient. The feelings evoked in the analyst are, however, a potential contribution to the analytic work. The analyst actually cannot and does not operate as "the surgeon, who puts aside all his feelings, even his human sympathy, and concentrates his mental forces on the single aim of performing the operation as skilfully as possible" (Freud, 1912, p. 115). The analyst uses modulated feelings to further the analytic process. The analyst does have emotional responses which are not wholly neutral and which are sometimes quite alien to his or her own usual reactions to that patient or other patients. Neither Freud's surgical nor mirror metaphor is currently viewed as a literally appropriate technical recommendation. But the metaphor of the analyst's unconscious as a receptive organ tuned to the transmitting unconscious of the patient is particularly apt if considered in terms of bilateral affective communication. Such alien feelings are not simply transferred from the patient, as if the analyst were a container for the patient's feelings and ideas. The analyst's feelings are themselves complex responses, related to the analyst's empathy, identifications, conflicts, defenses, etc. The analyst's affective experience needs not only to be monitored, but to be analyzed so that the transference and the countertransference (actual or potential) can be clearly distinguished and understood. Unanalyzed countertransference impedes empathy, neutrality, and correct interpretation. The analyst should not confuse the patient's conflicts and experiences with his or her own reactions.

The analyst's boredom or lassitude is also a source of information about the patient and about countertransference tendencies and the "work-ego." When the patient senses the nonneutral, affective response on the part of the analyst, the patient may interpret the analyst's contribution to the problem. But whether the patient frets or gloats at the analyst's real or imagined excitement, anger, or reproach, the patient's reponses are never entirely determined by the analyst. The patient's transference and character are major determinants of the patient's affective response to the analyst's affective input. These affective responses are an important part of continuing analytic work upon the patient's conflicts and fantasies.

While these responses may be more overt, more pronounced, more intrusive and disruptive with very infantile personalities, borderline characters, and ego deviant patients, they are the focus of analytic work with all patients. It also follows that patients with affect intolerance, more serious affect impoverishment, so-called alexithymic tendencies, and those who convey emotion without having the conscious feeling may be just as difficult to treat as patients with labile affect or affect storms. Some patients use affect labels such as "sad" or "mad" without feeling or consistent meaning. Some patients can recognize affects in others far more readily than in themselves, or vice versa. This ability to recognize and empathize with the object's affects implies that the patient's affect disorder is probably determined by conflict and not by deficit.

Work with borderline patients and those with developmental deviations or deficits has led not only to reconsiderations of the influence of the preoedipal upon oedipal development, but also to the primary significance of very early disturbance. Affective dispositions such as basic trust, confident expectation, and feelings of optimism are all thought to arise in the preverbal phase, although their consolidation is influenced by subsequent development. Sound, secondary narcissism and confident self-esteem follow from earlier basic trust (Erikson, 1950; Mahler et al., 1975).

Entailing some conjecture, it is possible to relate certain affective reactions in the adult to preverbal, infantile tendencies and experience. The most careful analysis of transference and countertransference phenomena combined with knowledge of the specific patient's infantile life and a knowledge of affect development are necessary to arrive at a reasonable assumption concerning preverbal affect dispositions. Based upon adult analytic data, reconstructions of such adult affect constellations have been attempted. A number of such affect reconstructions have converged on the oral phase, e.g., the character traits of poise (Rangell, 1954); smugness (Arlow, 1957); serenity (Winnicott, 1958); and enthusiasm (Greenson, 1962). Greenacre (1941) noted the predisposition to anxiety and aggression and regarded the psychosomatic, physiological manifestations of affects in the psychoanalytic situation as possibly representing the repetition of preverbal experience which had never been previously verbalized.

Freud had already detected, very early in the development of psychoanalysis, the preoedipal antecedent of guilt, the "germ of guilt" that was a residue of the death of his brother Julius. It is probable that the loss of this sibling and the birth of his next sibling, powerfully influencing both infant and caregiver, contributed to his lifelong depressive tendencies (Blum, 1977). In this connection, Emde (1980) noted, "complex affect states of anxiety and depression, each have their own hierarchical developmental histories, their own propensities for sustained mood, and their own signal affect systems" (p. 72).

Such tendencies, e.g., anxiety or depressive proclivities, pessimistic or optimistic attitudes, good humor, wittiness, irony, are all closely related to character. In some instances, character, affect tendencies, and mood tend to converge as in the depressive character. The attitude of pessimistic despondency is associated with sadness and depressive mood. Weinshel (1970) regarded moods as psychological structures which bind affects and which have a genetic relationship to unconscious early events, i.e., memories which are the genetic nuclei for the moods. Moods tend to distort reality, color cognitive and perceptual processes, and inevitably involve a selection of linked memories. In Arlow's (1977) view, moods are structured affective states perpetuated by the continuing influence of unconscious fantasy. Perception, anticipation, and subsequent experience are shaped by unconscious fantasy. The affect, object relationship, and ideas as well as memories are embedded in the unconscious fantasy without sharp distinction between a central persisting affect and a mood. I would additionally note that the mood may be related to the influence of unconscious traumas, current object relations, and the transference. Moods evoke reactions in others, and these reactions may be significant to the features and functions of the mood. Countertransference, or the analyst's characterological affect disposition, can anchor a mood as in the case of the critical analyst and the depressive, self-reproachful patient. Moods are complex, affect-laden, compromise formations which peculiarly influence the range, expression, and regulation of specific affects. Moods bind and express intense affects related to contemporary experience linked to unconscious conflict and trauma. Insofar as affect state and mood are tied to character, such traits may be close to or quite removed from unconscious conflicts, fantasies, and/or traumatic memories. Individuals may be genetically predisposed to particular moods which resist analytic change. Psychoanalytic technique now encompasses the analysis of both character and symptoms. But the analysis of moods which are well-integrated into the personality and associated with ego syntonic character traits may present formidable challenges.

Characteristic affective dispositions and moods are also associated with behavior patterns. Both hypomanic acting out and the psychomotor retardation of depression can seriously interfere with analytic work as well as reality adaptation. Character attitudes and associated characteristic affects, such as the case of the patient who has only one affect—anger, e.g., *The Last Angry Man*—will hardly be exclusive to the analytic transference. The anger may have become enmeshed in secondary gain and pain and in complex adaptation to life. In the extra transference sphere, these patients tend to provoke their own angry altercations. In the transference relationship, characteristic affect dispositions may be important to considerations of the so-called mix and match of patient and analyst. If both patient and analyst tend to be angry, obsessive, or depressive, with characteristic, isolated, or depressive affect, if both use sarcastic humor as defense, if the feelings of one tend regularly to a contagious or distancing effect on the other, then that particular match will be bound to have some influence, however subtle, upon the analytic process. At the same time, the analysis of typical affective responses and moods will be a pathway toward character analysis. And beyond moment-to-moment affects, the mood of the patient in the analytic situation invites careful analytic scrutiny.

Moods are, of course, subject to the influence of the transference-countertransference field and to both analytic and extra-analytic influence. Psychic stimuli and drugs may alter mood; e.g., Freud had noted the mood elevation associated with his smoking cigars. Underlying fantasies often appear to be very important to understanding and to interpreting moods. The fantasies may condense actual traumas, originally associated with overwhelming affects. The blend of affects and prevailing affect tone may also be linked to specific self and object representations.

A brief example here illuminates the technical significance of such unconscious trauma, elaborated in fantasy, and contributing to the complex mood disturbance. A male merchant reported business problems, and that he was in an awful mood, later described as a "shitty mood." He was irritable, pessimistic, dour, and sour; nothing was right or bright. Business was "slow as shit," and he might go bankrupt; he could be up "shit creek without a paddle," or sink into quicksand, a bottomless pit of shit. His dreams further depicted his inner fantasy life. In a recent dream he was sinking into an overflowing toilet, and at the time of the aggravated mood disturbance, he dreamed of three words, "Merde, Verde, Palente." He associated these words, respectively, to the French word for feces, to green diarrhea, and to heaps of excrement. He would be bankrupt, or rich, with lots of greenbacks and plenty of money. He would have security with his love objects, or lose them and his own self worth. The words also magically referred to murder and fertilizing manure, death and rebirth.

The patient was guilty over success and afraid of failure. Unconscious fantasies of oedipal victory, and defeat, and narcissistic mortification were regressively represented in scatalogical language. He was also attempting to master the trauma of childhood object loss, identifying with his idealized and devalued parents, and with their verbal imprecations and interdictions. The patient's guilt and low self-esteem were associated with a fecal self image. His feelings of loss and failure could be clarified and interpreted in the context of his unconscious fantasies with alleviation of his negative mood. His tendency to perceive the world through jaundiced eyes and to anticipate failure in the transference and in life was mitigated with his mood change. However, his predisposition to a negative basic mood with self and object denigration was deeply rooted in his character, and subject to regressive reactivation.

For most patients, the capacity to tolerate and modulate moods and feelings, to unmask and recover hitherto inaccessible feelings, and to endure a wide range of emotions constitutes a major dimension of analytic progress. Changes in the defense organization of the ego, e.g., in isolation and reversal, more realistic, stable self and object representations, more mature superego standards, values, and reliable function, all contribute to and are simultaneously influenced by affective functions and their role in the total personality. The analysis of unconscious conflict and fantasy liberates affective potentials and promotes progressive transformation of regressive, resomatized affective states. Clarification, interpretation, and genetic reconstruction, associated with the application of insight to the working through of pathogenic, affect-laden conflict, remain the most significant aspects of analytic technique.

Affect recognition and reexperience in the transference are integrated with new cognitive understanding and ego regulation. Advancing insight changes automatic anxiety to signal anxiety. Insight provides new perspectives on affective states in relation to conflict, structure, and development. The resolution of unconscious conflict facilitates appropriate experience and expression of affect. The capacity to tolerate and modulate affect is related to the affective component of analytic insight. Cognitive insight without appropriate affect and the experience of emotional conviction is not likely to facilitate structural change (Blum, 1979). Further, the assimilation of insight leads to ego mastery and modulation of affects and to structural change that influences all affective experiences.

Deficit and Related Questions

Biogenetic predispositions are doubtless of great importance and always interact with the shaping affective responses of the caregivers and with all other aspects of development. Major issues in the treatment of severe disorders of affect involve (1) patients with poor communication of affect through language in a verbal treatment; (2) the epigenetic and continuing influence in later life of innate affect dispositions; (3) the transformation of preverbal, affective constellations never before symbolized or verbalized into linguistic communication; (4) integration of somatic, subjective, and expressive dimensions of affect; (5) the limits to affective exchange imposed by the analytic situation and process; and (5) tendencies toward regression, resomatization, and disorganization of affective processes.

The patient does not see the analyst's gaze, facial expression, or gestures, and hears clarifications and interpretations rather dispassionately rendered. The language of interpretation tends to be less emotional and excitable than the affective communication of free association or the affect exchanges of ordinary discourse. Depending also upon overall personality structure and ego resources, many forms of affect disorder are best treated in psychoanalysis. Others might benefit from expressive psychotherapy with face-to-face affective exchanges or supportive recognition and relationship approaches for those patients with very severe disorder. Some patients can be analyzed only after education in affect recognition, clarification, and verbal expression in preparatory psychotherapy. Some patients benefit most from relatively unmodified analysis with expression, identification, and clarification of affects in the context of reliable empathy and consistent interpretation. Those patients with primary affect disorder and significant biogenetic determinants may provide important leads for further research. Techniques yet to be devised for such patients may combine analytic and neurobiological considerations. Many patients with constricted, isolated, or labile affect, or lacking in affect recognition and regulation, may show major improvement after analysis, and with further "living through." The differentiation of a possible primary affect disorder from disturbance secondary to conflict and regression may be extremely difficult or clinically impossible. A primary affect disorder also represents a vulnerability to structural disorder and trauma, and is inevitably alloyed with intrapsychic conflict. Specific affect disorders, and the changes effected by psychoanalysis, and therapeutic applications of psychoanalysis remain major areas for further analytic research.

REFERENCES

ARLOW, J. A. (1957). On smugness. *Int. J. Psychoanal.,* 38:1–8.

——— (1977). Affects and the psychoanalytic situation. *Int. J. Psychoanal.,* 58:157–170.

BLUM, H. P. (1977). The prototype of preoedipal reconstruction. *J. Amer. Psychoanal. Assn.,* 25:757–785.

——— (1979). The curative and creative aspects of insight. *J. Amer. Psychoanal. Assn., Suppl.,* 27:41–69.

——— (1986). Countertransference: concepts and controversies. In *Essays in Honor of Charles Brenner, M.D.* Hillsdale, N.J.: Analytic Press.

Brenner, C. (1974). On the nature and development of affects. *Psychoanal. Q.*, 43:532–556.
——— (1975). Affects and psychic conflict. *Psychoanal. Q.*, 44:5–28.
Breuer, J. & Freud, S. (1895). Studies on hysteria. *S. E.*, 2.
Ekman, P. et al. (1972). *Emotion in the Human Face: Guidelines for Research and an Integration of Findings.* New York: Pergamon Press.
Emde, R. N. (1980). Toward a psychoanalytic theory of affect. In *The Course of Life,* Vol. 1, ed. S. Greenspan & G. Pollock. Washington: U.S. Government Printing Office, pp. 85–112.
——— (1983). The prerepresentational self and its affective core. *Psychoanal. Study Child,* 38:165–192.
Erikson, E. H. (1950). *Childhood and Society.* New York: Norton.
Fenichel, O. (1941). The ego and the affects. In *The Collected Papers of Otto Fenichel,* 2:215–227. New York: Norton, 1954.
Freud, S. (1894). The neuro-psychoses of defense. *S. E.*, 3.
——— (1895). On the grounds for detaching a particular syndrome from neurosthenia under the description 'anxiety neurosis.' *S. E.*, 3.
——— (1912). Recommendations to physicians practising psychoanalysis. *S. E.*, 12.
——— (1916–17). Introductory lectures on psychoanalysis. *S. E.*, 15 & 16.
——— (1926). Inhibitions, symptoms and anxiety. *S. E.*, 20.
——— (1940). An outline of psychoanalysis. *S. E.*, 23.
Glover, E. (1939). The psychoanalysis of affects. In *On the Early Development of Mind.* New York: Int. Univ. Press, 1956, pp. 297–306.
Greenacre, P. (1941). The predisposition to anxiety. *Psychoanal. Q.*, 10:66–95.
Greene, A. (1977). Conceptions of affect. *Int. J. Psychoanal.*, 58:129–156.
Greenson, R. R. (1962). On enthusiasm. *J. Amer. Psychoanal. Assn.*, 10:3–21.
Jacobson, E. (1953). The affects and their pleasure-unpleasure qualities, in relation to the psychic discharge processes. In *Drives, Affect, Behavior,* ed. R. M. Loewenstein. New York: Int. Univ. Press.
Kernberg, O. F. (1976). *Object Relations Theory and Clinical Psychoanalysis.* New York: Aronson.
Loewald, H. W. (1974). In Panel: Toward a theory of affects. P. Castelnuovo-Tedesco, Reporter. *J. Amer. Psychoanal. Assn.*, 22:612–625.
Mahler, M. S., Pine, F. & Bergman, A. (1975). *The Psychological Birth of the Human Infant.* New York: Basic Books.
Pulver, S. (1971). Can affects be unconscious? *Int. J. Psychoanal.*, 52:347–354.
Rangell, L. (1954). The psychology of poise. *Int. J. Psychoanal.*, 35:313–332.
——— (1974). In Panel: Toward a theory of affects. P. Castelnuovo-Tedesco, Reporter. *J. Amer. Psychoanal. Assn.*, 22:612–625.
——— (1978). On understanding and treating anxiety and it derivatives. *Int. J. Psychoanal.*, 59:229–236.
Rapaport, D. (1953). On the psychoanalytic theory of affects. *Int. J. Psychoanal.*, 34:177–198.
Sandler, J. & Sandler, A. (1978). On the development of object relationships and affects. *Int. J. Psychoanal.*, 59:285–296.
Schafer, R. (1964). The clinical analysis of affects. *J. Amer. Psychoanal. Assn.*, 12:275–299.

SCHUR, M. (1969). Affects and cognition. *Int. J. Psychoanal.,* 50:647–653.
SHAPIRO, T. (1974). The development and distortions of empathy. *Psychoanal. Q.,* 43:4–25.
SPITZ, R. A. (1965). *The First Year of Life.* New York: Int. Univ. Press.
STERN, D. N. (1985). *The Interpersonal World of the Infant.* New York: Basic Books.
WEINSHEL, E. (1970). Some psychoanalytic considerations on moods. *Int. J. Psychoanal.,* 51:313–319.
WINNICOTT, D. W. (1958). The capacity to be alone. *Int. J. Psychoanal.,* 39:416–420.

23 The Hemlocks
Roslyn Estates, NY 11576

THE SIGNIFICANCE OF A THEORY OF AFFECT FOR PSYCHOANALYTIC TECHNIQUE

MICHAEL FRANZ BASCH, M.D.

Although Freud was very much aware of the centrality of affect for psychoanalytic treatment and cure, his confusion of neurotic with normal development led to a metatheory that has limited the flexible use of affect in psychoanalytic technique. This essay, using both a clinical example and a summary of the pertinent literature, seeks to demonstrate the advantage of an explanatory or metatheory based on both the power of information (rather than on psychic energy) and on an understanding of what recent research in normal development, especially insofar as it relates to affect, has taught us. Such a theory will lead to an expansion of psychoanalytic technique that does no violence to Freud's clinical findings while expanding the efficacy and applicability of the psychoanalytic method.

GEORGE W., A 43-year-old businessman, came into analysis for what he initially described as a sexual problem.[1] He was no longer attracted to his wife of 20 years, but, for the past 5 years, had been carrying on a clandestine relationship with a young woman whom he found sexually gratifying. However, he had no wish to divorce his wife, he respected her and cared for her as a person. Together they had established what was now a successful business, and they had both been very involved in raising their four children. Mr. W. said that to leave his wife would be to turn his back on his own history; his and his wife's lives were so intertwined that to leave her would be "like cutting off my right arm." Yet, he said, it was becoming increasingly painful to lead a double life.

Professor of Psychiatry, Rush Medical College, Training and Supervising Analyst, Institute for Psychoanalysis, Chicago, Ill.

[1]This clinical example is an abbreviated version of a case dealt with at greater length in a forthcoming book entitled: *Practicing Psychotherapy: A Casebook.* New York: Basic Books, in press.

Once the analysis was under way, Mr. W. described his relationship with both women in greater detail. He felt that his wife took him for granted. As he experienced their relationship, it was always the task at hand that was the focus of her attention. He was grateful for her organized, efficient ways, which kept household and business functioning so well, but felt she made no effort to come to understand him. She had no sympathy for what she called "navel-gazers." Her philosophy was that personal problems, whether caused by past or present events, were to be dealt with by immersing oneself in those things that one could do something about. He recognized that in what he experienced as her disregard for his needs, she was very much like his mother, although, strangely enough to him, he had married his wife because he thought her to be very different from this parent. His mother had been a vapid, anxious, and reclusive person, absorbed in herself and her multiple ailments, who functioned poorly and rejected his efforts for emotional closeness. He remembered quite accurately first being aware of making a commitment to the woman who was to become his wife, who was at that time just one of several women he was dating, when he came to her apartment one Sunday to help her repair a malfunctioning automatic dishwasher, only to find that she had already located the problem and fixed it herself. He was conscious at the time of thinking that she could be a real partner, unlike his mother who was a drag on his father. Ruefully he speculated that he must have assumed that his future wife's independence and efficacy implied that, unlike his mother, she could and would also be interested in and emotionally involved with him.

Mr. W. tried to be scrupulously fair to his wife and always let me know that the fault for his dissatisfaction in the marriage lay with him. So, he explained, that his wife was not a "cold fish." On the contrary, she was more than a willing sexual partner, and that, paradoxically, he found problematic. Although initially he had found his wife-to-be attractive and sexually exciting, almost immediately after their marriage that interest disappeared. He was only able to achieve an erection and perform sexually with her by first arousing himself with fantasies of various women of his acquaintance whom he pictured either tenderly seducing him or surprising him and overwhelming him with sexual desire. In recent years he found that, much to his wife's distress, he could only perform intercourse infrequently, perhaps once or twice a month, and then only, he told me, if he planned their coupling in such a way that within a few hours he could visit his mistress. So, for example, when he and his wife were away on vacation, he found himself impotent with her, though he felt sexual urges that he would release with solitary masturbation. At times like this, he dutifully forced himself to satisfy his wife's needs manually or through cunnilingus, but derived no sexual pleasure from that.

His mistress, judging from his description, was a young woman with a borderline character, who depended on the stimulation of the moment for her sense of self. As Mr. W. described it, when he was with her she focused totally on him and his needs and, for a while, he could feel whole. Always on guard with his wife, constantly observing himself to see if he was living up to what was expected of a mature, devoted husband, with his girlfriend he felt he could be himself without fear of being shamed. With her, he could clown around, act boyish, confess his fears, and indulge himself freely sexually without regard to what she might want from him—whatever he did seemed to please and satisfy her. It did not trouble him that his mistress had other lovers who, as he also did, helped to support her financially. What mattered to him was that when he was with her he experienced her as totally devoted to him.

The increasingly detailed introspective examination of his experiences in the analysis led to our recognition that anger intruded on any attempt at intimacy with his wife. The more ardent she was, the angrier he became inwardly, thinking he was being used, while his own needs had to be buried behind a façade of pseudomaturity. If he let the child within him show, he anticipated her scorn and contempt for his neediness.

As the analysis deepened and the initial positive, idealizing father transference gave way to a repetition of earlier experiences, anger came into the transference. He turned his obligations to me in terms of the fee and the limits of the appointment time, as well as my periodic absences for vacations or conferences, and any lapses in my attentiveness or cordiality toward him, into evidence that my interest in him was only pretended, and that I with him, like he with his wife, was putting on a charade so as not to let my true, selfish nature be revealed.

Through the interpretation of the negative mother transference it became possible to link his anger genetically to his mother's seeming inability to respond to his needs. And, eventually, as he could separate mother and wife, his emotional relationship generally and his sexual relationship particularly with the latter became much more satisfying to him.

As the above case vignette illustrates, there was never any question of decreased sexual desire in this patient. It was the difference in the unconscious affective reaction to his wife and mistress respectively that governed Mr. W.'s sexual behavior with each of these women. The improvement as a result of this psychoanalysis is explained by the fact that once analysis resolved the negative mother transference the patient had had toward his wife, his affective position vis-à-vis the latter was significantly altered and, among other things, permitted her to become an object of his sexual interest.

Freud was always aware of the centrality of affect for psychoanalytic treatment: "to suppress the development of affect is the true aim of repression" (Freud, 1915, p. 178). Yet, central as affect is and always has been for the practice of psychoanalysis, Rapaport (1953) concluded in his classic paper on the subject: "We do not possess a systematic statement of the psychoanalytic theory of affects" (p. 476). Nor, for the following reason, will we ever have a *psychoanalytic* theory of affect.

The psychoanalytic method reveals the unconscious meaning behind the thoughts and other behaviors of human beings. It does not, as analysts from Freud through Kohut have thought (Bacal and Newman, 1990), provide the data on which to base either a general psychology or a theory of normal human development. Freud's analogy justifying extrapolation from pathology to normal development, namely, that only when a waterglass breaks does it reveal where its seams are located, is misleading. Identifying the fault lines in a glass tumbler does not tell us how glass is made—how the various constituents are mixed, fired, and so on. Similarly, though we uncover and interpret the meaning of the content and affect of our patients' transferences to us, that does not then tell us how affect and cognition developed. However, today we can turn to the work of investigators of normal human development, especially to the exploration of the preverbal period, not for *psychoanalytic* theories of affect, cognition and learning but for viable theories of affect, cognition, and learning that are useful to every scientist interested in human behavior and its antecedents. In Freud's day, the information to construct valid theories of human development was not available; indeed, it was Freud's demonstration that the child is truly father to the man that made the study of the early years of life a legitimate concern for the scientific community. Since then, the work of Vigotsky, Piaget, Bruner, and many others regarding cognition and learning has become familiar to psychoanalysts. However, these studies have not been that useful to us because, as I certainly heard repeatedly as a student and many times since then, they do not tell us about affect—and the mobilization of affect and its working through in the transference is focal for our work. It is therefore very important for psychoanalysis that a viable theory of affect development was proposed by Tomkins (1962-63), a theory that has held up well under experimental testing since then.

Darwin (1872) already investigated facial expressions in

man and animals, and concluded that they were remarkably similar, especially when man and the nonhuman primates were compared. He believed that certain basic facial expressions were inherited and inherent, representing dispositions to engage in one or another form of survival behavior. These expressions were originally part of larger action patterns, but evolved into an independent signaling or communicative function, which was important for social adaptation. Duchenne, also in the nineteenth century, showed that the various facial expressions indicative of affect are automatic and stereotyped. Duchenne electrically stimulated the face of a man insensitive to pain and was able to produce and photograph facial expressions typical for various emotional states by activating trigger areas for various muscle groups. More recently, Chevalier-Skolnikoff cited the neurologic evidence explaining Duchenne's findings, which indicates that "facial expressions of emotion are mediated by subcortical structures, relatively stereotyped in form" (Ekman, 1973, p. 54).

Silvan Tomkins (1962-63), the founder of modern affect theory, basing himself on Darwin's work, identified and systematically described the facial features of the following eight basic affects, each with a range from mild to intense expression, present either at birth or shortly thereafter: surprise/startle; enjoyment/joy; distress/anguish; contempt/disgust (now separated by Tomkins into disgust and dissmell); anger/rage; fear/terror; shame/humiliation. Sadness, which Tomkins considers a variant of distress, also seems to qualify as a separate, basic affect. Douglas Detrick (personal communication) suggests that understimulation/boredom should be added to this list.

Tomkins's work lets us answer a question that is very important for psychoanalysis, which, after all, emphasizes the psychological import of the earliest experiences. An infant's cognitive development is such that objectification of events and reflection on its experience is not yet a possibility. Why then do infants already express affect appropriate to their subjective experience? That is, how does a baby "know" it is happy, angry, etc.? According to Tomkins (1962-63, 1970, 1980, 1981), the affective reaction to stimulation is, initially, not a response to the quality or nature of the stimulus as such, but is, rather, selectively triggered by the intensity, the duration, and the shape formed by the rise and fall of the stimulus as it impinges on the nervous system. So, for example, whether the stimulus is sound, light, or touch, practically from the first day of life, if the number and frequency of nerve impulses set up by the excitation fall within the infant's optimal range for stimulation, the baby's face will assume an expression of interest. If the excitation is above the optimal level, there will first be a reaction of surprise; and then, if stimulus intensity is maintained steadily at a higher than optimal rate for a length of time, distress, anger, and fear make their appearance. Joy will be registered whenever a sharp rise in stimulation is followed by a sudden drop. (So, for example, father, having playfully tossed his baby daughter in the air, catches her; and the baby laughs—not because she knows she is safe after having been endangered, but because there has been a sudden decrease in the stimulus input produced by the act of tossing her up, letting her fall for a distance, and then suddenly interrupting her descent when she is caught.)

The work of Darwin and Tomkins demonstrates that the affective response is initially a genetically encoded reflex phenomenon. Although the affective response is a total bodily response, in humans the face has become the prime communicator of affective states, with each specific affect reflex expressing itself by temporarily taking over the group of voluntary muscles that together give rise to the prototypical expressions associated with it. Once affect is identified as an adaptive behavior, a form of communication mediated by the autonomic nervous system and relying primarily on chemical transmission of messages, a form of communication that is both more general and rapid in its effects than is the transmission of signals in the associational cortex (Ekman, 1973; Ekman et al., 1983; Rose, 1973), it ceases to be a mysterious event and takes its proper place among physiological processes and their psychologic manifestations (Basch, 1976a, 1983a, 1988).

Words like interest, joy, and anger are so connected to adult self-conscious reflection that it may seem adultomorphic to attribute such experiences to infants. This is no longer a problem if affect, like cognition, is thought of in terms of a maturational line. Then, though the words may be the same, what they are meant to describe is not. Previously (Basch, 1983a) I have postulated a distinction among affect, feeling, and emotion. I reserve the term affect for the group of biological responses to stimulation described by Tomkins. Feeling, as I think of it, comes into being only later, around 15 to 24 months, when the involuntary basic affective reaction begins to be related to a concept of the self. To be able to say, "I am angry," is to have already abstracted and objectified the affective reaction. Emotion, a further step in affective maturation, results when feeling states are joined with experience to give personal meaning to complex concepts such as love, hate, and happiness. The final maturational step in affective development in this schema is the capacity for empathic understanding—that is, affective communication that goes beyond the self-referential.

How does the affect theory of Tomkins and his students affect psychoanalytic technique? In and of itself it makes little difference. Psychoanalysts, following Freud, have always been aware of the importance of affect—their patients' and their own. However, it is the underlying theory of how human beings develop and how the mental apparatus (brain) functions that governs how the observed, affectively laden associations of the patient are interpreted. As someone has said, there are no "immaculate perceptions." The meaning of what we hear and our reaction to it are governed by our expectations, that is, the orienting and explanatory theories we carry into the consulting room. It is here that we run into difficulties. Freud, as we know, equated development, including the evolving affective relationship of child to parent with the oedipus complex: "psycho-analysis has shown us, to our growing astonishment, the enormously important part played by what is known as the 'Oedipus complex'—that is, the emotional relation of a child to its two parents—in the mental life of human beings . . . the Oedipus complex is the psychical correlate of two fundamental biological facts: the long period of the human child's dependence, and the remarkable way in which its sexual life reaches a first climax on the third to fifth year of life, and then, after a period of inhibition, sets in again at puberty" (Freud, 1924, p. 208). The resolution of the oedipus complex is the watershed of maturity for Freud. The vicissitudes of psychosexual development—the progression from the oral, to the anal, to the phallic, and ultimately to the genital phase of psychosexuality constitutes the psychoanalytic theory of development. Freud explained the roots of his theory of human development by adducing a biological metatheory known to us as the dual instinct theory—consisting at first of sexual and self-preservative instincts, later of sexual and aggressive instincts. For Freud, the brain (Freud, 1895) or mental apparatus (Freud, 1900) had as its function the transformation and discharge of these postulated sexual and aggressive biological substances. The very nature of this mission brought the organism into conflict with the demands of society, represented in infancy and childhood by the parents who, in the interest of their and society's preservation, had to oppose this heedless search for pleasure through any behavior that would permit instinctual discharge. Freud essentially concluded that the symptoms the patient brought into analysis were the outcome of an unsuccessful accommodation between the need for discharge and the demands of the environment and/or the superego. The analyst's function was to assist the patient in tracing, through analysis of the symptoms in the transference, the repressed unconscious reasons for this failure, so that understanding might free the patient to find acceptable instinctual gratification in his daily life. Affect for

Freud was simply a qualitative manifestation of instinctual discharge or frustration—positive affect denoted discharge, negative affect its blockage.

It is the analyst's metatheory, the explanation of human development that the analyst brings with him to the consulting room, that determines his technique.

Freud's theory, taken to its logical conclusions, has led to what is now usually called "traditional" or "classic" psychoanalytic technique. It mandates an analytic posture in which the analyst is ever alert for the patient's attempt to discharge sexual or aggressive energy through transference gratification and requires that the analyst continuously monitor himself to try to ensure that these attempts are thwarted through a neutral, abstinent position on his part.

I have elsewhere dealt with the origin of Freud's metapsychology and summarized the literature that definitively establishes that Freud's metatheoretical speculations regarding the nature and origin of instinct and its transformation into energy have found no basis in the now voluminous experimental and theoretical work done in the area of neurobiology (Basch, 1975, 1976b, 1977, 1984, 1989). It so happens that though the theory is false, it does not significantly interfere with the psychoanalysis of patients suffering from psychoneuroses, the patients that formed Freud's data base. The reason for that is that the psychoneurotic patient's affective development is essentially not impaired; indeed, it is the intense but misplaced affect that, when repression fails, gives rise first to symptoms and then becomes transferred to the analyst. It is the reconnection of the now displaced affect with what in the past was experienced as traumatic that is the essence of genetic reconstruction, insight, and psychoanalytic cure of the psychoneurotic patient. Although it is epistemologically invalid to use for proof of the theory (metapsychology) the phenomenon (the clinical course) that that theory is meant to explain (Basch, 1973), it is the undoubted efficacy of traditional psychoanalytic methodology when applied to psychoneurotic patients (Basch, 1988) that has led generations of analysts to conclude that Freud's theory is correct, and that the approach so successful for the psychoneurotic patient is generally applicable. However, in a patient like Mr. W., whose primary defense against anxiety was not secondary repression but, rather, disavowal (Freud, 1927), in whom, therefore, memory was not blocked from affect, but rather, affect from memory (Basch, 1983b), the traditional methodology would have proved to be ineffective. The analyst's affective abstinence that serves us so well with the psychoneurotic patient would only have played into the defense of a patient like Mr. W., a patient with a narcissistic character disorder. Since disavowal interferes with affective recognition and maturation in the area of the patient's pathology, it is pointless to play the waiting game and trust that, sooner or later, the patient will transfer what needs to be analyzed. In these cases the analyst has to actively intervene in helping the patient to see what is not there, and by the analyst's activity first mobilizing, and then interpreting, the patient's shame about his need for an affective response pave the way for the genetic reconstruction of what accounts for the affective arrest. The clinical rationale and technique for such work was described by Kohut (1971, 1984), and I have elsewhere given a more extensive illustration of its course (Basch, 1988, pp. 239-258).

What enabled me to analyze Mr. W. was not a grasp of twentieth-century affect theory per se, but the formulation of a metatheory that both accommodates and accounts for what we have learned about affect in recent years. What must change is the concept of the brain as an energy discharging organ. The brain is an organ that generates information and guides behavior accordingly (Wiener, 1948; Fields and Abbott, 1963; Buckley, 1968; Rose, 1973; Campbell, 1982). Instincts, as we understand that term today, are inherited transformation rules that guide, but do not determine, the process by which information necessary for the survival of the individual and (indirectly) the species is generated (Basch,

1984). Psychosexuality, the focus of Freud's exploration of the unconscious, is only one sector of human development: behavior is also governed by attachment needs—as emphasized in the writings of many analysts, from Ferenczi to Klein, Bowlby and Kohut (Greenberg and Mitchell, 1983; Bacal and Newman, 1990)—as well as a need to exercise initiative and creativity. Psychosexuality and the need to discharge sexual tension (an aggressive instinct or a need to discharge aggressive tension is no longer believed by biologists to be a tenable concept [Basch, 1975]) cannot subsume the need for attachment, creativity, and/or initiative. It is the brain's ordering function and the search for competence and the attendant effectance pleasure that govern human mental life from beginning to end (White, 1959; Papoušek, 1969; Broucek, 1979), and form the final common pathway for all instinctual needs. It is only when the psychoanalytic theory of unconscious human motivation is revised on the basis of these findings that the affect theory of Tomkins and those who have extended his work becomes useful for the practicing analyst. It is the affective reaction attached to events that both guides subsequent behavior—positive affect inclining toward repetition of that or similar events, negative affect predisposing the organism toward avoidance—and communicates to those concerned the subjective state of, for example, the infant, the child, or the patient, and indirectly signals that individual's needs. In psychoanalysis, the affect associated with both transference repetition and the defense against the transference gives the analyst indispensable data as to the patient's development. How, as an analyst, one responds to those needs, that is, the effect of affect theory on technique, depends on what sort of information one's anticipatory theories regarding human development will permit one to generate.

REFERENCES

BACAL, H. A. & NEWMAN, K. M. (1990). *Theories of Object Relations: Bridges to Self-Psychology.* New York: Columbia Univ. Press.

BASCH, M. F. (1973). Psychoanalysis and theory formation. *The Annual of Psychoanalysis,* 1:39–52. New York: Quadrangle.

——— (1975). Toward a theory that encompasses depression: A revision of existing causal hypotheses in psychoanalysis. In *Depression and Human Existence,* ed. E. J Anthony & T. Benedek. Boston: Little, Brown, pp. 485–534.

——— (1976a). The concept of affect: A re-examination. *J. Amer. Psychoanal. Assn.,* 24:759–777.

——— (1976b). Psychoanalysis and communication science. *The Annual of Psychoanalysis,* 4:385–421.

——— (1977). Developmental psychology and explanatory theory in psychoanalysis. *The Annual of Psychoanalysis,* 5:229–263.

——— (1983a). Empathic understanding: A review of the concept and some theoretical considerations. *J. Amer. Psychoanal. Assn.,* 31:101–126.

——— (1983b). The perception of reality and the disavowal of meaning. *The Annual of Psychoanalysis,* 11:125–154. New York: Int. Univ. Press.

——— (1984). Selfobjects and selfobject transference: Theoretical implications. In *Kohut's Legacy,* ed. P. E. Stepansky & A. Goldberg. Hillsdale, N.J.: Analytic Press, pp. 21–41.

——— (1988). *Understanding Psychotherapy: The Science Behind the Art.* New York: Basic Books.

——— (1989). A comparison of Freud and Kohut: Apostasy or synergy? In *Self Psychology: Comparisons and Contrasts,* ed. D. W. Detrick & S. P. Detrick. Hillsdale, N.J.: Analytic Press, pp. 3–22.

BROUCEK, F. (1979). Efficacy in infancy: A review of some experimental studies and their possible implications for clinical theory. *Int. J. Psychoanal.,* 60:311–316.

BUCKLEY, W., Ed. (1968). *Modern Systems Research for the Behavioral Scientist.* Chicago: Aldine Publishing Company.

CAMPBELL, J. (1982). *Grammatical Man.* New York: Simon and Schuster.

DARWIN, C. (1872). *The Expression of the Emotions in Man and Animals.* Chicago: Univ. Chicago Press, 1965.

EKMAN, P., Ed. (1973). *Darwin and Facial Expression.* New York & London: Academic Press.

——— LEVENSON, R. W., & FRIESEN, W. V. (1983). Evidence for autonomic reactions in specific emotions. *Science,* Sept. 16, 221(4616):1208–1210.

FIELDS, W. S. & ABBOTT, W., Eds. (1963). *Information and Storage and Neural Control.* Springfield: Charles C. Thomas.

FREUD, S. (1895). Project for a scientific psychology. *S. E.,* 1:281–397.

——— (1900). The interpretation of dreams. *S. E.,* 5.

——— (1915). The unconscious. *S. E.,* 14:159–204.

——— (1924). A short account of psycho-analysis. *S. E.,* 19:191–209.

——— (1927). Fetishism. *S. E.,* 21:152–157.

GREENBERG, J. B. & MITCHELL, S. A. (1983). *Object Relations in Psychoanalytic Theory.* Cambridge: Harvard Univ. Press.

KOHUT, H. (1971). *The Analysis of the Self.* New York: Int. Univ. Press.

——— (1984). *How Does Analysis Cure?* Chicago & London: Univ. Chicago Press.

LASHLEY, K. (1958). Cerebral organization and behavior. In *The Brain and Human Behavior,* ed. H. C. Solomon et al. Baltimore: Williams & Wilkins, pp. 1–18.

Papoušek, H. (1969). Individual variability in learned responses in human infants. In *Brain and Early Behaviour,* ed. R. J. Robinson. London & New York: Academic Press, pp. 251-266.
Rapaport, D. (1953). On the psychoanalytic theory of affects. In *Collected Papers,* ed. M. M. Gill. New York: Columbia Univ. Press, 1967, pp. 476-512.
Rose, S. (1973). *The Conscious Brain.* London: Weidenfeld & Nicolson.
Tomkins, S. S. (1962-63). *Affect, Imagery, Consciousness,* 2 Vols. New York: Springer.
——— (1970). Affects as the primary motivational system. In *Feelings and Emotions,* ed. M. B. Arnold. New York: Academic Press, pp. 101-110.
——— (1980). Affect as amplification: Some modification in theory. In *Emotions: Theory, Research and Experience,* ed. R. Plutchik & H. Kellerman. New York: Academic Press, pp. 141-164.
——— (1981). The quest for primary motives: Biography and autobiography of an idea. *J. Personal. & Soc. Psychol.,* 41:306-329.
White, R. W. (1959). Motivation reconsidered: The concept of competence. *Psychol. Rev.,* 66:297-333.
Wiener, N. (1948). *Cybernetics.* Cambridge: MIT Press, 1961.

55 East Washington Street
Chicago, IL 60602-2234

A PSYCHOANALYTIC THEORY OF AFFECTS

CHARLES BRENNER, M.D.

The theory of affects proposed by the author (Brenner, 1982) is briefly reviewed with special reference to the role of depressive affect in triggering conflict. Its usefulness in practice is explained and illustrated.

AFFECTS CAN BE studied in many different ways. One can compare affective display or expression in various animals, including man, as Darwin (1872) did. One can study them neurophysiologically, as Cannon (1929) and his associates did in cats. One can study them developmentally in humans, as Emde (1989) and others have done (Emde and Buschbaum, 1989). Or one can study them as they appear in humans after the age at which mental development in general and speech in particular are sufficiently well developed to make it possible to use the psychoanalytic method in a dependable way.

The psychoanalytic method thus applied has generated much useful data concerning the nature and role of affects in mental life. Perhaps the reason that relatively few analysts have tried to generalize about affects from psychoanalytic data is that Freud himself never did so to any extent. He considered affects to be phenomena that are of secondary importance in mental life. What he believed to be of primary importance are the vicissitudes of the drives and it was they that interested him the most. Affects, he said, are discharge phenomena that are consequences of the discharge and/or lack of discharge of drive energies. What distinguishes one affect from another, he believed, is an inherited factor, acquired in the remote past. As Freud put it, the core of each affect is attributable to "the repetition of some particular significant experience . . . in the

Training and Supervising Analyst, New York Psychoanalytic Institute.

prehistory not of the individual but of the species" (Freud, 1916–17, p. 396). Freud maintained that traumatic events had produced affects in the human species as they produce hysterical attacks in individuals.

Freud did, however, devote a great deal of attention to one affect, anxiety. He realized very early how important a role anxiety plays in mental illness and formulated a theory of anxiety on the basis of his clinical observations. For many years he maintained that if too much libido is undischarged for too long a time, it changes into anxiety, at least in many individuals, i.e., that anxiety is altered or transformed libido, something which is not true for any other affect. Later Freud (1926) modified his theory of anxiety and of its role in mental conflict on the basis of greater clinical experience, i.e., in the light of fuller data. He suggested that any influx of stimuli too great for the mental apparatus to master or discharge otherwise generates anxiety automatically. This formulation, though different from the first, still gives anxiety a special place among affects. In addition, and perhaps more importantly, Freud linked defense exclusively to anxiety, giving up the notion he had had previously that the earliest and most important instances of repression appear early in life independently of anxiety (Arlow and Brenner, 1964). Thus anxiety held a unique place in Freud's ideas about affects, both with respect to what can produce it and with respect to its role in mental conflict.

The contributions of several later authors should also be mentioned at this point, since they are pertinent to the ideas to be presented here. Glover (1947) suggested that affects may profitably be classified into two groups, the pleasurable and the unpleasurable. Katan (1972) suggested that it is preferable to speak of distress rather than anxiety before a child has reached a certain stage of mental development. Novey (1959), Lewin (1961, 1965), and Schur (1969) all called attention to the intimate association between affects and ideas. Pulver (1974) maintained the validity of the concept of unconscious affects, a concept that Freud had explicitly rejected in his discussion of guilt. One can speak of an unconscious need to punish oneself, said Freud, but one cannot, if one is scientifically scrupulous, speak of an unconscious sense of guilt (Freud, 1923). Finally, Jacobson (1953) called attention to the fact that not just anxiety but affects in general are related to the maturation and development of ego and superego.

Classification

It must be emphasized that the sensation of pleasure and/or unpleasure is not in itself the affect. Only the combination of pleasure and/or unpleasure *and* an idea or ideas qualifies as an affect. If we attempt to classify affects, the correctness of this view becomes apparent at once. Whether pleasurable or unpleasurable, one criterion to be used in classifying affects must be the intensity of the pleasurable-unpleasurable sensation. In the case of pleasurable affects, for example, one speaks of contentment only when the pleasure sensation is of slight or moderate intensity and of ecstasy only when the intensity of pleasure is very great. With appropriate alterations the same is true of unpleasurable affects. Worry is an affect whose unpleasure is of low intensity; terror, one whose unpleasure is of high intensity. Given an equal intensity of pleasure, however, what decides whether we call an affect contentment or triumph will depend on the ideational content of the affect in question. If an affect is to be properly labeled contentment, its ideational content must involve some version of "I'm happy with things as they are." To be justified in labeling an affect triumph, on the other hand, one must be able to identify its ideational content as one or another version of "I've won!"

Note that the definition of affect that underlies the scheme of classification of affects just referred to imposes no limitations of a developmental nature. Does contentment always refer to a universal, prototypical experience of being in a loving mother's arms, perhaps after a satisfying feed? Maybe, maybe not. The individual ideational content can be determined only from each patient's associations. Should it turn out that "I'm happy with things as they are" always has the meaning, whether conscious or unconscious, "I'm happy to feel as I did when I was a baby in mother's arms," we would be justified in using this genetic feature of the affect as part of the definition of the affect, contentment. The same if the ideational content of triumph, as another example, always and for everyone involves thoughts of oedipal victory. At the present time one can say only that the existence of universal, genetic determinants of affects remains to be proven. We have no doubt that for each individual the ideational content of her or his affects is importantly determined by genetic factors, i.e., by her or his early childhood experiences. It remains to be discovered whether these show sufficient uniformity from person to person to justify including genetic factors in defining affects.

What one can say for certain is that no affects are ever identical from person to person. Sensations of pleasure and unpleasure may be the same for one person as another. We have no basis for asserting that they are not, any more than we have for asserting that they are. The ideational component of an affect must be unique for each individual, however. Whatever the affect, whether joy or jealousy, rage or sexual excitement, happiness or misery, pleasurable anticipation or anxiety, or any other, the ideational content of each will be unique. One can usefully classify affects on the basis of common elements from person to person, but when one is trying to understand a particular patient one is primarily interested in the intensity and ideational content of that person's affects and only secondarily interested in what they have in common with the affects of others.

Affects and Mental Conflict

Conflicts are of central importance in mental development and functioning. It is the principal task of every analysis to understand the nature and origin of a patient's major conflicts. Since conflicts are triggered by unpleasure, psychoanalysts, beginning with Freud, have paid much more attention to unpleasurable affects than to pleasurable ones.

The unpleasurable affect that interested Freud more than any other is anxiety. He defined anxiety as an anticipation of danger and he conceived the relationship among drive derivative (instinctual wish), anxiety, and defense in the following way (Freud, 1926). Whenever a drive derivative arouses a great degree of anxiety, defenses are instituted to avoid, eliminate, or mitigate the anxiety. The drive derivative may be repressed, it may be regressively altered, it may be changed from passive to active or vice versa, it may be projected, i.e., attributed to someone other than oneself, a reaction formation may appear, etc. The statement that anxiety triggers conflict means that anxiety is the occasion for instituting defense.

Freud's discussion of anxiety and his elucidation of its role in conflict was a major step forward in the development of psychoanalysis. Psychoanalytic data that have accumulated in subsequent years support a revision that places a less exclusive emphasis on anxiety as the trigger of conflict, however. The data indicate that it is more precise to say that, beginning early in childhood, whenever a drive derivative is associated with intense unpleasure it gives rise to conflict and defense (Brenner, 1975, 1976, 1982). As noted above, defense may take many forms and its function is to eliminate or minimize unpleasure. The unpleasure in question can be usefully divided into two categories, anxiety and depressive affect.

Anxiety is best defined as unpleasure plus danger, i.e., as unpleasure plus the idea that a calamity is impending, that it is about to happen. This corresponds to what is often called signal anxiety. What I suggest is that anxiety is always a signal of calamity (Brenner, 1953). Whether the expected calamity is object loss, loss of love, castration, punishment, or some combination of the four, unpleasure associated with such an anticipation is what is or should be meant by anxiety. As Freud pointed out in 1926, the dangers feared in childhood in connection with drive derivatives do in fact fall into one or the other of the categories just mentioned. It is for this reason that the vocabulary of analysis includes the terms separation anxiety, fear of loss of love, castration anxiety, and fear of punishment.

The association of anxiety with childhood drive derivatives and its consequences are familiar to every analyst. The association of depressive affect with childhood drive derivatives is less familiar, yet it is as common and its consequences are of great clinical significance.

Depressive affect is unpleasure plus the idea that a calamity has already occurred, that it is a current fact of life. There are times in the life of every child when it anticipates or expects that what it wishes will result in a dreadful calamity, e.g., that it will be deserted, or banished, or unloved, castrated, or punished in any one or all of these ways. As noted above, this is what is meant by anxiety associated with a drive derivative. There are other times in every child's life when it is convinced that it *is* deserted, that it *is* unwanted and unloved, that it *has been* castrated, or that it *is being* punished for the same or other instinctual derivatives. This sort of belief does not give rise to anxiety, to the anticipation of calamity. It results in one or another variety of depressive affect or misery rather than to one or another variety of anxiety.

As in the case of anxiety, when depressive affect associated with a drive derivative is intense, it triggers conflict and defense, defense whose function is to mitigate depressive affect, not anxiety. If a girl in the oedipal phase of development is convinced that she has been castrated because of one or another of her "bad" instinctual wishes (= drive derivatives), her conviction gives rise to depressive affect and in the subsequent conflict the defenses serve to mitigate her depressive affect.

It should be noted that Rangell (1978) advanced arguments to contradict the view that conflict is triggered by unpleasure and that the unpleasure may be either anxiety or depressive affect. According to him, the only affect that can trigger conflict is anxiety. He argued as follows. Intense unpleasure of whatever sort, he said, is itself a danger, the danger being that the unpleasure will get worse, will never stop, or will recur. According to Rangell, danger always begets anxiety and since unpleasure is a danger, unpleasure gives rise to anxiety. Thus unpleasure equals danger, danger begets anxiety, and it is the anxiety which, in fact, initiates defense in every instance.

What Rangell presents as a painstaking analysis of psychic events seems in fact to involve an assumption that begs the question at issue. It is his view that the ideational content of unpleasure cannot be that a calamity has occurred. It can only be that a calamity impends. An intensely unpleasurable affect, says Rangell, can never have the ideational content that one is abandoned, or unloved, or, for that matter, punished or castrated. It is only the prospect for the future that counts in psychic conflict, according to Rangell, never the past or the present. It is difficult to see what data, psychoanalytic or other, support such an extreme view.

The fact is that the calamities of childhood that are connected with the drive derivatives of that period of life give rise to misery (= depressive affect) as often as they cause anxiety, and clinical experience has shown the value of making the distinction between the two in one's interpretative work with patients in analysis. The clinical vignette in Brenner (1991) is an example of the usefulness of the view presented here of the role of depressive affect in psychic conflict. Another example, presented in more detail, is to be found in Hoffman (in press). Others may be expected to appear in the literature as time goes on. The following clinical notes will serve to convey to the reader the sort of observations that are to the point.

The patient is a professional, in his 30s, who has been in analysis for several years. Many aspects of his complicated symptomatology were related to conflicts triggered by anxiety. Competition with other men, whether physical or professional, aroused intense castration anxiety, anxiety related to childhood fantasies of competing for his mother's love with his father and/or two older brothers. As would be expected, it was only after considerable analytic work that he became aware of how afraid he still was of such competition. But this was not all. As analysis progressed he also became aware that some of his childhood wishes made him feel terrible about himself. They made him feel he was the worst person in the world. These were wishes occasioned by the birth of his sister, three years his junior. He was convinced by his parents' reaction to his sister's birth that they neither loved nor wanted him. His self-punitive and self-destructive behavior in later childhood and adult life, his sexual difficulties with women, whom he wished to make feel as miserably unhappy and rejected as he had felt as a child, his dedication to helping the waifs and orphans of our society, and his counterphobic Robinson-Crusoe-like fantasies and behavior, all were related to the depressive affect of his early childhood and to the conflicts triggered by it. The anxieties of his childhood had to be understood and interpreted in his analysis, but so did the depressive affect and its role in his childhood instinctual conflicts.

It should be added that, as I have noted elsewhere, anxiety and depressive affect are always intermingled, sometimes in unexpected ways. In the case of the patient just referred to, for example, the patient's conviction that his mother did not love him after his sister's birth (depressive affect) was mixed with the anxiety associated with the vengeful, sadistic wishes to which his feeling of being unloved gave rise. By the time he was in analysis as an adult, it was impossible to separate his misery associated with his conviction that he was unloved from the anxiety associated with his sadistic, vengeful desire for revenge. The two were inextricably intertwined.

Summary

Affects are complex mental phenomena that consist of sensations of pleasure and/or unpleasure and an idea or ideas. Neither the pleasure-unpleasure sensation nor the idea alone constitutes an affect or emotion as a feature of mental life. Only the combination of the two is what constitutes an affect. It must be added that either the idea or the pleasure-unpleasure sensation may be unconscious. If both are unconscious, one is dealing with an unconscious affect. If the pleasure-unpleasure sensation is unconscious, but the idea is conscious, one is dealing with what has, till now, usually been called isolation of affect by analysts. If the reverse is true, one is dealing with an unexplained mood or with "free-floating" anxiety or other affect.

To turn to the role of affects in mental conflict, the two unpleasurable affects that regularly precipitate conflict associated with childhood drive derivatives are anxiety and depressive affect. The former is unpleasure plus the idea that a calamity impends. The latter is unpleasure plus the idea that a calamity has happened, that it is part of one's current life.

The clinical consequences of this modification of the view that anxiety is the only affect that triggers mental conflict due to childhood drive derivatives are of considerable significance (Brenner, 1976, 1982). Among other things, it throws new light on mental life and development in girls during the oedipal phase, on superego development and functioning, and on the psychopathology of depressive illness in later life. This new light has led to a better understanding of many problems frequently met with in analytic practice and to more accurate and more useful ways in which to convey that understanding to patients.

REFERENCES

Arlow, J. A. & Brenner, C. (1964). *Psychoanalytic Concepts and the Structural Theory.* New York: Int. Univ. Press.

Brenner, C. (1953). An addendum to Freud's theory of anxiety. *Int. J. Psychoanal.,* 34:18–24.

——— (1975). Affects and psychic conflict. *Psychoanal. Q.,* 44:5–28.

——— (1976). *Psychoanalytic Technique and Psychic Conflict.* New York: Int. Univ. Press.

——— (1982). *The Mind in Conflict.* New York: Int. Univ. Press.
——— (1991). A psychoanalytic perspective on depression. *J. Amer. Psychoanal. Assn.,* 39:25–43.
CANNON, W. B. (1929). *Bodily Changes in Pain, Hunger, Fear, and Rage.* New York: Appleton.
DARWIN, C. (1872). *The Expression of the Emotions in Man and Animals.* New York: Philosophical Library, 1955.
EMDE, R. N. (1989). Toward a psychoanalytic theory of affect: I. In *The Course of Life,* Vol. 1, ed. S. I. Greenspan & G. H. Pollock. Washington: U.S. Government Printing Office.
——— & BUSCHBAUM, H. K. (1989). Toward a psychoanalytic theory of affect: II. In *The Course of Life,* Vol. 1, ed. S. I. Greenspan & G. H. Pollock. Washington: U.S. Government Printing Office.
FREUD, S. (1916–17). Introductory lecures on psychoanalysis. *S. E.,* 15 & 16.
——— (1923). The ego and the id. *S. E.,* 19:1–59.
——— (1926). Inhibitions, symptoms and anxiety. *S. E.,* 20:75–174.
GLOVER, E. (1947). Basic mental concepts: Their clinical and theoretical value. *Psychoanal. Q.,* 16:482–506.
JACOBSON, E. (1953). The affects and their pleasure-unpleasure qualities in relation to the psychic discharge processes. In *Drives, Affects, Behavior,* ed. R. M. Loewenstein. New York: Int. Univ. Press.
KATAN, A. (1972). The infant's first reaction to strangers: distress or anxiety? *Int. J. Psychoanal.,* 53:501–503.
LEWIN, B. D. (1961). Reflections on depression. *Psychoanal. Study Child,* 16:147–157.
——— (1965). Reflections on affect. In *Drives, Affects, Behavior,* ed. M. Schur. Madison, Conn.: Int. Univ. Press.
NOVEY, S. (1959). A clinical view of affect theory in psychoanalysis. *Int. J. Psychoanal.,* 40:94–104.
PULVER, S. E. (1974). Unconscious versus potential affects. *Psychoanal. Q.,* 43:77–84.
RANGELL, L. (1978). On understanding and treating anxiety and its derivatives. *Int. J. Psychoanal.,* 59:229–236.
SCHUR, M. (1969). Affects and cognition. *Int. J. Psychoanal.,* 50:647-653.

1040 Park Avenue
New York, NY 10028

III. INTEGRATIVE PERSPECTIVES

INTRODUCTION

THEODORE SHAPIRO AND ROBERT N. EMDE

Freud gained impetus from the philosophy and science of his time as he reformulated his models of the mind. He saw fit to use the then current work of linguists, philosophers, sociologists, psychologists, and biologists to complement the data he gathered in the psychoanalytic situation. His notions about groups heavily weighed on the sociologist Le Bon. His ideas about the death instinct were based on romantic philosophy then current, citing Schopenhauer, and also on the biological observations on lower organisms citing A. Weissmann and invoking Darwin as well. In his writings on negation and the antithetical meaning of primal words he borrowed from linguists and philologists as well as from his earlier interest in aphasia influenced by the neurologist Hughlings Jackson. Thus, from the beginning, Freud and other psychoanalysts reached out into the broader intellectual world and integrated ideas derived from the data of other disciplines in the surround. Reciprocally psychoanalysis then reinfluenced other sciences and humanistic endeavors.

The final section of our volume deals with integrative perspectives on affective experience. We offer five presentations devoted to the integrations of psychoanalysis and linguistics, cognitive psychology, and sociocultural, historical, and literary interpretations of love. The last essays on love may invite controversy, but each is anchored in a psychoanalytic perspective, while also using observations derived from literature and history.

The fact that we speak about emotions as well as experience them forces us into a nominalist position, rendering some uncertainty as to whether the inner experience of affect is well conveyed in words. We worry if the sensed uniqueness and nuance of our feelings correspond to the words used by the person speaking, including the psychoanalytic patient. The effects of nominalization and the necessity for translation into words for communication are central to the psychoanalytic perspective. Freud recognized this problem and made it explicit. Yet this transformation confounds our capacity to go further than words, unless we call for other intersubjective units of exchange. Psychoanalysis, looked at as a dialogue, produces a new and rich avenue to understanding the interactions that are currently expressed in the terminology of object relations and interpersonal encounters, as well as in transference, acting out, and enactments. The essay on "Words and Feelings" reviews such experiences and provides an opportunity for analytic insight stemming from linguistics. Linguistics, in turn, is enriched by psychoanalysis because of the special dialogue opportunities provided by the treatment setting. Data obtained in that way will help us understand metacommunication, deep intention, and the semiotics of human exchanges under special circumstances.

Among those who have witnessed the problems that occur following brain damage, there is nothing so vivid as the catastrophic reactions of dysphasics. Emotional storms in the absence of the modulating effects of words make us aware of the interplay of feeling and language in normals. More recently, neurologists and psychiatrists have learned there is a similar dissociation between affect and cognition in the capacity to designate knowledge about how to do things. Procedures and routines may be remembered and newly learned by stroke victims, but are not able to be articulated, verbalized, or even remembered semantically. These facts have caused a reevaluation of the cognitive status of remembering. While we are accustomed to hearing about categorical groupings of memory such as episodic and semantic memory, the notion of procedural memory is rather new. Its relevance to understanding the dual track of development in the predevelopment of the hippocampus and in the later grasp of *how* things are done versus *what* things are done are relevant to psychoanalysis. When we see enactments, transferential responses, or acting out, it may be that individuals may have stored experiences related to the past that have not been put into words. Is the act of putting these events into words a new mediational interference with a reflexlike way of responding to affect with action? In the essay on "Procedural Organization of Emotions," the author opens a new door to an integrative look at transferential phenomena. Analysts could also attend to the data presented as a basis for thinking about certain kinds of emotional behaviors emerging in the course of analysis and how they are stored in memory.

The remaining three essays are devoted to romantic love—they range from an exuberant "Hooray for Love" through an analytic essay on romantic erotic love, and they span issues of the interaction of psyche and culture, borrowing from and sorting the literature and psychology of contemporary humanism. The authors approach this most elusive and complex of human emotions with new boldness and also remind us of the underside of the exuberance of love. One author writes of the absence of a concept of romantic love in some cultures. Another contrasts the cultural response to "painful love affairs." Another writes about the powerful compound of passion that love is. All look at the "untender, unempathetic, unpleasant, and dangerous qualities of love." Thus, as in much of psychoanalysis, the familiar appearance gives way to constituent elemental forces that are less exuberant, less tender, darker, and more complicated than the surface behavior. On the other hand, the surface behavior has its tumultuous elements too. Abstinence in love and culturally specific demands can be analyzed into affective and cognitive components that give the ideas new vibrance.

That psychoanalysis has ignored love for so long, except in some of Freud's early writings, and that it has left the psychoanalytic perspective so uncertain, is a fact needing to be confronted. Those essays provide a significant beginning. One essay provides a useful encounter with the intensity of the experience by means of a description of a love affair during an analysis. Another paper contrasts the painful love affair from a person in our culture with that of a person in another culture. The contrast provides us with additional understanding of the relationship of love to objects, while at the same time it extracts what aspects of being in love transcend cultural differences. The relationship of love to core gender identity is a further benefit received from reading this piece.

Twentieth-century lovers have been affected by the powerful romantic literature from the Middle Ages that received its final formulation in the nineteenth century. These essays do much to advance our understanding of the psychoanalytic perspective on these issues and to bring love into center stage as a legitimate area of inquiry. It seems appropriate to round out this volume with essays on love, because they provide much that is enriching, forward-looking, communal and procreative for future studies of affect and its relationship to emotional attachment and human growth.

WORDS AND FEELINGS IN THE PSYCHOANALYTIC DIALOGUE

THEODORE SHAPIRO, M.D.

Psychoanalytic therapy requires that we render our feelings in words. Insofar as nominalization of feelings is required, we can apply a linguistic analysis to that process illuminating the range of effects that language has on these complex affective states. Syntactically, we notice the subject-object vectors of feelings. Semantically, we note the representational valence of affects as part of word definition. Pragmatically, the psychoanalytic situation provides a unique dialogic relationship not seen elsewhere. These parameters are elaborated for their significance to the process of psychoanalysis.

A CHARACTER IN A T. S. Eliot play fragment protests, "But I got to use words when I talk to you" (1930, p. 152). The painter Francis Bacon (1989) is quoted as saying, "If you can talk about it why paint it?" These are just a few of many pronouncements concerning the radical argument that affective experiences are nonverbal and therefore inexpressible in words. I refer to these positions initially to provide a counterpoint to the central assertion of this essay: We live in a largely nominalist world, and Freud and his progeny in psychoanalysis continue to demand turning feelings and experiences as they occur in various states of psychopathology and everyday life into words so that they may be dealt with rationally as propositions. This is so because we have a special interest in the affective emotional life of our patients and not despite it.

I will propose that psychoanalysts, especially Freud, were early interested in a cohesive theory of symbol formation that

Professor of Psychiatry, Professor of Psychiatry in Pediatrics, Cornell University Medical Center; Director of Child and Adolescent Psychiatry, Payne Whitney Clinic; Training and Supervising Analyst, the New York Psychoanalytic Institute.

linked affects with the derivatives of drive discharge represented as thought. Representational modes were highly elaborated in the topographic theory, especially in the dream book (1900) where Freud labored to determine the relationship between thing and word presentation and representation. However, when Freud (1923) switched to the structural theory and to the concept of signal anxiety (1926) he turned his focal interest to defense and compromise formation, neglecting the nuances of the mechanisms of symbol formation, only referring back to his earlier work.

The recent advances in linguistics provide an easy map of symbol formation that can be used with profit by psychoanalysts as we integrate a modern theory with our clinical postulates and observations. Indeed, psychoanalysis as a method, I will propose, can be viewed as a linguistic interchange emphasizing man's symbolizing role as he encodes simultaneously words and narratives as a means of both emotional expression and self-protection. As such, the rich opportunities provided by linguistic analysis apply. I will proceed to use a linguistic frame to explore:

1. The contrived dialogic arrangement that is necessary to do analysis
2. The role of the dynamic unconscious in symbol formation and language usage in analysis
3. Free association and transference from the vantage of a linguistic analysis.

In this pursuit the affective component of linguistic structures should emerge as a major means of comprehending the affect-laden elements of symbolic life as expressed in the analysis and offer a mutually enriching proposal where psychoanalysis gains and linguistics is broadened to consider a new, pragmatic sequence in the analytic method and process.

Having stated these preliminary notions, I will introduce some of the language of linguistics to see if some of the constructs of that somewhat arcane field can be melded with the language of psychoanalysis and determine if such a blend enriches our psychoanalytic understanding of how we deal with affects (Shapiro, 1979). Before I embark on purely linguistic matters, one thing is certain: In usual discourse, we generally employ other channels than speech (the phonetic shape of language) per se to lend emotional tone in the two person world and to communicate feelings. Some of these accompaniments may be excluded in telephone conversations (*gestural-mimetic features*) or computer-written material (*prosody or the musical contour of speech, and tonal variation*). On the other hand, what is lost in the latter two vehicles is exaggerated in theater where communication channels include gesture and mimesis, and prosody as well as the usual broadcast transmission in words. We also employ these more fully in the cadences of poetry. Siomopolous (1977) and others have commented on the aptness of the rhythms of poetry in conveying affects to supplement the verbal rendering of feelings in metaphors which stimulate images that refer to feelings as well as to things.

There are those (as noted above) who claim that music and the visual arts are not amenable to such reductions to language, but we also try to take nondiscursive forms and render them discursively. The students of music and art certainly use a language which makes us wonder whether there are not *synesthetic* significances among the different vehicles of expression. Designations such as a *pastoral symphony* elicit pastoral images as well as pastoral voices. The Blues induce another feeling state that goes beyond the low notes and cadences of that musical form. The words match the tones. In psychoanalysis, verbal communication is asked for from the very beginning: "Say what comes to mind!" the analyst requests. However, such a request does not keep the analyst from watching as well as listening. Indeed, we also ask for images and bodily feelings as well as thoughts and words, and they enrich the experience of the content to be explored. The analyst and the patient may experience the composite in an immediate empathic apprehension, but I proffer that the translation into a verbal form is necessary to understanding.

Although we study affects in the analytic field, empathically and in transference-countertransference modules, we dare not be misled by the false notion that words are mere labels or adornments that are arbitrarily appended to ideas and feelings. Instead, *words in use* are our most parsimonious means of rendering inner personal, subjective experience in a sound repeatable communicational system. This does not deny that there are other kinds of human communication, both proximal and far, that are important and are sensed as an "experience of community" with others, but not verbalized.

The *communion* of the religious group or the political rally, or the quiet sighing, grunting or scream of coitus, the nodding approval of the conversationalist, the commiseration and sense of unity with the bereft, all bring people together. Nonetheless, words and sentences derived from human codes and language also are a major vehicle of being together, emotionally as well as cognitively. The latter distinction between cognition and emotion is quite artificial and fraught with confusion. Indeed, we may argue that the distinction is artifactual—the result of scholars' need to make distinctions. Researchers too have exploited some of these splits in order to keep their fields simpler and clear of contamination from "nonessential data." Nonetheless, in life, feelings and thoughts are experienced together as wholes or units.

Mahoney (1987) notes that there are three forms of translation: *interlinguistic, intralinguistic,* and *semiotic.* The latter includes the translation of symbolic entities such as dream images into words; feelings into words. Thus the third of these modes is the most central to psychoanalysis and the one which analysts deal with most commonly. Indeed, Freud's (1900) treatment of dreams is apt in this argument because he noted that we never see the dream of the dreamer, but we hear the dream report. And the dream report in words is what we deal with analytically. Trying to reimage, rethink, and reunderstand the rebuslike nature of the relationship of the images and to translate them into common thought is a major task as we assume the surface has a deeper significance (Levy and Inderbitzin, 1990). Similarly, with feelings, since we never can be certain that the feeling tone expressed facially reflects the same feeling that is experienced. Necessarily, we use facial expression as well as descriptions of inner feeling states as important data in the analysis. Because the analyst-patient arrangement does not permit as careful a view of facial expression, the analyst may have to pay particular attention to the lilt of the voice, the prosodic variation, and the gestural accompaniments to "read" the emotion. But defenses against expression in any of the communicative channels may be selectively employed even in average discourse. If the patient wishes to hide, she does so, unless the involuntary expression is imminent or triggered by the analyst's tact or clumsiness. The notion of a "poker face" is too familiar and becomes a metaphor for dissimulation, *but* the "social smile" too is a dissimulation that hides, *but* less completely because we can often decipher how it differs from the full smile of enjoyment (Ekman et al., 1983).

This distinction between *expressed feelings* and *read feelings* as opposed to inferred feelings is crucial in clinical psychoanalysis and one of the areas in which its practice is unique because we can explore the experiential nuance and history of feelings as well as discrepancies between the read feelings from facial expression and experienced feelings. Indeed, this distinction can be seen as a developmental achievement in the second and third year as well. At the point when the child can dissimulate and pretend feelings we recognize that emotions as expressed may be dissociated from felt emotion—the pretend pout or smile to get one's way becomes social manipulation, just as the breakthrough of rage or laughter is unplanned and may signal a failure of mastery of feelings. The human possibility to hide or erupt perforce includes recognition that conscious and unconscious mechanisms may be at play. At the conscious level manipulative guile or even consideration of others may be at work, while affect may be isolated or displaced unconsciously from one content to another. Thus, as in the case of repressed or suppressed ideas, we are at times called upon not to permit expression to reveal inner states that may be affectively charged. The split-off affective tone of an ideational-affective complex may be expressed in a different setting by virtue of displacement (kicking the cat instead of the boss) or attached to another person by projection or, as Arlow (1953) notes, be expressed in pleasurable contentless masturbation, while unaware of the arousing ideas that are represented in disguised form in a dream.

Linguistics has its own formal traditions. It divides language into syntax, semantics, pragmatics, and its most applied anthropological branch, sociolinguistics. By and large, syntax does not interest psychoanalysts as much as the issues of reference as studied in semantics and the circumstances and models recently studied in pragmatics that describe how dialogues take place and how they are interpreted (Shapiro, 1986, 1988). The latter should be of special interest because of the somewhat "unnatural" arrangements of the psychoanalytic dialogue. Sociolinguistics deals with the differences in cultural expression and how members of each culture name the elements of their affective experiences and permit expression of feelings. For example, it is said that the poverty-stricken and poorly educated may use, or rely more heavily on, vehicles for the expression of their feelings that differ from those of the middle classes. It is an uncertain general observation that they tend more to action to express feelings. Some developmentally disabled children, too, have difficulty putting their feelings into words and mentally designating them for discourse that requires a delay between thought and action. The impulse-ridden, organically damaged child tends more often to short-circuit the mediating effect of cognition on emotion. We also might look at the concept of alexithymia as an example of not encoding emotion in language, but rather channeling affects into bodily ills as another variant on the inability to tolerate affects consciously. If we look at each of these areas of language study separately, we may be able to bring some order into how psychoanalytic thinking can be influenced and enriched by the data derived from linguistics and conversely where psychoanalysis might provide new directions for linguistic study.

Syntax and Psychoanalysis

Psychoanalysts could attend to this area well because, among other things, it provides the rules by which we verbally establish agency and object directedness, establishing the "I" as feeler. Indeed, the translation of Freud's *Ich* into ego may, according to some, be a Latin tragedy that has permitted English-speaking Freudians to forget agency and responsibility for actions by using the less personal Latin form. Schafer's (1976) notion of action language makes clear the need to "own one's feelings"—to be the "I" of the experience rather than be the passive victim of one's feelings. Fenichel (1941) too in his book on technique similarly alludes to the notion that patients come to therapy feeling as though they are victimized by their feelings.

Even in our more common forms of expression we create confusion about how we syntactically relate to emotion. There are common verbal forms such as "I *have* feelings too," "I have had (or seen) happiness," or there is the confusion of identity with one's feeling in "I am depressed," which seems to signify the identity of the feeling with the person. Then there is the ambiguity portrayed in being a victim of feelings or a receptacle of feelings in phrases such as "I was accosted by anger," "I am full of rage," or "he makes me angry."

All of these avoid the I as feeler and create semantically ambiguous references where the patient requires redirection to understand how these common forms represent defensive disavowals of responsibility as an agent. The analytic clinician should take into account these varying syntactic forms as traps from patients and clues to understanding their sense of plight because it reveals to the stance of the feeler as she casts herself as first, second, or third person. Is she the feeler, are you making her feel this way, or is she a third person observing her feelings? The obvious relation of these variables to object relations is central, but the clue is in the syntax and knowledge of a person's place if the proposition can direct the analytic interpretation.

Dahl (1978) uses a specific schema designed by de Rivera to pose a series of poles which derive from Freud's (1915) three polarities of subject-object, pleasure-unpleasure, active-passive dimensions. He uses terms such as "it, me; to and from" as important distinctions that delineate a person's discourse, creating the final common pathway of a number of decisions that emerge as "how to act toward someone." This scheme attempts to remove feelings from the romance of subjective depth and probes their relationship to inner objects and real people in a syntactic form. Each of the binary decisions that determines the end—i.e., how we act toward another—might be probed in the analytic process to determine abiding attitudes toward others or potentially in the transference. The following analytic confrontation can be considered for its integration of affect and interpersonal import: "You act injured and hurt each time I tell you that you feel victimized by your brother, and then you become quiet as if I am hurting you." Such a transference confrontation puts the affect in a syntactic field. The statement strikes parallels between current feelings in the therapeutic relationship and historical interpersonal feelings as well. It is a syntactic formula for recognizing future events and experiences. Dahl (1978) also has shown that analysts reveal their hidden wishes and countertransferential attitudes in specifically awkward grammatical constructs. I have observed the tendency of analysts to use hypothetical conditional constructions such as "You act as if. . ." in conveying reconstructions to patients. In this way, the analysts cover uncertainty and anxiety about their patients' acceptance of the ideas proposed.

Another vantage point derives from the development of agency in social relationships by social referencing (Klinnert et al., 1983; Sorce et al., 1985). The establishment of social referencing by reading affects begins in the second half of the first year. When a child is placed in a dilemma involving an ambiguous choice, she looks to mother or her surrogate for information that is read from facial emotional expression as to how to proceed. We not only socially regulate our behavior in relation to the feelings and signals of mothers, but we utilize feelings as an organizer of behavior as expressed in the words of others. Indeed, the developmental movement from responding to affective tone to being able to understand "no" as a prohibition to action is very well marked in the developmental sequences and has been studied as a hard-won achievement of the mediational power of words over motor impulse. The Soviet scientist Luria (1961) and his coworkers used a simple experiment requesting that children of 3 to 5 press a rubber bulb attached to a string gauge to record the pressure when they saw a certain color light. The younger they were, the more the children had trouble suppressing the squeeze until the light went on, and only the older children could obey linguistic interdictions of "no" to reregulate the actions. Moreover, only the oldest children could obey a change of rules in mid-experiment on linguistic command, e.g., "Now *don't* press when the light is red as before, but only when it is green."

Freud's concept of acting out is clearly derived from his central proposal that thought is trial action, utilizing small amounts of energy. Mature human organisms use thought and language profitably and do not waste action until further cognition and planning are completed. These require syntactic schemes that describe future direction. Again the analytic situation especially calls for a translation of action potentials into words. The words are syntactically arranged in order to convey a sequenced scheme of potential action that can be avowed as deriving from the self or projected onto others, "He made me do it!" or "She made me feel guilty," or "You don't want me to have pleasure." The voice and trajectory of each proposal define the potential action sequence as it is being formed, before it is done, so that analyst and patient can experience the direction of the aim together in a shared linguistic reference. In that way, both can weigh the consequences of wishes or inhibitions on adaptation and survival. Without syntax we have no verbal vectors, but vectors need designated starting points and ends, and thus we need a means of reference. I have suggested (Shapiro, 1988) that the notion of a drive having a source aim and object even posits a linguistic unconscious.

Semantics and Psychoanalysis

Semantically, words signify that they have meanings. They refer to feelings, things, areas in the world, and in fact, they also serve as action potentials that guide individual behavior. The distinction between and among signal, sign, and symbol has been utilized in psychoanalysis by Rosen (1961) and by Lacan (1956). *Signals* are based on contiguity between referent and reference and are the simplest of our symbolic systems. For example, a signal is represented in our psychoanalytic practice in the contiguity of the fetish to the female genital signaling recognition of an absent, hoped-for, male genital or the incidental remembrance in the screen memory which is an event *near to* the more frighteningly significant event that it signifies. Freud (1899) suggested it is the *sham* near the gold.

Signs are based on an iconic relationship to the signified, as the arrow shows direction or the purse stands for the female genitals insofar as each may be seen as a receptacle. *Symbols* in linguistic terms are based on arbitrary relationships; i.e., there is no intrinsic or structural reason why "R" stands for the sound it represents, except convention. The psychoanalytic symbol is closer to the sign; e.g., sometimes a cigar is a penis; sometimes a snake is a penis. The error of pars pro toto is a logical one, not one that precludes an associative psychological path based on iconic likeness (Shapiro, 1979).

This tripartite analysis of symbolic form should permit analysts to consider the degree of disguise in symbolic presentation and offer an opportunity to reconsider Freud's original mechanisms described in the dreamwork, turning into opposites, displacement, etc. In fact, there is some evidence that certain character styles habitually use metaphoric (pars pro toto symbols) or metanymic (displaced) associative mechanisms, the former using a sign relationship and the latter signal. We may refer to our enemies as snakes, which represents a metaphoric transformation based on sign function of partial similarity, e.g., trait of sliminess or deceptiveness. We may also refer to the President as the White House or the Queen as the Crown, which referents are based on contiguity or metonyms. A concept such as overdetermination is well rendered as polysemy (many referents or meanings attached to one sign). Reference and meaning, in general, may be grasped as a single process employing a number of mechanisms bringing together translation and semiotics, and even such diverse figures as Webster and Lacan. Webster, the classical lexicographer, offers denotative referents for words and in addition shows the context of use within our corpus of written examples of language. He is a traditional writer of dictionaries; Lacan reaches for the connotative and even more for the idiosyncratic referents that make the patient's ramblings meaningful. The common usage is less interesting in his translations.

Since patients start their communications in words we attend—i.e., common denotative references—we also have a more complex referential receiving system which is alerted to words as embedded in meanings that have affective valence. We hover about the verbal productions waiting for cues that signal affects. Indeed, our "pay dirt" in the clinical process involves "hearing better" than others the lodestone of affectively charged unconscious constellations and resistances to their exposure.

Affects may be generated in an analysis as a signal in contiguity with a word. For example, the patient may tell the analyst any number of disparaging or unpleasant facts about a spouse. Then if the analyst suggests that he or she sounds close to divorce, a flood of tears emerges. The word, divorce, may be seen as a signal to the affectively loaded idea of divorce as a signifier of danger to the patient.

The dream may be told and described as vivid, *but* the affect associated with the referent behind the image will emerge only as the patient using the free associative process uncovers the sign function of the image. The image accompanied by the affect now is linked to an unconscious residue up to now unknown.

The symbolically arbitrary relationship of the word to the thing does not mean that there are not significant affective components in the apparently simple definition of words. Linguists use a feature analysis as a way of defining symbols, potentially giving us a way of considering affect as a feature to be included in dictionary meaning (Shapiro, 1979). Words have dynamisms that should be included in such a feature analysis. Words are not just labels, for they may have strongly affective features which are mobilized when the hearer audits the word. There are, after all, words of approbrium which jar our sensibilities—nigger, kike, wop, mickey! All are emotion arousers as compared to calling someone Black, Jewish, Italian, or Irish. The latter group does not call up emergency emotions as do the former. Words and names are not merely interchangeable in the affective content. Feces is different from shit. Masturbation is different from "jerking off." Indeed, some of our comedians utilize the jarring, outrageous effect of specific words in order to titilate our emotions and stimulate these associated arousals. These examples reveal that the usual process of definition is achieved by providing roughly equivalent words to clarify meaning of the index word (what Mahoney calls intralinguistic translation). Analysts have had the experience of a bilingual patient using a word in his second language without effect on the emotions, while expression in his first language brings tears or laughter. This example provides simple evidence that emotions are linguistically as well as cognitively bound to sentences and complex thoughts. Anyone familiar with the film, *Citizen Kane,* will appreciate the evocative force of the word, "Rosebud." In analysis, we discover our patients' idiolect and in each of those personal languages their Rosebuds.

Freud (1905b) was correct when he suggested that comedy consists of loosening repression and permitting a rapid emergence of unconscious fantasy. Just as a bull rages at seeing red, we can stimulate rage in almost anybody if we knew their symbolic catalogue well enough to say the right things to trigger idiosyncratically significant emotion-thought complexes. Indeed, a common clinical situation was alluded to in the Dora case (Freud, 1905a) in which she went on interminably about how awful her father's deeds were. Instead of Freud criticizing her father along with her, he turned her complaint about and commented on how much she must love him for her to be so preoccupied with him. He thereby turned attention to another affective valence which he recognized in the symbolic significance of her overzealous negative preoccupation. In this instance a whole sequence of negative narratives pointed to a positive, but disappointed affective constellation: love. Indeed, the analyst's interpretation is often an exercise in naming an unnamed enemy, i.e., a warded-off emotion associated with an unconscious complex (Shapiro, 1970).

Let us turn now to the matter of how we name and categorize emotions, i.e., how we turn emotion into a shorthand verbal reference. There are a number of curious confusions in how we designate feelings. Moreover, cross-cultural distinctions and problems exist with regard to how we interpret expressed feelings, or how we attach feelings and affects to our notions of disorder, or even how we name affective disorders.

The word depression is used to designate everyday sadness and also major depressive disorders. Curiously, we also use the word melancholia to designate similar disorders. The latter calls up connotations of Galenic medicine with etiologic inferences about the role of black bile in the generation of dark moods. On the other hand, depression is associated with feeling low, heavy, leaden, etc. The clinical depression of the Western world has been found to correspond to the neurasthenia of China (Kleinman, 1980). Very similar components that define major depression in DSM III are interpreted by the Chinese in a way by a term that is out of use in the West. Similarly, the alexithymia that is postulated in the individual who cannot put his feelings into words, but sidetracks them into the soma, represents a cultural variation of how people are tagged as "different" because they use different mechanisms to deal with feelings. Indeed, my very word, sidetrack, reveals a Western cultural stereotype which seems to require that we experience our affects in the usual way, i.e., in a manner to which we in the West have become accustomed.

It was brought to my attention at a WHO meeting a number of years ago that Westerners frequently talked about *somatization* of feelings, but we were brought up short when our colleagues from India suggested that we may *psychologize* too much (see section on Sociolinguistics). These polarities bring to attention the fact that concepts of affect are frequently intermingled with cognitive organizations as well as a world perspective, and that although feelings have physiological and other components, they also are psychological, nominal entities. As we name them in the course of our experience, we also bring them into a domain where they can demand our attention and be considered, but not before categorical, nominal boundaries are drawn. The frequency range of colors is known as an empirical fact, but color naming varies from language to language. The functional use of such language is culture-bound. Similar nuances of emotional tone may be more or less differentiated in different cultures. Freud's notion of a pleasure-unpleasure dimension might be sufficient for some purposes, but more shades of affective tone are required for a psychoanalytic exploration because we anticipate that psychological-cognitive accompaniments of these variants will direct us to a better understanding of the person's emotion-eliciting circumstances.

Psychoanalytic and dynamic psychotherapeutic enterprises for some individuals are an attempt to bring into consonance feeling states and tones with specific cognitive elements, i.e., memories and experiences. The anticipatory anxiety that certain phobic individuals experience is indeed at times a cognitive misreading of events on the basis of unsaid and unknown, unconscious and irrational identifications between referents on the basis of their sign or signal function. The phobic object is avoided; i.e., the patient avoids circumstances and places which usually do not elicit fear. We see this referential confusion as a displacement of the feeling tone belonging to one constellation onto a different symbol in the service of defense to shield the patient from realizing the warded-off thoughts. Thus, an affect-laden mental complex can lead to a designative error using a sign or signal as a representation that stands for the danger. This is a nonshared new vocabulary that is noncommunal and idiosyncratic.

The obsession also can be seen as a linguistic event which represents another form of displacement that includes the compromise formation of unconscious organizations as thoughts intrude on consciousness in a barely disguised way, but the affect is isolated. These are all within our symbolic system and are linguistically relevant. That is why we listen so carefully to *how* people tell us about their lives and experiences, and why we are so tolerant of the *redundancy of the form* in the analytic situation. But we are not only listening to hear *what* is hidden, but also what emotions would be elicited if the unconscious fantasy were made conscious, thereby rendering a more complete "definition" that enhances understanding of the meaning of behavior.

I will mention, but briefly, other communicational channels for the expression of emotion and include music and other auditory experiences as well. Even within language we have a bevy of anomotopoetic expressions for feelings that carry the weight and impact of the feelings to which they refer. In fact, many expressions of strong emotion do not employ formal words, but the vocal accompaniments of emotional expressions. The *ach!* the *oy!* the *ahhhhh!* and the *aghh!* used in comic strips are related to actual nonword vocalizations that co-occur with certain feelings such as pain, fright, despair, or ecstasy. They are not words, and yet we can communicate with them. I have already mentioned the poetic in this vein and its imagistic language forms used to evoke feelings. On the gestural and mimetic side, we make commands and demands by raising or wagging our fingers. We point to things, and we accuse with our fingers as well. These have as much iconic significance as words do, and they may be expressed with words or alone. Indeed, the designation through gesture in emotional states as seen in analysis is probably more frequent than in our traditional discursive forms of discourse. One can immediately bring to mind the gesturing of the logician as he organizes, layers, counts, and cuts through the air, signifying the sequencing and margins of arguments as well.

The prosodic or paralinguistic features of language in speech reminds us that in traditional discourse and couch monologues these elements carry the emotional tone to the auditor analyst. These matters are very difficult to represent in the written language that records the semantic-syntactic production, but are certainly available clinically on the couch or on videotape. Indeed, the flow of associations may sometimes move from words to gesture (Needles, 1959) or may include gesturing in one way, while the person is talking about something else (Grand, 1977; Freedman, 1977). Observing a patient's foot wagging, or the replacement of the hands from one part of the torso to another, or the lack of animation in the hands, while the voice is animated, all give kinesthetic clues to what is going on in the patient's thoughts. The frequent play of a smile across the lips of the patient telling a horror story suggests that sadism might be a part of the unconscious structure to be dealt with. Thus, we watch and listen for dissonance, consonance, and sequential shifts in the vehicles of expression for clues to understanding how emotions hide in communicational sequences, just as the child analyst watches the change in play items, while the theme does not shift.

We move now from words and gestures and their meaning to the notion of a dynamic unconscious which influences surface activity. We move into an area of questioning how complex mental structures are organized and how we deal with *potential affects.* Freud (1915) struggled mightily in the initial phases of his work with the question of whether affects could be unconscious. He initially opted for the notion that only ideas were unconscious, and then finally admitted to the limited possibility of the unconscious wish for self-punishment. This notion has been adopted by some to mean unconscious guilt, but others even espouse the notion of a whole array of unconscious affects (Pulver, 1974). On the other hand, I would offer that there are structural mental organizations that are clearly cognitive. If brought to the surface, they would yield the expression of a full range of affects when their personal significance is integrated with the context and time of life of their emergence. Traditionally, guilt as an experience, or even anxiety and glee, are feature components of organized mental complexes when they are elicited or when derivative forms emerge. Thus, just as humans in the environment and internal objects regulate emotion, cognitive organizations determine which affect is to be expressed once basic affects are mentally arranged. Arlow (1977) noted about moods that they are "structured affective states evoked and perpetuated by the continuing influence of unconscious fantasy" (p. 164).

For example, moral masochism indicates that there is an unconscious dynamism in the form of a mental constellation that dictates self-destructive external surface behavior in the service of guilt. While these are not exactly coded into words, some feelings are acted on and interacting with mental organizations that have significance and emotional valence. Returning to the area of reference in semantics again, we have many superficial displays which refer to deeper emotional signifiers. Indeed, what a patient says on the surface only partially reveals what is meant. The choice of words hides too, thereby revealing the action of wish and defense, or compromise formation, but also displaying the interplay between superficial and deeper mental organization which perforce requires an assumption of a potential emotion. The proposal that meaning is coded along with affects utilizes a linguistic frame that is explicated in the analysis. The analyst names the unconscious referent or fantasy in a syntactic form designating conflict and elicits the experience of affect that is tied to the words we call an interpretation.

This brings us to the interposition of the defenses of repression, denial, displacement, and isolation, and how they may suggest varying feelings that are being avoided. In 1926, Freud posited that defense is instituted at the behest of the signal of anxiety. This notion has been expanded by Brenner (1982): it is not only anxiety, but depression that calls for defensive action.

Pragmatics in Clinical Psychoanalysis

The next large area of linguistic consideration to be addressed concerns emotion in psychoanalysis as *pragmatics* or the practical interactions between people in dialogue or polylogue. Within philosophy and then linguistics the concept of performatives and speech acts (Austin, 1962; Searle, 1969) were introduced, providing the opportunity to consider *intention* and *motive* in the language sciences (see Shapiro, 1979). One can appreciate that grammar is most easily isolated for study from human context and interaction because as mathematics, it is analytic and has a formal structure. Semantics adds the complication of referencing a world of things or ideas, but pragmatics, as defined by the new language theorists, requires human interaction or *language in use* as its study base. With every word expressed in an interaction we witness, or better still, infer, what is called illocutionary force. This rhetorical force is empowered either by social convention or by habitual practice—politeness, guile, cultural rules, etc. When use becomes too idiosyncratic, its force is only recognized by the few who know the individual speaker well. Loewenstein (1951) used the model of a developmental psychologist, Karl Buehler, as a parallel to psychoanalytic couch behavior. We not only *express* and *appeal* on the couch, but we also *propose*. When we arrive at the propositional aspects of language, we are free of the demand structure of the appeal and its associated needs to influence others in a ministration, but now only are we able to express those thoughts which are developmentally free of need for sharing of ideas and exchange. In analysis the pragmatic arrangement of patient and therapist is unusual. It is not a dialogue of mutual sharing as in the conversation—the patient is expected to free-associate and the analyst remains a receptive listener and is only sometimes a verbal contributor (Shapiro, 1988). Couch behavior in relation to permission for affect expression is similarly unique insofar as analysts are asked to interpret the meaning of the phrases in terms of their illocutionary force which includes affective valence as inferred as well as their face value or semanticity. Consider the patient who says, "I don't usually use such language" and then interposes street language or frank smut or sexually provocative words. Others say, "I mean to say . . ." or we hear the frequent locution, "You know. . . ." What is the patient trying to get across by these various locutions? What is the read-out for those expressions in terms of the status of the transference, or the status of unconscious constellations that are being expressed?

Pragmatics has taught us that the patron who looks at a seat in a theater and asks the person sitting next to the empty seat, "Is that seat empty?" is not only asking whether it is occupied, but is also saying, "I want to sit in it. May I sit in it?" A somewhat less circumlocutious way an individual might approach the seat is to say, "May I sit down?" to ask for permission, when a more direct request might be, "I want that seat!" Similarly, the father who states casually as his son walks into a room, "It's warm in here," is requesting that his son open the window. If the same utterance were to be delivered by the son as father entered the room, he might interpret the remark as insolent or arrogant and possibly become angry.

Let us return now to "I don't usually use such language." Is this some variety of appeal to the analyst suggesting that "I don't want you to think ill of me" or "I'm embarrassed to say what I think using the language of my thoughts?" The "I mean to say" probably and frequently refers to "I hope you don't take me wrong. This is not the meaning I wish to convey. I don't want you to infer that I am hostile, angry, lascivious, wanton, lewd, unsophisticated, prudish, or the like." Freud's (1925) essay on negation provides examples of how the associational path is intruded on rather than repression being effective, and the patient provides a negation in order to disavow the thought as his own. For that matter the patient is isolating the emotions that accompany the thought because of the awareness of the hearer as a judge—a transference figure.

Speech acts add richness to semantics by including interactive fields in which psychoanalysts reveal transference possibilities as well as stereotypic affective exchanges. We read how the patient feels about us at that point of the analysis by how she addresses us in the dyad. A sudden lapse into baby talk, lisping shyness, the aggressive tone, silence and obsequiousness, all have meaning in the transference. This ought to be looked at from the standpoint of *what do these behaviors stand for* and what do they add to our knowledge of the significance of her utterance in a traditional semantic way. We ask: what is being said that cannot be read from the grammar or the semantics of the words themselves, but must be a composite derived from context, tone, and illocutionary force as well. In the area of emotional expression the force of the feeling may be found in the context rather than in the sentence form, and indirection or, for that matter, excessive directiveness. Each may tell more about emotional status than the clean statement "I am sad."

A clinical experience of recent vintage may highlight the discussion. There is a current trend, especially among adolescents, that evaluative statements and emotions are expressed by irony. They say "bad" and mean "good"; they say "groovy" and mean "banal." In addition, a traditional or usual form of address may be associated with an appeal function without being stated in that form. *Sir* implies obsequiousness, *man* too much companionableness, *buddy* fawning friendship. It helps to know these things because sometimes what appears to be an unprovoked emotional storm may be instead a response to an unrequited appeal for attention or love.

I referred earlier to a woman in her 40s who was emotionally contained as she related endless details about her husband and home life, all of which had a negative, angry ring. The details also conveyed the sense of desperation of her dependent bond and lack of initiative as well as fear of and rage at this man. The analyst's summary comment or clarification, "You sound angry and desperate as if you would think of divorce, but can't do it," brought a flood of tears. Analytic statements of this sort, naming the idea expressed in another way, are frequent and attest to the binding of affects to designative shorthand naming of a set of ideas. Moreover, such simple generalizations in words have the further interpersonal impact of feeling understood, which provides a further sense of community.

Naming and interpretation go hand in hand (Shapiro, 1970), making the psychoanalytic process a linguistic event that can be analyzed by pragmatic tools. The fit of the words to the events described are clear in the misadventures known as incomplete or premature interpretations (Glover, 1955) in which the patient evades the unconscious and acquires a new obsessional defense rather than being fully relieved by understanding. The patient becomes part of the interpretive field as he or she feels relief. Sometimes the relief is similar to a tip of the tongue phenomenon—it only occurs on recall of the missing word or phrase.

The notion of a dynamic unconscious rather than a simple cognitive unconscious may receive some warrant from recent studies and discussions from cognitive sciences on memory (Erdelyi, 1990; Clyman, 1990). Although these investigators are not linguistics students, their distinction between implicit procedural and declarative symbolic knowledge is apt to psychoanalytic and pragmatic inquiry. Implicit procedural knowledge concerns knowing how to do something like drive a car, or behave at a social gathering; they are like dialogic rules. Many of these procedures have never been reencoded in language in a declarative form; i.e., we usually do not say the procedure to ourselves or others, we know how to do it. Indeed, declarative knowledge seems to be a later developmental landmark and as such it is lost in expressive aphasias. The proposition offered earlier in a more linguistic frame, that affective constellations are to be considered part of a feature analysis of meaning, could be understood pragmatically for psychoanalytic analysis as a procedural nonexpressed feature of memory that has not been declared, but can be recognized once the dynamic barrier is lifted in the two-person field by trust and transference.

The patient's tears on hearing the word, *divorce*, permits a dreaded idea into awareness for consideration between two people and now is available for reworking as an ego property—the tension of suppression/repression or isolation of affect is relieved.

Linguists could certainly take a lead from psychoanalysts by including affective determinants in their semantic and pragmatic definitions and illocutionary devices. On the other hand, analysts could certainly use such an analysis as a way of considering "potential affects" as linked to cognitively conscious, linguistic events.

Sociolinguistics

Sociolinguistic analysis is but a small step from pragmatics, because it too takes its data from language in use—this time in communities. Because the frame is larger, it may seem somewhat remote from the dyadic analytic field. Nonetheless, there are cautions and mechanisms to be learned. Common language groups share and even define ethnic separateness. However, discrete language groups also show a tendency to shift the meaning of words over time and from generation to generation. The word fag in the early nineteenth century was used to describe an under classman with menial duties for upper classmen in English boarding schools. By the mid-1940s, it referred to gays, but remember it also is used to refer to a cigarette and is used to describe fatigue as in "fagged out." Even within cultures, groups like adolescents develop their own idiolects confounding their adult auditors. Many of the words are used as affective referents (Shapiro, 1985).

It is not by chance that some anthropologists have used the words etic and emic, borrowed from phon*etic* and phon*emic,* to reference sequentially the universals and the particulars of cultural habits and practices. These structural notions derive from the linguistic notion that we all make sounds for speech (phonetic), but that there is a specific corpus of sounds (phonemes) that make up the specific acoustic shape of words in specific languages in order to signal meanings.

A recent series of studies (Badad et al., 1983) show that American school children return the social smile of strangers, while Israelis do not. The implications within each culture regarding shows of friendliness and sincerity are legion. I introduce this fact because we analyze individuals who use our common tongue in ways that mark them regionally, but also in ways that mark them culturally. This is especially so when we consider how they encode their affectivity. Are exuberance and expressiveness only the mark of the southern European or Latin American? Is restraint of emotion the mark of the Anglo-saxon, the Swede, or the Down Easterner? These stereotypes bear some notice, but we are also attuned to the specifics of an individual's style.

The analysis of an Afro-American who grew up in the South brought home the emic-etic problem whole cloth. She had an oedipal complex, no doubt, but her specific shame centered more fully on poverty rather than on the universals discovered or the specifics of being black in a white world. Such specificity suggested the need for careful attunement and empathy to her verbalizations and behavior, rather than to preconceived ideas.

Doi's (1973) concept of Amai brings home the notion that rearing practices may lead to powerful changes in the constellations of early relationships that count later in life. His emphasis on mother-son ties preoedipally has significant impact he claims on emotional life later. This should remind us of Kohut's (1977) almost casual comment that the closer we are to a person's cultural experience, the more empathic we can feel.

In a contrary vein, Hartmann et al. (1951) noted the completeness of Freudian metapsychology as a general plan of the vicissitudes of drives that must be adapted to cultural variation. In that sense, the etic is there in the paradigm and the analyst is moved to reduce data from the surface. Technically this requires a good working knowledge, not only of how resistances are organized in transferential enactments, but also of how much an individual exploits cultural variation for idiolectic reason.

The formal northern European is a stereotype, as is the hot-tempered southern European. However, within each culture there is variation. We have had enough experience in the United States with emigrés from middle Europe and elsewhere to understand that adaptation to a new language is but one feature of adaptation to cultural expressiveness. Linguistically, this can take many forms with respect to emotional expression.

The analyst must become accustomed to the exuberance that covers depression or the formal serenity that covers rage. If we yield to the notion that affects may, at times, not be encoded in words, we have also to agree that simple affective displays require understanding and even curtailing as a feature of civilized action in some communities.

Within the culture of the analysis itself, we create a refuge in which safety of expression is the claim, and yet we see patients fall into habitual patterns—no, we expect and welcome such regression, for without it we could not analyze. Thus, we expect that the vehicle of expression of emotion in adults will have been acted upon by experience that is culturocentric and idiosyncratic at the same time. We learn the codes of each. If we are familiar with the former specifically, it makes some of our tasks lighter, but the latter must be learned firsthand—in the analysis.

Summary

I have proposed that the clinical process of psychoanalysis can be viewed with some advantage as a subset of linguistic experiences using a specific method. As such, the general rules of linguistic analysis and understanding apply. Nonetheless, psychoanalysis may be viewed as a subcultural experience that requires special linguistic consideration in order to account for data derived from (1) the contrived communicative pattern of the analytic situation; (2) the theoretical underpinnings of the method that includes dynamic unconscious mental functioning; (3) free association and transference as special cases of discourse. In each of these three areas, we must account for the unique role of affective experience. The contrived clinical arrangement is designed to help the patient focus within and offers possibilities to experience affects that might otherwise be overlooked. The dynamic unconscious is held in abeyance by mechanisms that are responsive to affective signals. The transferences permit the unusual possibility of experiencing affects in new contexts which seem appropriate, but which soon can become ego-alien under the scrutiny of the observing ego.

Each domain is embedded with linguistic significance that can be illuminating for understanding of how language facilitates and permits affective expression and comprehension in the special circumstance of the analysis. The events discovered can then be studied in relation to the usual circumstances or dialogue in life. Contrariwise, psychoanalysis can also contribute to linguistic analysis by adding the dimension of a dynamic unconscious understanding of symbolic function as it occurs in life. More specifically, analysis forces linguistics to include affective valence in its definitional parameters.

There is no way that we can consider affective experience only from the vantage of the physiology of affect or the varying physiognomies that make up facial expressions accompanying feelings. We need a depth understanding of affects that includes how they are linked to conflictual constellations of ideas and the words we use. We also should be curious as to how affects deter cognitive and other expressions and how affects determine or modify object relations because they become the organizing feature that has the valence and countervalence that makes for significance and meaning. The language of affect and the study of the linguistic forms in analysis should be useful to systematically help psychoanalysts better grasp what they do and how they understand affective expression using a modern interdisciplinary model.

REFERENCES

ARLOW, J. A. (1953). Masturbation and symptom formation. *J. Amer. Psychoanal. Assn.*, 1:45–58

——— (1977). Affects and the psychoanalytic situation. *Int. J. Psychoanal.*, 58:157–170.

AUSTIN, J. L. (1962). *How to Do Things with Words.* New York: Oxford Univ. Press.

BACON, F. K. (1989). Quoted in New York *Times* Magazine, August 20. "Unnerving Art" by M. Kimmelman, pp. 41–76.

BADAD, Y. E., ALEXANDER, E. E., & BABAD, E. Y. (1983). Returning the smile of the stranger: Developmental patterns and socialization factors. *Monographs of the Society for Research in Child Development,* No. 203, Vol. 48, No. 5.

BRENNER, C. (1982). *The Mind in Conflict.* New York: Int. Univ. Press.

CLYMAN, R. B. (1990). *The Procedural Organization of Emotions.* New York: Int. Univ. Press.

DAHL, H. (1978). A classification of emotion words. *Psychoanal. Q.,* 1:269–270.

——— TELLER, V., MOSS, D., & TRUJILLO, M. (1978). Countertransference examples of the syntactic expression of warded off contents. *Psychoanal. Q.,* 47:339–363.

DOI, T. (1973). *The Anatomy of Dependence.* San Francisco: Kodansha International Publishers.

EKMAN, P., LEVENSON, R. W., & FRIESON, W. V. (1983). Autonomic nervous system activity distinguishes between emotions. *Science,* 221:1208–1210.

ELIOT, T. S. (1930). Sweeny agonistes. In *The Complete Poems of T. S. Eliot.* New York: Harcourt Brace.

EMDE, R. N. (1983). The prerepresentational self and its affective core. *Psychoanal. Study Child,* 38:165–192.

ERDELYI, M. H. (1990). Repression, reconstruction, and defense. In *Repression: Personality Style and Mechanism of Defense,* ed. J. Singer. Chicago: Univ. Chicago Press.

FENICHEL, O. (1941). *Problems of Psychoanalytic Technique.* New York: Psychoanalytic Quarterly.

FREEDMAN, N. (1977). *Hands, Words and Mind: Communicative Structures and Psychic Structures,* ed. N. Freedman & S. Grand. New York: Plenum Press.

FREUD, S. (1899). Screen memories. *S. E.,* 3.

——— (1900). The interpretation of dreams. *S. E.,* 4 & 5.

——— (1905a). Fragment of an analysis of a case of hysteria. *S. E.,* 7.

——— (1905b). Jokes and their relation to the unconscious. *S. E.,* 8.

——— (1915). The unconscious. *S. E.,* 14.
——— (1923). The ego and the id. *S. E.,* 19.
——— (1925). Negation. *S. E.,* 19.
——— (1926). Inhibitions, symptoms and anxiety. *S. E.,* 20.
——— (1940). An outline of psychoanalysis. *S. E.,* 23.
GLOVER, E. (1955). *The Technique of Psychoanalysis.* New York: Int. Univ. Press.
GRAND, S. (1977). On hand movements during speech. In *Communicative Structures and Psychic Structures,* ed. N. Freedman & S. Grand. New York: Plenum Press.
HARTMANN, H., KRIS, E., & LOEWENSTEIN, R. M. (1951). Some psychoanalytic comments on "culture and personality." In *Psychoanalysis and Culture,* ed. G. B. Wilbur & W. Muensterberger. New York: Int. Univ. Press.
KLEINMAN, A. (1980). *Patients and Healers in the Context of Culture.* Berkeley: Univ. California Press.
KLINNERT, M. D., CAMPOS, J. J., SORCE, J. F., EMDE, R. N., & SVEJDA, M. (1983). Emotions as behavior regulators. In *Emotion: Theory, Research and Experience,* ed. R. Plutchik & H. Kellerman. New York: Academic Press.
KOHUT, H. (1977). *The Restoration of the Self.* New York: Int. Univ. Press.
LACAN, J. (1956). *The Language of the Self.* Baltimore: Johns Hopkins University Press.
LEVY, S. & INDERBITZIN, L. (1990). The analytic surface. *J. Amer. Psychoanal. Assn.,* 38:329-349.
LOEWENSTEIN, R. M. (1951). The problem of interpretation. *Psychoanal. Q.,* 20:1-14.
LURIA, A. (1961). *The Role of Speech in the Regulation of Normal and Abnormal Behavior.* New York: Liveright.
MAHONEY, P. (1987). *Psychoanalysis and Discourse.* London: Tavistock.
NEEDLES, W. (1959). Gesticulation and speech. *Int. J. Psychoanal.,* 40:291-294.
PULVER, S. (1974). Unconscious versus potential affect. *Psychoanal. Q.,* 43:77-84.
ROSEN, V. H. (1961). Relevance of "style" to certain aspects of defense and the synthetic function of the ego. *Int. J. Psychoanal.,* 42:447-457.
SCHAFER, R. (1976). *A New Language for Psychoanalysis.* New Haven: Yale Univ. Press.
SEARLE, J. R. (1969). *Speech Acts: An Essay in the Philosophy of Language.* New York: Cambridge Univ. Press.
SHAPIRO, T. (1970). Interpretation and naming. *J. Amer. Psychoanal. Assn.,* 18:399-421.
——— (1979). *Clinical Psycholinguistics.* New York: Plenum Press.
——— (1985). Adolescent language. In *Adolescent Psychiatry*, ed. M. Sugar. Chicago: Univ. Chicago Press, 12:297-311.
——— (1986). Sign, symbol, and structural theory. In *Psychoanalysis: The Science of Mental Conflict.* Hillsdale, N.J.: Analytic Press.
——— (1988). *Language Structure and Psychoanalysis.* Madison, Ct.: Int. Univ. Press.
SIOMOPOLOUS, G. (1977). Poetry as affective communication. *Catron,* 46:499-513.
SORCE, J. F., EMDE, R. N., CAMPOS, J. J. & KLINNERT, M. D. (1985). Maternal emotional signaling. *Devel. Psychol.,* 21(1):195-200.

American Psychoanalytic Association
309 East 49 Street
New York, NY 10017

THE PROCEDURAL ORGANIZATION OF EMOTIONS: A CONTRIBUTION FROM COGNITIVE SCIENCE TO THE PSYCHOANALYTIC THEORY OF THERAPEUTIC ACTION

ROBERT B. CLYMAN, M.D.

Recent research in cognitive science has demonstrated that there are different types of memory processes. While declarative memory refers to memories for facts or events which can be recalled, procedural memories underlie skills yet encode information which cannot be recalled. This paper extends this distinction to the nature of emotions and emotional memories. Its implications for psychoanalytic theory are then examined, yielding fresh views of transference, defense, and treatment. Infantile amnesia is found to result partially from the immaturity of the declarative memory system, yet procedural memories encode transference expectations and provide continuity in emotional functioning from early childhood onward. In this light, psychoanalytic treatment is conceptualized as the modification of emotional procedures. Two general methods for modifying procedures are then described, which provide a new model, grounded in current memory research, for understanding therapeutic change through insight and through a new emotional experience with the psychoanalyst.

A CENTRAL QUESTION POSED by psychoanalytic developmental theory is how early experiences affect mental functioning, when few memories remain from early childhood. Freud's explanation, of course, was that memories are repressed during the resolution of the Oedipus complex. An alternative hypothesis, however, has been raised by recent

---

Post-Doctoral Research Fellow, Developmental Psychobiology Research Group, Department of Psychiatry, University of Colorado Health Sciences Center, Denver, CO.

The author gratefully acknowledges the thoughtful comments of Drs. Richard Bingham, Mardi Horowitz, Jacob Jacobson, John Kelly, Peter Mayerson, Homer Olsen, Theodore Shapiro, and, above all, Robert Emde, during the preparation of this paper.

research in cognitive science. We now know that there are multiple distinct memory processes which develop at different rates in childhood. In particular, one currently prominent hypothesis is that there are two distinct types of memory, termed procedural and declarative memory. Procedural memory refers to the information which underlies skills and forms early in childhood, and declarative memory refers to information which can be recalled consciously, such as recollections of facts or events, but forms only later in childhood. In this paper, the hypothesis will be presented that procedural memories underlie transference and defense, form early in childhood, and withstand the effects of infantile amnesia. By recasting portions of psychoanalytic theory in terms of modern memory research, we can take a fresh look at emotions and their organization, the interpretation of transference, and the theory of therapeutic action.

Multiple Memory Processes in the Brain

Clinical Amnesia

Procedural and declarative memory are dissociated when the hippocampus is damaged in a neurological syndrome called clinical amnesia, and this has provided a model system for research. Amnesic patients, despite their startling deficits—including being unable to remember that they met someone a few minutes before—can retain certain kinds of information (for reviews, see Richardson-Klavehn and Bjork, 1988; Mayes, 1988; Squire, 1987; Cermak, 1982; Lynch et al., 1984; Squire and Butters, 1984). While there have been a large number of studies to date, the findings will be illustrated using one important experiment. Cohen and colleagues (Cohen, 1984; Cohen et al., 1985) studied adults who were learning to solve the Tower of Hanoi puzzle. This puzzle consists of three vertical pegs on a board, and the left-most peg has five concentric rings of varying radii on it, so that a smaller ring always lies on top of a larger one. The task is to transfer all of the rings from the left peg to the right one. Only one ring can be moved at a time, and a larger ring cannot be placed on top of a smaller one. Amnesic patients, even though each time they work on the puzzle report that they have never seen it before, can learn to solve the puzzle and retain their skill over time as well as normal adults. In general, it has been shown that amnesic patients can acquire complex perceptual, motor, and cognitive skills and demonstrate conditioning and priming effects. The data are complex, and controversies remain as to the best way to explain the findings (for valuable discussions of these controversies, see Schacter, 1987, 1990; Richardson-Klavehn and Bjork, 1988; Roediger, 1990; Roediger et al., 1990). Squire and Cohen (1984; Cohen and Squire, 1980; Squire, 1986, 1987), however, have postulated that procedural knowledge is retained, while declarative knowledge is lost in clinical amnesia. This theory will be reviewed in detail in order to lay the groundwork for explicating a psychoanalytic theory of affects, transference, and treatment based on modern memory research.

Declarative and Procedural Knowledge

Declarative knowledge refers to information that can be learned, stored in memory, and later recalled. It stores memories for facts or events that have been experienced, and it is represented either in language or in sensory images, such as mental pictures. Declarative knowledge is symbolic, in that the thought always refers to something else, its meaning, or referent. Declarative knowledge, however, may be conscious, preconscious, or unconscious.

Procedural knowledge is different. We have many skills, but we are rarely conscious of the knowledge which underlies our skills. For example, we typically do not have to think where third gear is before we shift from second gear. We do not have to access consciously that information in order to shift gears. We can skillfully adjust our performance when a road is icy or a hill is steep precisely because we do not have to think about what we are going to do before we do it. This is procedural knowledge. It is the information we acquire when learning a skill. It is demonstrated by our performance, not by recalling facts or experiences. Procedures are flexible in that they can respond to multiple contingencies, and they are organized around obtaining goals.

Squire (1986) has suggested that procedures are encoded directly in the neural program which underlies the skill. This is not symbolic knowledge; procedurally encoded information does not stand for anything else. It cannot be stated in language directly, although the procedural program can be translated into declarative language. While declarative knowledge can be made conscious, procedural knowledge cannot. Declarative knowledge can be remembered; procedural knowledge can only be enacted. Declarative knowledge enables us to be aware of the outcome of our thought processes, but we are not conscious of how the procedures actually function.

Cohen and Squire (1980) hypothesize that amnesics' procedural knowledge is intact but that the declarative memory system is impaired. Amnesic patients know how to solve the Tower of Hanoi puzzle, but they have forgotten that they learned how. No memory of learning the puzzle nor memory that they can solve it is retained, but their skill, supported by procedural knowledge, is intact. Squire (1986) argues that the hippocampus is necessary for the consolidation and storage of declarative information. Because the hippocampus is damaged in clinical amnesia, declarative memory is impaired. But the procedural knowledge which supports the skill is unaffected. Complex procedures can organize how we think, even though the actual procedural mechanisms remain outside of conscious awareness. This is as true whether we are driving a car or, as I hope to show, negotiating our way within an emotionally complex relationship or our intrapsychic world of internalized objects.

Controlled and Automatic Procedures

Shiffrin and Schneider (1977; Schneider and Shiffrin, 1977; Shiffrin and Dumais, 1981), in their elegant studies of visual search mechanisms, have demonstrated that there are two types of procedures, controlled and automatic. Consider how we learn to shift gears. As is characteristic of controlled procedures, initially we are slow and our coordination is poor. The neophyte has to remind herself of the rules of the procedure (e.g., third gear is upwards, to the right and up) prior to executing the program. A great deal of attention is required. With practice, our skill improves and the procedure becomes automatic. A skillful driver's movements are fluid, rapid, and efficient, and she does not have to recall consciously the rules of the procedure in order to execute it. Indeed, Shiffrin and Schneider (1977; Schneider and Shiffrin, 1977) have demonstrated that automatic procedures do not require any attention, which is why we can accomplish more than one task simultaneously once the skill has become automatic. From a representational standpoint, the central distinction between controlled and automatic procedures is that the former requires that declarative knowledge be conscious during execution of the procedure. With automatic procedures, all of the information is encoded in procedural, or what is sometimes termed compiled (Neves and Anderson, 1984), form. In practice, the amount of attention required during execution of a procedure varies along a continuum (Anderson, 1985).

Controlled and automatic procedures each have advantages and disadvantages as ways of representing information in the brain. While controlled procedures are flexible and readily modified by altering the declarative input, they are slow and poorly coordinated. Automatic procedures, while smooth, rapid, and efficient, are difficult to modify. Once initiated, they tend to go to completion.

The capacity to select one procedure over possible alternatives is itself a procedure, and it has been referred to as a control structure (Rumelhart, 1984). The ability to shift to third gear is a procedure, but the procedure which decides when to shift gears is a control structure. The central research question here is how best to model the functioning of control structures. In keeping with one of the most exciting areas of current interest in cognitive science, Horowitz et al. (this volume) suggest that control structures are best modeled within the framework of parallel distributed processing (Rumelhart) et al., 1986; McClelland et al., 1986). While this is a key question for all theories of mental functioning, it will not be discussed further here, other than to speculate that a control structure itself may be controlled or automatic. Flexibility in intrapsychic processing refers to the ability of control structures to select the procedure which best fits a given situation, and this is as true in the emotional realm as it is in the cognitive, perceptual, or motoric realms. A central goal of all dynamic psychotherapies is to increase the flexibility of a person's emotional control structures.

The Development of Procedural and Declarative Knowledge in Early Childhood

Clinical amnesia dissociates procedural from declarative knowledge in adults, permitting their study. These two memory processes also develop separately. While the ability to store procedural knowledge is present soon after birth, the capacity for declarative representation does not mature until approximately the fifth year of life. This will have important implications for psychoanalytic theory.

The separate development of these two memory processes will be demonstrated by briefly examining two domains: Piaget's description of infant cognition, and the role of the developing hippocampus in the consolidation and storage of long-term memories. Piaget (1952) described the period from birth to 2 years of age as the "sensorimotor period," in which infants make use of sensorimotor schemas, which are goal-directed plans for action, such as reaching for an interesting mobile or engaging in a game of reciprocal smiling with a parent. Infants learn to coordinate their perceptions and actions, but they cannot yet think without acting. In Mandler's (1983) words, infancy "is a most un-Proustian life, not thought, only lived."

Piaget believed that the sensorimotor period ended around 2 years of age when the infant developed the capacity for recall, a central feature of the declarative memory system. The schemas of the sensorimotor period are perceptual-motor-affective procedures. They enable babies to interact with their parents, but infants cannot think about them in their absence. In the language of modern cognitive science, we would say that procedures are present soon after birth, but the declarative memory system does not emerge until the end of infancy (Mandler, 1983; Schacter and Moscovitch, 1984; Nadel and Zola-Morgan, 1984).

Although the capacity to form declarative memories begins by the end of infancy, the system is not fully functional until around the age of 5, when declarative memories can be consolidated and stored in a form which permits later retrieval. Preschool children are limited in their capacity to recall declarative memories, and adults have few memories from before the age of 5 (for a recent review, see Pillemer and White, 1989). Freud (1899, 1905) first described this phenomenon, termed it infantile amnesia, and theorized that repression blocked access to the memories of early childhood. We now know, however, that early childhood amnesia is more complex.

Nadel and Zola-Morgan (1984) suggest that postnatal hippocampal maturation underlies the growing capacity to store declarative information. At birth, the human hippocampus is immature. It develops throughout early childhood, undergoing major changes after 18 to 36 months (Jacobs and Nadel, 1985). The studies of adults with clinical amnesia indicate that the hippocampus is necessary for registration of declarative information. While other areas of the brain are probably involved in the storage of declarative information, the hippocampus is certainly part of the neuroanatomic pathway (Teyler and Fountain, 1987). Additionally, Mishkin and colleagues (1984; Bachevalier and Mishkin, 1984; Malamut et al., 1984) have demonstrated similar findings in nonhuman primates. When the amygdala and hippocampus are resected in Rhesus monkeys, they retain what these researchers call "habits" while losing memories based on recognition or associations. Furthermore, the habit system develops prior to the recognition system in nonhuman primates, quite analogously to the findings in humans.

Before the hippocampus is mature, young children are unable to store declarative memories in a fully retrievable form. While we begin developing procedures soon after birth, and can retain them throughout our lives, the declarative memory system is not fully functional until the end of the preschool years. Although repression clearly plays a role in early childhood amnesia, so does hippocampal immaturity. It is interesting to note (Emde, personal communication) that Freud (1915a) foreshadowed this research in his discussion of primal repression, which blocks initial access of instinctual derivatives into consciousness. According to Freud, the information which has been (primarily) repressed then draws conscious contents into the unconscious during secondary repression. Primal repression, then, results in an unconscious procedure which affects mental functioning, even though the information which underlies the procedure cannot itself be made conscious. Later it will be argued that clinical amnesia, early childhood amnesia, and repression are inextricably linked.

The Development of Emotional Procedures in Early Childhood

How is this related to emotional functioning and its development? We can now develop the concept of an emotional procedure, drawing from research on perceptual, motor, and cognitive procedures. This will provide a foundation for discussing transference, ego functions, and psychoanalytic treatment from a procedural perspective. This discussion will lead us to the conclusion that the emotional procedures which develop in infancy and early childhood can withstand the effects of early childhood amnesia and provide continuity in emotional functioning across the life-span, and that modification of maladaptive emotional procedures is central in psychoanalytic treatment.

Cognitive procedures organize how we think, and emotional procedures organize how we feel. Just as nonaffective information and experience are processed with cognitive procedures, emotional information and experiences are processed with emotional procedures. This is not to imply that cognition and emotion refer to disjoint sets of mental activities, as emotions typically (and often necessarily) involve cognition (see Horowitz et al. in this volume for a further discussion of this point of view).

The mental processes which culminate in an emotional state, as well as the consequences of that emotional state, are procedurally organized. Let us look first at how emotions organize subsequent behavior. When a baby experiences an incentive stimulus for an emotion, motoric procedures are initiated. If a frightening figure suddenly approaches, emotion will be expressed through contraction of facial musculature, a gasp of fear, and avoidant movements. The expression of emotion in the face is genetically governed (Izard, 1971; Ekman et al., 1972), and the other component processes may well be, too. Emotional procedures organize behavioral expressions through multiple channels such as gestures and vocalic intonations. This is accomplished outside of awareness and is procedurally organized. We use this clinically: when different channels carry contradictory messages, we infer the presence of hidden (multiple) emotions (for a discussion of this issue, see Shapiro in this volume). With development, emotions will influence not only how we act, but also how we think as well as how we process further emotional information and experience. Children will develop characteristic ways of thinking, feeling, perceiving, and acting in response to different emotions. The processes which govern these responses will be organized procedurally. Emotional procedures regulate our responses to emotional situations.

The processing of the antecedents of emotional experience are also procedurally organized. Affective procedures process the meaning, significance, or value of a stimulus to the individual (Arnold, 1960; Campos et al., 1989). A simple stimulus such as a loud noise may regularly elicit a specific emotion such as fear. More complex stimuli will require interpretation before the emotion is experienced. These emotional interpretive procedures are dramatically illustrated by the phenomenon of social referencing in the latter part of the first year (Campos and Stenberg, 1981; Feinman and Lewis, 1983; Klinnert et al., 1983). An infant, upon encountering uncertainty—for example, the approach of a toy robot which makes noise and flashes lights—will look to an adult for an emotional signal to use in regulating her behavior. If the adult expresses fear through facial expression or voice, the infant will not approach, but if she expresses interest or pleasure, the infant will be encouraged to approach the robot (Klinnert et al., 1986). With cognitive-emotional development, children will respond not only to external stimuli but to internal wishes, fears, and fantasies as well. Through regularities in the child's care-giving relationships, the child will come to interpret certain situations in characteristic ways. Both how the child tends to react to emotional situations and how those emotions constrain further thinking, feeling, and behavior will be encoded in affective procedures.

We can further our understanding of the procedural mechanisms of emotion processing by examining the concept of heuristics, which has been studied extensively in the cognitive realm (Kahneman et al., 1982). Heuristics are strategies employed to solve a problem or to reach a goal. For example, we make use of the clarity of a visual image in judging an object's distance (Tversky and Kahneman, 1982). Like all heuristics, this processing strategy developed through trial and error. It developed within a specific context, and it was not formed solely by inference (Polya, 1945). Like most heuristics, this strategy will work most of the time, and therefore it can be adaptive. However, heuristics often encode suboptimal solutions to problems (Tversky and Kahneman, 1982), and they can lead to systematic distortions in how information, and emotions, are processed.

Four features of cognitive heuristics which will be relevant to our discussion of emotional processing can be illustrated by returning to the Tower of Hanoi study (Cohen et al., 1985). First, amnesic patients had no difficulty generalizing their skill and transferring the rings to the middle peg instead of the right one, a task which requires different moves. Second, although the impaired subjects were unable to recognize intermediate positions along the way to the optimal solution (after they had learned to solve the puzzle), they were able to solve the puzzle from those intermediate positions. Third, the puzzle consists of a set of subproblems which are formally equivalent, although each subproblem requires different moves. Amnesic subjects learned to treat the subproblems equivalently. These three results, taken together, demonstrate that amnesic patients are able to develop interpretive procedures which extract regularities from the complex stimuli present in the Tower of Hanoi, and transform those rules into strategies for solving the puzzle. Fourth, nonamnesic comparison subjects' verbal reports lagged behind their acquisition of increasingly sophisticated, problem-solving strategies, demonstrating that their interpretive procedures and strategies developed without conscious declarative planning. These procedures and heuristic strategies are encoded procedurally and form in both amnesic and nonamnesic adults.

Just as subjects in the study can extract regularities from the puzzle and develop strategies for solving the problems it presents, young children can decipher the rules by which their families operate and develop strategies for meeting their needs within their families. In general, children do this in one of two ways. They may formulate their strategies consciously and then implement them. However, most of the time, young children develop their emotional procedures directly, without any intermediate declarative steps, just as both amnesic and nonamnesic subjects learned to see patterns in the Tower of Hanoi and developed strategies to solve those problems without intermediate, conscious, declarative processing. These interpretive procedures and heuristic strategies are encoded procedurally outside of conscious awareness. For example, some physically abused children are avoidant in their interpersonal interactions (George and Main, 1979), but they do not need to formulate these strategies consciously in order to implement them. Indeed, it may be the case that strategies which are developed unconsciouly have more motivational force than those which are consciously formulated when learned. Like all heuristic strategies, however, they may be adaptive in some contexts and not in others. Procedurally encoded, maladaptive heuristics will lead to systematic distortions in the subsequent processing of emotions and experience, just as ascertaining the distance of an object by the clarity of the image will occasionally lead to errors in judgment. Heuristics develop outside of awareness, are encoded procedurally, affect subsequent processing of emotions and experience, and may be adaptive depending on context.

Young children are not only interested in discovering how their family functions in order to meet their needs, but they are also concerned with moral rules, with what is considered right or fair in their families (Emde et al., 1988, and in press). They will decipher and encode these rules and develop heuristic strategies in order to act in accordance with them. With development, moral behavior will become regulated by moral emotions such as pride, shame, or guilt, and these emotions will incorporate the procedural heuristics which the child has developed.

Emotional heuristics, whether they are developed to help the child meet her needs or to act morally, are intrinsic components of the mental complexes we call emotions. Conscious feelings, which are also components of emotions, affect the course of mental functioning in part because they are inextricably linked to emotional heuristics.

Such a view makes sense of the difficult problem of unconscious emotions, which psychoanalysts and philosophers have grappled with since Freud (1915b, 1926; Pulver, 1971; Dilman, 1988). Emotions may be unconscious, in general, for one of two reasons. First, affects may be warded off defensively. Second, when controlled emotional procedures have become automatic with practice, the conscious feeling no longer needs to be experienced in order to execute the procedure, as conscious attention is no longer required. This is useful, as consciousness processes information and experience too slowly to support quick, adaptive responses to stimuli (Kihlstrom, 1987; Horowitz, 1988a). For both reasons, automatic defensive functioning can proceed without conscious awareness of the feeling state.

When emotions are activated, the component emotional heuristics are also engaged. Even if the feeling is unconscious, the activated emotional heuristics will affect the course of mental functioning and behavior. Within this frame, emotions, whether they are conscious or not, may play causal roles in mental functioning due to the activation of the procedurally encoded heuristics.

We can further our understanding of emotional procedures by taking another look at their development. Once again, we can benefit by examining how complex, cognitive, problem-solving skills develop. Anderson (1982) studied how students learn geometry. The problem they faced was to know when to apply which Euclidian axiom in order to prove various theorems. Anderson found that the students would repeat the axioms to themselves over and over, in different contexts, until the procedure became automatic and it was "intuitive" which axiom had to be applied in which situation. Each individual axiom had to be applied many times in multiple situations before the procedure became automatic. Similarly, new emotional procedures will be used in multiple situations. Isolation of affect, for example, may be useful in avoiding many different painful emotions. One procedure may come to serve multiple motivations or goals. For each goal, the control structure will develop heuristics which regularly initiate certain procedures in order to meet that goal. Multiple motivations or goals may characteristically initiate only a limited number of procedures. A process akin to natural selection may occur in development, where the different motivations "select" a procedure found to be useful, strengthening the procedural heuristics between the motivation or goal and the procedure which is initiated. However, this natural selection process yields a probabilistic hierarchy: All procedures survive, but those procedures which best fill open niches in the mental ecology become more likely to be implemented than others. Procedures which are selected are overdetermined in the sense that they can serve many goals and have been incorporated into multiple motivational structures. Different control structures, serving different goals and using multiple heuristics, will share a small number of procedures as their final common pathway. We observe the procedures which are selected as the patient's characteristic coping strategies.

The procedures which are selected are shaped by the interactional patterns within the family. Reiss (1989) has called these patterns the "practicing family," the array of repetitive interactions which occur within families. This type of representation has a special status, in that it reflects both the individual family members' procedures, as well as the precise dovetailing of procedural interactions which results from the procedures having formed in relation to each other. Both family therapists and psychoanalysts work with these patterns. Family therapists intervene directly by disrupting these precise transactional patterns during family therapy sessions. Sandler (1976), in his discussion of role responsiveness, has described these patterns within the context of transference-countertransference interactions. These procedural patterns are central to psychotherapeutic treatment.

A clinical example will illustrate these ideas. The vignette comes from ongoing research on moral development and affective representation in maltreated preschool children that Robert Emde, Helen Buchsbaum, Sheree Toth, Dante Cicchetti, and I are currently conducting. The study utilizes a technique developed by Buchsbaum and Emde (1990) and Bretherton et al. (1990), in which the first part of a story is told to a child using a doll family, and the child is then asked to complete the narrative. Story stems are designed to elicit specific issues such as empathy or restraint of aggression, or to challenge the child to make moral choices. The children's responses are then videotaped and coded blindly. In one of the stories, the boy is hungry but Mom warns him not to get too close to the stove. He cannot wait, and he knocks the pot of hot gravy off the stove and burns himself. Timmy, a 3½-year-old severely neglected boy, completed the story by having the mother doll clean up the mess. The mother then scolded the boy doll for being too close to the stove. In a painfully plaintive voice Timmy had the little boy respond: "But the gravy burned me." The mother in the story did not respond, and Timmy then had the boy take it upon himself to step away from the stove. In Timmy's other stories, the parents repeatedly ignored the boy's needs. Only rarely did Timmy have a child doll ask them for help.

Timmy's responses in this story reflect his procedural knowledge of how to cope with this situation. One can infer that he did not expect help from his parents, nor was it in his repertoire to seek help readily from them. He demonstrated his expectation of how parents behave and how he is likely to behave when he is hurt. But note that Timmy did not say: "This is how my mommy acts," or "I remember that my mommy didn't help me when I burned myself." He did not recall declarative memories of his experiences and then act in response to them. He knew how to behave in this situation, how to cope with burning himself, because he had built his experiences into procedural skills. When solving the Tower of Hanoi puzzle, the amnesic patient does not say: "I know how I solved the puzzle yesterday" because she does not recall how she solved it. That is precisely what the amnesic patient does not remember. But the patient can solve the puzzle based on her procedural knowledge. Analogously, Timmy could solve the emotional dilemma which confronted him by utilizing his procedural skills, without relying on his declarative memories. He has developed procedurally encoded coping skills which are adaptive in his family environment. Unfortunately, he has learned that parents are unhelpful, and this will take its toll in his life.

In summary, we have seen that emotional procedures organize our emotional lives. They organize how we interpret emotional situations and how we react emotionally to them. They can develop without intermediate conscious declarative processing, and, when automatic, they function outside of awareness. They are guided by procedurally encoded heuristics which are initially adaptive but may later lead to systematic distortions in the processing of information and experience. Those procedures which are selected in development are observed as the individual's characteristic coping strategies.

Emotional procedures develop prior to the declarative memory system in early childhood, are unaffected by hippocampal immaturity, and are retained across the boundary of early childhood amnesia. Emotional procedures provide organization and community in our emotional functioning across the life-span.

A number of authors have discussed these issues from related perspectives. Shapiro and Perry (1976) organized data which supported the idea of a discontinuity in mental functioning at the onset of latency, suggesting that the amnesia of early childhood reflects a different form of cognitive organization, similar to the recent discovery that the declarative memory system forms by the end of the preschool years. Piaget (1973), extending his work on cognition to affect, suggested that operational schemas underlie the individual's affective capabilities. Bowlby (1980) reconceptualized his view of attachment as the development of "internal working models" of self, other, and the attachment relationship. In discussing the superego, he noted that the rules of appraisal of action, thoughts, and feelings are applied automatically outside conscious awareness. Furthermore, he observed that all skills are slow to change, and he saw this reflected in the pace of dynamic psychotherapy and psychoanalysis. His ideas about internal working models have been extended by Main et al. (1985) in the demonstration of cross-generational continuities in insecure attachment patterns, and Bretherton (1985; in press; Bretherton et al., 1990) in linking internal working models to nonsymbolic capacities and motivational-behavioral control systems, thereby suggesting—in the language used here—that they are encoded procedurally. Stern (1989) has incorporated recent research on categorization (Rosch, 1983) and event representations (Nelson, 1986) into a view of internal working models informed by recent research in cognitive science.

Focusing more directly on psychoanalysis, Gedo (1988) emphasized the role of skill acquisition during treatment.

Lichtenberg (1983) saw infant memories as encoded in "perceptual-action-affect responses without symbolic representation." In his recent book, he suggested that procedural knowledge includes rules which govern perception, cognition, and affect, and he postulated that procedural knowledge underlies role enactments (Lichtenberg, 1989). The most extensive discussions of procedural models of emotional functioning can be found in the work of Horowitz and his colleagues (Horowitz, 1987, 1988a, 1988b, 1989; Horowitz et al. in this volume). This pioneering work has integrated research in cognitive science with psychoanalysis. The constructs of person schemas and role relationship models have promoted valuable new ways of understanding both psychoanalytic theory and individual psychopathology. I turn now to an examination of the implications of this new information about procedural knowledge for psychoanalysis.

Implications for Psychoanalytic Theory

We will begin with a brief discussion of selected psychoanalytic constructs from a procedural perspective. This will lay a foundation for a procedural view of how emotional procedures are modified in psychoanalysis. Bridging cognitive science and psychoanalysis affords each field the opportunity to modify its theories and generate new hypotheses based on insights from the other endeavor. It also serves to clarify areas of agreement and disagreement, hone our thinking, and help us notice phenomena we have often seen but not fully appreciated or understood. By translating familiar psychoanalytic ideas into the language of cognitive science, I hope that new light will be shed on our understanding of the mechanisms of change in psychoanalysis. I will begin with a discussion of transference.

Transference

> . . . the patient does not say that he remembers that he used to be defiant and critical towards his parents' au-

> thority; instead, he behaves in that way to the doctor. . . . The patient does not *remember* anything of what he has forgotten and repressed, but *acts* it out. He reproduces it not as a memory but as an action; he *repeats* it, without, of course, knowing that he is repeating it [Freud, 1914, p. 150].

Transference is the enactment of the emotional procedures learned in childhood. This idea is derived from a seminal paper by Matthew Erdelyi (in press). Independently, Grigsby and Hartlaub (1988) have suggested that character is represented procedurally. While transference enactments occasionally are based on controlled procedures operating on unconscious declarative information, more commonly they are manifestations of procedurally organized emotional skills.

Ego Functions, Defenses, Repression, and the Repetition Compulsion

Ego functions, defenses, repression, and the repetition compulsion can all be profitably viewed from the perspective of procedural knowledge. Let us begin with ego functions. Another way of viewing this construct would be to consider ego functions as affective control structures. A discussion of self and object constancy will illustrate the productiveness of this approach by casting them as procedural capacities of the well-functioning ego. Mahler (1968) offers a definition: "By object constancy we mean that the maternal image has become intrapsychically available to the child in the same way as the actual mother had been libidinally available—for sustenance, comfort, and love" (p. 222). But object constancy, along with self constancy, do not refer to the experience of a declarative image of mother or of oneself. Rather, they refer to a capacity to self-soothe, tolerate loneliness, and experience oneself as whole in the absence of the important other. They are sets of intrapsychic emotional procedures, organized into complex emotional control structures. The adult with a healthy capacity for self and object constancy does not recall the innumerable times her parents left her but returned to greet her warmly when she was young, or her many minor childhood injuries which were responded to with loving, attentive care, but she compiled those emotional experiences into proceduralized capacities for self and object constancy. Self and object constancy are operations the healthy ego can perform. Like all ego functions, they are emotional control structures.

Defenses, as a type of ego function, are affective procedures (Erdelyi, in press; Grigsby and Hartlaub, 1988). Repression, in particular, has the interesting property of making declarative knowledge of an experience unconscious without affecting the associated procedural memories (Erdelyi, in press). The procedural knowledge cannot be made unconscious, as it already is. Repression produces a circumscribed amnesia. It is adaptive in that it protects us from dysphoric emotions while permitting us to enact our emotional procedures. Just as declarative knowledge probably developed after procedural knowledge during the course of evolution (Squire, 1987), repression, too, is a product of evolution in that it took advantage of the fact that the brain stores memories in both procedural and declarative forms. Clinical amnesia, early childhood amnesia, and repression all preserve procedural knowledge despite loss of the associated declarative knowledge.

These ideas can be used to amplify our understanding of the repetition compulsion. To see this most clearly, consider another example of a nonaffective procedure. Think about a man who, after keeping his socks in his top drawer for ten years, suddenly decides to move them into the second drawer. After they are moved, he will probably find himself occasionally looking in the top drawer for his socks. The procedure which reaches for the socks had become automatic, and while its execution was smooth, rapid, and efficient, it is difficult to modify and hard to interrupt once initiated. This example illustrates that a procedure can encode not only an overall goal, such as obtaining socks, but also subgoals, such as opening the top drawer, which it tries to attain in order to reach the main goal. Automatization locks those subgoals in place. The more the procedures are automatic, the more constrained the individual is to use the kinds of strategies that he or she used at the time of automatization.

With this in mind, the repetition compulsion can be parsed into three components. The first two are familiar: Stereotypical behavior is repeated because we retain childhood wishes and goals, and the coping strategies and defenses which are repeated are maladaptive. What is new is that the maladaptive coping strategies function automatically. They do not require conscious attention to be enacted, and, because they are automatic, they are difficult to interrupt or modify. The degree to which emotional control structures and procedures are automatic is reflected in the severity of character pathology. The driven quality of the repetition compulsion in part reflects the automatic nature of the procedure, just as our hypothetical man feels "driven" to reach in the wrong drawer for his socks. When a narcissistic man acts contemptuously, he is trying to reach a maladaptive subgoal in order to obtain his adaptive overall goal, restoration of his injured self-esteem. His maladaptive strategy is repetitively reinvoked because it has been structuralized by automatization.

Therapeutic change in psychotherapy or psychoanalysis occurs not only through the relinquishment of childhood wishes and goals, but by modification of the procedures used to meet those goals. Inadequately functioning, automatic, emotional procedures have historically been dichotomized into those which reflect maladaptive compromise formations and those which reveal what Kohut (1977) and others have called structural deficits, such as an inability to test reality, self-soothe or modulate affect. However, all patients with character pathology have emotional procedures and control structures which are inadequate to handle life's exigencies. Structural change in psychoanalytic treatment always involves the modification and acquisition of new, more adaptive, emotional procedures. I turn now to a procedural view of how this occurs.

Therapeutic Action from a Procedural Perspective

I will speculate that there are two general ways procedures change. It will then be seen that psychoanalytic change through insight on the one hand, and through a new, empathic relationship with the analyst on the other, are manifestations, in the psychoanalytic domain, of how all procedures are modified.

The Role of Insight in Psychoanalytic Treatment

Consider how a simple procedure can be changed. Recall the fellow who kept looking for his socks in his top drawer. After he moved them to the second drawer, he had to remind himself of the new rule: "The socks are in the second drawer." He converted his previously automatic procedure into a controlled procedure. This enabled him to think before he acted. He made use of the new information and modified his actions accordingly. If he practices this controlled procedure, with time the new information will be compiled, and the new procedure will become automatic. Then he will no longer have to remind himself of the new declarative rule, and he will be able smoothly and efficiently to obtain socks from the second drawer. One general way to modify an automatic procedure is to convert it into a controlled procedure, modify the declarative rule on which the procedure is based, and develop a new controlled procedure in accordance with the new rule. If it is useful and practiced, the new procedure will become automatic.

Emotional procedures can also be modified in accordance with this model. Consider a simplified example of a man who, whenever he considers asking a woman out on a date, feels inhibited and cannot ask her out. Perhaps he fears retribution from his father. Over the years, the procedure has become automatic. He does not have to experience his fear in order to enact the automatic procedure, and conscious attention is no longer required.

How can we help him modify his emotional procedure? We typically initiate this by interrupting his automatic procedural enactment. This may be done by not fulfilling the role he, in his transference, expects of us, either through our action, inaction, or with a timely interpretation. This focuses his attention on his procedural enactment; in this case, his expectation of punishment. His maladaptive automatic procedure may have been initiated by only the merest trace of a dysphoric emotional signal, but because the procedure was automatic, he could execute it without consciously feeling afraid. In treatment, we help him to titrate that feeling back into awareness. We not only help him to tolerate those painful feelings, but we look at his declarative belief, what he fears his father will do, and we reality test it with him. Is it still true, if it ever was? With psychotherapeutic work his fear attenuates, and he can modify his expectations of what will happen if he asks a woman out on a date. In other words, he develops a new, more adaptive, controlled procedure. With practice, it will become automatic and he will no longer inhibit himself.

The transformation of automatic emotional procedures is an example of this general model of the modification of procedures through the use of intermediate, conscious, declarative processing. Our patient's automatic procedure was interrupted and converted into a controlled procedure, the belief was reality tested, his emotional state was characterized and tolerated, a new controlled procedure was developed, and with practice it became automatic. A key issue is that while cognitive procedures are modified by new information, emotional procedures are modified through insight. Insight is the emotional experience of new declarative information which has the power to change preexisting emotional procedures. It appears that only by emotionally experiencing the new information can neural emotional systems be engaged, thereby modifying the emotional heuristics. The formal method, however, is similar for all types of procedures.

Safety in the psychoanalytic situation enables the patient to hear the analyst's interpretations and not to ward them off defensively. The feeling of safety (Sandler, 1960) also makes it possible for the patient to recall painful memories. In both cases, however, we know that making the unconscious conscious, while useful, is not the goal of treatment. The goal, in this context, is to develop new, adaptive, automatic procedures; making the unconscious conscious is a means to that end. Indeed, genetic reconstructions from early childhood are not always possible because the hippocampus may have been too immature to consolidate and store declarative memories from that era. Only the procedural heuristics remain, and it is these which are modified during treatment.

New procedures, however, do not always replace old ones in treatment, a point also made by Horowitz et al. (1984). During and after psychoanalysis, new procedures often coexist with the old ones without replacing them. In intermediate stages of psychoanalysis as well as in more supportive treatments, we observe the new controlled procedure competing with the old, now only partially automatic procedure. This is similar to a tennis player who is learning a new serve. She will expend a great deal of attention in order to serve using the new controlled procedure in order to avoid using the old one. This occurs during psychoanalysis. Two procedures may coexist, but in a successful treatment, the new adaptive procedure is more regularly elicited. The reemergence of the old pathological procedure in regressed states reminds us that emotional skills become hierarchically organized in treatment, a view which has a long tradition in psychoanalytic theory (Freud, 1905; Spitz, 1959; Emde et al.,1976).

Working through, from this perspective, requires repeated interpretations of the transference in part because each procedure is linked to multiple motivational systems or goals through multiple emotional heuristics. Repeated transference interpretations are necessary to undo the effects of the natural selection process from childhood. As this is accomplished, new, more adaptive control structures emerge.

The Role of New Emotional Experience in Psychoanalytic Treatment

Procedures can also be modified directly without any intermediate, conscious, declarative processing, and this second general way procedures are altered is analogous to therapeutic change without insight in psychoanalysis. Once again we will benefit from examining how nonaffective procedures can be modified. Then I will review how emotional skills in childhood develop outside of conscious awareness. This will lead to a procedural view of what Kohut (1971, 1977) has called "transmuting internalization" and, from a developmental perspective, Emde (1990) has called "corrective empathic experience," the direct reworking of emotional procedures without the use of insight through a new empathic experience with the analyst.

Consider how we improve our athletic skills. When learning a new serve in tennis, for example, we often try out the new technique directly, without first saying to ourselves how we are going to serve. As Ryle (1949) has observed, we do not have to think before we act in order to act intelligently. Similarly, we have seen that children unconsciously infer the rules of relationships which operate in their family, without first stating those rules declaratively. They develop coping strategies without consciously planning them in advance. Like the nonamnesic subjects learning to solve the Tower of Hanoi, they often develop their strategies first and only later (if at all) reflect upon them.

Furthermore, children may learn more from how their parents act toward them than from how their parents tell them they should act. Commonsense homilies reflect this discrepancy between verbal comments and actual behavior: "Words are cheap," "Action speaks louder than words," and "Do as I say, not as I do." Semantic meaning is the channel most easily dissociated under conscious control from the complex of emotional expression, and it is the channel most readily doubted. A child who has been physically or sexually abused by a parent who proclaims love and concern for her experiences this dissociation between verbal comments and actual behavior. Although this is an extreme (albeit common) example, some degree of dissociation between verbal statements and actual behavior occurs in all families. The learning which accrues from such experiences occurs through the direct modification of emotional procedures without any intermediate conscious processing of declarative information.

In psychoanalysis, new emotional procedures develop directly through genuine emotional experience with the analyst, without insight functioning as a mediating process. People experiment with new ways of relating and new ways of processing their affective states directly, without interpretations or insight. This is supported by the safety of the psychoanalytic situation, just as a tennis player with a supportive teacher is more willing to try out a new serve. People develop new intrapsychic and interpersonal skills without being aware that they have done so. This is often observed during treatment.

The analyst's behavior is central to therapeutic action. It is only because the analyst does not behave in accordance with the patient's procedurally encoded role relationship models that the patient can change during treatment. This is most obvious for patients for whom "words are cheap." Because they suffered gross discrepancies between their parents' comments and behavior, the more primitive and fundamental power of action may be needed. An example would be making ourselves available for after hours calls when working with a patient whose capacity for object constancy is uncertain. What patients learn from the analyst's actions does not always need to be stated declaratively for it to be efficacious. Indeed, discussing the patient's experience of our actions too early may vitiate the intervention, sapping it of its emotional strength. Patients acquire new rules of relationships directly within the analytic relationship. Emotional heuristics are modified because the patient has a new emotional experience with the analyst.

One must be quite cautious, of course, in modifying technique based on new theory. All such modifications must pass through the crucible of clinical experience. These kinds of modifications in technique are not new, however; what the research offers is a way to model the occurrence of therapeutic change through a new emotional experience without insight acting as a mediating process.

Working through occurs not only through repeated insights, but by trying out new procedures in multiple domains. The new procedures must be practiced in order for them to be elicited automatically (for a related discussion, see Horowitz et al., 1984). Working through modifies emotional heuristics through repeated insights as well as through the direct modification of emotional heuristics by repeated practice.

Complex emotional skills change through a series of transactions between learning accrued through insight and learning acquired through direct procedural modification. Understanding both precedes and follows behavioral change. In psychoanalysis, change occurs through a complex interplay between insight and direct reworking of the emotional procedures within an empathic analytic relationship. Structural change in psychoanalysis is a transactional process. This is how all complex skills change.

Conclusions

This paper has brought insights from cognitive science to bear on some of the central questions of psychoanalytic theory.

Along the way some of the theory and data of cognitive science have been simplified, and there has been much speculation. The most important simplification, which exists in the cognitive literature, is in the notion of procedure. And many questions remain unanswered. Does the nature of procedures vary across neural systems? To what extent is Squire's (1986) hypothesis true that procedurally encoded information is represented directly in the neural program which controls the activity? How do procedures which are initially organized at a sensory-motor-affective level complexify into more complex cognitive-affective procedures while maintaining continuity in their functioning? How does discontinuity naturally occur in development, and, from a representational standpoint, how can it be introduced therapeutically? The most important set of speculations in the paper concerns the nature of emotional procedures. The empirical research has mostly ignored affect, yet it has been assumed here that emotional procedures and cognitive procedures are similar. Further research will clarify to what extent this is true.

This paper has translated familiar psychoanalytic concepts into the language of cognitive science. This is valuable in that it supports interdisciplinary communication and enables us to modify theory based on data collected in other fields. Bridging disciplines may serve to disconfirm psychoanalytic hypotheses, point to gaps in our knowledge, or broaden our conceptualizations. For example, the research indicates that not all that is unconscious is instinctual, dynamically repressed, or preconscious, as some unconscious knowledge is procedurally unconscious. When Freud described transference, current information about procedural and declarative knowledge was unavailable. The degree to which these constructs prove useful will be seen in the clarifications it offers, the new ideas that are generated, and the new research questions which can now be asked.

Emotions, we have seen, are procedurally organized, and heuristic strategies are essential components of emotions.

This makes ontological sense of the idea of unconscious emotions. When these emotional heuristics are suboptimal, they guide maladaptive defenses and coping strategies. Emotional procedures begin to develop in infancy and early childhood, are unaffected by hippocampal immaturity, and provide organization and continuity to our emotional lives. This is the foundation of transference, the enactment of the emotional procedures learned in childhood. The repetition compulsion, in part because it is based on automatic maladaptive procedures, is difficult to interrupt or modify. And clinical amnesia, early childhood amnesia, and repression all share the same property: Declarative knowledge is lost amidst retention of procedural knowledge. Clinical amnesia provides an experimental model in which to study phenomena of interest to psychoanalysts. Modeling structural change as the acquisition and modification of complex emotional skills provides a conceptual framework in which to conduct such research. Developmental psychology, neurobiology, cognitive psychology, and psychoanalysis can all contribute to our understanding of these processes.

These disciplines can also contribute to our understanding of psychoanalytic treatment. Psychoanalysis, we have seen, works through both insight and direct reworking of the emotional procedures which underlie transference. An automatic emotional procedure can be converted into a controlled procedure by interrupting the automatic procedural enactments, and the resulting controlled procedure can be modified through insight, permitting the development of a new, more adaptive controlled procedure. With practice, it will become automatic. This view places the uncovering of unconscious declarative memories within the context of the analytic goal of modifying maladaptive emotional procedures. These maladaptive, automatic, emotional procedures can also be reworked directly through a genuine emotional experience within an empathic analytic relationship without insight mediating the process. In practice, structural change is a transactional process. Both approaches are essential to psychotherapeutic change.

Emde (1983) has suggested that there is a prerepresentational "affective core of the self" which guarantees our sense of continuity across development in spite of the many ways we change. Intrinsic to the prerepresentational affective core are emotional procedures, which maintain consistency in our emotional experiences in spite of the many emotional and interpersonal contexts in which we live, as well as how we change with development. To modify these procedures is to change who we are, and this is not easily accomplished. It is the task which psychoanalysis continually confronts.

REFERENCES

ANDERSON, J. R. (1982). Acquisition of cognitive skill. *Psychol. Rev.,* 89:369–406.

——— (1983). *The Architecture of Cognition.* Cambridge, Mass.: Harvard Univ. Press.

——— (1985). *Cognitive Psychology and Its Implications.* New York: W. H. Freeman.

ARNOLD, M. B. (1960). *Emotion and Personality.* New York: Columbia Univ. Press.

BACHEVALIER, J. & MISHKIN, M. (1984). An early and a late developing system for learning and retention in infant monkeys. *Behav. Neurosci.,* 98:770–778.

BOWLBY, J. (1980). *Attachment and Loss,* Vol. 3. New York: Basic Books.

BRETHERTON, I. (1985). Attachment theory: Retrospect and prospect. In *Monographs of the Society for Research in Child Development,* ed. I. Bretherton & E. Walters, 50, Serial No. 209, pp. 3–35.

——— (in press). Open communication and internal working models. In *Nebraska Symposium on Motivation: Socioemotional Development,* ed. R. A. Thompson. Lincoln, Nebraska: Univ. Nebraska Press.

——— RIDGEWAY, D., & CASSIDY, J. (1990). The role of internal working models in the attachment relationship. In *Attachment during the Preschool Years: Research and Intervention,* ed. M. Greenberg, D. Cicchetti, & E. M. Cummings. Chicago: Univ. Chicago Press.

BUCHSBAUM, H. K. & EMDE, R. N. (1990). Play narratives in 36-month-old children. *Psychoanal. Study Child,* 45:129–155.

CAMPOS, J. J., CAMPOS, R. G., & BARRETT, K. C. (1989). Emergent themes in the study of emotional development and emotion regulation. *Develpm. Psychol.,* 25:394–402.

——— & STERNBERG, C. (1981). Perception, appraisal, and emotion. In *Infant Social Cognition,* ed. M. E. Lamb & L. R. Sherrod. Hillsdale, N.J.: Erlbaum.

CERMAK, L., Ed. (1982). *Human Memory and Amnesia.* Hillsdale, N.J.: Erlbaum.

COHEN, N. J. (1984). Preserved learning capacity in amnesia. In *Neuropsychology of Memory,* ed. L. R. Squire & N. Butters. New York: Guilford Press.

——— Eichenbaum, H., Deacedo, B. S. & Corkin, S. (1985). Different memory systems underlying acquisition of procedural and declarative knowledge. *Ann N.Y. Acad. Sci.,* 444:54–71.

——— & Squire, L. R. (1980). Preserved learning and retention of pattern-analyzing skill in amnesia. *Science,* 221:207–210.

Dilman, I. (1988). Intentions and the unconscious. In *Mind, Psychoanalysis and Science,* ed. P. Clark & C. Wright. Oxford: Basil Blackwell.

Ekman, P., Friesen, W., & Ellsworth, P. (1972). *Emotion in the Human Face.* New York: Pergamon Press.

Emde, R. N. (1983). The prerepresentational self and its affective core. *Psychoanal. Study Child,* 38:165–192.

——— (1990). Mobilizing fundamental modes of development. *J. Amer. Psychoanal. Assn.* 38:881–913.

——— Biringen, Z., Clyman, R. B., & Oppenheim, D. (in press). The moral self of infancy: Affective core and procedural knowledge. *Develpm. Rev.*

——— Gaensbauer, T. J., & Harmon, R. J. (1976). *Emotional Expression in Infancy.* New York: Int. Univ. Press.

——— Johnson, W. F., & Easterbrooks, M. A. (1988). The do's and don'ts of early moral development: Psychoanalytic tradition and current research. In *The Emergence of Morality,* ed. J. Kagan & S. Lamb. Chicago: Univ. Chicago Press, pp. 245–277.

Erdelyi, M. H. (in press). Repression, reconstruction, and defense. In *Repression: Personality Style and Mechanisms of Defense,* ed. J. Singer. Chicago: Univ. Chicago Press.

Feinman, S. & Lewis, M. (1983). Social referencing at ten months. *Child Develpm.,* 54:878–887.

Freud, S. (1899). Screen memories. *S. E.,* 23.

——— (1905). Three essays on the theory of sexuality. *S. E.,* 7.

——— (1914). Remembering, repeating and working-through. *S. E.,* 12.

——— (1915a). Repression. *S. E.,* 14.

——— (1915b). The unconscious. *S. E.,* 14.

——— (1926). Inhibitions, symptoms and anxiety. *S. E.,* 20.

Gedo, J. E. (1988). *The Mind in Disorder.* Hillsdale, N.J.: Analytic Press.

George, C. & Main, M. (1979). Social interactions of young abused children. *Child Develpm.,* 50:306–318.

Grigsby, J. & Hartlaub, G. H. (1988). The neural basis of memory and its relationship to character development. Presented to the Denver Psychoanalytic Society.

Horowitz, M. J. (1987). *States of Mind,* 2nd ed. New York: Plenum.

——— (1988a). *Introduction to Psychodynamics.* New York: Basic Books.

——— Ed. (1988b). *Psychodynamics and Cognition.* New York: Basic Books.

——— (1989). Relationship schema formulation. *Psychiatry,* 52:260–274.

——— Fridhandler, B., & Stinson, C. (1990). Person schemas and emotion. *This Monograph.*

——— Marmar, C., Krupnick, J., Wilner, N., Kaltreider, N., & Wallerstein, R. (1984). *Personality Styles and Brief Psychotherapy.* New York: Basic Books.

Izard, C. E. (1971). *The Face of Emotion.* Meredith, N.Y.: Appleton-Century-Crofts.

JACOBS, W. J. & NADEL, L. (1985). Stress-induced recovery of fears and phobias. *Psychol. Rev.,* 92:512–531.

KAHNEMAN, D., SLOVIC, P., & TVERSKY, A. (1982). *Judgment Under Uncertainty.* Cambridge: Cambridge Univ. Press.

KIHLSTROM, J. F. (1987). The cognitive unconscious. *Science,* 237:1445–1452.

KLINNERT, M. D., CAMPOS, J. J., SORCE, J. F., EMDE, R. N., & SVEJDA, M. (1983). Emotions as behavior regulators. In *Emotions in Early Development,* Vol. 2, ed. R. Plutchik & H. Kellerman. New York: Academic Press.

——— EMDE, R. N., BUTTERFIELD, P., & CAMPOS, J. J. (1986). Social referencing. *Develpm. Psychol.,* 22:427–432.

KOHUT, H. (1971). *The Analysis of the Self.* New York: Int. Univ. Press.

——— (1977). *The Restoration of the Self.* Madison, Conn.: Int. Univ. Press.

LICHTENBERG, J. D. (1983). *Psychoanalysis and Infant Research.* Hillsdale, N.J.: Analytic Press.

——— (1989). *Psychoanalysis and Motivation.* Hillsdale, N.J.: Analytic Press.

LYNCH, G., MCGAUGH, J. L., & WEINBERGER, N. M., Eds. (1984). *Neurobiology of Learning and Memory.* New York: Guilford Press.

MAHLER, M. S. (1968). *On Human Symbiosis and the Vicissitudes of Individuation.* New York: Int. Univ. Pres.

——— (1974). Symbiosis and individuation. *Psychoanal. Study Child,* 29:89–196.

MAIN, M., KAPLAN, N., & CASSIDY, J. (1985). Security in infancy, childhood, and adulthood. In *Monographs of the Society for Research in Child Development,* ed. I. Bretherton & E. Waters, 50, Serial No. 209, pp. 66–106.

MALAMUT, B. L., SAUNDERS, R. C., & MISHKIN, M. (1984). Monkeys with combined amygdalo-hippocampal lesions succeed in object discrimination learning despite 24-hour intertrial intervals. *Behav. Neurosci.,* 98:759–769.

MANDLER, J. M. (1983). Representation. In *Handbook of Child Psychology,* ed. J. H. Flavell & E. M. Markman. New York: John Wiley, pp. 420–494.

——— (1984). Representation and recall in infancy. In *Infant Memory,* ed. M. Moscovitch. New York: Plenum, pp. 75–101.

MAYES, A. R. (1988). *Human Organic Memory Disorders.* Cambridge: Cambridge Univ. Press.

MCCLELLAND, J. L., RUMELHART, D. E., & THE PDP RESEARCH GROUP (1986). *Parallel Distributed Processing,* Vol. 2. Cambridge, Mass.: MIT Press.

MISHKIN, M., MALAMUT, B. L., & BACHEVALIER, J. (1984). In *Neurobiology of Learning and Memory,* ed. G. Lynch, J. L. McGaugh, & N. M. Weinberger. New York: Guilford Press.

NADEL, L. & ZOLA-MORGAN, S. (1984). Infantile amnesia. In *Infant Memory,* ed. M. Moscovitch. New York: Plenum, pp. 145–172.

NELSON, K., Ed. (1986). *Event Knowledge.* Hillsdale, N.J.: Erlbaum.

NEVES, D. M. & ANDERSON, J. R. (1984). Knowledge compilation. In *Cognitive Skills and Their Acquisition,* ed. J. R. Anderson. Hillsdale, N.J.: Erlbaum.

PIAGET, J. (1936). *The Origins of Intelligence in Children.* New York: Int. Univ. Press, 1952.

——— (1973). The affective unconscious and the cognitive unconscious. *J. Amer. Psychoanal. Assn.,* 21:249–261.

PILLEMER, D. B. & WHITE, S. H. (1989). Childhood events recalled by children and adults. *Advances in Child Development and Behavior,* 21:297–340.

POLYA, G. (1945). *How to Solve It.* Garden City, N.Y.: Doubleday.
PULVER, S. E. (1971). Can affects be unconscious? *Int. J. Psychoanal.,* 52:347-354.
REISS, D. (1989). The represented and practicing family. In *Relationship Disturbances in Early Childhood,* ed. A. J. Sameroff & R. N. Emde. New York: Basic Books.
RICHARDSON-KLAVEHN, A. & BJORK, R. A. (1988). Measures of memory. *Ann. Rev. Psychol.,* 39:475-543.
ROEDIGER, H. L. (1990). Implicit memory. *Amer. Psychologist,* 45:1043-1056.
——— RAJARAM, S., & SRINIVAS, K. (1990). Specifying criteria for postulating memory systems. In *The Development and Neural Bases of Higher Cognitive Functions,* Vol. 608, ed. A. Diamond. New York: New York Academy of Sciences.
ROSCH, E. (1983). Prototype classification and logical classification. In *New Trends in Conceptual Representation,* ed. E. K. Scholnick. Hillsdale, N.J.: Erlbaum.
RUMELHART, D. E. (1984). Schemata and the cognitive system. In *Handbook of Social Cognition,* Vol. 1, ed. R. S. Wyer, Jr. & T. K. Srull. Hillsdale, N.J.: Erlbaum.
——— MCCLELLAND, J. L., & THE PDP RESEARCH GROUP (1986). *Parallel Distributed Processing,* Vol. 1. Cambridge, Mass.: MIT Press.
RYLE, G. (1949). *The Concept of Mind.* New York: Barnes & Nobles.
SANDLER, J. (1960). The background of safety. *Int. J. Psychoanal.,* 41:352-365.
——— (1976). Countertransference and role-responsiveness. *Int. Rev. Psychoanal.* 3:43-47.
SCHACTER, D. L. (1987). Implicit memory. *J. Exper. Psychol.,* 13:501-518.
——— (1990). Perceptual representation systems and implicit memory. In *The Development and Neural Bases of Higher Cognitive Functions,* Vol. 608, ed. A. Diamond. New York: New York Academy of Science.
——— & MOSCOVITCH, M. (1984). Infants, amnesia and dissociable memory systems. In *Infant Memory,* ed. M. Moscovitch. New York: Plenum, pp. 173-216.
SCHNEIDER, W. & SHIFFRIN, R. M. (1977). Controlled and automatic processing: I. *Psychol. Rev.,* 84:1-66.
SHAPIRO, T. (1990). Words and feelings. *This Monograph.*
——— & PERRY, R. (1976). Latency revisited. *Psychoanal. Study Child,* 31:79-105.
SHIFFRIN, R. M. & DUMAIS, S. T. (1981). The development of automatism. In *Cognitive Skills and Their Acquisition,* ed. J. R. Anderson. Hillsdale, N.J.: Erlbaum.
——— R. M. & SCHNEIDER, W. (1977). Controlled and automatic human information processing: II. *Psychol. Rev.,* 84:127-190.
SPITZ, R. A. (1959). *A Genetic Field Theory of Ego Formation.* New York: Int. Univ. Press.
SQUIRE, L. R. (1986). Mechanisms of memory. *Science,* 232:1612-1619.
——— (1987). *Memory and Brain.* New York: Oxford Univ. Press.
——— & BUTTERS, N., Eds. (1984). *Neuropsychology of Memory.* New York: Guilford Press.
——— & COHEN, N. J. (1984). Human memory and amnesia. In *Neurobiology of*

Learning and Memory, ed. G. Lynch, J. L. McGaugh, & N. M. Weinberger. New York: Guilford Press.

STERN, D. N. (1985). *The Interpersonal World of the Infant.* New York: Basic Books.

——— (1989). The representation of relational patterns. In *Relationship Disturbances in Early Childhood,* ed. A. J. Sameroff & R. N. Emde. New York: Basic Books.

TEYLER, T. J. & FOUNTAIN, S. B. (1987). Neuronal plasticity in the mammalian brain. *Child Develpm.,* 58:698–712.

TVERSKY, A. & KAHNEMAN, D. (1982). Judgment under uncertainty. In *Judgment Under Uncertainty: Heuristics and Biases,* ed. D. Kahneman, P. Slovic, & A. Tversky. Cambridge: Cambridge Univ. Press.

WHITE, S. H. & PILLEMER, D. B. (1979). Childhood amnesia and development of a socially accessible memory system. In *Functional Disorders of Memory,* ed. J. Kohlstrom & F. Evans. Hillsdale, N.J.: Erlbaum.

University of Colorado Health Sciences Center
Box C-268-69
4200 East Ninth Street
Denver, CO 80262

ROMANTIC LOVE: AT THE INTERSECTION OF THE PSYCHE AND THE CULTURAL UNCONSCIOUS

ETHEL SPECTOR PERSON, M.D.

Not a primary affect, but a powerful compound passion, in which affective and cognitive components are inextricably intertwined, romantic love is best conceptualized as a creative synthesis of many diverse feelings, impulses, and wishes which come to be focused on one person alone, the idealized beloved. The best evidence that romantic love is not hard-wired into the emotional repertoire of humanity but is a cultural construct is the fact that there are so many cultures in which it is virtually absent.

Romantic love provides a premiere case study of the way in which the cultural unconscious (by which I mean the stamp impressed by a given culture upon expressions of drive and affect) intersects with the psyche to create important cultural narratives. Fantasy-based, romantic love appears to be a cultural innovation of the medieval world that borrowed both from the world of Islam and the Marian revival within the Catholic Church. Redefined in the nineteenth century, romantic love continues to exert a major effect on the imaginative lives and behavior of those of us in the West.

The psychological predisposition to love is probably located in the intimacy of the infant-mother dyad and is related to the child's dependence on an idealization of its parents, culminating in the oedipus complex. The ingenuity of the cultural innovation of romantic love is that it brings together into one story line—the story of idealized mutual love—the possibility of simultaneously fulfilling many disparate wishes, fantasies, and needs. As a cultural construct, it appears to have as much to do with the resolution of issues of authority and personal autonomy as with narcissistic repair or the disposition of libido.

WHATEVER WE MAY think of it, professionally or personally, romantic love is the single most powerful passion in many contemporary lives. Generally assumed to be a passion

Training and Supervising Psychoanalyst at the Columbia University Center for Psychoanalytic Training and Research; Professor of Clinical Psychiatry, Columbia University.

which will inevitably fade, love may in fact have an outcome which is redemptive and exalting—or utterly destructive. Perhaps as a way of taming it, reducing it, even denying its existence as a singular and extraordinary force, analysts sometimes depict love as no more than a nucleus of physical passion around which a cluster of other feelings—admiration, respect, affection, intimacy, commitment, and approbation—cohere. And certainly it is true, at least in our culture, that passionate love does generally comprise both carnal passion and affectionate bonding. But its defining purpose is ultimately neither sexual nor companionate. It is not reducible to sexual passion and it is more than a "mature" commitment to affectionate bonding. To think that is to miss out on the opportunity for many psychoanalytic insights, as well as an understanding of the intersection between culture and psyche.

The real core of passionate love, as distinguished from carnal love or affectionate bonding, is the lover's idealization of and yearning for an Other, as revealed through the urgency to be with the beloved; it is *this* nucleus that draws to itself the aggregate of other feelings. Alberoni captures the essence of passionate love when he describes it as "a terrible force . . . that leads to our fusion and makes each of us irreplaceable and unique for the other. . . . And this happens even against our will, even though we continue for a long time to believe that we can do without the one we love and can find that same happiness in another person" (1983, pp. 12–13).

Nothing seems more real or important to lovers than their longing to be with the beloved. Strange to think, then, that such a seemingly primordial emotion is not universal but is specific to individual cultures. And yet this is so. While there are those who consider affectionate bonding as well-nigh universal—indeed some classifications name it as a primary affect—romantic love, for all its intensity of emotion, is not primary, not one of those universal affects depicted by Darwin, Izard, and others as central to the human condition and bound up with the survival of the species.

The best evidence that romantic love is not hard-wired into the emotional repertoire of humanity is the fact that there are so many cultures in which it is virtually absent. The sociologist William Goode (1959) suggests that romantic love occurs on a continuum: At one end of the continuum, romantic love receives negative social sanction and is regarded as a comic or tragic abnormality (as it is in Japan and China), while at the other end, it would be considered disgraceful to marry without love (as, for example, in much of contemporary Western society). As Goode points out, these facts are consonant with two different but not inconsistent hypotheses about the nature of love. Either love is "a universal psychosocial possibility" (p. 41) the flowering of which is largely dependent on positive sanction, or else it depends entirely on specific structural factors (I would take this to mean certain cultural configurations and the presence of romantic role models). However, we do know that even in cultures and situations where love is negatively sanctioned, there are frequent occurrences of full-blown, and on occasion death-defying, love, for example, in the case of Abelard and Heloise, whose passionate sexual love flew in the face of the precepts of the church. Goode (p. 41) cites a number of other examples of romantic love in unlikely circumstances, including the Bible stories of Jacob's love for Rachel, Michal's for David, and most notably of all, Solomon's for Shulamith (as depicted in the Song of Songs). These examples are in support of Goode's first hypothesis: Love, if not a hard-wired emotion, is certainly a universal psychological possibility, a potential which may be cultivated (as in our own culture), or largely suppressed (as it is in most tribal cultures), but may sometimes, even against great odds, appear spontaneously, thus revealing its roots in some universal aspect of the human condition. (The psychological predisposition to love is probably located in the intimacy of the infant-mother dyad and is related to the child's dependence on and idealization of its parents, culminating in the oedipus complex.)

As a large-scale phenomenon, however, love is a product mainly of the West, a cultural construct which first appeared in eleventh-century Provence (a point agreed upon in most historical accounts of romantic love; see, for example, de Rougemont, 1956; Campbell, 1968; Lewis, 1936). According to Lewis, "We are tempted to treat 'courtly love' as a mere episode in literary history—an episode that we have finished with as we have finished with the peculiarities of Skaldic verse or Euphuistic prose. In fact, however, an unmistakable continuity connects the Provencal love story with the love poetry of the late Middle Ages, and thence, through Petrarch and many others, with that of the present day" (p. 3). In contrast, he argues, such a phenomenon as romantic love was extremely rare, if not unknown, in classical antiquity and in the Dark Ages. Its steady rise since then parallels and, in my view, was strongly affected by the West's increasing emphasis on individuality as a primary value. In Western culture today, with religion on the wane and the cult of radical individuality correspondingly on the rise, love more and more has come to be invoked as the major route to happiness, as well as a principal device for solving the problem of meaning.

Not a primary affect, then, but a powerful compound passion in which affective and cognitive components are inextricably intertwined, romantic love is best conceptualized as a creative synthesis, or a dynamic constellation, of many diverse feelings, impulses, and wishes which come to be focused on one person alone, the idealized beloved. Romantic passion, sanctioned (and for the most part generated) by cultural prescription, unites these impulses, wishes, and needs, which in other cultures would find alternate modes of expression, and be dispersed among different objects. (For example, in some other culture, sex might be shared with a spouse, intimacy with a friend, idealization reserved for God, and meaning derived through religion.)

Love stories, the narratives that bind these impulses and wishes together and give voice to the surrounding culture's attitudes toward love, are for the most part a product of the West, and it is through them that so many of us in the West have learned to seek romantic love. Without cultural sanction—which is expressed through such stories—romantic love is very rare, and those who experience it do so at risk not only of certain intrinsic psychic perils, as is the case with all lovers, but of social punishment and ostracism as well.

Freud was deeply aware of the profound impact love has on the lives of those of us in Western culture, asserting that "Sexual love is undoubtedly one of the chief things in life, and the union of mental and bodily satisfaction in the enjoyment of love is one of its culminating peaks. Apart from a few queer fanatics, all the world knows this and conducts its life accordingly; science alone is too delicate to admit it" (1915, pp. 169–170). But Freud was hesitant to address love's power (or indeed to tackle the study of any of the emotions); by way of an explanation he said that he thought it "not easy to deal scientifically with feelings." He believed that beyond describing the physiological state that accompanies them "nothing remains but to fall back on the ideational content which is most readily associated with the feeling" (1930, p. 65). He had previously remarked that there were certain enigmatic features about being in love (or under hypnosis) "which we must recognize as unexplained and mysterious" (1921, p. 115). So it is that Freud, despite his major insights into the nature of love, never followed through on his original intention to explore love in the same rigorous, systematic fashion he had treated dreams (Bergmann, 1980).

Subsequent generations of analysts have also eschewed the study of romantic love, because like Freud (and like most lovers as well) they sense that there is something ineffable in love, ultimately mysterious, that defies dissection. Then, too, analysts have been most comfortable theorizing about things they believed to be immutable, ahistorical, such as humankind's instinctual endowment (though, as it turns out, even the expression of sex has some cultural variability). Moreover, as some analysts have argued in defense of their reluctance to theorize love, each love affair is so complex—take, as only one example, the dynamics of the unconscious selection of the love object (Arlow, 1980)—that we are necessarily limited in the generalizations we will be able to make. Still, despite the lover's belief in the uniqueness of his love, and despite the corresponding belief on the part of analysts that each individual's experience of love varies drastically in intensity, feeling tone, and meaning, there is a sufficient pool of identifiable characteristics common to all lovers' experience to justify using the psychoanalytic approach to understand it.

Love is not only amenable to being understood within a psychoanalytic framework, however; it is itself a means to further understanding, for it can provide unique insights into the meaning of many extremely complex psychological phenomena, among them both transference and narcissism. Freud's insights into love as a refinding (or re-edition) of earlier ties have helped shape transference theory, and his view of love as narcissistic gratification brought about indirectly through glorification (idealization) of the beloved has had profound implications for our understanding of narcissism. Love, according to Freud, is a means of healing the narcissistic wounds left over from childhood. But its effects can be more radical still, resulting in the dedifferentiation of personality, with the potential (not always realized) for deep inner change, for a new structuralization. The observation that love is a transformative event, though routinely made by poets, has just begun to be theorized within the psychoanalytic enterprise (Person, 1988a).

No one approaching the study of love from the psychoanalytic stance, however, can afford to ignore either the cultural and historical contingencies that give it form or the existential longings it assuages. Romantic love, insofar as it draws upon the fantasies and narratives that permeate the surrounding culture, resists any reductive theorizing that would explain it exclusively in terms of drive and psychosexual development. And it similarly resists being explained merely as a cultural artifact, since, as already suggested, it may appear in cultures in which the quest for romantic love is either absent or anathema. Although the variable status of love in different cultural milieus and historical epochs has been viewed as an impediment to theorizing, this cultural variability has its own relevance to psychoanalysis, leading as it does to a consideration of what might best be called the "cultural unconscious"—the stamp left by a given culture upon expressions of drive and affect. By cultural unconscious, I do not mean to imply any universal cultural content; quite the contrary, I refer to those stories and narratives specific to a particular culture that are internalized in such a way as to shape the individual's (unconscious or preconscious) choice of a life path, modes of gratification, and priority of values.

Through its sanction of particular methods of discharge and its provision of a storehouse of meaningful narratives and myths with which to organize instinctual and cognitive life, the cultural milieu encourages, ignores, or even suppresses the potential for romantic love. The Duc de Rochefoucauld's oft-quoted maxim that people would not love had they never heard of love has some merit. It does not, however, discredit love, as appeared to be the Duc's intent; rather his maxim highlights the fact that the expression (and content) of our dearest longings depends not only upon instinctual life and individual development but also upon the cherished myths and goals around which a culture coheres.

Romantic love, then, can be considered as a good case study of the intersection between the personal (universal) unconscious and the cultural (contingent) unconscious. It draws attention to a particular "community of daydreams" (Sachs, 1942) by which the composite passion we call romantic love is shaped. Whereas in primary (or wired-in) affects, interpersonal interactions are simply the triggers for biological reactions which are then guided into culturally validated channels, in the less biologically mandated, composite passions (such as romantic love), cultural factors enter into their very organization, codification, and expression. For example, romantic love may be held in the realm of the ideal with no expectation of carnal enactment (as with the troubadours), or may be experienced as a passion that is expected to be expressed carnally (as within our own culture).

What I propose to do is to give a brief historical account of the way in which love stories (and lived loves) enter into Western thought and history, culminating in romantic love as we understand and experience it today in the West—as prelude (and prerequisite) to marriage, the beloved both desired *and* sought as a matter of course. Having looked at love in historical perspective, I will turn to what I regard as its key psychological components: idealization of and yearning for union with the beloved. I will argue that these core factors indicate that the primary motor force in love can best be understood, not in terms of libido, but in terms of narcissistic issues: the regulation of self-esteem, projection of the ego ideal onto the beloved, and the search for an ideal self.

I will try to show that while the choice of the beloved is decisively influenced by the imagination acting on early life experience, the initial impulse to fall in love is additionally shaped by the impact on the imagination of those love stories, myths, and values that are characteristic of our culture. While romantic love may on occasion be the spontaneous imaginative creation of a particular individual without sanction from the surrounding culture, it appears much more regularly in cultures that provide ready-made scripts for love.

Love in the West

Within our own culture romantic love has by now achieved mythic status, but that is a relatively recent development. We have only to look at the history of romantic love in Western culture as it is revealed in the prototypical love stories of each successive era to realize that popular conceptions and expectations of love have undergone a sea change over the centuries—further evidence still of love's variability as a function of the culture. (This section draws not only upon my own reading, but also on Tanner, 1979, and Fiedler, 1966.) As already noted, until the Middle Ages, there are relatively few love stories. There's the Song of Songs, of course, one of the most beautiful love poems ever written; various Greek and Roman myths centered around the gods and goddesses, which depict love as capricious and for the most part destructive; and then the *Iliad* which, although not *about* love, is set in motion *by* love—the adulterous love of Paris for Helen being the precipitating factor for the Trojan War.

While these works tell us that romantic love did indeed exist in earlier epochs, it did not become an important cultural (and literary) concern until the Middle Ages, when it began to flourish with particular vigor in the troubadour culture of Southern France, though not in the form with which most of us are familiar today. Believed to draw its inspiration in part from the Sufi tradition of mystical eroticism, and in part from the increasing emphasis on Madonna worship, the origins of the troubadour tradition have never been fully explained. Whatever impelled it into existence, the troubadour tradition promulgated a very special kind of romantic love, in which the love relationship was to be kept in the realm of the ideal, leading neither to carnal knowledge nor to marriage. By circumscribing its expression and its effects so carefully, this tradition managed to celebrate individual passion without sanctioning any breach of the social order.

In the literature of the age of chivalry, the figure of the beloved is *always* married, but to someone other than the would-be lover. However adulterous the longings expressed in the prototypical love songs of the medieval troubadours, the love they described remained chaste. Although the knight might long intensely for the lady, he respected his commitment to his lord (generally the lady's husband) too much to do anything to violate that bond. Consequently, the knight had no thought of expressing his love in the flesh, for to do so would have meant compromising his allegiance to his liege lord who was also, within the hierarchical order of medieval society, his symbolic father.

This idealized version of love remained a cultural option for some centuries. Take the extreme case of Dante, who, like the troubadours, never attempted to realize his love for Beatrice in any earth-bound way. Instead he immortalized his love for her in the *Vita Nuova* and *The Divine Comedy,* this despite the fact that he saw her only three times in his life (the first time when they were both 9) and he never met her. We know little of his life, but we do know that he mourned her early death and that her memory became the inspiration for his life's work.

Even in the Middle Ages, however, the theme of love which is adulterous not just in longing but in actuality was not unknown; in fact, it is frequently invoked—always in an admonitory mode. In the Arthurian legends which were so popular then, Guinevere deceived her husband King Arthur with that great knight, Sir Lancelot, only to end her life in a nunnery, while Lancelot wound up in a hermitage. Even more of a cautionary (but perhaps also subversively inspirational) tale is that of Tristan, the nephew of King Mark of Cornwall, who was sent to Ireland to escort his uncle's bride-to-be, Isolde, but betraying his uncle, fell in love with her himself. These two illicit lovers would find release for themselves only in death, in the Liebestod.

Romantic love continues to appear mainly in the guise of adulterous love in the literature of successive generations. As such, it was generally portrayed as something more to be cautioned against than celebrated, a force at odds with the social order. Even Shakespeare, one of the great love poets of all time, made adultery and its earth-shattering consequences one of his major themes. And even when he portrayed love in other guises, the pure love of Romeo and Juliet, for example, it was still seen as a force that could destroy lives.

Adultery continued as a major theme in virtually all Restoration drama, but seems to have fallen from favor as a topic of much interest to the rationalists of the eighteenth century (though girls like Pamela and Clarissa did have to fight off the advances of lustful, loving lords as they served as examples of middle-class sexual modesty).

Adultery reappeared as a major theme in many of the great nineteenth-century novels, for example, *The Red and the Black, Madame Bovary, Anna Karenina,* and *The Ambassadors,* the manifest content of all these works continuing in the cautionary mode, with the adulterous lovers paying a great price (up to and including death) for their flouting of the social order. There is considerable sympathy for their suffering, however, and if only because of the frequency and intensity with which these adulterous longings are evoked on the pages of the great writers of the nineteenth century, one senses something subversive in the air, a major assault on the rules of possession both in the private and public spheres. Indeed, adultery became so prominent a theme of Western literature that, as Denis de Rougemont put it, were we "to judge by literature adultery would seem to be one of the most remarkable of occupations in Europe and America" (1956, p. 16). Adultery appears to be emblematic of a larger issue: the extent to which the flowering of the cult of individuality, with its legitimatization of individual desire, would preempt the claims of society, of the "fathers." At the dawn of the age of free enterprise, reform, and revolution, the values of communality were eroding as the valuation of the individual increased. Only in a society inclined to celebrate the autonomy and self-assertion of the individual, it would appear, could the ideal of realized romantic love flourish.

And soon enough, a momentous change did occur in the way westerners regarded romantic love. No longer pictured just in its adulterous form, love was domesticated, to the point that it was judged to be the necessary precursor to marriage, which itself was redefined. Marriage was originally a legal transaction designed to implement social necessities and provide a stable environment for child raising. In society's upper echelons it was used to unite kingdoms, to cement alliances, and to regulate the exchange of wealth and property. But eventually marriage came to be seen as the natural culmination and institutionalization of love, a sacrament between two individuals more than a social contract, with love as the birthright of all. This new concept of love is surely a remarkable change from the older ones in which romantic yearning was either idealized and chaste, with *no* consequences in the outer world, or adulterous and impure, with disastrous consequences. What had been the anomalous experiences of a chosen or, alternately, cursed few, came to be seen as a universal experience, devoutly to be wished by all, and, moreover, the only proper basis for entering into marriage.

According to the historian Lawrence Stone (1988), this shift arose out of the romantic movement that began in the late eighteenth century, was consolidated with the flowering of that movement in the nineteenth century, and won general acceptance only in our own. The dissemination of the new ideology of love depended upon the unprecedented availability of the written word in the nineteenth century, courtesy of the institution of the lending library as well as the greater affordability of books and periodicals. Love stories came to constitute much of what was written about in both the novel and the popular press. For a long time, the tone remained cautionary, with the theme of adultery and its consequences continuing to be central to literary depictions of love. By the late nineteenth century, romance had become a "sentimental love religion," love the pursuit of every man and every woman—in fiction, thence in life. As happens more than occasionally, perhaps even systematically, life was imitating art.

Not just historians, but artists too have acknowledged love's debt to love stories. According to Dante, the adulterous lovers Paolo and Francesca whom he encounters in the second circle of hell are in a direct literary line with Lancelot and Guinevere, for it is in reading about those earlier transgressors that they themselves came to feel the spark of love.

Flaubert too was aware that the longing for love can be catalyzed by reading about it. In *Madame Bovary* (1857), Emma's desire for romance, her taste for "Sighs in the moonlight, long embraces, hands bathed in lovers' tears—all the fevers of the flesh and the languors of love" (p. 66) appear to have been acquired by her devouring of novels, specifically those of Honorè de Balzac and George Sand, and her sensuality in general to be a direct result of her convent-girl immersion in the mystic languors of the Catholic Church.

Secondhand though Emma's passion may be, and she herself a petite bourgeois of the provinces with little to distinguish her from the society around her except the intensity of her longing to escape it, still we are moved by her. Flaubert's heroine is tragic precisely because her passion is so great. The literature that inspired her notions of love was not always first-rate, her means of expressing her passion hackneyed, its object an unworthy cad, but by sheer intensity of emotion she transcends her circumstances. "Deep down all the while, she was waiting for something to happen. Like a sailor in distress, she kept casting desperate glances over the solitary waste of her life, seeking some white sail in the distant mists of the horizon. She had no idea by what wind it would reach her, toward what shore it would bear her, or what kind of craft it would be—tiny boat or towering vessel, laden with heartbreaks or filled to the gunwales with rapture" (pp. 69–70). We sense in Emma those impulses (endemic in individualistic societies) toward radical change, specifically toward self-transformation and the melioration of the solitariness of the self, which are among the motivating factors for all lovers, however unworthy their objects. And so we see how a particular cultural construct, the popular love story, itself a product of important but not fully articulated cultural aims, can shape the expression of an individual's hopes, wishful fantasies, and behaviors.

The Motive Force in Romantic Love: Idealization and the Ideal Self

As the story of Emma Bovary makes clear, love itself is in part a cultural construct, a learned phenomenon transmitted through the oral and written culture of our times. But as with Emma, it is far more than that. Cultural narratives (or prescriptives) only take root if and when they offer us the opportunity to gratify wishes and needs that originate in instinctual and affective life and ramify during the course of our psychological development. What, then, are the psychic needs satisfied by love?

Despite the general agreement that the defining feature of passionate love is the urgency of the lover's longing for the beloved, the origins of that intense force remained wholly obscure until Freud (1905) intuited that love is a refinding (p. 222). Any and all surface indicators to the contrary, Freud recognized the continuity of emotional life from infancy through maturity (beginning, it is now believed, in the ties the child has to its mother), and saw how it was expressed in the lover's choice of a love object. It was his genius to understand that all the lover's unfulfilled yearnings, dating from earliest life, are carried over to the beloved, who is, by virtue of this transference, experienced as the source of all good—hence the enormous importance of the beloved for the lover.

Freud did not come to this formulation of the phenomenon of refinding in love through any study of lovers, but rather through his study of patients and the erotic transferences they formed (1915). His observations in the consulting room enabled him to see that the object of both transference and romantic love is a re-edition of the original love objects of childhood. And while he recommended that the analyst bring the erotic transference to the attention of the patient, so that she would understand that she had fallen in love with him only as a means of resisting the process of analysis, he also understood the very real power of transference love, which he acknowledged by comparing it to romantic love—also a re-edition of one's earliest love, a refinding.

In this, Freud's first formulation of love, he made an important discovery, but one that still locates the central mechanism of love within libidinal development. However, there is now a growing feeling in psychoanalysis that the true provenance of love is elsewhere, that sex cannot fully explain love. For one thing, the sexual drive is universal, but romantic love is not, and so often, even in our own culture where love is highly valued, there are many passionate sexual encounters which are devoid of love. Conversely, there are many instances of romantic love in which sex plays little or no role. Balint (1948) describes romantic love as making use of "genital sexuality only as a stock on which to graft something essentially different" (p. 36), and goes on to say that what is unique consists of idealization, tenderness, and a special form of identification—a position which has gained ascendancy within psychoanalysis.

But if love is not fueled by an instinct tied to sex and reproduction, we must find some other way to account for its urgency and priority of importance. It is again in Freud's own work that we find the key to understanding the nonsexual source of love's urgency. Through his studies on narcissism, Freud demonstrated that the lover's union with the idealized beloved would provide for the restoration of a grander self, a self experienced as both more perfect and more powerful than at any time since infancy. "He [man] is not willing to forgo the narcissistic perfection of his childhood; and when, . . . he can no longer retain that perfection, he seeks to recover it in the new form of an ego ideal" (Freud, 1914, p. 94). Love is, in part, a roundabout quest for perfection, for the restoration of one's lost narcissism.

Reik (1941), observing that idealization was the central distinctive feature in romantic love, proposed that idealization of the beloved was a kind of reaction formation against an underlying envy and jealousy. His formulation suggests an ego motive in place of an id motive as the energy fueling romantic love. Formulations such as these have achieved increasing credibility because of the ongoing work of a number of analysts who have established the prevalence and importance of ego motives in addition to instinctual ones. According to Sandler (1989), the discrepancy between actual and ideal self representations gives rise to painful feelings. Sandler argues that it is this psychic pain which becomes a motive force in behavior, as the individual strives to overcome his pain and attain a basic state of well-being. Though Sandler does not specifically refer to love, he observes that "the presence of an ideal object may be just as much a part of the ideal state as the ideal self" (p. 98). And romantic love surely does offer one modality for achieving an ideal state.

This conceptualization of romantic love, based on narcissistic restitution, echoes that of the philosophers (the search for one's other half as described in Plato) and of the sociologists (Alberoni's description that love "originates in an extreme depression, an inability to find something that has value in everyday life" [1983, p. 69]).

Chasseguet-Smirgel (1984) also proposes the ego ideal as the source of a major motivational system, in my reading giving it priority over drive (Person, 1988b). In the beginning of life, the child's narcissism is vested in himself—he is his own ideal as it were. Only when he realizes that his survival depends upon another does he project part of his narcissism onto the other in the form of an ego ideal. Chasseguet-Smirgel suggests that the wish for union with the original narcissistic object (the mother) is fundamentally a desire to retrieve a lost narcissistic unity. The oedipus complex, in her view, later becomes the agency through which the child can hope to assuage the longing for wholeness, for perfection. Though she does not deny the centrality of the oedipus complex, she reinterprets its incestuous wishes in the light of this longing for perfection, so that the meaning of incestuous wishes is seen to go beyond the sexual, the instinctual.

In the case of the boy, when he acknowledges the genital universe of the father—and with it, his own genital inadequacy by comparison—he perforce postpones his sexual ambitions until he grows up and becomes like his father. According to Chasseguet-Smirgel, "He places his narcissism in his father who thus becomes his model, that is to say, his aim for identification" (1984, p. 27). His father embodies his ego ideal. For Chasseguet-Smirgel, the ego ideal implies that there is a "plan," "hope," and "promise for the future," which can compensate for the lack of narcissistic gratification in the present, a solution which is in conformity with the demands of the reality principle since it defers immediate discharge and satisfaction in favor of an ongoing adaptation and future rewards.

Chasseguet-Smirgel's account of the development of the ego ideal is quite easy to adapt to our understanding of the psychology of love. Although her focus is on idealization of, and identification with, the same-sex parent, one can easily posit that in romantic love the ego ideal finally achieves satisfaction through the granting of the incestuous wish (itself the product of a wish for narcissistic unity) by way of union with the beloved (a displacement of the original incestuous object).

The notion of romantic love as narcissistic repair goes a long way to explain the sense of peace, of rightness, that is so prominent a feature of requited love. Contemporary theorists (Bergmann, 1980; Person, 1988a; Viederman, 1988) explicitly posit what is only implied in Freud: namely, that lovers attempt to undo the unhappy past. If, as Freud (1908) suggested, the "motive forces of phantasies are unsatisfied wishes, and every single phantasy is the fulfilment of a wish, a correction of unsatisfying reality" (p. 146), then love, which is an imaginative act, a "fantasy" of a kind, can be seen as a means of reversing the disappointments of early life, of gratifying unfulfilled and forbidden childhood wishes—all at an unconscious level, of course. Primary among these delayed gratifications is the oedipal victory that can finally be effected when the lover takes possession of his beloved, thereby restoring his lost omnipotence. Achieving union with the beloved allows him to identify with the victorious rivals of his childhood and assuages his wounded narcissism (Bergmann, 1989; Person, 1988a; Viederman, 1988). Romantic love does not result, as originally believed, in a diminution of the self; rather it results in self-expansion. Hope for restitution, for release from one's sense of inadequacy, is the fuel of love, wholeness and exaltation the reward when love is reciprocated.

While romantic love subsumes many different aims (sex, intimacy, priority) under its umbrella, it is the lover's quest for union with the idealized beloved that is primary. Although some have claimed that happiness is the goal (and motivator) of love, this claim cannot suffice insofar as we know that some lovers will sacrifice all hope of conventional happiness for the sake of their love and may even be prepared to die for it. Love is better understood as the pursuit not of happiness but of the beloved, possession of whom is the guarantor of self-esteem. The motivation in romantic love appears to have more to do with issues of narcissism, regulation of self-esteem, and the search for meaning (as a major adaptive strategy) than with either sex or attachment (though romantic love coopts both to serve its own purposes).

Love as an Agent of Transformation

Yet if this were all there is to love—new gratifications for old urges, new solutions to old problems—then love would be, as many claim, no more than narcissism à deux, and Freud correct in his contention that the so-called selflessness of love is no more than the disguise under the cover of which Eros and Narcissus seek their own gratifications. However, love is not merely a closed loop, as is sometimes postulated even within the framework of ego psychology. We know that the lover's sense of well-being is something more than a transient instinctual gratification or narcissistic exaltation, because psychic change (restructuralization) may endure even when a love affair ends. Certainly it is true that love is a process born of internal psychic need, but as an act of the imagination, it transcends need and sometimes culminates in internal change.

There are many ways in which such permanent change appears to be effected in realized love. Successful love is not only a re-edition of the past but, often, a permanent renunciation of the past (as with Romeo and Juliet). Love has the power to break old ties to family and friends, alter religious and ethnic affiliations, change social class and political preference, and in the case of those lovers who discover by way of their beloved their life's work or mission bring new purpose and meaning to life. At the most minimal level love may simply result in an expansion of interest; she may discover basketball, he ballet; he may instruct her in the intricacies of politics while learning something of the joys of literature from her, and these new interests may survive the departure of the one who introduced them. But regardless of whether any of the external interests or circumstances of one's life undergo alteration, love, even transient, unsuccessful love, can cause profound inner change.

In the throes of love, the lover feels himself to be enlarged, expanded. This new sense of self appears to be mediated through the series of new identifications that are catalyzed by falling in love. Such identifications are not just regressive but progressive in nature as well. As already noted, in their regressive and restorative aspect, they permit the lover to enjoy the pleasure of identifying with the victors of the oedipal period (or of a sibling rivalry for parental favor), and so to complete some of the psychological work left unfinished from that phase. But in their progressive aspect, new identifications change the lover's sense of self. The lover's ability to project his ego ideal onto the beloved and through reintrojection to assuage his longings for goodness and perfection results in the identification of self with the other (or the self representation with the object representation) that is the hallmark of love (and an important paradigm for understanding any psychic change).

Through identification with an idealized other, and through the idealized reflection of himself which he can see in the eyes of his beloved, the lover finds his best self, and may as a consequence be moved to acts of pure altruism and even renunciation which further expand his sense of his own worth. Sometimes this expanded sense of self survives even when the love does not.

Moreover, the lover forms an entirely new identification with the beloved as a pair, a merging of two identities that reverberates with all the important "psychic" couples of one's life, real and imaginary. Psychologically, the lover condenses two powerful images, that of mother and child (with himself playing both roles), and that of the parental couple. By making these simultaneous identifications, he is able to assimilate within himself partial and contradictory images. The sense of self is enlarged and integrated at a new level, and the lover empowered beyond the usual.

These new identifications may result in a significant reordering of one's values and priorities (sometimes a crossing of internal psychological boundaries); hence the opportunity to liberate the self from the constrictions of the past. The lover is emboldened to start new projects, take new risks, and embark on a new phase of life. It is not unusual for lovers to feel that they have been reborn, or given a second (or third or whatever) chance at life.

Closely related to identification yet slightly different from it, empathy is an act of the imagination which enables one to feel *with* one's beloved (instead of feeling *like* the beloved). Empathy allows the lover to move out of the tiresome trap of the self, to affirm another consciousness as a separate but equal center to the universe; it facilitates a deep interest in the inwardness of another, an ability to move beyond the limits of one's own consciousness and see the world through other eyes. (The phrase "falling in love" may implicitly convey that one is falling *out of* the confines of the self.) This too can be a wonderful liberation, an experience that permanently alters the self, regardless of the outcome of the love that made it possible. At its best, through the imaginative acts of identification and empathy, love expands us, ennobles us, moves us beyond the limits of our own consciousness.

If sufficiently profound, the lover's mutual identification may be understood as the psychological counterpart of the philosopher's concept of merging. Here one sees that love serves not only psychological needs but existential ones as well. Passionate love attempts to overcome the pain of separation, separateness, and the felt inadequacies of the solitary self through a sense of merger with the other. Successful lovers establish a union characterized by ongoing warmth, commitment, intimacy, reciprocity, and some degree of mutual identification. If they are lucky enough to enjoy a *passionate* love as well, their feelings of union will be interspersed with ecstatic moments of merger. It is for this reason that love is so often likened to a religion of two; in love, as in religion, there is an object of worship, a means of communion, and even a route to transcendence. To some degree, then, love has preempted religion's lock on personal transformation (conversion, rebirth, redemption), and perhaps on meaningfulness as well.

Idealization, Imagination, and Cultural Narratives

Thus far, I have given a brief history of the way love has evolved in the West and described the psychic roots of love in the individual's developmental history. What remains to be explored is the way cultural processes (in additon to early family experiences) impact on the development of love. To understand the link between cultural narrative and love it is necessary to look more fully at the role of imagination in romantic love.

One of the best descriptions of how the content of our idealizations is formed, both psychically and culturally, and its relationship to how the beloved is selected, comes to us not from a psychoanalyst but from a man of letters. Toward the end of his life, H. G. Wells tried to come to grips with the question of why we love whom we love and in so doing gave us a brilliant account of how each of us forms an unconscious image of an idealized other:

> I think that in every human mind, possibly from an extremely early age, there exists a continually growing and continually more subtle complex of expectation and hope: an aggregation of lovely and exciting thoughts; conceptions of encounter and reaction picked up from observation, descriptions, drama; reveries of understanding and reciprocity: which I will call the Lover-Shadow . . . I think it is almost as essential in our lives as our self-consciousness. It is *other* consciousness. . . .
>
> When we make love, we are trying to make another human being concentrate for us an impersonation or at least a symbol of the Lover-Shadow in our minds; and when we are in love it means we have found in someone the presentation of the promise of some, at least, of the main qualities of our Lover-Shadow. The beloved person is for a time identified with the dream, attains a vividness that captures the role, and seems to leave anything outside it unilluminated [Wells, pp. 53–55].

Wells is clear that our choice of lovers has to do with our own internal psychic processes—with imagination, in short. The processes leading up to that choice begin by our creating within our minds that complex of qualities that seems to us to constitute our ideal love. We each of course have different priorities, generally unconscious, for those qualities essential to our own image of the Lover-Shadow (see Arlow, 1980; Person, 1988a), the ideal love. Whatever the shape of the Lover-Shadow we finally create, we then, by another imaginative act, transform some living creature into the embodiment of this product of our minds. (We "try" to make another human being into an "impersonation . . . of the Lover-Shadow.")

Wells does not explain, because no one can, how the imagination performs this alchemy. But as Wells intuits, the would-be lover senses the potential power of the beloved; he senses the beloved can touch him, fulfill him, gratify him in some unique way. The loved one elicits some yearning, some need in the lover, which he believes that only the loved one and no one and nothing else will be able to fulfill.

What is the story, the plot line, in which the beloved is assigned the leading role? As I have already suggested, the act of love draws on some widespread if not universal fantasies engendered during developmental life. In love is born anew the dream of fulfilling the half-forgotten, inevitably frustrated, wishes for perfect harmony and complete mutuality—wishes that are re-editions of the buried fantasy of obtaining the perfect mother who would love unerringly and unceasingly—and many other fantasies as well. Romantic love is a creative synthesis precisely because it provides an overarching narrative into which many subordinate fantasies—for example, the fantasy of the perfect mother—can be incorporated. But each lover does not—could not—invent the love story for himself.

Lovers incorporate into their imaginative longings what they observe in the culture around them—and love stories have long been an important part of our cultural heritage. It has been said that "the noble lover loves love stories" (the poet Gottfried, quoted by Campbell, p. 42). It would seem rather, as I have already suggested, that love stories create lovers. The longing for romantic love often crystallizes in the context of emulation and envy of other lovers whether encountered in real life, in books, or on the silver screen. In other words, the prevailing cultural narratives or the prevailing "community of daydreams" provide ready made love stories.

It is perhaps not too far-fetched to analogize the role of the love story in the potential lover's life to the role Schafer (1983) gives to the interpretive metaphor in the analytic treatment situation. As he puts it, "The metaphor creates an experience one has never had before. It is an experience one has not realized by oneself. The metaphor does, of course, suggest certain constituent experience of which one may have been more or less dimly aware. . . . One may say, therefore, that the metaphor *speaks* for these constituents, on the existence of which much of its appeal depends, but in its organizing and implicitly rendering these constituents in its new way it is a creation rather than a mere paraphrase or new edition" (pp. 127–128). In this scenario, the analytic patient makes creative use of the analyst's interpretive metaphor. So it is with the lover and the love story.

Love exerts enormous power over the lover not only because it provides the vehicle for instinctual gratification, but also because it stabilizes self-esteem and provides meaning. The imaginative valuation and idealization of an object coupled with one's union to that object is a psychic strategem mobilized to stabilize self-esteem and establish meaning. This latter dynamic is not, of course, limited to romantic love. The same mechanism is at work in religion, in the passionate love of God; a similar one is at play in any passionate devotion to a person or cause whether political, religious, or artistic. For example, in religious communities, the narrative proposes a God who is divine, devotion and closeness to whom are the prevalent routes for establishing a sense of goodness, of rightness, of self-esteem, and of meaning. The ideal self is achieved through dedication to and worship of God.

Each idealized pursuit—nationalism, religion, love—has a slightly different psychology. Insofar as different cultures may generate different needs and propose different methods of assuaging them, we would anticipate different cultural narratives and a propensity to different idealized pursuits. A comparison between religion and romantic love, and the nature of idealization in each, is illustrative. Though there are great similarities between religion and romantic love, there are equally important differences. In religion there is generally a consensus as to the attributes of God; in romantic love, while love itself may be culturally sanctioned, the choice of a particular love object is more a product of the individual imagination. Brehm (1988) gives an elegant account of this difference, concluding that "it seems a reasonable proposition that, at least within a certain range of belief and practices, the passionate lover of God is far more integrated into and supported by a social network than is the individual whose passionate love is directed toward another human being. Consequently, a mystic's conception of God typically has more social reality and appears (to the faithful) less imaginative than does a passionate lover's image of the beloved" (p. 248).

What is celebrated in romantic love is man's uniqueness, his individuality, his propensity for self-will as opposed to the capacity for self-abnegation (as a means of participating in God's divinity), which religion celebrates. The historical appearance of romantic love marks the beginning of a shift from an authoritarian, traditional, God-oriented society to an individual-centered one. Campbell (1968) goes so far as to suggest that "of all the modes of experience by which the individual might be carried away from the safety of well-trodden grounds to the danger of the unknown . . . the erotic [mode of feeling] was the first to waken Gothic man from his childhood slumber in authority" (p. 2).

Romantic love, then, as we know it in the West, is related to the rise of individuality; it is an instrument of self-will and self-transformation—and also a product of those psychic forces. Without self-will (self-assertion) there is no capacity for psychological separation from a preexisting tie and therefore no possibility for establishing a new preeminent relationship.

Romantic love cannot be so important in cultures that value conformity and authority as it is in those that value differentiation and autonomy. In Japan, for example, conformity and identification with the group are valued above all, and romantic love is a rare occurrence, disapproved of and feared (Keene, 1978, p. 253). However, the Japanese do celebrate one highly romantic convention: lovers who cannot be together in life join each other in death—by suicide. For the Japanese, self-will, because of its potential for social disruptiveness, cannot easily exist within the cultural framework. Consequently, the only acceptable outlet for love (one of the ultimate manifestations of self-will) is doomed love, in which the lovers, by dying for their love, simultaneously assert and extinguish the self, thus insuring the primacy of the group over selfish claims of the lover. The Japanese weep at stories of doomed lovers' suicides, and thereby vicariously indulge, romanticize, and exorcise those impulses within themselves. This means of channeling illicit desires is not so different from the celebration of chaste, doomed love which was the defining feature of Troubadour culture, or the punishment of adulterous love which was the stuff of Arthurian romance. During the Middle Ages, when the valuation of autonomy was coming into its ascendancy but the individual's behavior was still bound by strict laws of fealty and obligation, it made perfect sense for the culture to have arrived at a means of acknowledging the peremptoriness of love, and, through the literary convention of the Liebestod, punishing it.

Conclusion: The Intersection between Culture and Psyche

Though we often take romantic love for granted, it is generally agreed that it is a creation of the poet troubadours of eleventh-century France. While I have tried to show that love is an invention (or discovery) that elegantly brings together our needs for bonding, intimacy, sexuality, and a passionate idealized "cause," I have also argued that our belief in the legitimacy of the pursuit of realized passionate love is only possible because we inhabit an individualistic society. The gradual changes in Western love stories parallel a loosening of authoritarian bonds. While it is unclear what historical forces came together that allowed the medieval imagination to create romantic love, that creative synthesis has proved decisive for the future psychological development of individuals and for Western culture. If C. S. Lewis is to be believed, "French poets, in the eleventh century . . . were the first to express . . . that romantic species of passion which English poets were still writing about in the nineteenth. They effected a change which has left no corner of our ethics, our imagination, or our daily life untouched, and they erected impassable barriers between us and the classical past or the Oriental present. Compared with this revolution the Renaissance is a mere ripple in the surface of literature" (p. 4).

Lewis's conclusion is certainly a largish one, but one that he defends admirably. However, the question for psychoanalysts is the way in which such dramatic cultural shifts shed light on fundamental psychoanalytic questions—and the obverse, too: what it is that psychoanalytic theory can contribute to our understanding of cultural shifts.

The changing history of love in literature and lives tells us something about the nature of idealization and the shifting (and adaptive) role it plays in human life. There are many cultures in which the self (if indeed there exists in those cultures anything like what we regard as the self) is not so problematic a construct, I speak of cultures in which individuals fit into predetermined and extremely defined roles, which automatically provide strong bonds with group or tribe or God through which to realize themselves and achieve meaning (Morgenthau and Person, 1978). In our own culture these bonds have weakened, and while we congratulate ourselves for having escaped the demands of a repressive, authoritarian social order, we now find ourselves trying to assuage the hunger of the inner self for the validation and identity it once found through conformity to those external demands. Without a socially determined role to which to adhere, self-esteem becomes problematic and the individual must work out some form of personal satisfaction (usually invoking idealization of one or another pursuit) in order to stabilize self-esteem and achieve an ideal state (in Sandler's sense).

Despite some intrinsic paradoxes and limitations (Person, 1988a), romantic love through its creation of an idealized Other provides many of us with a meaningful center in a shifting world, a culturally available schema for stabilizing self-esteem and establishing meaning, and a mode for effecting internal change. As such, romantic love provides gratification not only for primary (instinctual) needs, such as sex and attachment, but also for psychological needs generated within a given cultural milieu. Romantic love is also, for psychoanalysts, a premiere case study of the way in which the cultural unconscious intersects with the psyche to create new stories with corollary shifts in the way the self is construed and in the adaptations and gratifications that are sought.

REFERENCES

ALBERONI, F. (1983). *Falling in Love,* tr. L. Venuti. New York: Random House.
ARLOW, J. A. (1980). Object and object choice. *Psychoanal. Q.,* 49:109–133.
BALINT, M. (1948). On genital love. *Int. J. Psychoanal.,* 29:34–40.
BERGMANN, M. S. (1980). On the intrapsychic function of falling in love. *Psychoanal. Q.,* 49:56–77.
——— (1989). Freud's three theories of love in the light of later developments. *J. Amer. Psychoanal. Assn.,* 36:653–672.
BREHM, S. (1988). Passionate love. In *The Psychology of Love,* ed. R. J. Sternberg & M. L. Barnes. New Haven: Yale Univ. Press, pp. 233–263.
CAMPBELL, J. (1968). *Creative Mythology*. New York: Penguin Books.
CHASSEGUET-SMIRGEL, J. (1984). *Creativity of Perversion.* New York: Norton.
DARWIN, C. R. (1872). *The Expression of Emotions in Man and Animals.* London: John Murray.
DE ROUGEMONT, D. (1956). *Love in the Western World.* New York: Pantheon Books.
FIEDLER, L. (1966). *Love and Death in the American Novel.* New York: Stein and Day.
FLAUBERT, G. (1857). *Madame Bovary.* New York: Random House, 1957.
FREUD, S. (1905). Three essays on the theory of sexuality. *S. E.,* 9:141–153.
——— (1908). Creative writers and day-dreaming. *S. E.,* 9:141–153.
——— (1914). On narcissism. *S. E.,* 14:67–102.
——— (1915). Observations on transference-love. *S. E.,* 12:157–143.
——— (1921). Group psychology and the analysis of the ego. *S. E.,* 18:65–143.
——— (1930). Civilization and its discontents. *S. E.,* 21:54–145.

GOODE, W. J. (1959). The theoretical importance of love. *Amer. Sociol. Rev.,* 24:34–47.
IZARD, C. E. (1977). *Human Emotions.* New York: Plenum Press.
KEENE, D.C. (1978). *World within Walls.* New York: Grove Press.
LEWIS, C. S. (1936). *The Allegory of Love.* New York: Oxford Univ. Press, 1985.
MORGENTHAU, H. & PERSON, E. (1978). The roots of narcissism. *Partisan Rev.,* 45:337–347.
PERSON, E. S. (1988a). *Dreams of Love and Fateful Encounters.* New York: Norton.
——— (1988b). Review of "Creativity and Perversion" by Chasseguet-Smirgel. *J. Amer. Psychoanal. Assn.,* 36:1067–1071.
REIK, T. C. (1941). *Of Lust and Love.* New York: Aronson, 1984.
SACHS, H. (1942). The community of daydreams. In *The Creative Unconscious.* Cambridge, Mass.: Sci-Art Publishers.
SANDLER, J. (1989). Toward a reconsideration of the psychoanalytic theory of motivation. In *Psychoanalysis: Toward the Second Century,* ed. A. Cooper, O. Kernberg, & E. S. Person. New Haven: Yale Univ. Press, pp. 91–110.
SCHAFER, R. (1983). *The Analytic Attitude.* New York: Basic Books.
STONE, L. (1988). Passionate attachments in the west in historical perspective. In *Passionate Attachments,* ed. W. Gaylin & E. S. Person. New York: Free Press, pp. 15–26.
TANNER, T. (1979). *Adultery in the Novel.* Baltimore: Johns Hopkins Univ. Press.
VIEDERMAN, M. (1988). The nature of passionate love. In *Passionate Attachments,* ed. W. Gaylin & E. S. Person. New York: Free Press, pp. 1–14.
WELLS, H. G. (1984). *H. G. Wells in Love: Postscript to an Experiment in Autobiography,* ed. G. P. Wells. Boston: Little, Brown.

135 Central Park West
New York, NY 10023

HOORAY FOR LOVE

ROBERT J. STOLLER, M.D.

"Love" is a word that supposedly links an affect homogeneous enough from episode to episode or from person to person or from culture to culture to be recognized by anyone as being, clearly, love. The cautious psychoanalyst, however, knows—not the least from being unable to define love—that there really is little homogeneity. Nonetheless, analytic investigators are now facing this problem. In order to examine an aspect of the concept "love," a fragment from the report of a woman of our culture in a painful love affair is placed next to a fragment from a Sambia (New Guinea) woman. As we would expect, untender, unempathic, unpleasant, and dangerous qualities—in the form of memories and scripts—immediately appear amid the tender emotions. The roots of these unloving affects can be found in the forces that, transcending cultures, create gender identity in males and females, and give us hints as to why love is often so unloving.

"SEXUALITY," "ROMANCE," "LOVE": words that should be easy for the psychoanalyst, for they refer to direct, reportable experiences with visible behavioral consequences. Words that draw on common knowledge requiring at the start neither the microscope of analytic treatment nor the dark glass of metapsychology. But these are words not easy to encompass. So I shall play lightly with them; no try for definitive statements. ("Romance" and "love," being subjectively recognized feeling states, can rightfully, I think, be considered affects, as does, perhaps, an aspect of "sexuality": erotic excitement.)

Professor of Psychiatry, University of California Medical School, Los Angeles, Calif.

I am indebted to Professor Gilbert Herdt for sharing with me both his Sambia findings and his Sambia friends and for his invaluable help with the Sambia text in this paper.

Sexuality

Hearing the word, one has no precise idea what is meant. Recall the history of Freud's search for understanding "sexuality." He starts, for instance, with "libido" having its usual meaning—erotic desire—and ends with Eros, where "sexuality" means *anything* that happens, mental or otherwise, to *any* living tissue. (Reik [1945] remarks on this: "People have always differentiated between love and sex. . . . Only in psychoanalysis the word [sex] extended its meaning and became a hodge-podge expression. . . . To the same unjustified and unjustifiable extension was the word libido subjected" [p. 16].)

Even early on, when Freud's thinking was less spectacular, he used "sexuality" equally for masculinity and femininity, erotic excitement, sensuality, pleasure, unpleasure, reduction of tension, and heightened tension. "Sexuality" covers so much, then, that it covers almost nothing, giving too much license to theory-making. How about restricting "sexuality" to domains long recognized: gender identity and erotic excitement? And shall we also include romance and love?

Here are ideas useful for mapping the territory, even if they are truisms, folk wisdom mostly antecedent to psychoanalytic insights.

Romance. Romance has no connotation of constancy (not that it does not, rarely, persist through a life-long relationship). Nor of commitment, insight, and patience. Its altruism is spectacular and superficial. (The flaccid word for this description is "narcissism," which tells us nothing.) It is a positive transference, erotic or not, and is likely to fade, though it may rarely, with time and understanding, transmute into something quieter. As with transference-in-treatment, romance is heavy with scripts: performance in a spotlight. (Romance is, in the song's words, "falling in love with love." Erotomania is its most dramatic form.) It is a sweet pathology ("madness").

Though romance, love, and erotic behavior sometimes come together, they draw from very different fantasy systems.

Romance resembles a wonderfully well-told joke: the "natural" hostility between people is for the moment subdued, surmounted, transformed, with success celebrated by the mutual applause we call "romance" or "humor." Being momentary, it allows for quick exit.

Love. "Love"—to stay with the obvious—is a word like "happiness," "joy," "beauty," "art," "goodness," "sincerity," "kindness," or "wisdom"; it can stand for so many different experiences, have such different dynamic structures, be used for such different purposes. It is, until one gets descriptively precise, recklessly amorphous. As with "affects," every moment of love is at least a bit different from every other moment of love. Though, given such parameters, finding a definition is hopeless, we all know enough about love to sense a few of its dynamics. (In this fragment, I am not considering the grosser pathologies of love, though where mutuality ends and aberrance starts is hard to measure.)

What differentiates the love we admire from romance? This above all: minimal fetishizing. Which implies, in varying amounts, empathy; identification; the need to need and the need to be needed; high-pleasure altruism; reduced inventing of the other to fit our primordial fantasies; not too much ego ideal or other idealizations; the capacity to survive one's own and the other's rage and fear (stoically, with good spirits, even with humor); curiosity: the unending antidote to boredom; respect: admiring and unmalicious envy (that is, pride in the other's qualities); capacity to keep one's boundaries in the midst of merging; constructive guilt; happy vulunerability. Mutuality, obviously.

Note that these qualities can be there whether the relationship is erotic (heterosexual, homosexual, openly perverse—e.g., consensual SM) or not. It can fit friendships with either sex, can even include animals, vocations, avocations, one's relationship to art—anything where admiration and rage can thrive together. It is quite unrelated to the grand orgasms of Reich's system. It is not even the same as compatibility. And it is rare.

How amazing that "the synthetic function of the ego" can put all these pieces together and come up with an affect we experience as a unity (see Freud, 1912, pp. 180–181).

Case Material

1. Fay is terribly shy and unendingly consumed with thoughts of sex, romance, love, and a marriage filled with the presence of husband, pregnancies, babies, and a housewifery that does not enslave her. If it did not debilitate her, she says, she would lie in bed masturbating, day and night. Yet, the only daydreams that give the needed excitement, as different from the "nice" daydreams that satisfy the happy desires for love and marriage, are "dirty" variants of this: a cold, silent, unknown, faceless man who passes on the street, looks up her skirt (gust of wind, stepping off bus, etc.), and stares at her genitals; she is without underwear. He gets excited. So she gets excited. They have violent but cold, silent intercourse, never to meet again.

It is not the purpose of this essay to link Fay's infancy and childhood to the adult forms of her erotic desire. I want rather to report the precise words of the ordinary. You will be disoriented if you read the following expecting to find it remarkable. Instead, think how often you have heard comparable; found it reported in histories, ethnographies, biographies, autobiographies, novels, jokes, songs, dramas, comedies, dance, paintings, seen it in the anguished statements of feminists and in the scripts of pornographers. Our assignment here is, then, to note the details of the affects/scripts that underlie our words "romance," "love," and "erotic excitement." Then I shall link them to a description of masculinity and femininity different from that used in classical analytic theory.

In the following, we are several years into treatment (not analysis):

F: Jason and I are back together. He did do the things that I needed, reluctantly but mechanically well, lacking feeling. Clinically, "Okay," like a doctor. When he came in [her bedroom], I just wanted to hug him, but he went straight to the clitoris. [She has, throughout the months of their affair, complained that she cannot get excited without foreplay; foreplay would signal she is wanted, is seen as a real, desired person. An important element in this benevolence would be his awareness that she likes clitoral stimulation. But he ignored this, despite her asking, pleading, scolding. She is referring here to his hasty, perfunctory, affectless—"clinically"—giving her clitoris this time a short rub.] It's the same thing—lack of foreplay. I know it's better [this time]; at least he did it. But by the second day, it was less each time. . . . He woke up in a panic, shaking in his sleep. He had a terrible dream. He and I were on a pleasure cruise ship. We were given seed pods that we were to nurture. Then I told him it wasn't really a pleasure cruise. These were the Queen's babies. We had to make sure that they hatched. The Queen was a queen bee, and the babies turned into insects that were trying to devour us. He was trying to kill them when he woke up.

S: His doing what you want is frightening him?

F: Why is it so frightening to him? He hardly even recognizes that it scares him. He won't tell me what his fantasies are. Maybe he fantasizes I'm a whore: I *have* given him massages. I might have told him [that she sold sex several years ago, in a massage parlor] long [months] ago, but he's never brought it up and I've never brought it up again.

S: What does he imagine a clitoris feels or fantasizes? Or is the question why does he not want to produce the sexual excitement you want? Or: why, why, why? I don't know what the questions are. "If a woman says, 'Please love me,' why is he unable to?" That's what you want to know?

F: I think I know. He knows it makes me feel loving toward him. It draws him to feeling loving toward me, and he's afraid of that.

S: Erotic love produces bad seeds that turn into bees?

F: Killer bees. He told me this story long ago: the male bee exists only to fertilize the queen. After they have sex, she bites off his head and eats him. And he goes, "It makes sense, because that way the male bee (his proteins, or whatever) go to seeds, the next generation of bees, nothing goes to waste." On the same night he told the bee story, there was a TV program about this woman who was really a bee-woman, a sexy woman who turned into a devouring monster.

S: So it may not be fantasies about your anatomy or your clitoris but rather your excitement [that worries him].

F: I think so. Because when he did that with the clitoris, it was like he knew he did less kissing beforehand than usual [and so "did that with the clitoris" only to pay a debt]. He broke off the kiss that was really getting me turned on in order to go for the clitoris, right? So he knew that he can get away with that [i.e., get her excited by friction without regard to her as a responsive person] and still not generate the love that I wanted. But he did generate it anyway. Afterward, I was feeling. . . . I had tears running out of my eyes. And he did too. So he was feeling the same way. Exposed and naked and vulnerable, in a good sense. Scary for both of us.

S: Was this just the other night?

F: The bee story and television show was long ago, the tears a few nights ago. He had the dream after we went to sleep. Then he woke up in a panic. We just held each other, and then he climbed on top of me and immediately stuck it in, I guess for comfort, and I let him do it. I sensed that that other part [kiss, clitoris: love] must have scared him so badly that he wanted to do it the old way to be safe. So I let him. And he stopped without climax. He just wanted that little. . . . It really wasn't out of turn-on or excitement.

S: He lost his erection?

F: No, he didn't.

S: He didn't want to come?

F: I don't think so. He told me the dream first, and I could see that he wanted to do it ["stick it in for comfort"]. I felt I was comforting him. There wasn't much turn-on [for her], because I was so disturbed by his dream. I thought, "Oh, shit! Just when he's taken that small step." I was almost glad that he didn't come, because that way [in coming] he would have gotten away with turning this dangerous thing into an excitement. Instead of doing that, he just was seeking comfort. I think he thinks about marriage a lot. Like he'll sing [hums *Here Comes the Bride*] as we're walking down the street. Then, after we had sex that time, that bee thing, he sings "Now I'm going to get married." I go, "What?" Then he just sang some other part of the song. Maybe he thinks if he gives me too much love, I'm going to want to marry him. I want to say, "I certainly wouldn't marry you." Aren't there spiders that kill their mates? The Black Widow. That's why she's called "The Widow." She sucks all the blood out of him. What could be killing about my desire?

S: You have to tell me. Why do you think you're a vampire? We haven't talked about that for a long time, but by God you used to tell me a lot about vampires! If you want to understand why a man might be afraid of sex with you, then you would have to see that someone senses it in you. They can't know of your [vampire] fantasy, but they may have an unconscious or subliminal sense that what turns you on is something hostile toward men. What they won't know is you are hostile toward men, and a vampire, because you were beaten up in your childhood, first [figuratively] by men [father] and then [literally] by boys [in the schoolyard]. Right?

F: Right.

S: Revenge: [when masturbating] "I'm not going to have any love for that man [the faceless stranger], and if I feel some love, I lose my excitement during the fantasy. [She cannot climax in masturbation until any loving details are dropped.] I'm going to really give it back to him."

Professor Gilbert Herdt for years and I for days have worked with members of a New Guinea tribe, the Sambia, to understand how they created in their males the brutality and courage necessary to preserve themselves from their cruel environment and the savage wars they engaged in with neighboring villages. Though culturally far removed from the west, the Sambia share with us fundamental dynamics of masculinity and femininity and of erotic behavior. Let me review studies of two of Herdt's friends, a woman and a man I had the opportunity to interview with him (in addition to sharing with him, over several years, the details of his work with them). In this way, we can test ideas on our versions of the affects romance, love, and erotic excitement against theirs: whether Fay and Jason, though unique, are nonetheless recognizable not only in other lovers in our world but also in these natives. In other words, dare we generalize, across cultures, the dynamics of romance, love, and erotic excitement?[1]

2. The first is (at the time she speaks here, 1979) a woman, Penjukwi, married, with two children. As a child and early adolescent, she had tender, romantic fantasies of sweet, gentle intimacies with a boy her age. Her romantic impulses (reported more fully elsewhere [Herdt and Stoller, 1990]) are indis-

---

[1]I resist the temptation to indulge the psychoanalyst's venial sin: finding the universe in an *n* of one.

tinguishable to us from what we hear from women in our culture (and not from men in either place). Here is an example she told us: Herdt and I are talking with her. He, translating, reviews for me in her presence what she was saying. (Fay would appreciate Penjukwi's daydream. And Jason, as you will see, is a Sambia manque.)

H: So, I've been asking her about her favorite erotic daydream, the only one, as far as I know, she has now. This is the daydream. She's a young girl of, say 8 to 10, 11; not yet to puberty. And she is with a boy her age. They're near the village where she was born. On that side of the village there are flowers, bamboo, and grass—it's a nice place. And they've been playing with some children in the morning. They tell these others to occupy themselves while P. and the boy go off to do something. At this point she does not know what is going to happen.

S: But she does know. In this society everybody knows about sex, at an early age.

H: No, no they don't.

S: Children—

H: No.

S: They do not know about intercourse?

H: No. The implication is that the boy is stronger than she is and knows more about sex than she does. And so they go off. . . . And it's the two of them alone. This happened several times [in reality] with a boy she grew up with. And so [in the daydream] they go out to collect ferns and insects to eat. But the boy has something different in mind. He begins to look at her sexuality. That is, he is looking at her intensely, which means in this culture that he wants her, desires her.

S: [Interrupts.] This has nothing to do with her daydream but with the culture: he looks where—face, eyes . . . ?

H: At her face—

S: She knows he's looking at her face and she turns her eyes down. . . .

H: And smiles—

S: Because at that age she recognizes what that look means?

H: In the daydream.

S: Yeah.

H: And she smiles.

S: What smile—what kind of smile?

H: Well, I imagine, a charming smile.

S: Shy, innocent—understand, but doesn't understand?

H: It means, "I accept your desire."

S: "I do understand"?

H: Yeah, that is, "I will be your desirable object." She started having this daydream when first having sex with her husband. She was very afraid. When she saw his penis she was very afraid. It was so big.

S: That was the first one she'd ever seen? Like that [erect]? [Pause.] Not crucial———

H: Yeah, I don't know[2] and I'd have to think it out. . . . That's when she had this daydream. And in it she sees a little boy's penis. First she's a bit frightened.

S: A little boy's erect penis?

H: Yeah, a little boy's erect penis. The boy looks at her strongly, and she smiles in response. Then he says, "Look at my penis." She looks. He removes his grass skirt and she sees his erect penis.

S: And she sees one then for the first time.

H: For the first time. And she is frightened at first, but then feels okay. Then, in one version he pushes her down, lays on top of her, puts his penis partly in her still immature vagina. In another version [these have been told in earlier interviews] they lay down together and it's a little less

[2]H. adds years later "I'm 99 percent sure that as an adult woman, P. had never before seen an adult erect penis."

> rough. The story line is that she wants him, but he's also very firm and he's pushing her. But it's not a rape, not that. She wants him [to do it that way]. And in reality she is using the daydream [to protect her] when she sees the [her husband's, the first time, when frightened, angered, and with the pain of first intercourse] erect penis.

After menarche, which makes a woman there eligible for marriage, there were for her as yet no such specific plans, though she was a desirable woman because of her physical beauty (and a dangerous one because of culturally aberrant, openly displayed independence and intelligence). One night, before dawn, several warriors accompanying the one who was to be her husband left their village, slipped down the mountain path, crossed the bridge over the wildly flooding river, climbed up the other side, and raced into the sleeping village where Penjukwi lived. They tore her from her hut, beat off her defenders. Down the path, across the bridge—grappling her so she could not save herself in death by throwing herself in the river—up to their village, and into her husband-to-be's hut. There, with his companions on guard outside, he forced himself on her, effectively a rape. This occupied several days, a rare but legitimate entry into the extended process that marriage is for the Sambia. Not much romance, but up there, not that aberrant either.

3. The next case is, however, aberrant for them. Imano is a gentle man, and for that he is not necessarily admired in a culture that cannot, because of its warfare, survive without ferocious masculinity. His peers measure his failure in the fact that he is happy with both his wives and treats them with respect. Unknown, consciously, to his comrades, he also loves his wives' bodies, over which he enthusiastically lingers in foreplay. And—as different from the other men, who are frightened into rapid-fire intercourse by women's anatomy and juices—Imano waits pleasurably in intercourse until his

wives' climax. (The other men claim not to know or care if women have the capacity for orgasm.)

Herdt, reading this material in manuscript, adds: "In fact, Imano tells us [H. and S.] that the peak of his sexual excitement is his wife's orgasm: a report so remarkable that the anthropologist [Herdt] and his translator [Weiyu] had to overcome their own disbelief enough to *hear* Imano repeat the same feeling to them long enough to be convinced of its authenticity."

As we consider erotic behavior in other times and places, can we pretend that these savages are more savage with their ladies than some cultured gents of our acquaintance? The Fays and Jasons of our world are, in erotic dynamics—the men on the run, the women yearning—not so far from the Sambia. We all know people identical in their erotic tastes and practices to Herdt's fierce warriors/hunters/killers.

Historians say that romantic love was invented in the hothouse atmosphere of the twelfth to thirteenth century Languedoc court. Penjukwi daydreaming—and hardly a troubadour—lets us dismiss that notion. People anywhere anytime can emit romance. (Herdt adds: "even daring to violate the canons of their society [as Penjukwi did] to do this.")

Elaborating the Sambians' Theory

"Romance" and "love" are subjects that, properly, analysts have pretty much avoided until recently. (Reik [1944, 1945] is a hot, ironic, forgotten, incisive, iconoclastic, opinionated exception. Kernberg [1974a, 1974b, 1977, in press] and Person [1988] are present-day important contributors.) I think of two reasons. First, agreement on definitions or clinical descriptions of these emotions does not exist. Second,though other subjective states can be closely examined psychoanalytically to tease out component parts below the surface, "romance" somewhat, and "love" largely, tempt us to treat romance romantically and love lovingly. These subjects melt the myelin of ordinarily tough-minded investigators.

Suppose, following what we expect of human behavior, we look to see to what extent are "romance" and "love" states of defense, that is, neurotic structures. All analysts will suspect romance, with its connotations of impermanence and youth, but some may look coldly on looking coldly at "love." Still, if we stick to the clinical and avoid the temptation to romanticize (dramatize, mystify) or to work from our personal good or bad luck with these adventures, we can examine *each* real-world example of love or romance. The test will be to find cases in which, contrary to the defense hypothesis, "romance" is purely romance and "love" is purely love. (I join those who doubt that we shall find any.)

Every comedian since at least the fifth century B.C. notes that love and erotic excitement are rarely well-mated. Repeating this wisdom, let me review the Sambia situation. (For details, see Herdt [1981] and Stoller and Herdt [1982, 1985].) Therewith, we can pick up on a few elements in the structure of love that also, in a different way, are essential for erotic excitement. In doing so, I shall point to aspects of gender identity that mix with romance, love, and erotic excitement.

You will see that, to repeat, beneath the surface expressions of culture lie the same dynamics that energize our western convictions. We return to the Sambia. (As you study this, recall Jason's dream and Fay's reactions to him.)

Females are the natural sex, whether humans or other fauna, and the most at home in nature. Therefore, nothing need be done in nature or culture to bring about their maturation, reproductive capacity, or feminine psychology. Their fundament is the *tingu*, the blood organ at the center of their biology and psychology. Its presence directs the development of what our world calls "female sexuality": anatomy, biology, reproduction, erotic desire, femininity. Sambia believe, therefore, that culture need not provide a method to bring forth female sexuality; it creates itself naturally, inevitably.

On the other hand, "male sexuality" is uncertain, in its development, its outcome, its stability. The problem is there from the start: males also have a *tingu*, that core female organ. (It is, however, infertile.) As with females, it is inherited from mother. Conception, for the Sambia, is a cumulative process, not a big bang: the couple must have intercourse many times to build up enough semen for a fetus. That semen produces the biology and psychology of a man's maleness and masculinity. The ineffable quality of admirable masculinity is *jerungdu*, an untranslatable word that means prowess, strength, courage, forcefulness. (As with other great explanatory systems, such as religions, this story has loose ends, such as why the so-male semen will, in the female, produce muscle and bone as it does in males, but also in time milk.)

Yet men do not *create* semen. As different from women, who create blood, men only *store* semen (in an organ, the *keriku-keriku*). Semen, unlike blood, is not physiologically replenished. (See below.)

So, every male begins life with a natural, permanent, essential defect. He has the organ of female sexuality inherited from his mother: the *tingu*. To mitigate its effects requires unending vigilance, rituals, and practices secret and public. Example: the copious spitting men do on saying the words for female genitals. Example: after intercourse, a man will go into the forest, find an appropriate tree, such as the aerial root of a pandanus, and suck the white, sticky sap that flows when the root is cut. Example: also after intercourse, a man will secretly lacerate his nares with razor-sharp grasses to release blood, the inescapable femaleness that threatens *jerungdu*.

The main techniques, however, for creating the masculinity and maleness that could otherwise not develop are the initiations boys must undergo. (If they refused, they would be killed.) In the first-stage initiation, the boys are terrorized physically and emotionally to introduce them to what they will face as warriors and hunters. They are also taught that females, especially their menses, are polluting. But *any* intimacy with women, not just touching their blood or speaking their sex, puts you at risk for weakness, unmanliness, disease, and death. Even food cooked by a female is dangerous, the more so the more closely she is related. (Freud [1918]: "Wherever primitive man has set up a taboo he fears some danger and it cannot be disputed that a generalized dread of women is expressed in all these rules of avoidance. Perhaps this dread is based on the fact that woman is different from man, for ever incomprehensible and mysterious, strange and therefore apparently hostile. The man is afraid of being weakned [sic] by the woman, infected with her femininity and of then showing himself incapable" [pp. 198–199]. Freud says this is castration anxiety; I think the castration is more primal: amputation of *identity*.)

But the ultimate teaching of the first-stage initiation is that there can be no true maleness and no *jerungdu* unless boys ingest (the equivalent of what we call "androgen"): semen. Since they cannot manufacture it, they must drink semen—as often and as much as possible—or there will be no puberty, no adolescence, no ability to father children, no full adult maleness. So, at the deepest and most mysterious moment of the initiation, the boys are told that they must perform fellatio on the bachelors, the young men who have reached puberty. Then, for several years, the boys are to regularly drink semen and at the same time remain isolated from females, the more tabooed the more closely related (no easy task, considering the denseness of living in a mountainous, rain-forest-enclosed, primitive village). The men harangue the boys, during the weeks of this initiation, with the dangers of women's bodies and desires, erotic and otherwise.

Why the high excitement/danger/emergency atmosphere that attends almost every moment of the initiation? Because: *It is Almost Too Late*. The boys, the men say, have been living too intimately, too exclusively, too long with females in these first years of life, the men being less present, what with hunting and warrior responsibilities and spending so much time in the men's house away from the women and the care of children. Contact with women puts males—men and boys—at risk for being feminine, not masculine. (Imano exemplifies the consequences of succumbing to what is remembered down the millenia as the Sirens' Song.)

Recall our late-twentieth century, western-scientific theory of gender identity, identical in essence with the Sambia explanation: femaleness is the nature state in all animals, including humans. For full maleness and masculinity to occur, a male substance—androgens—must be added.

As I compare the Sambia beliefs and rituals on masculinity and femininity to revisionist psychoanalytic positions such as mine, it is as if the Sambia had read the new texts, which go, in brief, like this. The first stage in gender identity development for both sexes is one in which the infant only gradually separates from mother. She is, in this description, scarcely distinguished as a separate person, at first hardly at all and only later (and never completely) more fully. This means, then, that the first stage is not one in which mother is treated as a separate object—heterosexual in boys and homosexual in girls—but rather mostly as a part of oneself ("identification"). Freud's position is the opposite: the natural state biologically and psychologically is maleness.

In the Sambia and in the newer psychoanalytic version, not only do we need androgens for biologic maleness, but a radical intrapsychic and interpersonal ("social") effort must be made to overcome the effects of the female within the boy (the *tingu* in the Sambia and the "identification" in us). "Symbiosis anxiety" and "merging anxiety" are the (awkward) terms I use for the compelling affect/fantasy system that energizes this shift from being at one with mother to being two people and consider it an aspect of Mahler's "separation-individuation."

In working out this challenge to separate, I believe that girls must succeed both in the face of and with the help of the fact that they belong to the same class—female—as their mothers. Boys, however, have a radically different problem in regard to gender identity: they must create/discover themselves—outside "identification"—as a different sex. In order to succeed, males must, as the Sambia also discovered, erect an internalized, automatized, desired barrier against the primordial draw back to the frustration-less Garden. We know what the Sambia men know: if that process of gender separation is impeded by a mother who tries to sustain for years a merged relationship with her son, extreme femininity results (Stoller, 1968, 1975a, 1985b).[3]

Sambia men respond to their sense that mothers and sons have been too much merged. They recognize it is late in the game and stage a massive separation ritual—first stage initiation—with equally massive indoctrination. (Except in degree, in doing so they do as do other cultures/religions.) They thereby provide the next generation with the symbiosis barrier—beware the mortal danger of intimacy with women—needed for the culture to survive its brutal physical (nonhuman and human) circumstances. It is easy—we need no scholarly demonstration here—to see how, throughout history and in all cultures, masculinity has been shaped by the same dynamics with the same resultant deformations. Recall Fay's lament and Jason's dream for one more account of the consequences of this process (figs. 1–3).

[3]You may not like this theory because it calls more on merging than you can grant occurs in infants (Stern, 1985). Even so, you can probably see that most—all?—cultures demand, as do the Sambia and ours, that masculinity, in males, have a macho, anti-female, anti-feminine, fetishizing, forceful vigilance. Though girls must also, to separate, resist the impulse to return to mother and must also appreciate separateness, they are less likely to be humiliated for that "weakness" and need not invent a gender identity alien from mother's: they are—say the cultures—charming, delightful, lovely, soft, sweet, i.e., admirable and acceptable, when they cuddle well. The same in a boy is bad.

FIGURE 1. Mother-son symbiosis. (Photograph by Stoller.)

FIGURE 2. Precipitous separation/individuation: a boy, early in the initiation process, is blocked by his mentor from seeing or experiencing females. From now until years later, females will be taboo. (Photograph by Herdt.)

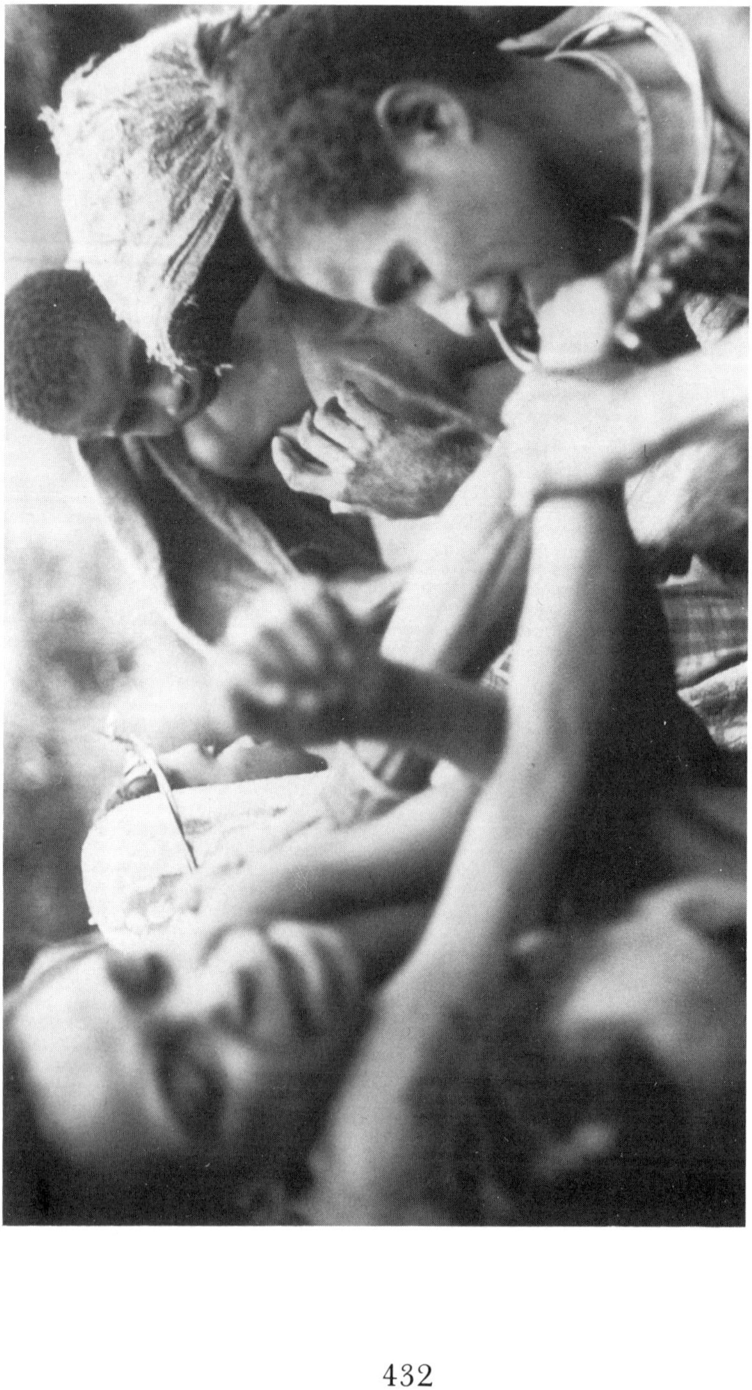

FIGURE 3. Precipitous separation/individuation: at this moment, the boys are being torn forever more from their frantic mothers' grasp. (Photograph by Herdt.)

Discussion

Let us return to romance, love, erotic excitement, and the common knowledge of the erotic incompatibility between men and women and the incompatibility, in males more than females, between erotic excitement and love. The two misfortunes are connected. (To keep this discussion from being endless, let us restrict our view to heterosexuality.) Their psychodynamic linkage becomes visible in daydreams, which take most tangible form in pornography.

Pornography, being purchased in the billions of pieces a year, provides a substantial sample, in the statistical sense, on which to base conclusions. Despite overlapping tastes between heterosexual men and women, it is no secret that most women prefer scripts that include tenderness, intimacy, caring, and mutuality. So much is this so that it is not generally recognized that women buy, for their "erotica"[4]—again, in uncounted numbers—tales of love and romance in books, movies, TV, the theater, opera, and popular songs. On the other hand, we know, in their tastes in pornography, men prefer fetishes; that is, dehumanized objects; that is, creatures that are not only anatomically exaggerated but psychically empty.

A woman's aphrodisiac is a man's soporific, marking differences in erotism so great that you would think human reproduction was invented by a madman. The classic American myth—the cowboy story—contains the same elements, wherein the warm, loving, would-be-enfolding schoolmarm (or whore-with-a-heart-of-gold) tries to get the stiff, guntoting, tall-in-the-saddle, laconic, isolate cowboy to warm up to love and, transformed, settle down to being a faithful husband, farmer, law-abiding sheriff, or other form of castrate.

What goes on? The experience emphasized herein[5] is the

[4]Radical feminist politics decrees that this material is not pornography.

[5]In this discussion, I leave out what some of us, from Freud on, consider a necessary but not yet well-measured cause of male-female erotic differences: biologic factors, especially processes run by sex hormones.

merging state from which infants must escape, boys in a different way from girls. And this must be accomplished in the first years of life so that the later separating and individuating of oedipal resolution can proceed. That done, boys can come to a later and safer version of closeness to females. (Whatever problems girls have in freeing themselves from mother, they do not need a gender-type barrier to let them know they are separate from their mothers.) That the exact forms expressed by the barrier to symbiosis—the exact forms of masculinity and of relating to women—depend on the exact nature of the course of preoedipal and oedipal development is discussion beyond the function of this essay. That the fear of intimacy with women helps explain why perversions are infrequently found in women (Stoller, 1975b) is another aspect of the struggle against merging that cannot be considered here.

Conclusions

With this revision, we turn the first part of Freud's theory of sexuality on its head. Biology does not favor maleness: a mammal will look and act pretty much female, regardless of chromosomes, unless androgens are added. (Androgen insensitivity syndrome is the paradigm [reviewed in Money and Erhardt, 1972].) And, in the nonbiologic aspects of gender identity, masculinity—the Sambia and our pornographers know—does not result unless a special "structure"—the barrier to merging—is created. The rest of "sexual" development may, more or less, follow Freud's description, for instance, that the boy's first object choice is heterosexual while the girl's is homosexual; or that the girl must, to be heterosexual, turn to her father. But since "sexual" development starts before the infant is fully individuated, then all that follows in our theory takes on a different cast.

The business of merging in infancy is in the later motions of romance or of love, where, I think, it is relived. Romance is merging, temporary. Love is merging, more extensive. Erotic excitement draws one toward merging, short-acting. The new (postoedipal) versions appear as fantasies, promises that this time it will work. Lovers stare deeply into each other's eyes—an act of trust, intimacy, and merging that has more hope and more risk in it than even the merging of their genitals. Except in types such as those who know the art of swooning (controlled, dramatized merging), people with sufficient ego boundaries easily recover back to separateness.

That merging recaptures the bliss of infancy relates it to the form of fetishizing we call "idealization." The problem with idealizing, in addition to it not being the truth, is that it must be sustained with unbroken vigilance, lest the negative side, with its angers, pop the bubble.

Men have, then, quite a problem: to be loving, romantic, and accepting of women's bodies and souls is to let oneself be vulnerable, not one of the qualities for which masculinity is praised by most men and the cultures they try to command. No wonder love and romance so easily inhibit erotic potency. (1) They threaten one with full intimacy; (2) with idealization—fetish-making—they excuse one from intimacy (e.g., "She's too pure for me to do *that* to her").

This explanation, I think, better fits the observed facts than does Freud's, with its wistful bigotry about women "having little sense of justice . . . no doubt related to the predominance of envy in their mental life" or their being "weaker in their social interests and as having less capacity for sublimating their instincts than men" (Freud, 1932, p. 134). (His beliefs may be manifestations of the above dynamics in action.) *Tingu* fear, the delicious Mystery men proclaim: how can these weak, sentimental, instinct-ridden creatures be so dangerous?

I have discussed elsewhere how hostility and anxiety (hostility is a primary defense against anxiety) energize erotic excitement (Stoller, 1975b, 1985a). The same exercise could be performed on romance and love: you have hostility—the desire to harm—buried in even their purest expressions. (Reik said it decades ago [1944].) Daydreams and pornography confirm the obvious.

Without good mothering and good fathering, from infancy on, that would take into account these dynamics, it will not be easy, by political, legal, economic, religious, treatment, or even ethical means, to correct the baleful consequences of these gender issues.

And hardly a nod here to joy, fun, reparation, gratitude, quietude, laughter, curiosity engaged and satisfied, tenderness, care, commitment, good humor, rest, safety: then home, to sleep.

S: Why are you shaking?
F: I don't know. Love, love.
S: Hooray for love.

REFERENCES

FREUD, S. (1912). On the universal tendency to debasement in the sphere of love. *S.E.*, 11.
——— (1915). The unconscious. *S.E.*, 14.
——— (1918). The taboo of virginity. *S.E.*, 11.
——— (1932). Femininity. *S.E.*, 22.
HERDT, G. H. (1981). *Guardians of the Flutes*. New York: McGraw-Hill.
——— & STOLLER, R. J. (1990). *Intimate Communications*. New York: Columbia Univ. Press.
KERNBERG, O. F. (1974a). Barriers to falling and remaining in love. *J. Amer. Psychoanal. Assn.*, 22:486–511.
——— (1974b). Mature love: Prerequisites and characteristics. *J. Amer. Psychoanal. Assn.*, 22:743–768.
——— (1977). Boundaries and structures in love relations. *J. Amer. Psychoanal. Assn.*, 25:81–114.
——— (in press). Perversity and love in the relationship of the couple. In *The Perverse and Near-Perverse in Everyday Life: New Psychoanalytic Perspectives*, ed. G. I. Fogel & W. A. Meyers. New Haven: Yale Univ. Press.
MONEY, J. & ERHARDT, A. A. (1972). *Man & Woman Boy & Girl*. Baltimore: Johns Hopkins Univ. Press.
PERSON, E. S. (1988). *Dreams of Love and Fateful Encounters*. New York: Norton.
REIK, T. (1944). *A Psychologist Looks at Love*. New York: Farrar & Rinehart.
——— (1945). *Psychology of Sex Relations*. New York: Rinehart.
STERN, D. N. (1985). *The Interpersonal World of the Infant*. New York: Basic Books.

STOLLER, R. J. (1968). *Sex and Gender*. New York: Science House.
——— (1975a). *Sex and Gender*, Vol. 2. London: Hogarth Press.
——— (1975b). *Perversion*. New Haven: Yale Univ. Press.
——— (1985a). *Observing the Erotic Imagination*. New Haven: Yale Univ. Press.
——— (1985b). *Presentations of Gender*. New Haven: Yale Univ. Press.
——— & HERDT, G. H. (1982). The development of masculinity: A cross-cultural contribution. *J. Amer. Psychoanal. Assn.*, 30:29–59.
——— ——— (1985). Theories of origins of male homosexuality. *Arch. Gen. Psychiat.*, 42:399–404.

UCLA School of Medicine
760 Westwood Plaza
Los Angeles, CA 90024

A PSYCHOANALYTIC ESSAY ON ROMANTIC, EROTIC LOVE

JOHN MUNDER ROSS, PH.D.

I have attempted to conceptualize passionate love from a psychoanalytic perspective. Having noted psychoanlysis' long-standing reluctance to confront adult love, I have turned to the love poetry of different cultures and the more modern philosophers of love for more detailed descriptions of its phenomenology. With these depictions in mind, such love can be defined as a complex and somewhat conflictual affective disposition, rather like a mood, evoked by the image of another person and characterized by periods of passionate excitement and intimate repose.

A variety of both pleasurable and unpleasurable affects are entertained in romantic love, which derive from its both sensory and illusory wellsprings, from the opportunities it affords for sensual satisfaction and spiritual overreaching. These affects are activated in response to states of desire and satiety and as modes of communication with and knowledge of the other. They are accompanied and facilitated by the capacity for genital primacy and cognitive components in love—specifically the lover's capacity to express himself or herself in genital orgasm and then to create and dwell in metaphors about the lovers' sexual encounters. Whatever its infantile precursors and however regressive it can be at times, love emerges perforce as a late adolescent or young adult phenomenon. At this juncture, the prepotency of romantic love moves the individual to disengage from the injunctions and desexualized idealizations of his parental images and to reorganize the superego constructs based on these—to create his or her own ethic. Thus, while there may be other routes to maturity, embracing the feeling of being in love helps a person grow up.

MY OBJECTIVE IS to define romantic and erotic love from a psychoanalytic perspective. Since this issue is on affects, my emphasis will be primarily on the affective components in passionate love and only secondarily on the drive derivatives,

Clinical Associate Professor of Psychology in Psychiatry at Cornell Medical College, and Faculty of the Psychoanalytic Institute at New York University Medical Center.

dynamics, genetic antecedents, cognitive factors, structural and developmental prerequisites of the experience. I will draw from philosophers of love such as Augustine, de Chardin, Stendhal, Paz, Barthes, Gasset, Auden, and others as well as love poets from a variety of cultures and eras to fill a remarkable void in clinical psychoanalysis: a careful examination of the phenomenology of passion. In a word, paraphrasing Cherubino in *The Marriage of Figaro,* I will first ask "What does love *feel* like?[1]

A Clinical Case in Point

Perhaps it is the fact that our analytic patients seek us out because of inhibitions in love and work, but rarely does the psychoanalyst have the opportunity to observe romantic love in full flower. So I count myself lucky indeed to have received the narrative of Dr. A., an analyst from Los Angeles, about a 28-year-old investment banker, Mr. V., and how he fell "hopelessly in love." Dr. A. had spoken with me at length about my interest in male psychology and the conflicts inherent in heterosexual love and agreed to take careful notes on the unfolding of his patient's love affair.

Having first sought help to deal with compulsions, affective inhibitions, mild perverse trends, self-sabotage, and a general malaise, Mr. V. had been in analysis with Dr. A. for 2½ years when he met Rachel at a firm picnic. He had had several lovers since his college years, but never had this young man been "so taken by a woman."

He found Rachel's touch at once electrifying and calming. And when they had intercourse, after a premature ejaculation on his very first attempt, Mr. V. described her vagina in a

[1]In this paper, I shall not adhere to the medieval proscription that romantic love remain unrequited, having as its object an idealized beloved. Instead I will follow the more modern conceit whereby romance can survive and indeed be enhanced by its consummation. Thus the terms "romantic love," "erotic love," and "passionate love" will be used more or less interchangeably.

variety of oxymorons. It was like "living velvet ivory," and he "slipped into its possessive warmth," he said, as if he had always belonged there. Sexual union and orgasm were rivaled only by the hour or so of postcoital bliss during which these lovers revealed to each other their innermost "secrets." Between meetings, his longing for Rachel was delicious and unbearable, and Mr. V. found himself frozen at street corners or doors to meeting rooms, fixed on her image, mournful and triumphant at once. Perhaps, the young man reflected, analysis, in shredding outmoded defenses, had primed him to fall in love. He had been ready.

Nonetheless, despite these heights of ecstasy and periods of suspended repose, as the love affair progressed into its sixth month, this inconsistently passionate man found himself, as if inexplicably, avoiding the pleasures of intercourse with his girlfriend. They were living together most of the time now, but a barrier seemed to have inserted itself between the two, like the sword dividing Tristan from his Isolde (see Loewald, 1951).

A dream then brought to light one level of Mr. V.'s dreaded desires. In it, he dove with other children into a "great gulf." He emerged as if uncertain of his body—of what lay beneath the neck—and found himself crossing his old school's soccer field (pun intended, he indicated in his associations), but making his way not to the boys' but rather to the girls' changing or locker room (again, the puns). In his associations he talked of the eerie feeling he had come to notice after penetration. When he let himself "really go," sensing with his body and not seeing in his mind's eye, he felt wedded to his love. It was, he said, as if their pubic hair and bones were enmeshed and squashed together. Rachel's breasts seemed to seep into his own chest, to penetrate *him* yet to become his own possession. Upon climaxing, he found himself in an altered state, "weirdly" longing to take in her moistened vagina with his penis yet fighting off unnamed fears and becoming even physically chilled and anxious. Finally, as he associated to the act of intercourse, Mr. V. remarked on his long-standing inability to weep, to his surprise equating the watering of his eyes with the lubrication of a woman's genitals. The dream further reminded him of a memory involving water and potential drowning to which I will refer shortly.

Mr. V. now understood that he wanted to be as beautiful and bountiful as his lover. He yearned to incorporate her. He wished to be a woman. Contemplating the illusion of their interpenetration in the safety of analytic reflection with a male analyst, he wondered whether he would reemerge from Rachel as a man—ambitious and powerful and, one day, rich.

Perhaps his analyst "knew" women, in much the same way as Mr. V. did. Had not the self-revealing hero of Janet Malcolm's *Psychoanalysis: The Impossible Profession* (1981), the workmanlike amalgam portrayed by her as the "typical" psychoanalyst, had not "Dr. Aaron Green" confessed the source of his failure to speak or write more? To do so, he lamented, would be symbolically to fulfill a treasured but shameful wish—to parade himself as a "beautiful woman," and this before the gaze of others, analysts, who presumably "saw into people's souls."

Not only his sex but his self seemed somehow at stake. Even as Mr. V. now played with exchanging sexual identities with Rachel, he resisted what he felt to be simply her smothering envelopment of him. Sunday mornings, with the rare respite they provided, ironically proved the most disquieting. As Rachel lay bathed in her bed, having encircled herself and Mr. V., it seemed to him, with all her things—clothes, papers, magazines, cats, Sunday food and drink—he felt a fuzziness closing in. He was compelled to drag himself away, preferring the weights at the local health club or some last minute job from the office to the unbounded lovemaking which such leisurely interludes afforded and which, during frenetically scheduled weeks, he otherwise craved. There was some ineffable danger, V. sensed, as if invited into Rachel's welcoming arms, he might never escape intact and get about his business. He needed to resist her hold and "define" himself.

With uncertainty about his sexual identity and fears of engulfment, Mr. V. again "lost" himself in Rachel. However, he now began to complain bitterly of the demands made on his time by his junior position in a pressured profession. Whereas in the past, Mr. V. had tried obsessively to comply with the tasks set him, now he found himself becoming dangerously oblivious to them. He grew more casual about his hours and efforts during them, and his bosses, demanding a filial devotion to making money, were increasingly stung by his ill-concealed diffidence. The patient had asked for it, and eventually, rather regretfully, they suggested that he seek a position elsewhere.

In part, further analysis revealed, Mr. V.'s failure at work bespoke a typical acting out of oedipal guilt. He dared not try to have it all—professional success along with a loving woman—because of the murderous aggression toward and identification with his father which these conquests implied and the castration they invited as a retaliation. And so he had unconsciously worked to undermine at least one of his triumphs.

Mr. V.'s father hunger—with its *preoedipal* roots and resonances throughout development—had also moved him to place obstacles in love's path. Acting out, Mr. V. sought the very punishment he feared and ironically, he noted, the further illusion of security, the felt structure, which its "hard" presence afforded him. At 3 years, he recalled, left with his maiden aunt in Florida for several months while his father established a new residence, taking the patient's mother away with him, Mr. V. had fallen into a pool and nearly drowned. As he associated to it, the incident yielded a screen memory for the pitfalls of erotic entanglements in the absence of sustaining father love and reliable inner authority.

His seductive mother and her sister had suffused Mr. V.

with a sense of unending entitlement, so that he felt constantly at risk with women. And in an unusual way: He was fearful of deluding himself into thinking that he was indeed "his majesty the baby," an infant afloat in the "oceans of boundless love," tiny in being so important, potentially lost in being cherished. He needed to feel the restraining anchor of an authoritarian, external male presence, one like that of his tyrannical but remote father in reality, if he were to be self-assured enough to let himself go with a woman. Otherwise, he was afraid to feel love. Thus in a subsequent elaboration of the memory, Mr. V. found himself wondering whether he had been pushed into the pool by an older boy and rescued by his uncle (the mother's other sibling) who then punished the perpetrator.

In so many words, then, he required the safe moorings offered by what Schafer (1960) has called the "loving and beloved superego" in order to venture forth into the "seas" he yearned to explore.

The next challenge came when Mr. V. secured himself an even better job, and Rachel continued to love him. After a brief flurry, once again they made love infrequently now—"maybe weekly," he said pointedly, like "an old married couple." Instead of acting out in work, his actions serving to discharge and obscure his inner tensions, Mr. V. brought his conflict closer to home. He now enlivened his love life by manufacturing dramas in the manifest transference, aimed at provoking his analyst (a man in his 50s) to take him to task. Rachel and this "stern" older male, who tore him from her bed in the early morning hours which he had long ago requested or who deprived her by taking the money the couple needed for their revels, became rivals for his heart—a heart now in full-fledged oedipal conflict, positive and negative. Mr. V.'s loyalty to Rachel seemed to vie with his duty to Dr. A. and his longing to depend forever on his forbearance and beneficence. Like Tristan with King Mark, Mr. V. kept creeping back to pay his reluctant homage and, often belatedly, his bill—money he felt he also owed to his woman. Ironically, the conflict heightened his love; Mr. V. found that his passion for Rachel grew even as he felt more morally and lovingly bound to his analyst.

Still neither genetic reference point—oedipal or preoedipal—could account for the sense of ultimate peril and the moral drama injected again and again by Mr. V. into his passion, as if to keep the flame alive. Something in the way of an age-specific agenda, a young adult life crisis, seemed to be at work.

Psychoanalytic Contributions

Psychoanalysis was designed by Freud to be a psychology of love. Yet it has had more to say about the childish precursors of what has been called mature "genitality" than about Eros in adult life. Not all sexuality is infantile sexuality after all, yet our analytic literature almost makes it seem so.

Rarely describing in detail our adult patients' current erotic experiences, we have pretty much taken heterosexuality, and the conflicts and passions associated with it, for granted. Instead, clinical analysts and theoreticians have dwelled on the pathways toward its achievement and on the fixations surviving into biological adulthood as perversions, inversions, and symptoms compromising its full expression.

We have avoided identifying or conceptualizing what it is that is sexy about sex. Either passionate love is confounded with the marriage bond and the long-standing affection of the couple. Or else it is viewed skeptically as an immature and maladaptive variant of the "real [adult] thing." How ironic these oversights are, since romantic bliss and erotic consummation are what our adult patients often consciously crave and what we as practitioners must try to help them attain.

Responding to this void, several psychoanalysts have written books on love in the last few years (Benjamin, 1988; Bergmann, 1987; Kakar and Ross, 1987; Kernberg, in preparation; Person, 1988). Omitted from the 1968 edition, "love" has at last been inserted into the revised glossary of *Psychoanalytic Terms and Concepts* (1990), with its passionate and sexual form described as a special subset of the larger case. Still, psychoanalysts have repeatedly betrayed their faintheartedness in approaching a subject arguably at the very heart of their inquiry.

Whatever the lackluster denouement to their relationship as husband and wife, Sigmund Freud's voluminous letters to his fiancée Martha figure among the most poignant exemplars of passionate feeling in the Western world. Nonetheless, Freud's later and more official pronouncements on love tell a different story in different terms.

In what was to become an established canon, Freud came to search out the infantile prototypes of adult passions (see also Arlow, 1980). All passionate feeling was tied to sexuality, first of all—to the evolving sequence of bodily zones and modes through which libido expressed itself—and secondly, to the persons or objects who had first gratified its various modes of expression. The loves of the adult man or woman were viewed basically as transfigurations—more or less inhibited by later moral and realistic constraints—of these primal instinctual encounters. Thus, all love might ultimately be reduced to a sort of transference love (Freud, 1915b; Bergmann, 1987), parental images in whole or part imposing themselves on and rediscovered in the present.

Freud saw in love certain "economic problems." In "The Three Essays on Sexuality" (1950b) he hypothesized the bifurcation of libido into two currents—the sensual (*Sinnlichkeit*) and affectionate (*Zärtlichkeit*) and emphasized the tension generated by their coexistence and inevitable opposition. It was only with adolescence that the two diverging trends could be reconciled (1921). From early on the child struggled to safeguard *his* guardians from feeling the full brunt of his intense and imperious desires for them. This made for persistent fixations on the primitive pleasures and persons of the past and for inevitable frustrations and intrapsychic tension and prohibition, the nature of which was clarified with the structural model (1923).

Incestuous in origin, "forced upon us by nature" but "repugnant to morality" (Freud, 1900), the child's amorous wishes were inherently fraught with dynamic conflict. Freud's case histories (1905a, 1909a, 1909b, 1918) are all of them infantile love stories, therefore inevitably tales of unrequited love. Engendering guilt and frustration, more often than not repressed, giving rise to anxiety, inhibitions, and symptoms—the loves which Freud describes are thus quintessentially neurotic. There are no heights of ecstasy here, no deep fulfillment, no reaching beyond the moment for the ineffable and unattainable.

In fact, moving as these woebegone accounts are, Freud seems merely to assume the existence of the sort of love in which a measure of libidinal gratification is possible and never makes its experiential qualities and, through the analysis of these, its determinants explicit. In other words, passionate, erotic, romantic love can only be inferred in Freud's writings from its negatives (see also Balint, 1948).

Freud was no stranger to passion, of course, and some of what he had to say about love echoes its more poetic interpreters. For example, stressing its origins in self-love, Freud noted that object love in adolescence and adulthood tended to deplete or otherwise weaken the self, touching on themes evident in twelfth-century poems on the subject (Freud,1914b). In pondering the development of a capacity for passion in late adolescence, Freud (1921) alluded to the exaltations and sublimation of feeling described by the Romantic poets: "The depth to which anyone is in love, as contrasted with his purely sensual desire, may be measured by the size of the share taken by the aim-inhibited instincts of affection" (p. 112). Yet Freud himself did not elucidate the specifics of love's phenomenology.

From the very start, analysts have focused mostly on the content of the love relationship—the dynamics, the unconscious fantasies involved, the points of fixation, the infantile objects—rather than the form and quality of romantic feeling. Ironically enough, they have left *affect* out of their understanding of love. Unlike their approach to symptoms, when it comes to love, analysts have not proceeded "from the surface."

In addition to its genetic and dynamic determinants and, to a lesser degree, its economics and structure, early theorists also attempted to explain love in terms of its teleology. Following Freud's lead in "The Three Essays," Ferenczi (1924), Reich (1927, 1929), and especially Abraham (1925) constructed a theory of genitality, the attainment of which came to be seen as the sine qua non of mature sexual and overall ego functioning (cf. N. Ross, 1970). Ferenczi came closest to real life when he described what he called an amphimixis, a coalescing of pregenital aims in sexual union, all these component instincts being subsumed under the primacy of genital pleasure and penetration. This, in its turn, subserved the reproductive aim of the individual and the preservation of the species (see Freud, 1905b). With his interest in both epigenesis and character, Abraham posited the genital type as the highest of characterological levels in his hierarchy—an ideal type omitted by Freud in his own personality classification.

Once more, particularly in the heyday of id psychology, the focus was on libidinal impulses rather than feelings—albeit this time on the functions of sexual love. More important, again the experience of sensual love eluded careful observation. Eroticism was confounded with the overarching purposes served by sex—integration of the drive organization as far as the individual was concerned and survival for the species. Making love came to mean making a family, as it had a millenium earlier in the Western world, that is, before the aesthetic "invention" of romance.

A number of later contributors questioned the invariable link between genital gratification and the bond of love. Balint (1948, 1956), for example, saw the attainment of a sort of genital identification and consequent "equanimity" as a prerequisite for mature love. However, he then proceeded to the ironic conclusion that for such an ideal individual passion might very well become an unnecessary hindrance. Rather than tame and adaptive, genital love potentially imperiled an individual's well-being with the haunting threat of regression, a return to a state of primitive and illusory union wherein reality testing was simply swept away. We have learned love—Balint implied in Bergmann's reading (1987)—and should also learn to live without it!

In a similar vein, Binstock (1973) stressed the crossing over of gender boundaries in heterosexual encounters but went on to warn of the perils posed by the lovers' longings for and illusions of Liebestod, the love death, with its dependent and bisexual ramifications. Lovers, he suggested, reach their highest plateau when they can contemplate life without the other and give up more concrete expressions of their bisexual and symbiotic yearnings. Nathaniel Ross (1970) called into question the facile equation of orgasmic capacity and psychosocial maturity. He pointed to the fact that borderline and psychotic patients often reveal a great capacity for genital pleasure while higher functioning neurotics, who are capable of devotion to people and of consequent forbearance, might tend toward sexual inhibition. Eissler (1963) and Bak (1973) also took a less than sunny view of sexual love, likening its longings to those in mourning and melancholia and the ultimately unattainable object of such yearnings to the refound but lost love objects of the infantile past.

Thus, while they proved closer to the poets in emphasizing just how unruly and dangerous are the passions of lovers, the rationalism of these later theorists, wending its way back to to psychoanalysis' roots in the pre-Romantic Enlightenment, moved them to pull back. They, too, withdrew from immersing themselves in a scrutiny of their subject. Such love, they continued, can be deceptive and disruptive. Some even seemed to verge on the Sophoclean ideal articulated in Plato's *Republic*—a life free from Aphrodite's savage enslavement.

In recent years, analysts have returned to the Romantic, and romantic, view of love. In the spirit of Wordsworth's "The Prelude," Altman (1977), Bergmann (1971, 1980, 1986), van der Waals (1965), Grunberger (1971), Chasseguet-Smirgel (1983), Kernberg (1974, 1977), Person (1988), and Kakar and Ross (1987) have all granted a legitimate place to the "spontaneous overflow of powerful feelings" which occurs in love as in poetic inspiration. Several of these authors have looked somewhat more carefully at what real and fictional lovers have had to say about what they feel.

Beginning with Bergmann in 1971, analysts have stressed the interpenetration of self and other in passionate love. With this meeting there also emerges an interplay of idealization and identification. Thus, falling in love makes for an expansion, rather than depletion, of the sense of self and for an awareness of the complex nature of the beloved.

The crossing of boundaries in mature love harkens back to the "dual unity" of mother and child described by Mahler et al. (1975). However, it also involves much more than a revival of this symbiosis. What is called forth in love is not a primitive fusion, effacing self and object representations alike, but rather a union of two more defined and sexually differentiated persons (see Kakar and Ross, 1987). So love's crossing over is also a transcendence of the limits of gender, reminiscent of Plato's androgynes, a completion of an inevitably incomplete self made possible, ironically, by the essential or bedrock integrity of that self (as Binstock had suggested). When this is missing, according to Kernberg (1977), the lover is either fled from altogether or is confounded with an aspect of the self, becoming its narcissistic extension in a variation on what Stendahl (1842) dubbed "vanity love."

"Mature" romantic love, in Kernberg's analysis, also requires transgression, a symbolic sally, at least, across generational barriers into the forbidden domain of sensuality, the arena of the primal scene. Therein the lover rediscovers and revels in the once hidden sexuality of the parents and that of the imaginative oedipal child she or he once was. Kernberg especially has seen in such sexual love, arising at the close of adolescence and ushering in young adulthood, though sometimes lost thereafter, certain genetic preconditions and emotional consequences. Freud to the contrary, each love affair, amounting to a forbidden encounter, may drain otherwise inexhaustible reservoirs of incest just a little. Symbolic violations of the taboo ease the conflict and expose the defenses it calls up for what they are. Like most analysts, however, even Kernberg also fails to spell out the uses of adult love for further development.

With the exception of Person's thematic book, Bergmann's exhaustive review of the literature, psychoanalytic and otherwise, and Kakar and Ross's exegesis of various *Tales of Love, Sex and Danger,* once again these authors have omitted to look at love itself. The poets' musings, their patients' voices, and the sort of descriptions of sex to be found even in books like the Kinsey survey (1948) or Hite (1976, 1981) reports on men and women, with all their methodological problems, are absent or muted in these generalized accounts and theories.

Why have analysts so persistently, perhaps phobically, avoided confronting the passions, at once sensual and spiritual, expressed in adult sex and love? Most of the speculations about this glaring omission center on Freud biography (see Bergmann, 1987). Following Bernfeld (1949), Eissler (1951), for example, traced Freud's reticence to the trauma that ensued upon his falling in love with Gisela Fluss when he was 16 years old. Bergmann has pointed out that Freud believed passionate love to be shortlived, because his own infatuation with Martha waned after their wedding.

In this vein, Harold Blum (personal communication) has refuted Swales's contention that Freud had an affair with his sister-in-law, Minna, while vacationing in Italy. According to Blum, Freud remained chaste and monogamous, making his way to Rome while she went to the sanitarium for reasons other than having an abortion, as Swales had inferred.

In fact, it was on this very trip that Freud first visited Michelangelo's Moses at San Pietro in Vincoli, Blum continues, beginning his lifelong fascination and evolving identification with the Hebrew patriarch. Likening the statue to one in a niche of the Catholic church in Moravia to which his seductive nursemaid took him as a young boy, Blum has remarked on the sensual currents in Freud's "flirtation" with Christianity.

Like Moses, I would add, Freud eventually repudiated the temptations of the Golden Calf, the Bacchanalian icons and sensuous metaphors of what was for him a more concrete, decadent, hedonistic religion—a regressive revival of the idol worship and pantheism repudiated by the Jews. Behind the Christianity which Freud repudiated lurked the illicit and unconsciouly incestuous sensuality proffered by the banished caretaker and seductress. Like Moses, Freud went it alone. He may have replaced the temptations of Aunt Minna's body with a more lofty mission and an idea, more or less "disembodied," so that he and psychoanalysis were thereafter lost to love—unsublimated love, that is, love on earth.

Still, why the enduring reluctance of analysts after him? In his preface to the famed article on this very statue (1914a), published pseudonymously, Freud offers more clues about the sources of his and his discipline's abiding uneasiness with passionate feeling. When it comes to a work of art, Freud tells us, he is incapable of deriving pleasure without first "understanding" it; and by such understanding, he means conscious reflection and conceptualization. In all matters of the heart, Freud seems to imply, casual explanation is to precede rather than follow from aesthetic experiencing, careful description, and an exegesis of "the text" in and of itself—"the thing" itself, in Wallace Stevens' words. Thus, music eludes Freud's ken and his interest—music, perhaps the elemental form of romantic expression, its muse envied repeatedly by poets doomed to sing love's praises in mere words.

Freud and we after him have been mistrustful of affect without ideation. Indeed, the essence of analytic technique as Freud first conceived it was to replace other modes of expression with "word presentations" and, in making the unconscious conscious, to subject the primary process to the sway of reason and discretion (1900). Later, with his structural model, he declared, "where id is, there shall ego be" (1923).

From the psychoanalytic vantage, as from that of the social order, the desire and longing for another person inevitably threatens the status quo, the institutions and lawfulness which regulate and contain interactions among people, and so ideologies of all stripes have been loath to give it free rein. And, while impelling some of its highest attainments, the emotions of love threaten the rule of mind, disturbing psychoanalysts as they have the majority of so many philosophers who have pondered it from Plato to the present.

Affect theory in general has found but a belated and tenuous footing amidst the instinctual drives and psychic structures of our model, and analysts have had to be guided by observations and theories outside their orbit. Similarly, with the elucidation of romantic love, analytic thinkers have had to begin by turning to pursuits other than their own.

Love Stories and Love Theories

The Mr. V.s of our clinical universe are also rather rare. For most people, in midlife certainly, neurotic and mundane entanglements have come to subdue feeling or abort romance before it can flower. Lovers themselves have little libido left over for transferences and rarely seek or stick out treatment. The conflicts evoked in the transference may also interfere with the individual's inability to fall in love outside the analytic situation once in it. And, in the countertransference, once again envy rears its ugly head. Muted, mostly middle-aged or older, undemonstrative by virtue of training and disposition, many analysts begrudge their patients their passions—especially the younger ones. Reflexively, and with a certain surreptitious narcissism, we tend to refer these back to the transference and our own person, as if giving true love the lie.

So most of the accounts of love that come the way of clinicians are retrospective or subject to dulling scrutiny and self-consciousness. Because of this paucity of data from practice, we analysts have been forced to turn to the Annas and Vronskys enduring in the literary imagination for more multifaceted and dynamic portraits of love's complexities. "Applied analysis" has been with us from the start. Without an *Oedipus Rex,* we may wonder, would there have been, ten years after he reflected on the play, an "oedipus complex" (Freud, 1900, 1910, 1985)?

In this spirit, I will cull from some of the great love stories and poetry of the Western, Sanskrit, and Perso-Islamic literatures (see Kakar and Ross, 1987). I will also refer to some of the more modern philosophers of love. Now and then, I will venture even farther back in time to the Greeks or the poetry of Virgil—to eras predating the conceptualization and elaboration of romantic love as a distinct form.

The aim in these excursions is to tease out certain repetitive *motives,* to distill some of the recurrent themes in love's phenomenology. There is a male bias in these generalizations, derived as they are from authors who are mostly men. Yet it is my conviction that much of what they have to say about feelings of love cuts across sex differences and individual variations. My focus is also on the emotions evoked in a heterosexual encounter, though, interestingly, several of the major contributors—Auden or Barthes, for instance—were acknowledged homosexuals.

When it comes to erotic love, as opposed to recreation, there is no such thing as "safe sex." Danger, the great love stories tell us, is an integral aspect of sexual love. Such passion is by nature perilous—"peril in [the lover's] eye," in the words of the poets, its bliss "tragic," and filled with "anguish most sharp." From the time romantic love was, as some say, "discovered" or at least catalogued as such by the poets around the twelfth century, love's celebrators have also told of its inevitable terrors. According to Shakespeare's 129th sonnet: "All this the world knows; yet none knows well / To shun this heaven that leads men to this hell."

The lover, according to poets as diverse as the twelfth-century Persian Nizami or the Jansenist Racine, finds himself in an "altered state," one of heightened sensibility and intense pleasure. Love is a sort of waking dream, according to John Donne. Much as Freud suggested in his narcissism paper (1914b), it has been seen as a sort of sublime madness, wresting the individual from the safety and self-satisfaction of his filial, social, and moral anchorage. In so doing, the feverish incorporation of the beloved's promised replenishment offers exhilaration and an immortality not unlike union with the Godhead. In the words of Teilhard de Chardin (1972), lovers seek "one another in the light and darkness of the soul; the pull is toward mutual sensibility and completion, in which preoccupation with preserving the species gradually dissolves in the greater intoxication of two people creating the world" (cf. Freud, 1905b; Abraham, 1925). Like addicts, such lovers dread the return to normal consciousness.

This is not to say that the lovers' state is one of unalloyed joy. Quite the contrary, such sensual and emotional excitement trenches all too quickly on pain—as Freud (1924) implied. (One analyst, William Evans [1953], went so far as to suggest that love stories merely provided a pretext for masochistic gratification.) Indeed, as Keats repeatedly rendered it, romantic love is fraught from the start with suffering. This is so because, while elevating the self through union with the other, love paradoxically threatens to infantilize, debase, and deplete this self because it has been rendered no longer whole in itself.

Especially in the absence of what has become one's "better half" (Tolstoy's *Anna Karenina*), the lover experiences an excruciating incompleteness. But even when reciprocated by an ideal lover, no love could truly be requited because of the intangibility and inaccessibility of the beloved's spirit, because his or her innermost thoughts and feelings remain essentially unknowable. An intrepid Cupid might at last snare his Psyche only to find that her soul—now indistinguishable from his own—eludes him after all. Kept from their heroines, soldiers and courtiers like Shakespeare's Antony and Romeo, Virgil's Aeneas, Beroul's Tristan, Nizami's Quays, and others, all become fools for love—abject, infantile, effeminate, entirely lost to themselves. Thus, more recently, Auden (1973) speaks of Tristan's and Isolde's urge to be one when they are doomed to add up to two, and Octavio Paz (Kernberg, 1977) of the penetrable body and impenetrable consciousness. Ultimately, the lover recognizes that "this state where there is no twoness in response to joy or sorrow" (Bhavabhuti) is but another instance of what the Hindus call *maya* —another mortal illusion. In our less fanciful terms, two persons have two personalities.

Nor, the courtiers of Aquitaine and others after them averred, could true love exist within the institution of marriage, whose sexuality indeed but subserved the teleology of reproduction. Tender, pleasant, but by its very nature inhibited, socialized and familiar lovemaking falls short of the mark. In contrast, free from constraining paternalistic sanctions and obligations, outside kinship and genealogical systems of deference, risky and uncertain, first love, an unrequited love or a treacherous, adulterous liaison paradoxically proved to be more full and *pure*. In these contexts, each moment of ecstasy (from ek-stasis, to be outside the self in the world) amounted to an orgasmic *little death*, as transport of pleasure foreshadowing the final love death, the Liebestod concluding most of the paradigmatic love stories of all cultures, but particularly our own Western one, according to Denis de Rougemont (1956). The stories of *Tristan and Isolde, Aida, Romeo and*

Juliet, and *Layla and Majnun* are filled with dread, haunted from the start by their tragic conclusion.

In love as in religion, the mystical union (*unio mystica*) does not come easily in a secular world, often demanding the ultimate sacrifice—martyrdom, the immolation of one self in the immortality of the two. Challenging the economic and feudal order (in derivatives of what we analysts infer to be the oedipal level) and yielding up his individuality (within the preoedipal dyad), the romantic lover of fiction is a revolutionary and a mystic who invites death in the act of passion.

Thus, two interwoven elements in love, as it has been fictionalized and conceptualized, have to do with inherent emotional violence—the lovers' defiance of the guardians of social order who erect barriers to its consummation and their willingness to risk all, to suicide in quest for union with the beloved. As one patient of mine put it, "Damn them all—the experience is so exquisite that it's worth the hurt and loss."

There are some—Sartre (1956), for instance, Reik (1944), or Stoller (1979)—who have accented the lovers' hateful, vindictive, embittered feelings and urges to avenge old hurts through domination on the lover's part. Sullerot (1979) sees even in a woman's shows of selfless enslavement her effort to control absolutely a man's emotions—his pleasure, his excitement, his expressions of his guilt. And hell, of course, has no fury like a woman scorned—to which the wrath of Dido, Phaedra, Medea, and other spurned lovers provides testimony. Certainly there are destructive aims in the imperious desires lovers feel for each other—in their urges to conquer and consume, to possess and devour. The affective corollaries of Freud's hypothetical *Sinnlichkeit* are undeniable, and love can, as Freud (1915a) himself suggested, turn quickly enough to hate, particularly when frustrated. With two sets of drives, moreover, libidinal and aggressive, both of whose derivatives find the same object, it is inevitable that a lover should want both to join and to destroy his or her lover. In the words of

Roland Barthes (1978), "I want to possess, fiercely, but I also know how to give, actively. . . . I see the other with double vision; sometimes as object, sometimes as subject; I hesitate between my tyranny and oblation. I am condemned to be a saint or a monster; unable to be one, unwilling to be the other."

Or to quote one patient, a woman who had recently broken up with her lover of one year: "I had a dream that I was going down on Billy. I love this, as you know—always did with men. I was sucking harder and harder, and Billy was going wild with pleasure. And then suddenly he was hurting, too, and asking me to stop." Asked what came to mind, Ms. P. replied, "Power." Indeed, in real life, it is this sort of ambivalence which most often brings romance to an untoward close.

Nonetheless, with exceptions here and there—Isolde poised with the young lover's sword above the beautiful Tristan in his bath—the stories of true love are remarkably devoid of frank acts of aggression on the lovers' part toward each other. In this, certain sex differences do come into play. Rather than abuse his lady, the male hero will flee instead, betraying her for other women and for "king and country." In contrast, a woman finds herself ingesting the man whose heart she has won or cursing him when he abandons her for another. But, for the most part, hostile feelings are banished from the dyad, whose preservation is safeguarded by the play of idealization and identification and the overriding sense of cherishing and perpetual *longing.* These processes and imperatives further secure the affectionate ties that keep desire from being self-serving.

Nor is romantic love all *Sturm und Drang.* The burning torments of unrequited or unconsummated love, the sharp stabs of jealous possession, and the high pitch of supreme joy—the *höchste Lust* of Wagner's Isolde—describe but one of its incarnations. However intense or multiple the lovers' orgasms may be, they occupy only moments in their relationship. Love is characterized as well by a near "religious" *intimacy*, by postcoital discourses of sentiment occurring upon "tolerant and enchanted slope(s)," where, Auden (1976, p. 131) tells us, "Grave the vision Venus sends / Of supernatural sympathy / Universal love and hope." In such contemplative and tender states of mind, the lover's sentiment toward the beloved is captured best in the words of Augustine as the feeling that "I want you to be."

Where the love is found to be hollow or unreal, of course, feelings of depression and disgust follow sexual union. And even where this love proves "true," sadness enters the picture in the form of the "postcoitum triste," expressing as it does the sense of loss in intercourse and a lover's inevitable ambivalence about having given himself (or herself) so utterly to another.

Alas, even when they succeed in escaping society's intrusions on their intimacy, the lovers themselves—especially the men—fear its *entrapment.* So they act to attenuate it. Thus, for instance, Tolstoy's Vronsky, Shakespeare's Antony, Beroul's Tristan, the God Krishna of Jayadeva's Sanskrit poetry, the paradigmatic sufi Majnun of Nizami's Persian epic, Virgil's Aeneas—all literature's warriors turned lovers—at one time or another try to escape the hold of their love's beauty. They do so variously and with varying degrees of success, calling upon martial duty or else lapsing into peccadilloes with other, lesser women in order essentially to reestablish their freedom, virility, and responsibility. Sometimes, too, love is felt to grow stale or the beloved's faults reviled, boredom and contempt for her being exaggerated and exploited to defend against the prepotency of desire and grip of longing.

Thus it is really Anna Karenina's mesmerizing and womanly beauty, not her flaws, her once cavalier lover, Vronsky, resents. The real danger lies for him, a man without a father, in the rupture of those tenuous filial and fraternal lifelines from woman and mother to masculine selfhood and professional advancement.

Where the fatherless Vronsky fails to "save himself from

love," incidentally, the scion and patriarch Aeneas succeeds in wresting himself from Dido's hold, revisiting his beloved father Anchises as a shade, honoring his own son, and pursuing his destiny as the founding father of Rome. It was only with Anchises' death that Aeneas was able to begin the affair in the first place. Eventually he casts off the womanly robes in which Dido giddily dresses him because of the paternal principles that are the father's heir and, most specifically, the duty owed to a son who has come to embody these.

At this point, I shall summarize at least some of the affects and sustained emotional states associated with "falling" and "being" in love: a sense of abiding *danger*; *pleasure* and *ecstasy*; divine *madness*; exquisite *pain*; protracted *suffering*; *defiance*; *suicidal* despair; a measure of inherent *hostility* and *hatred*; intense feelings of *desire*; a *cherishing* of the beloved, accompanied by gratitude and surprise in response to his or her very existence; an undercurrent of trembling and *longing*. Appetitive states and consummatory acts give rise to *intense excitement*, passions whose pitch is unequaled in almost any other activity (except possibly war or religious entrancement). These alternate with periods of equally remarkable *repose* when the lovers, having satisfied their desires and longings for the moment, become intimate in their alert inactivity (Wolff, 1965) and can peruse each other's countenance and explore their innermost thoughts and feelings.

As Michael Balint (1948) noted, both such states—passionate and intimate—compromise the lovers' reality testing. Either the longed-for lover comes to envelop the universe with his or her presence, or else this world becomes "garbed with beauty to his taste" so that its dangers and demands fade into the background. In such a frame of mind, in which the ordinary exigencies of reality are subsumed by love's spiritual heights and sensual demands, it becomes difficult indeed to go about one's business. Feeling *entrapped, distracted,* and controlled by their passion, lovers resent loving and being loved; inevitably they become *ambivalent* and try to wriggle free.

And so romantic love is also dogged by the sense that it *cannot last.* It is a "quick bright thing," all to soon "devoured by the jaws of death," "fire and powder [which] as they kiss, consume." When not destroyed from the outside, passion burns itself out (as Freud himself stressed).

For these reasons, perhaps, many of literature's protagonists have been relatively *young* lovers. Romantic heroines and heroes are repeatedly depicted as girls and boys poised on the brink of adulthood, taken by the ideal other as by sensual self-discovery before they come into their own as adult men and women. In their physical and intellectual prime, these young lovers collapse before instinctual tides which might have served worldly ambition but end up sweeping them beyond social convention, leaving them there to their own fatal devices.

Yet there are notable exceptions here and there, especially in the stories of adulterers rendered impolitic and childish by their quest for rejuvenation—Anna forsaking her motherhood; Antony enthralled and unmanned by the sorceress Cleopatra; Phaedra possessed by her yearning for her priggish stepson Hippolytus, whom she likens to the philandering Theseus as a young initiate. And certainly these figures are as passionate and heroic as Tristan and Isolde, Abelard and Heloise, Romeo and Juliet. Where passionate love is rekindled later in life, the lover suffers a second adolescence, with spouse, family, and other sources of adult duty representing parental figures and injunctions not easily disregarded. Love at midlife both rejuvenates a lover and makes him or her incautious. Conflict and the potential for tragedy are immediately apparent.

Thus the fictive tales of doomed young love, perhaps at any actual age, are, as Freud also lamented, mostly *short* stories. As Turgenev's actual short story by that name reveals, "First Love," especially, is charged with both self-discovery in the unknown and recapitulatory regression, often reaching psychosexual climaxes not repeated in life. Past and present, illusion and reality converge on and find a new synthesis in the sensual romantic encounter. After all those years of onanistic imagining, the late adolescent can identify at last with his or her parent in their sexual role and marvel at the fact that intercourse is possible, indeed real. As Nabokov (1966) put it in *Speak Memory*, recalling his first sexual encounter, "I parted the fabric of fancy; I tasted reality."

A Psychoanalytic Definition

From depictions outside psychoanalysis, it becomes clear that romantic love cannot be reduced to one or more instinctual impulses. Nor can this phenomenon be conceptualized even as a single affect, whose underlying determinants are already more various and complex. Passionate love must be seen essentially as a complex and sustained affective disposition, structurally rather like a mood (Jacobson, 1971) in its amalgamation of emotion, fantasy, and perception, but specifically object-directed and impelled. The state of love is characterized essentially by the concatenation of desire and longing (the affective derivatives of Freud's sensual and tender libidinal currents), in which the lover's paradoxical aim is to possess or devour a specific person, while simultaneously preserving his or her existence. ("You can have your cake and eat it too," as Bob Dylan (1969) put it in his love song, "Lay, Lady, Lay.") Contradictory emotions and sensations, which point to revived but also current conflicts, accompany falling and being in love.

With some notable exceptions—unrequited love, for instance, or certain religious ecstasies—romantic love eventually becomes also erotic love. It is tied to and expressed in genital sexuality, either in fantasy or, better, in reality. In fact, for the most part nowadays, romantic love progresses in stages, each altering and deepening the constellation of feelings of which it is composed. The first, exemplified in Freud's letters to Martha, is that of love which is as yet unconsummated—love that has not found its realization in actual sex. For some—the courtiers of Aquitaine, for instance—this represents its final and even its highest form. For others, to echo Coleridge (1817) in his critique of *Romeo and Juliet*, such love is still mere "fancy," a state in which the lover is not comprehended as a whole individual with idiosyncratic emotional needs, sensual preferences, and spiritual ambitions to which the lover must attune, but rather as an infantile, part or split object—as an idea or ideal. With a sexual meeting, "imagination," put into practice, replaces the two-dimensional fantasy. The lover is *known* as a real and variegated person, with sexual and other responses of his or her own. Subject to another level of idealization (Kernberg, 1974), he or she is still experienced as much more than real.

Being in love is thus more than a repetition. Eroticism of this kind is a quest reminiscent of, but not reducible to, earlier object relationships involving both sensuality and attachment. It represents, if you will, a search for "intersubjective" communion. In the wake of infatuation and passion, ambivalence and then forgiveness, compassion and gratitude are entertained and the intimacy of the lovers becomes invested with feelings of empathy and mutuality. It is now that love's tender current eddies in to quell a self-protective hostility.

Romantic love is not simply synonymous with what we commonly call *genital primacy,* since it also involves an illusory or psychic reaching after the "soul" of the beloved. The capacity for genital feeling and a personal capacity for and knowledge of orgasm in intercourse are necessary but not sufficient. Ideational and symbolic elements come into play, and, as in artistic creativity, the romantic lover requires a capacity for *metaphor.* Immediate sensation is vital yet deliberately endowed by a lover with meanings and attainments beyond the momentary gratification.

In states of love, then, both concrete sensations and the

emotions which these call up are subject to intellectual reflection. The romantic lover feels deeply and simultaneously thinks about what he is feeling. His capacity to ponder his desires and to wonder about them suggests both a measure of realism about himself and his lover and the ability, as if hypothetically, to make of them, singly and in concert, much more than they are. Romantic love is a feeling which is simply not accessible to the intellectually immature individual. Rash as they are, the lovers' emotions are not merely regressive but rather fall within the province of the sophisticated adult.

Romantic love is marked by periods of passionate excitement—exquisite fulfillment, intense frustration, rage, and epiphanies (like the orgasm) when opposites can conjoin in an explosion of undefined yearning and sensation (hence passion's particular emotional stamp and the various oxymorons used to depict it—"tragic bliss," "sweet sorrow," etc.). At the same time, however, this form of love has its more quiescent periods, interludes of libidinal satiety yet of sustained and suspended interest in the other—intervals, that is, of the highest form of intimacy (Ross, 1989). Whereas uniting has been the objective of love's more passionate phases, there are times when the lover's interest is in letting himself as individual be known and learning about the other as a distinct and highly differentiated person (or object). There is an integral quality in these emotional polarities—passionate intensity and intimate repose. The love object endures both levels of exaltation and proves to be the same person in either state. Indeed, memories of the one experience serve to enrich the other.

Idealization in concert with identification contribute to the altered state of consciousness occurring when one is in love. The environment surrounding the lovers may even be invested with the vitality of their relationship. However, no matter how stimulated and alive the lover may feel, his state of mind is not to be equated with simple "happiness." It is charged with feelings of sadness, anxiety, and inevitable loss, all of these affects bespeaking the impossibility, danger, and death-defying abandon of the union sought.

Love does not easily endure within the confines of most adult lives; the dyadic exchanges of love cannot be sustained in a workaday world; its time is limited. The easing of self-boundaries, heightened appetitive states, acceptance of vulnerability, illusions of "transcendence" (Kernberg, 1974), and immersion in affect all compromise reality testing and the capacity for alloplastic adaptation. Concern over these matters conspires with the conflictual meanings love inevitably comes to assume, because of its resonance with the infantile neurosis and its objects, to tip the balance once more toward the side of emotional inhibition.

Defenses and consequent compromise formations are evoked to contend with the dangers, both imagined and real, which are inherent in this condition. The individual returns, both grudgingly and thankfully, to "normal consciousness." In our culture, if not in others where marriage had and has a more frankly economic impetus, romantic love opens its doors to readmit third persons and is reorganized into what we analysts have commonly called "mature love."

Within this context, suspending daily concerns and making use of fantasy, established partners can periodically act to renew their erotic love for each other. Yet it is doubtful whether certain critical preconditions having to do with danger, obstacles in love's path, a sense of transgression and transcendence are present in such encounters. Without them, it becomes difficult to sustain a passionate intensity which is warranted by the situation itself and therefore which has a life of its own. The individual differences in this regard are considerable.

Against this backdrop, I will now consider love's developmental preconditions and ramifications.

Some Developmental Prototypes and Preconditions

Reacting to its irrationality, most analysts have underscored the regressive aspects of romantic love. However, a further elaboration of its phenomenology reveals just how delicate an achievement it is—sexually, interpersonally, and imaginatively.

As many have stressed, sensuous and sensually various as eroticism first is, it does require the ultimate subordination of pregenital aims and pleasures under the dominance of genital gratification. Now there is sex, and there is sex—as descriptive surveys like the Hite reports (1976, 1981) reveal. If a man and a woman are successfully to express a more high-minded sexual love (*höchste Lust*) in sexual activity, they must be conversant with their own and their partner's anatomy and responsiveness. A man, in particular, must have the control to delay his orgasm until either a woman reaches her climax in intercourse or he recognizes the need ultimately for other forms of stimulation. Both partners must exercise empathy in reacting erotically to the flush of excitement in the other person without exploiting this as a defensive screen obscuring their own arousal because of the conflicts associated with it. In other words, in genuine romantic unions, sexual pleasures are shared ones. And the lovers must be comfortable enough with their bodies to reveal all during forepleasure and intercourse and then to stay close, to settle into each other, to cuddle and converse afterwards. Failure along the way can engender disappointments, mistrust, and narcissistic wounds which accumulate to destroy the lovers' passion for each other.

Successful sex presupposes an early age-specific sensuousness in the infantile and later preoedipal exchanges of parent and child, a reasonable resolution of oedipal conflict, and a pleasurable masturbatory history during the coming of age in puberty and early adolescence. If a mother loves her child, his or her body and bodily products sufficiently, then she can teach him or her to enjoy rather than hide his or her physical self and its secretions, to reveal these wishes and sensations in the expectation of their being accepted and enjoyed and understood and of receiving pleasure from others. Elsewhere (Ross, 1986, 1990a) I have further suggested that the father plays significant roles in consolidating the body images of both boys and girls in ways that allow a lover to tolerate the illusions of sexual dissolution, expansion, and transient transformation which accompany orgasm.

As far as oedipal development is concerned, not only must the stress fall on the positive and heterosexual denouement to the conflict, but the child must have struck a balance between repression and expression. With the unfolding of the oedipal complex, autoeroticism is enriched by fantasy and becomes masturbation proper. The initial objects of this fantasy have eventually to fade into the unconscious if a child is to feel free enough to indulge in dreamy self-stimulation accompanied by images of love objects less close to home. Acts of incest or visual and tactile overstimulation during and just after the oedipal period, along with a disturbed sexual relationship between the parents, can make for the sort of frank fixations which have a compensatory and inhibiting effect on children. No longer free to fantasize, because they are sexually unprotected, such children must redouble their efforts to anaesthetize and constrict themselves—to the point that in their adulthood capacities for romantic and erotic love, even for sexual sensation, all calling up incestuous yearnings, become out of the question.

Lastly with regard to sex, the reverielike masturbation of the oedipal child is not the real thing—however taken we adults may be by a little boy's or girl's precocious sensuality and declarations of love. Such arousal does not typically eventuate in orgasm, much less in mutual satisfaction. Surveys from Kinsey's (1948) to Masters and Johnson (1966) or Hite's (1976, 1981) have suggested that for both men and women (though particularly the former) a healthy history of masturbation to orgasm, self-exploration, and, finally, either homo- or heteroerotic pubescent sex play prepare the way for more fully realized heterosexual encounters later in adolescence. A prior personal knowledge of orgasm—or at least the male's of ejaculation—alone or in the company of another person facilitates the sensual and interpersonal refinement of what otherwise eludes consciousness as the mere discharge of tensions. Some individuals need to learn about their and other's sexuality in less charged experimental sex before concentrating their energies on a true love—while others, in the manner of Juliet, can rush as if virginally into their first lover's arms and adapt to their own and the other's desires. Sex differences probably come into play here—in the Hite surveys, 99 percent of men masturbated in contrast to 82 percent of women—because of the man's need to overcome his castration anxiety, repetitively reassuring himself of his bodily integrity in the wake of orgasm, as well as the myths and restrictions attaching until now to female sexuality and muting its expression.

Second, for love to pass beyond narcissistically impelled fantasy and infatuation to a more wholehearted form of idealization, the lover must have cultivated the ability for devotion to and fascination with a person other than him- or herself. In our jargon, object constancy—the ability to sustain the object's integrated image in its absence or during states of ambivalence (Fraiberg, 1969)—must have been secured early on. Indeed, it must be well enough in place to weather the revival of quasi-symbiotic trends during orgasm and at other moments in loving. So the lover must have had his or her satisfactory phase-specific symbiosis and separation-individuation (Mahler et al., 1975) along with the periods in infancy described by Stern (1985) during which objects apart from the self are perceived as having their own contours and life—interludes described by Wolff (1965) as intervals of alert inactivity.

In point of fact, however, the romantic lover must have passed well beyond these early stages in the evolution of object relations—subsequent milestones overlooked by most analysts writing on the subject. Early on, by conversing "to" them, mothers help toddlers begin to talk about their feelings. These interchanges then provide the basis for friendships in later childhood in which the child learns how to find gratification simply in making himself known and in knowing another person as best he or she can—knowing more and more about the details of that person's life and personality and identifying with these particulars. The onrush of the drives in adolescence further infuses these friendships, cutting across the genders now with intensity, urgency, a sense of priority. The capacity for friendship is, then, another developmental precondition for love.

All lovers aspire to the music of "immortal souls" beyond the "muddy vesture of decay"—as Lorenzo muses to Jessica in Shakespeare's *Merchant of Venice.* Groping for words to communicate feeling to the other, all are poets. Granting poetic license, simultaneously love requires a capacity for metaphor, in which all manner of emotional longings find satisfaction in a sexual union with the beloved, which, in its turn, takes on spiritual meanings, which, in their turn, the lover tries to represent and articulate. The capacity for concrete sensual pleasure must be there but, with it, the ability as well to dwell on the illusions of mystical union accompanying eroticism. When the one order of feeling—concrete sensation or spiritual questing—predominates to the exclusion of the other, the beauty and value of the real person of the beloved suffer, and love can founder.

Thus, from the cognitive point of view as from that of the drives, it follows that romantic love is, at the very least, a late adolescent phenomenon. "Impossible" urges to reunite with the mother in toddlerhood, unrequited incestuous yearnings later on, fantasy and unfulfilled onanistic preoccupations prepare the way for love's imaginative aspirations and inevitable felt deprivations. Still, representational thought, symbolic communication, an interest in the world are rudimentary prerequisites. Beyond this, it is formal operations and the inclination to proceed beyond immediate sensation by making the most of it—the proclivity to think about thinking (Inhelder and Piaget, 1958) and *feeling*—which provide the epistemological backdrop for the exaltations of the romantic lover.

Falling in love also gives expression to the turmoil of late adolescence and young adulthood. With this come certain developmental consequences in addition to the preconditions particular to this stage in the life cycle.

Perhaps most important in terms of psychic structure, passionate love demands a moral or ethical accommodation—a reorganization of the superego so that it can countenance hitherto forbidden wishes as well as feeling states. The discovery of the need to be loved and to love erotically gentles our consciences, making us more tolerant and more aware of ourselves and others. In a subsequent paper (Ross, 1990b) I shall explore the moral individuation that derives specifically from the dislocation of the tie to the father and of the ego ideal (see Blos, 1985) which are set in motion when a man falls in love with a woman for the first time.

Finally, not all loves are revivals, not all lovers "revenants." They are also irreducible—new people, new and unique. They bring distinct personal histories, teach new knowledge, expand experience in unexpected ways. The lover must be prepared, sure enough of his or her own psychosocial identity, to take them in (Erikson, 1963, 1969).

Why for so many individuals romantic love does not often survive late adolescence and youth is a question probably beyond this paper's scope. At no time thereafter does a responsible individual have the leisure and energy to expend on love—so pressing are the demands of what the Hindus have called the householder phase in the life cycle. We tend to become more pragmatic and at times rather concrete in our thinking as we get older—less inclined to the metaphoric abstractions of the lover. Yet, emotionally and perhaps biologically, we need our passion, to "forget" life's stresses and to stimulate the immune system. So we are at least episodically moved to create conditions within or outside a marriage for its expression—"quality time" in the case of a married couple. In midlife loving makes one young again.

Conclusion

I have attempted to conceptualize passionate love from a psychoanalytic perspective. Having noted psychoanalysis' longstanding reluctance to confront adult love, I have turned elsewhere for more detailed descriptions of its phenomenology. With these in mind, such love can be defined as a complex and somewhat conflictual affective disposition, rather like a mood, evoked by the image of another person and characterized by periods of passionate excitement and intimate repose.

A variety of both pleasurable and unpleasurable affects are entertained in romantic love, which derive from its both sensory and illusory wellsprings, from the opportunities it affords for sensual satisfaction and spiritual overreaching. These affects are activated in response to states of desire and satiety and as modes of communication with and knowledge of the other. They are accompanied and facilitated by the capacity for genital primacy and cognitive components in love—specifically the lover's capacity to express himself or herself in genital orgasm and then to create and dwell in metaphors about the lovers' sexual encounters. Whatever its infantile precursors and however regressive it can be at times, love emerges perforce as a late adolescent or young adult phenomenon. At this juncture, the prepotency of romantic love moves the individual to disengage from the injunctions and desexualized idealizations of his parental images and to reorganize the superego constructs based on these—to create his or her own ethic. Thus, while there may be other routes to maturity, embracing the feeling of being in love helps a person grow up.

REFERENCES

ABRAHAM, K. (1925). Character-formation on the genital level of the libido. In *Selected Papers on Psycho-Analysis*. London: Hogarth Press, 1949, pp. 407-417.

ALTMAN, L. (1977). Some vicissitudes of love. *J. Amer. Psychoanal. Assn.*, 25: 35-52.

ARLOW, J. A. (1980). Object concept and object choice. *Psychoanal. Q.*, 49:104-133.

AUDEN, W. H. (1973). *Forewords and Afterwords*. London: Faber and Faber.

——— (1976). *Collected Poems*. New York: Random House.

BAK, R. (1973). Being in love and object loss. *Int. J. Psychoanal.,*. 54:1-7.

BALINT, M. (1948). On genital love. *Int. J. Psychoanal.*, 29:34-40.

——— (1956). Perversions and genitality. In *Perversions, Psychodynamics, and Theory*, ed. S. Lorand. New York: Gramercy Books.

BARTHES, R. (1978). *A Lover's Discourse*. New York: Hill and Wang.

BENJAMIN, J. (1988). *The Bonds of Love*. New York: Pantheon Books.

BERGMANN, M. S. (1971). Psychoanalytic observations on the capacity to love. In *Separation-Individuation: Essays in Honor of Margaret Mahler*, ed. J. B. McDevitt & C. G. Settlage. New York: Int. Univ. Press.

——— (1980). On the intrapsychic function of falling in love. *Psychoanal. Q.*, 49:56-76.

——— (1986). Transference love and love in real life. *Int. J. Psychoanal. Psychother.*, 11:27-45.

——— (1987). *The Anatomy of Loving*. New York: Columbia Univ. Press.

BERNFELD, S. (1949). Freud's scientific beginnings. *Amer. Imago*, 6:163-196.

BHAVABHUTI (8th century AD). *Uttara Rama Carita* (The Later Story of Rama). In *Six Sanskrit Plays*. Bombay: Asia, 1964.

BINSTOCK, W. A. (1973). On the two forms of intimacy. *J. Amer. Psychoanal. Assn.*, 21:93-107.

BLOS, P. (1985). *Son and Father*. New York: Free Press.

BLUM, H. P. (1989). Personal communication.

CHASSEGUET-SMIRGEL, J. (1983). Perversions and the universal law. *Int. Rev. Psychoanal.*, 10:293-301.

COLERIDGE, S. T. (1817). *Biographia Literaria*, ed. J. Shawcross. Oxford Univ. Press, 1965.

DE ROUGEMONT, D. (1956). *Love in the Western World*. New York: Doubleday.

DYLAN, B. (1969). "Lay, Lady, Lay." *Nashville Skyline*.

EISSLER, K. R. (1951). An unknown autobiographical letter by Freud and a short comment. *Int. J. Psychoanal.*, 32:319-324.

——— (1963). *Goethe: A Psychoanalytic Study 1775-1786*. Detroit: Wayne Univ. Press.

ERIKSON, E. H. (1963). *Childhood and Society*. New York: Norton.

——— (1969). *Gandhi's Truth*. New York: Norton.

EVANS, W. N. (1953). Two kinds of romantic love. *Psychoanal. Q.*, 22:75-85.

FERENCZI, S. (1924). *Thalassa: A Theory of Genitality*. New York: Norton, 1968.

FINE, B. D. & MOORE, B. E. (1990). *Psychoanalytic Terms and Concepts*. New Haven: Yale Univ. Press.

FRAIBERG, S. (1969). Libidinal object constancy and mental representations. *Psychoanal. Study Child,* 24:9–47.
FREUD, S. (1900). The intepretation of dreams. *S. E.,* 4 & 5.
——— (1905a). Fragment of an analysis of a case of hysteria. *S. E.,* 7:3–122.
——— (1905b). Three essays on the theory of sexuality. *S. E.,* 7:135–243.
——— (1909a). Analysis of a phobia in a five-year-old boy. *S. E.,* 10:3–149.
——— (1909b). Notes upon a case of obsessional neurosis. *S. E.,* 10:153–318.
——— (1910). A special type of object choice made by men. *S. E.,* 11:163–176.
——— (1914a). The Moses of Michelangelo. *S. E.,* 13:211–238.
——— (1914b). On narcissism. *S. E.,* 14:69–102.
——— (1915a). Instincts and their vicissitudes. *S. E.,* 14:109–158.
——— (1915b). Observations on transference love. *S. E.,* 12:157–171.
——— (1918). From the history of an infantile neurosis. *S. E.,* 17:3–123.
——— (1921). Group psychology and the analysis of the ego. *S. E.,* 18:67–143.
——— (1923). The ego and the id. *S. E.,* 19:3–66.
——— (1924). The economic problem of masochism. *S. E.,* 19:157–170.
——— (1925). Some psychical consequences of the anatomical distinction between the sexes. *S. E.,* 19:243–258.
——— (1926). Inhibitions, symptoms and anxiety. *S. E.,* 20:77–175.
——— (1985). *The Complete Letters of Sigmund Freud to Wilhelm Fliess, 1887–1905,* ed. J. M. Masson. Cambridge: Belknap Press of Harvard Univ. Press.
GRUNBERGER, B. (1971). Narcissism. In *Psychoanalytic Essays.* New York: Int. Univ. Press.
HITE, S. (1976). *The Hite Report on Female Sexuality.* New York: Dell, 1976.
——— (1981). *The Hite Report on Male Sexuality.* New York: Random House.
INHELDER, B. & PIAGET, J. (1958). *The Growth of Logical Thinking from Childhood to Adolescence.* New York: Basic Books.
JACOBSON, E. (1971). *Depression.* New York: Int. Univ. Press.
JONES, E. (1957). *The Life and Work of Sigmund Freud,* 3 Vols. New York: Basic Books.
KAKAR, S. & ROSS, J. M. (1987). *Tales of Love, Sex and Danger.* New York: Basil Blackwell.
KERNBERG, O. F. (1974). Mature love: prerequisites and characteristics. *J. Amer. Psychoanal. Assn.,* 22:743–768.
——— (1977). Boundaries and structure in love relations. *J. Amer. Psychoanal. Assn.,* 25:81–114.
KINSEY, A. C. (1948). *Sexual Behavior in the Human Male.* Philadelphia: W. B. Saunders.
LEWIN, B. D. (1952). The oral triad. In *Selected Papers,* ed. J. A. Arlow. New York: Psychoanalytic Quarterly, 1973.
LOEWALD, H. W. (1951). Ego and reality. *Int. J. Psychoanal.,* 32:10–18.
MAHLER, M. S., PINE, F., & BERGMAN, A. (1975). *The Psychological Birth of the Human Infant.* New York: Basic Books.
MALCOLM, J. (1981). *Psychoanalysis: The Impossible Profession.* New York: Knopf.
MASTERS, W. H. & JOHNSON, V. E. (1966). *Human Sexual Response.* Boston: Little, Brown.

Nabokov, V. (1966). *Speak Memory.* New York: Putnam & Sons.
Nizami (1141–1203?) *The Story of Layla and Majnun,* tr. and ed. R. Gelpke. Boulder, Colo.: Shambhala, 1978.
Ortega y Gasset, J. (1957). *On Love,* tr. T. Talbot. New York: Greenwich Editions.
Person, E. S. (1988). *Dreams of Love and Fateful Encounters.* New York: Norton.
Racine, J. (1677). *Phaedre,* tr. J. Caincross. New York: Penguin Books, 1983.
Reich, W. (1927). *The Function of the Orgasm.* New York: Oregon Institute Press, 1942.
——— (1929). The genital character and the neurotic character. In *The Psychoanalytic Reader,* ed. R. Fliess. New York: Int. Univ. Press.
Reik, T. (1944). *A Psychologist Looks at Love.* New York: Farrar & Rinehart.
Ross, J. M. (1986). Beyond the phallic illusion. In *The Psychology of Men*, ed. G. Fogel, F. M. Lane, & R. S. Liebert. New York: Basic Books.
——— (1989). On intimacy. Panel, 15th Annual Conference of the Regional Council of the Psychoanalytic Societies of Greater New York and Philadelphia.
——— (1990a). The eye of the beholder. In *New Dimensions in Adult Development,* ed. C. Colarusso & R. Nemiroff. New York: Basic Books.
——— (1990b). The role of the father representation in romantic love. Delivered before the Denver Psychoanalytic Society.
Ross, N. (1970). The primacy of sexuality in the light of ego psychology. *J. Amer. Psychoanal. Assn.,* 18:267–284.
Sartre, J. P. (1956). *Being and Nothingness.* New York: Philosophical Library.
Schafer, R. (1960). The loving and beloved superego in Freud's structural theory *Psychoanal., Study Child,* 15:163–188.
Stendhal, H. B. (1842). *On Love,* 3rd ed. New York: Liveright, 1947.
Stern, D. N. (1985). *The Interpersonal World of the Infant.* New York: Basic Books.
Stoller, R. (1979). *Sexual Excitement.* New York: Pantheon Books.
Sullerot, E. (1979). *Women on Love: Eight Centuries of Feminine Writing.* New York: Doubleday.
Teilhard de Chardin, P. (1972). *On Love.* New York: Harper & Row.
Tolstoy, L. (1878). *Anna Karenina.* New York: Penguin Books, 1986.
Turgenev, I. (1860). *First Love And Other Stories.* New York: Oxford Univ. Press.
van der Waals, H. G. (1965). Problems of narcissism. *Bull. Menninger Clin.,* 29:243–275.
Wolff, P. H. (1965). The development of attention in young infants. *Annu. N.Y. Acad. Sci.,* 118:815–830.
Wordsworth, W. (1800). *The Prelude.* New York: Modern Library.

243 West End Avenue
New York, NY 10023

NAME INDEX

SUBJECT INDEX